Crossing the Current

Crossing the Current

Aftermaths of War along the Huallaga River

Richard Kernaghan

Stanford University Press
Stanford, California

STANFORD UNIVERSITY PRESS
Stanford, California

Printed in the United States of America on acid-free,
archival-quality paper

Library of Congress Cataloging-in-Publication Data

Names: Kernaghan, Richard, author.
Title: Crossing the current : aftermaths of war along the Huallaga River /
Richard Kernaghan.
Description: Stanford, California : Stanford University Press, 2022. |
Includes bibliographical references and index.
Identifiers: LCCN 2021061741 (print) | LCCN 2021061742 (ebook) |
ISBN 9781503603295 (cloth) | ISBN 9781503633407 (paperback) |
ISBN 9781503633414 (ebook)
Subjects: LCSH: War and society—Peru—Huallaga River Valley. |
Political violence—Peru—Huallaga River Valley. | Insurgency—Peru—
Huallaga River Valley. | Huallaga River Valley (Peru)—Social conditions. |
Huallaga River Valley (Peru)—Politics and government.
Classification: LCC HN350.H79 K47 2022 (print) |
LCC HN350.H79 (ebook) |
DDC 303.6/60985—dc23/eng/20220107
LC record available at https://lccn.loc.gov/2021061741
LC ebook record available at https://lccn.loc.gov/2021061742

Visit crossingthecurrent.net for additional media and fieldwork material.

Cover art: Richard Kernaghan
Cover design: Emma Christine Hall

For Orlando and Hazel

contents

CONTENTS

CHAPTER NINE
cloud to clod
269

Crossing the Current

FIGURE 1.1. Huallaga River

malecón huallaga

Pressing on for the lowest point, for the ever-most grave, the river with a first cut partitions the valley into two earthen terrains. Only later will these two sides, these moving siblings always lagging far behind currents that hold them apart, become left and right. Orientation appears but only after the initial cut and then only because of gravity's sway. Does the Huallaga come first? Or do not other smaller streams anticipate its arrival? Tributaries that descend as blades from hills of variable distances, to slice up each side into smaller sections, as they lunge and lunge toward their eventual dive into the mighty Huallaga, where they mix their waters with its waters, into pools whirling round in infinite shades of brown, to swell currents already on their journey down to that faraway encounter where they too will dilute and mix and lose themselves in swirls of color . . .

once, into the Marañón and then again,

as they merge with the Ucayali.

On the second morning she arrived to speak with me in that cement room, Tina described events of recent date: a story where remnants of the war continued the war far from town in the deep beyond of the Huallaga's left bank. She told me of a place called Bijao, the new frontier she said of timber extraction, where her son-in-law and her daughter had tried their intrepid hands at logging almost two years before. In the extended interlude of waning fury an opportunity arose to uproot all remaining hardwoods from the left bank, not only the majestic mahoganies but the mohenas and the tornillos soon to vanish from the forest. And so, in hopes of securing a livelihood for their future family, they had to venture to that faraway place before it was too late, all the more pressing now because of a pregnancy moving into month five. Because of that baby already on its way, they had a future to think about. And what high expectations her son-in-law had pinned on logging, Tina said, as his new family's way forward.

If only she had not insisted. . . . If only Sabine had heeded her mother's advice and admonitions. But her husband's hopes were her hopes. Where he goes, Sabine said, I will go. Telling Tina, *no*, she would *not* stay behind. *Not* to tend to her infant son. *Not* in excess concern for a child to come. And so, when they left, she set out with them: crossing the Huallaga, picking up a trail just beyond the left-side hamlet of Bambú, to begin the five-hour journey to Bijao. They were a crew of six: Ítalo and Sabine, with Abel—the then boyfriend and eventual husband of Sabine's younger sister, Margo—plus three young men Ítalo had recruited to give them a hand.

They had been gone a week when Tina received a folded note, delivered to her house on Malecón Huallaga. It was from Sabine and what it said set Tina at ease. Not to worry, her daughter wrote. They had found an abundance of trees. They were all working in what was a beautiful place.

For several weeks Tina heard nothing more, until one afternoon, after spending the day in the nearby city of Tingo María, she returned home to learn her daughter had suffered a terrible accident. While the men were off felling trees, Sabine was occupying herself with chores at the camp when she slipped on wet ground, falling hard. That first day she said nothing when the men returned late in the afternoon, nothing at all about the bleeding. Day two the hemorrhaging had not stopped, but only when Ítalo noticed how pale Sabine looked did she tell him what had happened and that she feared she was losing their child. Ítalo knew then even more was a stake. And with all the haste they could muster Ítalo, Abel, and one of the workers, named Machín, carried Sabine in a stretcher on the long journey back to town.

When they reached the house, Tina was not there, and her husband, Wilson, had no money to give. So Ítalo and Abel ran door to door, asking friends and neighbors for contributions to pay for urgent care. By the time Tina arrived, they had already departed for the hospital in Tingo María, where doctors would confirm their worst for the child and insist on forcing a miscarriage to save the mother. Tina learned the sad news only later that evening upon her daughter's return to the house on Malecón Huallaga.

The rhythms of timber extraction did not allow time off for Ítalo to grieve. And with the other two men he departed, early the following morning, again for Bijao, leaving Sabine in Tina's care. The work crew was now down to five, yet the hazards they faced were only beginning to emerge. A couple of days later two armed men appeared at the camp. They wanted to know: Who among them was named Ítalo Santos? When Ítalo stepped forward, they told him they were from the Communist Party of Peru, that they needed him to buy provisions. They handed him a list with one hundred soles cash, saying that if that were not enough, he would have to make up the difference. Ítalo agreed and, promising to dispatch one of his crew, called out to Machín, asking him to come over. When Machín walked up and Ítalo had explained the errand, the armed men turned to him with this warning: *Si tú no llegas, vaya alistando tu cuello.* "If you do not return, you might as well begin preparing your neck."

Machín left right away, taking the two other workers along to help carry back the supplies. In town he checked on prices only to discover he would need upward of 250 soles to complete the list. Short on cash and frightened by what the *senderistas*—the men from Sendero Luminoso, Shining Path—might do if he dared to show up short handed, Machín decided it was better to stay put.

Two days passed, when back at the camp, Sendero dropped in once again. This time three armed men climbed up to the spot where Ítalo was milling with a "Where's Machín? He better start getting that neck ready, because he will not be giving us the slip." That was all they said before turning about and heading back down the hill.

Ítalo asked Abel to go find out what was causing the delay: "These guys are pressuring us here, and we don't want problems." Besides, without the help of their crew, the work had slowed to an excruciating pace. So Abel took the trail, descending to the Huallaga River, crossed over and into the town. In no time he had tracked down Machín, who admitted he was scared, too scared to return to the camp. Abel urged him to reconsider. "We're really close to finishing, and then we can all come home together." But Machín would not budge, reluctant to give up his distance from Bijao, the only thing separating him from Sendero's retribution. And in his refusal, there was an intimation of the prevailing political moment, expressed in terms of territorial control. For several streets over, the army had a well-fortified base, with the headquarters of the police nearby—and against neither one nor the other could Sendero gather the will, much less sufficient force, to attack. Such was the moment: suddenly the town, unlike years not so long ago, seemed to offer a modest degree of protection.

Later that evening Machín showed up unexpectedly at Tina's house with his spirits now high and, to Abel's surprise, his mind now changed. Thanks to an old debt he had managed to collect, they could acquire the rest of the provisions, and with money to spare! "Let's go back tomorrow," he said, "but tonight we should celebrate, and it will be my treat." Machín and Abel opened a bottle, that became two, and on and on, so much so, that the next morning they woke too hung over to complete the list of supplies, much less travel. When the day after that arrived and they were not even making motions of getting ready to go, Tina began to scold: "Abel! Ítalo is out there alone in the *monte*. What are you still doing here?"

By this time Sabine was feeling stronger. Three weeks had passed since her fall, eighteen days since losing her unborn child. Worried about her husband, she told her mother she would go with Abel, Machín, and the others when they left for the camp. "*Hija*," said Tina, "are you crazy? That's a terrible idea. You *are not* going." But Sabine insisted: "Yes, *mamá*, I *am*."

Since it was already close to noon, Abel, Machín, and Sabine decided to spend what remained of the day packing and resting up so they could depart for Bijao early the next morning. Tina recalled that day, how at Sabine's request she had prepared her daughter's favorite food for lunch, and when they were about sit down to eat, they heard a loud banging outside. When they opened the front door, Ítalo stood before them, the last person they had expected to see and drunk as could be. His right hand was heavily bandaged, but he did not want, or was not able, to explain. No, no, nothing had happened, was all he said before his words dissolved into a deep, deep sob. Tina told Sabine to douse him with water; that will bring him to. Even then Ítalo did not talk. He just headed to a room in the back and collapsed on a bed.

Four hours later, Ítalo woke, and finding his wife lying next to him, he told her that he could have been killed. He was all alone at the camp when five men showed up, armed with Kalashnikov rifles, what Tina described to me as "little machine guns, AKM." Figuring out who was who, out there, was not straightforward. If the war had already receded from the town, across the river it raged on in ways that still felt familiar: in minor details on which the fate of worlds seemed to turn. They were armed with AKM; surely that must have meant Sendero? But Tina insisted that no: they could not have been senderistas—their hair was cut way too short. They must have been Servicio de inteligencia. Rather than express my doubts, I wondered aloud if they might have been an elite group of army commandos stationed in Tingo María. Tina nodded, before going on:

"Anyway, they arrived more or less around one in the afternoon, and to Ítalo they said, 'Hey, *concha tu madre*, get over here. . . . You are a *terruco*.'"

The word *terruco* was an off-the-cuff expression for *terrorista*/terrorist, though I had heard people from the countryside more commonly use the diminutive *tuco*, which seemed to carry less sting and even a certain tinge of endearment. In the Huallaga neither Tina nor anyone else claimed to know the origins of the word.[1] And while from afar it would seem fair, if not incumbent, to search into shadowy ancestries of Indo-European languages where *terror* and *territory* might appear inextricably linked,[2] when I say *terruco* out loud, again and again, it sounds awfully close to *terrón,* a clod of earth, and even more so to another word for clod: *terruño,* which is also natal place, or more colloquially still, a plot of land. What tied all these distinct gradations of sense to one another? The answer seemed important, and especially so in the Huallaga Valley, where for many years, simply making a living from the soil or the forest was to leave oneself open to accusation. Here, however, the lead-in phrase *concha tu madre* / motherfucker set the tone for everything that would follow.

"I am not a terruco"—Ítalo insisted.

"You are a logger!"—(They did find him milling.)

"I am a logger, yes."

"Well then, loggers are terrucos."

Tina conveyed, compressed there into this ever-so-brief dialogue,[3] what had once been a frequent scene of counterinsurgency and, more broadly too, what had commonly happened when one fatefully came face-to-face with one of the sides at war: questioning under extreme duress. Questioning that crafted brute syllogisms repeated again and again to draw equivalences, again and again, between persons and things that would not have been equal otherwise in less turbulent, political times—times when armed men would not show up without warning. Questioning that made those equations, no matter how dubious, stick through threats of impending harm—concha tu madre—perhaps even death. At least out there and at that moment when Ítalo was alone and unable to defend any other claim, just as long as they all had their weapons trained on him.

One of the men, which Tina was now calling *commandos*, pulled out a combat knife and, stepping forward, brought its serrated blade up to Ítalo's face. "Here all loggers are terrucos," he said, passing the blade's cool metal back and forth, with a soft stroking motion, to make his point, across Ítalo's right cheek:

"You must be a terruco too."

For a brief second the commando stepped back, time enough for Ítalo to raise his right hand to cover his face, but immediately the guy leaned back in, pressing the blade's sharp teeth into Ítalo's hand, cutting deep and drawing blood.

"If I chopped you up and dumped you right here," the commando said, "it would cost me not a thing. Nothing would happen." Then the man said, *this time*, they would let him off with a warning, but only in exchange for his word: "Look, if someone comes this way, concha tu madre, you have not crossed paths with us. You have not seen us. Are we agreed?"

All this Ítalo told Sabine, alone in their bedroom. All this is what Sabine then relayed to her mother, before announcing she would return to the logging camp. "But you are frail," Tina pleaded with her. "No, mother, no matter what, I am going. I cannot stay. . . . If they kill us, they can kill us both."

That was but the beginning of what Tina shared with me, that second morning after meeting for the very first time, back in 2002—the second moment we spoke of her life and about the many histories that touched her, passed through her, that pushed her along. As I will later describe, Tina was introduced to me by a distant cousin Mauro, as a result of my brief role as a researcher for Peru's national truth commission.[4] And though Tina had already given her personal testimony to a local representative of that timely documentary project, about the family members she had lost in the war, Mauro had asked her to speak with me about the broader contexts and events of the conflict, explaining too—though I believe this was not altogether news to her—that I had already visited her town many times and had lived there too, off and on, in recent years. Yet, out of all of what Tina shared that second day, what resonated most, so much so that it has persisted with me ever since, was the overwhelming impression of an impossible place, set at an unfathomable remove—out there: across the river, folded in haze, straining sight but also looking back—an eye clouded over, deep in the left bank, to where everyday events of war had withdrawn so that they might continue. Out there—where Tina, and other people too, would tell me I could not go, not for any length of time—a turbulence persisted to interrupt and render impracticable any and all attempts at securing livelihoods viable and enduring. A turbulence still familiar to this town and palpable too, because of all that had happened before, because of all the war had left in its wake.

This much Tina would have me know: over there, on the other side of the Huallaga River, events still moved in heady swings and swerves that always seemed to turn dire. For what became of the intense hopes and strivings her daughter and son-in-law had wagered on logging deep in the left bank? Something near total loss, Tina said. For not one day after returning to the camp, Sendero summoned Ítalo and Abel to a meeting for area loggers. There they would learn about taxes they would have to pay on every shipment, but the real problem was what happened next. On the trail back to their camp, an army patrol lay in wait to surprise them and force them to lead soldiers back to the very place where the senderistas lingered still, where the patrol would launch an attack and where one of the senderistas in the fury of battle would catch a glimpse of Ítalo. And it was nothing short of astonishing that, despite all that, Ítalo and Abel managed to make it back to their camp, physically unharmed but knowing all too well what they had to do.

"No, Sabine, no; we must go. No time to explain. No time to grab your things."

The crew abandoned the left bank, leaving behind everything in their haste: cargos of timber and all their equipment. Yet taking with them, in their retreat, their lives but also something new, for now Sendero had Ítalo in their sights as a traitor, as a *soplón*, and they would not let him go. And so Sabine and Ítalo had no choice but to run. No choice but to flag down a car on the highway, with no time to pack, say good-byes. No choice but to leave the Upper Huallaga altogether, because withdrawing to another region of the country and starting over there was the only way to escape the Party's vindictive reach. Ítalo, to my knowledge, never did return, and though I know all of Tina's other children and most of her closest kin, to this day I have never met Sabine—though Tina does tell me that she goes to visit her now and again in the city of Pucallpa.

Flight on a moment's notice: a situation that before had hovered so close it became familiar enough to haunt each and every day. On a moment's notice, the command might come to run. And run you could. People would tell you how senseless it would be to do anything else. How intrepid and reckless it would be to stay put and not heed a threat of imminent death. And yet the airs of the intrepid and reckless were precisely what populated so many stories of the recent past, when people spoke as if everyone seemed to be seeking fortunes that, except for the extended embrace of their dreams, far outsized the possibilities of their present circumstances. People spoke as if most everyone seemed willing to take their chances until the moment tides turned. And yet those times were now decidedly in the past, here and now in this town, all the while that *over there*, they *somehow* carried on. Here and now, in that cement room near the center of town, Tina sat across from me, rather than out there on the river where she had worked for so many years, the last few with Sabine helping at her side. Even so and even here in that room, with walls reverberating the morning sounds of traffic in and near the plaza, she was in movement, always in movement, and especially so when she launched into a story, like the one she told that day and of which I have relayed barely a fragment.

Tina spoke to me of events from 2000. She spoke of them two years later, when we first coincided: already a moment when political circumstances region-wide were changing in ways that felt new. She spoke of a turbulence unbearable over there. She spoke as if, out there, in a place named Bijao, time were still a weather most foul. And yet between the here in town and a recent out there deep in the Huallaga's left bank, the broader political modifications under way expressed themselves most overtly underfoot and overhead, which is to say, in altered situations of territory.

By the year 2000, the left bank of the river remained sparsely inhabited. The most visible effects of the army's empty-the-countryside operations lingered on in the sheer dearth of people. The movement to populate the left bank once again had barely begun, such that two years later when I met Tina, she was only starting to speak of it. Even so, by the year 2000 a generalizing tendency of the coming territorial shifts could be discerned—a year when far away in Lima, the fraudulent reelection of Alberto Fujimori to the presidency roiled national politics, leading to the widespread discontent that would precipitate his flight from the country and the installation of a transitional government.[5] In the Upper Huallaga, meanwhile, a tenuous arc could be sketched, marking off the slow retreat of military conflict. The hostilities that had once persisted on both sides of the river would gradually become confined to the left bank and, with every passing year, to ever-more-specific regions and ever-smaller sectors of that other side. And at every point along that sweeping line of retreat, the legal relations that entangled people with actual, material terrains would remain unsettled.

Malecón: a thin dirt road, sometimes no more than a path from which one could look out across the water, from where I could see rolling hills, row after row, ridge after reclining ridge, until they converged with faraway horizons. Somewhere in between the malecón and that receding, and most removed, line were the things I heard about but could not directly experience. What I could do was look out at the expanse and weigh what came back in the distances that could not collapse, those rolling hills, those clouds and how they pressed on, one into the other.

Every town bordering the Huallaga has its malecón: a ridge of earth running alongside the river where a road appears to ride that raised bank in its gradual decline toward low-lying places where canoes gather at water's edge. Whether ridge or road, the malecón of the community where Tina lives traces the entire west side of town, drawing from the south a northward line that slopes downward, block after block, heading toward the main port in its slow fall to the water. The house of Tina's family sits beside that road, such that in the years to come to visit her at home meant coming face-to-face with the river and looking, even if for the briefest of moments, at the currents and beyond them to the other side.

So many times arriving at Tina's house, so many times gazing out across the river from Malecón Huallaga.

In the mid-1990s, in what were her later years as a *botera*, or river canoe operator, years when she ferried people and their things back and forth between La Roca, on the right bank, and Venenillo, on the left, Tina would leave Sabine in charge whenever she had errands to attend to in town. The story Tina told me on our second day recounted Sabine's decision to break out on her own. A chance to craft a livelihood with her husband and future family, a chance that ended in misery. Tina, when I first met her in the early 2000s, had her own hopes set on faring somewhat better. She told me that soon she would leave her work as a ferry operator. She had her sights trained on the left bank of the Huallaga, where in a place called Magdalena she would recover her father's farm in order to try her hand as a *campesina* once again.

Tina would be going back to the land. Nevertheless, the geographic features of the left bank barely appeared in the story of what her daughter and daughter's husband had faced only two years prior. Even as lines of territory were roughly intimated, their legal situations too, through a handful of topological figures—hills, trails, ravines, the river (always the river), Tina relayed few details of the landscape itself and almost nothing of what hovered overhead. And yet if political time turns on territory somehow, material terrains themselves perhaps should not be disregarded: not the grounds underfoot or their particular alignment with what presses down from above. For every iteration of political climate expresses a precise relation, an alliance even, between earth and sky.

To ask, in a political sense, what time it is—here and also over there—is to ask what the weather is like—here but also over there. The weather as a momentary yet prevailing political climate is what people in the Huallaga would in casual conversation refer to as *la situación*, a phrase often weighted in tones more somber than the words surrounding it. Sometimes, to tell the time is but a matter of looking up at the skies for army or police helicopters that might still appear. Or for the Cessnas that no longer do, thanks in part to a region-wide no-fly zone, previously enforced by the Peruvian Air Force and, as one might have learned, with occasional help from some CIA contractors. What's in or what's not in the sky can reveal something tangible about the moment—here as well as over there.

Political time can appear in a fleeting atmospheric convergence, whereby movements of air—winds and clouds with their pressures and precipitations—momentarily reach down to touch the earth. It might also name how material terrains simultaneously further and condition political circumstances—circumstances that unfold as historically specific denotations that ramify rumors of how this is this and how that is that. *Legal topographies* will be the notion I lean on to turn attention toward empirical relations, where lived encounters sometime brush uncomfortably close or where they sometimes are held in check instead as critical distances—palpable expanses across which visible and audible gestures might be conveyed, voids with vibratory charges that are far more often contemplated in silence. The notion of legal topographies asks about commands and threats and so many seizures that leave stings behind to fester, from which claims might later swell as an assertion of rights or as an appeal to unmet obligations. Above all, it points to where one can go—depending on who one is in a prevailing political moment—so as to tease out how empirical relations become implicated in material things and in what surrounds them.

Here in the Upper Huallaga Valley, the extent to which relations of territory and terrain have shifted may resonate in stories told of the war, which render, if faintly, their former outlines. Other intimations may come in fragments ever so small. Through the material traces of historical events that haunt ordinary lives and fieldwork encounters too. Through the abrasions that some bodies accrue as they wear long, thin, and out. In the accidents that happen and the woundings that linger on in senses both mutable and irreversible. In the ways some bodies mend, and in the ways some circumstances refuse to go back to what they were, but without for all that disappearing. The forgotten back injury that returns to keep a *mototaxi* driver off the streets. The limp sounding off in a *cocalero*'s every step. The timber beam that dropped to smash a raft operator's thumb. Tina's persistent fears of falling. In each of these fragments something of the past endures, sometimes offering glimpses of what might best be forgotten.

All histories have senses that are reversible, which run alongside others irretrievable, on account of what cannot be undone, and on account of the choices that now become constrained to their aftermaths. I have attempted with this book to follow some of those senses, ethnographically, from moments when the Upper Huallaga remained roiled in wakes of war: to trace what returns, while noting what quietly persists amid all that which does not repeat. This book thus strives to move ever closer to the region's riverine terrains: to what is most obvious and to all that shimmers beside and through the obvious as a semblance of something at once there and no longer there. The approach I have favored here takes inspiration from anthropology, understood as an intellectual tradition, which does not hold to national boundaries or care much about affirming disciplinary distinctions. What I appreciate about that tradition, and what keeps pulling me toward it, are those strands that assert an empiricist orientation by privileging events and relations through a strong sensibility for aesthetics.[6] Those strands understand ethnography to be an expressive task, which pushes description to the point where it acquires conceptual resonances, to that point where images unexpectedly emerge. For me ethnography entails finding a way of working that closely aligns with a place of inquiry. By persisting with that place, a process of sorts can take shape, which might allow for the particular, ever-shifting, features of that place to teach singular ways of working. The writing of this book bears the traces of that teaching; above all it conveys a patience, which I might describe as a deliberate hover—not because that's how I would have wanted it but because that was what the place of inquiry repeatedly imposed. And yet, in moving slow, if only because the place interrupted my best attempts to move fast, I have stumbled onto a principle or two about what ethnography demands, as I grasp it and as I would practice it—not because it is better in some generalizable way but, hopefully, because it can express something different, somehow.

Fieldwork generates fragments. Ethnographic writing explores those fragments with a patient piecing and re-piecing together. Where that examination does not belittle those pieces but affirms their partiality, it may, sometimes, tap into a kind of latent force. To do that—to find that force of the fragment—perhaps all that is needed is a little creative autonomy, some breathing room to compose. What's more, since efforts of recollection, continually striving to remember what has just happened, occupy no minor part of fieldwork and fieldwork-based writing, returning to that place, again and again, to grasp how it is changing, while also reaching toward receding moments of pasts that are largely unknown, amid storms that come and go, can create the impression of percolating back and forth through strata of time. This happens in hearing stories people share. It happens in the silences they also keep. It transpires as well in what can be strongly felt without words rising up or falling into place. For even if there is no escape from being carried off in presents that always pass, ethnographic writing moves along cusps of experience, while trying to grasp at other moments now gone: listening, sensing, gauging with a sideways glance.

The place to where I have been returning is a coca-growing region on the eastern slopes of the Andes of central Peru, known as the Upper Huallaga Valley, which beginning in the early 1980s became a stronghold of the Maoist Shining Path.[7] That setting has encouraged me to think about how war couples with forgetting. Or in another phrasing: how prior military conflicts (with their repetitions of the same, secret societies, atmospherics of threat and command) come to inhere in postwar landscapes in ways not altogether evident. In this book I am concerned with how the presents of war and postwar pass and how, in passing, they introduce changes, of which in the Upper Huallaga many of the most prominent have been territorial. Where spatial prohibitions have waxed and waned. Where, between town and country, the very material surfaces upon which transit happens have demanded vigilance—because precarious and ever vulnerable to sabotage. Where in the countryside the insurgency claimed dominion over all property in land, all the while thwarting road construction and repair. Where army forts arrived, starting in the towns and spreading from there, to re-order the lay of the valley and what flowed across it in their wake. *All this* so that later the departure of war might be easily read—as if through some mere reversal of sense—in the rehabilitation of a trunk highway or in the proliferation of dirt roads, reaching out to what had been the most politically remote of hamlets. In the retitling of rural land too, and in the slow shuttering of counterinsurgency bases. *All this* within the onset of new times that allowed so little space to reflect on how the past lingered, woven so thoroughly into the landscapes of aftermath, or why it was that now most anywhere could feel safe to go, even in the dark of night.

These varied and variable expressions of shifting territory suggest that the specificities of political time can be discerned through careful attention to configurations of matter and movement and to the events that bring them together. The notion *legal topographies* refers to the empirical relations that emerge through those events to reveal how political time meets terrain, where presents of war and postwar, in their very passing, continually bring earth and sky into ephemeral alliance.

This book has emerged out of materials gathered during multiple fieldwork visits to two Huallaga towns prominent in the Peruvian government's counterinsurgency war with Shining Path: Nuevo Progreso and Aucayacu. Though separated by a mere forty-five kilometers, throughout the conflict the social distance between them seemed appreciable even though in some respects they have shared many enduring characteristics. Both towns fall pressed, as it were, between the region's main overland thoroughfare—the Marginal Highway—and the river that gives the valley its name; both have small populations, numbering but several thousand. Their respective significance, historical but also topographic, resides elsewhere: in their tangled relations with the hamlets and rural expanses that surround them, most important, those that lie on other side of the Huallaga River: the so-called *margen izquierda* or left bank.

For a good twenty years, spanning the early 1980s and, in some corners, until the mid-2000s, the left bank was another political world. *Zona roja*: where Sendero Luminoso organized rural hamlets into bases of political and logistical support. The left bank was also where coca could be grown in fields far less accessible to the police and the US Drug Enforcement Administration (DEA). Because the river impeded easy entry and made all who crossed extremely visible and thus exposed to ambush, surprise raids were harder to pull off, requiring helicopters and specially trained teams that could slip in and out. The river also lent a hand to the insurgency's goal of shaping the composition of rural communities, whether that meant keeping tabs on who moved back and forth between the Huallaga's shores or banishing under threat of death or, if it came to that, killing, those the Party deemed socially undesirable. Such areas of Shining Path influence existed on the right bank too, especially in the hills farthest from the highway. But those places proved far more susceptible to armed intervention by Peruvian police or military, which hindered the insurgency's territorial expansion. The right bank, if always vulnerable throughout the war, fell more fully into the sphere of state influence. This was especially true for the towns, which had police stations, administrative offices of local and national government, and eventually, with the declaration of emergency rule, bases of the army. Thus, when rural communities on the left bank looked out across the river's currents, toward Nuevo Progreso or Aucayacu, they faced island outposts of the

Peruvian state. In this manner the Huallaga became the threshold separating one political world from another, a moving material line, laden
with turbulence.

The river is arguably what first shapes the region's legal topographies.
Even when that source goes unacknowledged, the Huallaga's material
force resonates in specific routes that roads follow, in shifting physical
contours of towns and shoreline farms, no less than in regimes of properties set at a remove from the river's basin, beyond the reach of seasonal
floods. Here the question of how the river relates to its tributaries reappears. For if the Marginal Highway would by the mid-1970s displace the
Huallaga as the preferred transportation route through the valley, most
of the major locations and settlements though which the road passed (and
passes to this day) were named for small streams. These were places where
traffic in the earliest years of the road had no choice but to slow and often stop, to contend with the steady flows of low water—descending toward the Huallaga—places that, following intense rains, could become
impassable until a series of small bridges were finally built to lift the road
up and over. This is all to say the empirical relations of legal topography
cannot be separated from the same material terrains, which produce and
impinge upon them, not without altering characteristics that are essential
to them. Political time moves through those relations precisely at those
points where earth and sky entwine. If so, perhaps it is only in intersections of matter, image, and sensation that those movements can be most
tangibly grasped.

Again: What do I mean by *political time*? Sometimes I mean the utilitarian bent of the present and how its particular distribution of unequal
rights and obligations becomes common sense. Sometimes I mean *time as
weather*: that Hobbesian all against all fury of civil unrest, which haunts
enduring ties between people and property (the very things they would
call their own), threatening to sever and dissolve them. Sometimes I mean
the little contracts people make with their everyday environments so
they might blend in: the "reciprocal topographies" people establish when
they appear and carry themselves as current expedience demands, which
takes on a heightened urgency in eras of war and immediate postwar,
where eliding certain distinctions and even camouflaging (parts of selves,

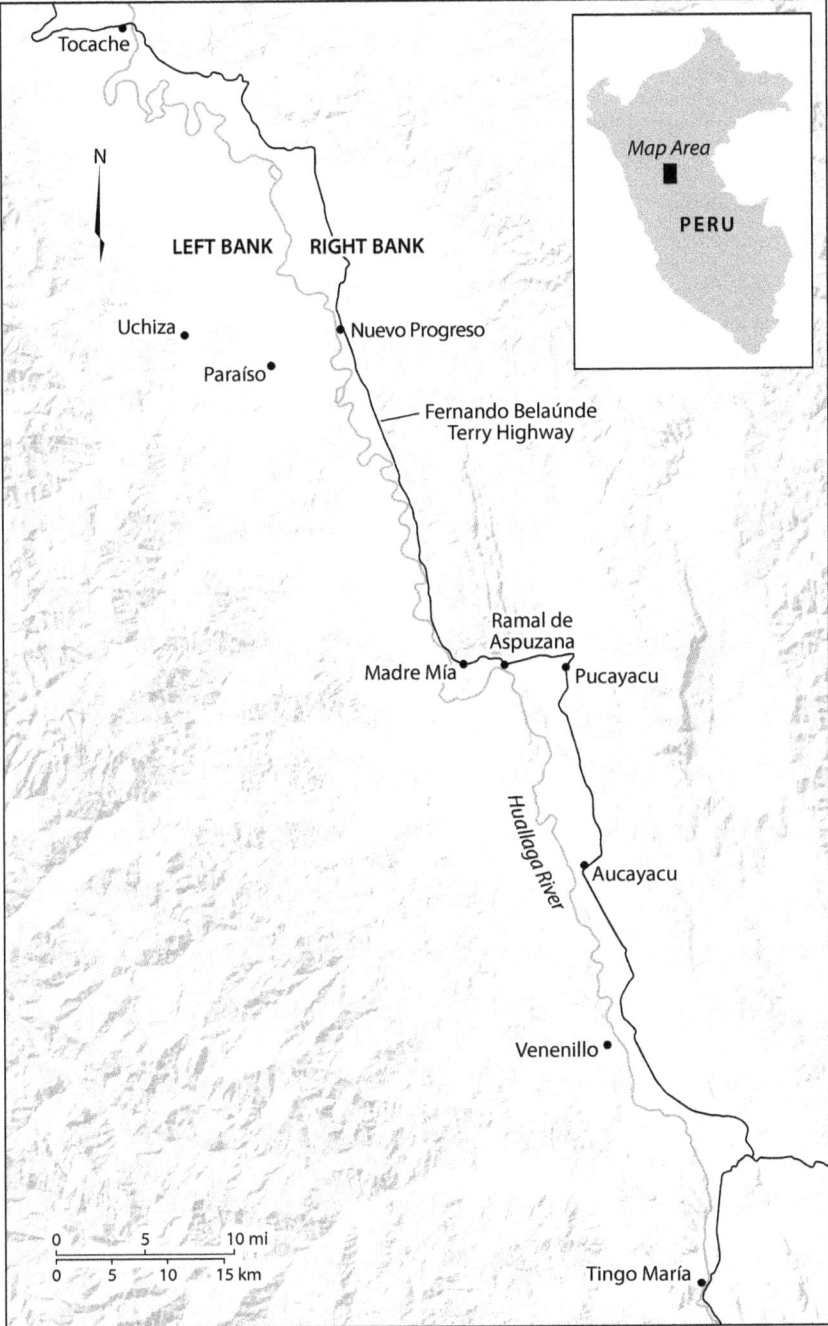

Tocache

N

LEFT BANK   RIGHT BANK

Uchiza

Paraíso

Nuevo Progreso

Fernando Belaúnde
Terry Highway

Ramal de
Aspuzana

Madre Mía   Pucayacu

Huallaga River

Aucayacu

Venenillo

Tingo María

Map Area

PERU

0	5	10 mi
0	5	10	15 km

sympathies, and deeds) become imperative, given the legal-existential risks and inducements of the situation.[8] Sometimes I mean a specific positioning within and toward a lived milieu, which in aftermaths of war entails a palpable reorientation or a shifting of axes—here subtle, there drastic—toward geographic settings, including the movements that may be made through those terrains. From this side of the river to that. Ahead, round that next kink in the road. And now, coming into view over there, that hill: strange how it no longer seems somehow better to just look away.

With or without war, fashioning a livelihood in the Huallaga Valley has demanded finding ways of transiting between town and country. Shining Path would first emerge during the early 1980s as a rural power that quickly aimed its sights on the towns. The army would then set up shop, first in the towns, and from there—through its ever-expanding archipelago of forts—extend a net of surveillance, capture, and slaughter into the countryside. In its rage, the insurgent-counterinsurgent conflict tensed geographic continuities that had formerly woven town to country, twisting the hierarchical relations that bound them, interjecting material and affective rifts that could at times appear to sever those ties altogether.

What the army and Shining Path brought to bear is no longer visible in the terrain. And though you cannot take photographs of that aspect of the past, it persists nonetheless, mostly in silence. The mute, oblivious insistence of political foundings—always failed but working somehow in and on the present as it unfolds—is what I call *prehistory*.[9] Something happened far beyond what ever could be spoken, something felt on occasion still as a chaos—a time as weather—that must be screened off, if one is ever to have a life. Something from all that insists still as an oblivion of political community, beyond what can be known.[10]

With and without war, everyday fortunes in the Huallaga Valley have depended on reliable transportation between local worlds urban and rural, so some have preferred livelihoods that could directly provide for and satisfy that persistent need—as the operators of small canoes and rafts and as the drivers of cars, vans, pickup trucks, or, more recently, the ever-ubiquitous mototaxi. Doing so has lent these *transportistas*—such as Tina and Wilson, Hugo and Pedro, Reynaldo and Don Florentín, and so many more—an intimate grasp on the events and broader predicaments of the war and on what transpired in their wake. Readily they would tell about impossible situations they once had to navigate—threading precarious paths between insurgents and armed agents of the Peruvian state— even if the specific circumstances, and their own place within them, were surely far more complicated.

My research for this book focused on everyday movements between town and country—through a series of fieldwork visits to the Huallaga Valley beginning in 2010 and culminating in 2015. During those visits, which lasted several weeks, some as long as two months, I collected life histories of transportistas, learning from them what I could about how the war and its passing affected not only the rhythms and tasks of transit but the ways people worked the land as they made claims to it. I also spent extended stretches taking photographs and short videos at the crossings of rivers, town ports, roads, bridges, and other settings of rural transportation. This book draws on events from earlier stays in the Huallaga Valley as well: from 2002, 2005, 2006, and from others still, predating the circumstances out of which the project, I would soon call "Semblance in Terrain," eventually arose.

One crucial feature of all ethnographic research is that it is never fully over. The experiences and encounters one absorbs during fieldwork are never definitively put away. To the contrary, they reveal their force and enduring significance precisely through the insistence with which they can rise up unexpectedly. Ethnography writes from the hauntings of the very materials that fieldwork gathers.

I made my first visit to the Upper Huallaga in the mid-1990s, and I have returned there, if not every year, frequently enough to have perceived the gradual fall away from overt war. Within that arc of slow passing, I have caught glimpses of modifications in political time. Those temporal shifts have been local in the extreme, and because they manifest primarily as atmospheric phenomena, they can be grasped only up close. One might say "in person." If how they unfold can be subtle, they are palpable, nonetheless, and sometimes surprise for the extent to which they may alter a sense of the place.

During the late 1990s two constraints with profound implications— prohibitions on speaking and obstacles to movement—shaped my initial research in the Huallaga, an era immediately following a twenty-year cocaine boom,[11] the subject of my first book, *Coca's Gone*. Back then everything seemed to turn on two sorts of limits. What one should not say or ask. Where one could and should not go. Hindrances to ordinary communication resonated as well in conditions of visibility, judging from common sense doled out as everyday friendly advice: one should not be *seen* talking to this person or that, or *seen* traveling to rural communities unless unaccompanied by someone who lived nearby. There was effectively only one public road—where stranger sociality was expected but also strained—the north-south Marginal Highway, fine to travel on during daytime but sketchy at night. To get off it between the main towns at any time could be charged. To linger along those rural roadside expanses, seemingly deserted yet teeming as if with fateful potentials, was something that seemed to unnerve, and even frighten, the townspeople I knew. Their assumption was that in such lands political control was at best fluid, that along those stretches Shining Path influence persisted and that, therefore, those places would be closed to outsiders. Their nervousness spread all the more when major dates approached from either of the two reigning civic calendars—state and insurgent—set side by side to scrape and grate. On those days, townspeople assured, it was preferable to stay inside and not to travel at all.

Back then, most news from the countryside arrived by word of mouth, where it might be picked up by a local radio station or conveyed by phone: residential landlines were only then beginning to become common. In towns north of Tingo María—Aucayacu, Nuevo Progreso, Uchiza, Tocache—the breathing room for representation, if I can call it that, felt tight and at times unbearably rarefied. On the streets and other places public and outdoors, it often seemed better not to engage in notation of any kind. Two episodes immediately come to mind: ready images jumping forward when I recall those early years. One happened late one morning in Aucayacu, just as the blazing sun coaxed residents near the town's center to abandon streets in favor of the shade of cement interiors. I am not certain of the year, probably near the end of 1998, but I was talking with my friend Mariela, at the counter of her bodega, when a group of young soldiers from the base, five maybe six teenagers, scrambled past her store—in a blur of black T-shirts and shorts, dingy canvas sneakers, with rifles strapped to shoulders and clutched tight—racing down the last block to the plaza to interrupt what had been a desolate quiet. The sudden tumult pulled us to the door, where we found others peering out from the doorways of nearby storefronts. Mariela called over to a shop-keeper friend, asking what was up. "A teenage boy is sitting in the plaza . . . and he's drawing!" No one seemed to know who the young guy was, but we soon learned that he ran when he sensed the commotion of sol-diers heading toward him. Though he ultimately escaped their pursuit, his desire to flee lent weight to the deduction, which immediately took hold among the shopkeepers on Mariela's block, that he must have been making a sketch of city hall and for Sendero too, who they imagined to be planning an attack from some remote hamlet in the hills, where this boy, whom they did not recognize, no doubt lived. On the face of it, their rapid judgment struck me as absurd, but it was a provocation to thought, all the same, leaving me to wonder why *here*, and why *now*. To pick a spot on a park bench, pull out a pen, and begin to sketch was not only deeply suspicious. It was to take a plunge into the roiling currents of counter-insurgency, which could get you shot or, maybe worse, hauled off to the base. Precisely here. And precisely now.

The other episode occurred about a year later, this time in Uchiza. I am sitting at a restaurant with Ediberto, a traveling salesman who peddles sundry goods to remote hamlets—small things: toothbrushes, soaps, tiny packets of shampoo, AA batteries for finger flashlights, but also larger bundles, perhaps sheets and blankets, that he packed up and lugged over a shoulder, as long as he knew they would sell. Running into "Eddy" outside the central market of Uchiza surprised us both, as our paths had until then crossed only in Tocache: always at the same rundown hotel just off the Plaza de Armas, where I rented a room, where he stayed when-ever passing through, and where we had many animated conversations, below a TV set screwed high up on the wall, blaring away. There, sitting on one of two rotting couches, he would reminisce, dispense advice, and argue points of local narco history, as he rested up between jaunts to the countryside north of Tocache. Always catching rides to the next village, always up toward Juanjuí before turning round and retracing steps to

Tocache once again, always carrying his wares, up and down the Marginal Highway, back when that extended stretch of road was still unpaved and often impassable because of the rains, mud, and ever-moving earth.

People who knew Eddy well called him "Happy Dólar," a colorful term of affection, pulling on another not-so-distant life. The hotel owner's wife explained with a smile, and with Eddy nodding all the while, that he had worked as an "accountant" in the village of Campanilla for el loco Limoniel himself: Demetrio Chávez Peñaherrera, better known as Vaticano.[12] Whenever a plane landed from Colombia, and in those days, the early 1990s, their arrival was always imminent, Eddy would tally up each and every bill to make sure all was square before bricks of *pasta básica*, unrefined cocaine, could be loaded on board. *Contando tarjeta*, he called it, and every time Eddy opened the first bag, box, or suitcase of cash, so captivating was the look of delight, so intense the glow that came over his face, that a nickname not only rose up but made an irrefutable and lasting claim on the man.

On the day of our chance encounter in Uchiza, Happy Dólar had unnamed people to see, unspecified affairs to resolve. Not wanting to linger in the glaring sun, we agreed to meet up once he was free. I would find him at his friend's restaurant, Eddy said, giving me directions. Several hours later, now early evening, there he was, crouching over a beer at a table, pressed up against a wall, with his friend tending to the counter in front. The place was small with six tables, mostly empty, though after I arrived, others would begin to trickle in. As I pulled up a chair, Eddy launched into telling me about this and about that—"*Look*, here's what we're working with now," he says, pulling out a gold metallic watch for me to see. "*They're knockoffs!*"—and pushing tales too, from other times when he had passed through Uchiza. Eddy shared, as he often did at the hotel, but here talking softly, almost a whisper, as if for our ears alone, things he had never shared before—the three years served in Lurigancho prison for his ties to Vaticano, all behind him now because he had paid handsomely to get his record fixed. Eddy shared and with details I would not want to forget, because so precise. It was like that time he told me about narco radio operators and how back in the 1980s they would avoid common Huallaga place-names, speaking in code: "Los discos" for Tocache,

"Las aguas" for Pizana, "La U" for Uchiza, "La iglesia" for Campanilla, "Las Ramas," for Ramal de Aspuzana, and on and on.

So I pulled a spiral notebook from my bag, but no sooner had I set it on the table did Eddy give me a hard look and say in words slow and firm: "Put . . . that . . . away," sweeping the room behind me with the dart of his eyes, reminding me of all those ears that must have been zeroing in just then on our conversation. All because my spiral notebook had come into view. "Guarda . . . eso": I can hear those words still— an image at the ready—but only now do I discover in them that point where a general prohibition on speaking might narrow its scope to make visibly evident the documentation of what was being said. All because jotting down someone else's words attracted unwanted attention. All because unwanted attention conjured vague threats. All because just as soon as my notebook was removed from sight, Eddy picked the same thread right back up and barreled on about the "huge injustice" that had been done to El Loco (Vaticano), adamant too that never again would he let himself get mixed up in *huevadas* (stupid stuff), and then pivoting for a moment, as if to catch his breath, to his current concerns and curiosities, like the tiny glass bottle he pulled from a pocket and shook to reveal a clear liquid inside, before storing it away once again. "*Pusanga* [love magic] . . . I buy these for three soles and sell them for fifty, sometimes sixty. That, right there, is my ability." In this way Eddy would weave back and forth between two distinct times and two different lives and livelihoods, keeping them separate, as if one did not, should not, touch the other.

After three beers, and an hour altogether, Happy Dólar got up to go. I walked him over to the counter where Eddy introduced me to his friend. While ringing up the bill, the restaurant owner alluded with a smirk to their shared years of excitement and plenty, which compared unfavorably with his present-day situation: stuck in Uchiza, abandoned by the drug economy when its heady swirl moved on. Eddy, however, claimed to feel nothing of the sort. Being an itinerant merchant brought him satisfaction. Far better to wander from hamlet to hamlet than have a prison sentence dangling overhead. And with that he walked out of the restaurant and down the street, alone, leaving me and the owner, lingering in the doorway to follow him for a moment with our glances as he withdrew, those three beers manifesting now in the slight stumble they added to his step.

Five days later I am back in Tocache where rumor has it that Happy Dólar is under arrest: three kilos of *cloro*, refined cocaine, found hidden in his wares. A merchant friend of Eddy's tells me, up to twenty years in Castro Castro await him now, saying that the police must have been keeping close tabs on his movements. Now that recent trip to Uchiza, well off his beaten path, makes a different kind of sense, reminding me of what my *traquetera* friend Yéssica once confided: in the Huallaga every legal business was but a front for something else.

Several months have passed when I run into Happy Dólar again. I have not seen him since Uchiza, and once again we cross paths in Tocache. He insists it was all a rumor, that he was never arrested, but will say nothing more. I think, surely something must have happened, and far more than Happy Dólar wants to let on, but for however little I know him, I know well enough not to press.

Perhaps these images—a boy who flees because he sketched, the spiral notebook I set on a table and then quickly withdrew—are less important for how they hover as memories available for voluntary recall. That they might strike some momentary analogy to a present, passing circumstance seems less significant too than how as dominant memories they haunt, providing sparks to post-fieldwork writing. For it is writing that can strive to turn such images into portals—portals that can point to other regions far larger, which linger alongside what is obvious and most manifest.

The depleted air for representation, which persisted throughout the latter half of the 1990s, also shaped my experience of taking pictures. Still then, in those years, over photography, vague threats seemed to hang: for committing that local, Huallaga-specific, crime of snitching. Or, what was for practical purposes the same, merely giving off the appearance of possibly being a soplón. And while I found I could take photographs in public—rare was the occasion that anyone actually advised me to stop—doing so felt licit and welcome only for certain formal occasions: private parties, school dances, and civic parade competitions. In all other moments, the threat that lingered over photography felt strong enough to generate noise, which in the absence of anyone saying anything

FIGURE I.2. Happy Dólar, field notes sketch

about it, could be unsettling and even disruptive. Often when taking pictures, I found I could barely concentrate. I struggled to take the time and care analog photography demanded. Always working rushed left me largely dissatisfied with the results. Perhaps that is why I also took to drawing small images alongside the words that were my field notes back then. Returning to them now, I am surprised to discover this drawing of Happy Dólar, sketched fast on a piece of white bond paper and then pasted into my black hardcover journal, barely a doodle. And I am even more surprised to discover in this drawing, less any exact resemblance than an expressive trace of Happy Dólar himself. A certain air and a carriage too—that heavy slouch of his, sliding softly—that somehow trues to that person I once knew.

Perhaps the most striking and personally difficult constraint of that initial period of extended fieldwork, mid- to late 1990s, was the imperative to keep detailed notes within circumstances where at any moment I might get stopped and told to hand over my things. Such pressures contributed to writing down much less than I might have otherwise recorded. They also resulted in a certain cryptic quality that accrued to notes that diligently avoided details traceable to actual people and to what they might have told me. I suspect such pressures also opened up spaces for small drawings to take shape, beside words that were too few and that conveyed far too little. What is certain is that, bit by bit, in glimpses afforded by subsequent visits, I would come to see, but even more so come to feel, how the circumstances that gave rise to those pressures and to other constraints began to change: first in 2002, then in 2005 and 2006, again in 2010, and all the more decisively since, as the war dipped ever further into the past. No longer would everything turn so obviously, so stridently, on what one could not say and on where one should not go.

Here it is essential to mention that the military features of the conflict persisted in the Upper Huallaga, long after they had subsided elsewhere in the country and did not seem to come to full stop, even then, until the capture of the regional leader of Shining Path in 2012: Camarada Artemio—a figure for many years shrouded in mystery, within a political organization famed for extreme secrecy.[13] All the while, a separate, antagonistic faction of the same Maoist insurgency has continued to carry out armed actions in a different coca-growing region to the south.[14] In other words, there was no national unity to an internal conflict that acquired a national scope. There were many wars, many places, many times.

The Upper Huallaga was significant foremost for the international dimension it brought to the conflict because of the strategic place it held within the global cocaine economy. From the late 1970s to the end of the 1980s, the region was considered the epicenter of illicit cocaine production and trade in Peru—the place where coca was grown and partially refined for clandestine shipment to the Medellín and Cali cartels of Colombia.[15] This is what gave the Upper Huallaga a notoriety that distinguished it early on from other parts of the valley and soon too from other fronts of the war. Such fame tended, however, to obscure a high deal of situational variance from locale to locale, which could only be discerned nearby. How each place became interwoven—deeply, fleetingly, or on occasion barely at all—with the extraordinary, extra-local forces that seemed to take hold of the region was not simply obvious but difficult to appreciate, because never transparent, and prohibitive too, because frequently laden with threat.

From afar, the tropical landscapes through which the Huallaga's waters descend could always be separated, as they commonly are, into three geographic areas—Upper, Central, Lower—designating stretches of river but also distinct social milieus. The "Upper" portion of the valley was where Shining Path, during the 1980s, established an enduring presence in rural expanses north of the city of Tingo María in Huánuco and running as far as, but not quite reaching, the town of Juanjuí in San Martín. This was an area the Peruvian state had previously set aside for rural settlement programs, when successive national governments of the 1960s and 1970s appropriated vast tracts of forest—often repossessed from absentee landowners—and redistributed them as smaller plots to anyone who would homestead, grow crops, and, above all, stay put.[16] Lost in that modern history of colonization were the indigenous, forest-dwelling peoples who had thrived in prior centuries along the banks of the Huallaga and nearby streams.[17] If memory of that former presence persevered among migrants who later arrived from neighboring highlands and lower regions of the Huallaga, it was at most in a bare recognition of not being original to the place.[18] Across this upper portion of the valley settler communities arose, yet without imposing uniformity. Palpable were differences between locales, whether for the social, historical, administrative, and economic ties that specific towns kept with the countryside immediately surrounding them, or for the distinctive lay of floodplains of individual tributaries that, in gathering hamlets and farms, comprised tiny micro-regions all on their own.[19] That is to say, "situational variance" up close responded far more to circumstances that *crosscut*, rather than followed, the Huallaga's winding currents—even as the course of that broad moving line would continue to orient national and extra-national readings of area geography.

From afar, political circumstances could look quite different too. When the Truth and Reconciliation Commission was created in 2001 to investigate the armed conflict over the two-decade period spanning 1980 to 2000,[20] the implication was that the era of political violence was over and that with the fall of the presidential regime of Alberto Fujimori the war had reached a definitive end. The commission gathered testimonies, as well as textual, photographic, and audiovisual materials for a massive archive, which served as the evidential basis for analyses, conclusions, and recommendations contained in an all-encompassing final report delivered to the national government.[21] Across twelve volumes and multiple annexes, that report represented an extraordinary undertaking, which sought not only to document what had happened but to investigate the specific sociohistorical contexts surrounding the outbreak and territorial unfolding of overt hostilities. The promise was enormous. The sweep was breathtaking. And yet the immediate political message of the commission would be conveyed less by the final report in its entirety than by a three-page preface, which plotted the causes and consequences of the era of political violence.[22] Out of this ordered, communicable core—filtered of crucial, even perplexing, details that appeared in later chapters and unfettered by ambiguities and ramifications that might have complicated public reception—a streamlined story emerged about the war, from which heated debates and many scholarly inquiries would borrow essential coordinates.

Here an ever-so-concise reading of history would turn on a small set of claims:

That the origins of political violence should be traced to the decision by the leadership of Shining Path to launch armed struggle in May 1980.

Or that the conflict's mortal toll, in the commission's numerical reckoning, exceeded sixty-nine thousand: almost double previous estimates.

Or that from this unexpectedly high number of fatalities, three out of every four were peasants who spoke Quechua—indicating that

those who had borne the brunt of the violence were disproportion-
ately from the Andean highlands or from remote rural communities
historically denied equal participation in the political community of
the nation.

Or that the Maoist insurgency was responsible for an absolute (if
narrow) majority of all lives lost.[23]

These were but a handful of the commission's numerous findings. Yet, as
overarching statements, they sufficed to provide a rhetorical ground that
could be returned to again and again, not only for separating victims from
victimizers and adjudicating ultimate blame but for extending a moral
sense to how the nation, *as a whole*, should reflect on the war. That so
many could perish without broad awareness, much less acknowledgment,
from national society—or rather from that portion geographically situated
in affluent areas of coastal cities, especially Lima, which enjoyed greater
protections of political belonging—was not only appalling. It suggested
the era of violence had been marked by a generalized oblivion, especially
among the country's most privileged and least scathed.

A similar disregard extended to the Upper Huallaga, even if the region aligned poorly with a framing of history that ignored the social
and economic significance of coca and cocaine. Tucked deeper into the
final report, if mostly under the watchword *narcotráfico*, there would
be stark acknowledgment that cocaine had been a collective phenomenon of consequence throughout the war.[24] Yet in the commission's more
public pronouncements, it barely appeared, and almost never with ad-
equate appreciation of the degree to which the outlawed, criminalized
trade responded quite directly to long-standing failures, exclusions, and
structural violences of the country's legal economy. It was as if a moral
sense were harder to reckon where warfare merged with cocaine's social
horizons. Those horizons also made things harder to count. The Upper
Huallaga had been a major front of the armed conflict, and yet reliable
measures, much less quantifiable bases of comparison with other regions,
were elusive and guesswork at best.[25] The difficulty stemmed in part from
the secrecies essential to what had been a flourishing, illicit frontier of

capitalism: from the anonymous, roving character of people and groups actively involved in the trade to the harsh penalties locally for anyone suspected of sharing vital information. Social exclusions and hierarchies prevailing elsewhere in Peru found vivid echoes in the Huallaga, but these did not map onto language practices in a manner that could provide ready insight as to who had been most targeted for wartime misfortune. Many who traveled seasonally from the nearby highlands of central Peru to labor in the valley's coca fields could understand and even speak Quechua, though increasingly few as their sole mode of verbal expression. Spanish, meanwhile, tended to be dominant among the area's more permanent residents—settlers and children of settlers who had come originally in search of land but who later followed opportunities created by the global demand for cocaine. Singular, surprisingly vital worlds formed in proximity to the commodity chains of illicit production and trade. That those worlds did not, and could not, partake of the everyday transparencies and protections promised by legal society hardly severed their ties to the nation at large. The social integrations they entailed were merely less apparent and more actively concealed.

Secrecies and threats permeating the cocaine economy offer a partial explanation for the profound oblivion that would persist nationally as to what had transpired in the Upper Huallaga. And yet there was a larger problem of fit with what became an authoritative national reading of the war's origins and outcomes—which, again, were more plural than commonly admitted. For it was not at all clear that the outbreak of political violence in the region could be tied to Shining Path, not at first and not entirely. Several years before the Maoist insurgency commenced its first armed actions in the Upper Huallaga, the national government had declared a state of legal exception over the region.[26] Yielding to pressures from the US embassy for more aggressive measures against expanding cultivations of coca and a burgeoning commerce in unrefined cocaine, the police had begun large-scale, often violent, interdiction campaigns against area farms: destroying harvests, stealing equipment, beating up whoever got in the way. Rural farmers responded by collectively organizing around the defense of their right to grow coca, leading to a series of valley-wide strikes.[27] These circumstances created favorable conditions for the entrance of Shining Path, whose clandestine militants encountered rural communities under constant predation from state security forces— in tandem at times with agents of the DEA—and feeling unfairly treated too, when not swindled, in their dealings with cocaine traders. Shining Path would by the late 1980s develop a wide social base, while exercising significant political and territorial control over much of the countryside. And yet among people I met, who had lived through the worst years of the war, most concurred that enthusiasm for the Maoist movement did not last. Support for Shining Path would endure in rural areas, even as its rule became increasingly forced: under local Party authorities described as domineering, exacting, at times disloyal, and always too quick to kill. Unlike other parts of the country, however, where local civil defense patrols or *ronderos* were credited with reversing the advance of Shining Path and for that cast at times in the role of national heroes,[28] rural communities here did not arm themselves to confront Sendero directly. Even so, most said that despite what had been a rather grim state of affairs, when viewed in retrospect, the insurgency was by no means responsible for the preponderance of death. In the Huallaga, they insisted, the army had killed far more, fighting terror with a terror all the greater still.

Such basic discrepancies about how the conflict unfolded in the Upper Huallaga, when compared with other fronts of the war, have gone generally unremarked. And that distance from the region's political circumstances is symptomatic too of the scant attention they have received in most historical accounts of an era of political violence, considered effectively over by the year 2000, if not before. Shining Path would pursue military and political activities in the Upper Huallaga for another decade to come. In the meantime, nationally, there would be less debate on how the conflict began and drew to a close than a competition of common sense over what should be remembered and how. There would be definitional clashes too over what to call those who took part, how to describe what they did and why, and over who deserved public sympathy and even recompense for losses suffered. Indeed, contests over what should anchor the proper terms of historical reference have been a constant of postwar politics in Peru.[29]

Anchoring reference—grasped as a political problem—applies not to dates alone but to any word or phrase that pretends to secure a ground in language from which to make candid claims about empirical worlds: here, over there, yesterday, today, this year and that. The problem is integral to political life and as such not new, especially not to theorists of civil war. For good reason Thomas Hobbes went to pains, at the beginning of his works, to nail down the predicates for the universe of terms that informed his philosophical propositions and their assertions about the fundamental characteristics of political community. That the connective tissues between words and what they name were not only fragile but critical to the constitution of a political body was also something Carl Schmitt would repeatedly underscore, noting on one occasion "Thomas Hobbes' pessimistic maxim that even arithmetic and geometric certainties become problematic if they fall within the sphere of the political: the intense friend-enemy distinction."[30] Here one notes a warning about the depths to which political life might fall, if factions became so opposed that between them nothing, nothing beyond hostility, could be held in common: not agreement as to numbers and what their laws might say, not even on when to call this whole a circle and that a square. Vulnerable to the tumults of collective life, the power of reference would also seem to draw on a certain turbulence or oscillation within language itself: between statements of *denotation*, expressing what simply *is*—rising somehow from empirical things as they objectively are— and statements of *designation,* affixing names from some elsewhere, that is, from a minimal distance such that what names might never be identical to what gets named.[31] The turbulence internal to language is paradoxical because at one moment it can appear self-contained and at another dependent on social worlds: to their shifting political states of affairs, including the actual terrains on which they move.

Names and naming are crucial to events of war and, all the more, if "killing is," as Edmund Leach succinctly phrased it, "a classificatory operation."[32] Names and naming are also one way the violence of those events may linger on after killing has largely stopped. And so, war entails, among other things, pitched battles for reference, battles of attrition that can always be picked up again, and then again, long after military strife subsides. Such contests would seem to become even more fraught, and strident, when national societies confront political violence from within,[33] where anchoring reference ultimately becomes at once a matter of gravity and the gravest of all matters.

That is why when writing about the Upper Huallaga certain challenges have appeared. How to portray a tumultuous period without firm bounds: that locally no one could fully know, that nationally most were oblivious to and that many have now "forgotten"? How to return to regions of that lingering past, without converting reflections on specific events of the war into so many moral and moralizing accounts? Perhaps attempts to describe histories of the conflict could unfold as a telling of political time. Or maybe at the very least the question of how those histories enter into relation with constellations of memory and forgetting could be posed, but without making the common, the good, or the obvious sense of events the limit where inquiry should stop. Perhaps the very question of oblivion could be pursued by moving ever closer to the specific places where the military conflict once hovered and where, in wakes it left behind, intersections of matter, sensation, image can still conjure up something of the war: through claims and contemplations that persist, sometimes to intimate rights and obligations, though never without doubts as to what might still obtain. This is to ask how time and history might entwine.

I see this book as an effort to explore aftermaths of Peru's internal war through the territorial transformations of a specific region. In so doing I have not automatically presumed that the ever-growing distance from times of conflict can permit a more discerning vision or effective judgment. I have not presupposed among those the war affected, that victims could always be separated from perpetrators, or even where they could, that such terms, if but designations of character, would convey enough about the agility of those pulled into the conflict or about the aleatory conditions they faced then and in what has followed. To the extent this book looks retrospectively at historical events, it does not seek to ascribe blame, nor does it dwell, as a guiding purpose, on the failures, fortunes, brutalities, or follies of wartime generations.[34] Nor does it turn the national truth commission into an explicit object of concern.[35] The histories seem too vast, multiple, and entangled to try to condense them, even when restricted to the Upper Huallaga Valley alone.

What this book does do is linger with fragments of fieldwork through which those histories still insist. Given that events change in valence, depending on the specific readings to which they are constrained, I have wondered if rendering those histories as different readings of political time necessarily entails the anticipation of how things might have unfolded differently. Allowing for other outcomes unsettles the frames readings often impose, because selecting for what can be grasped, synthesized, and repeated from what happened will always be easier than contending with the enormity of what actually did. In such thoughts I have come upon an aspiration that feels somehow worthy: that tellings of political time should remain open not only to every possible sense and to every possible trajectory but to imagining a place, no matter how far out of reach, where they might appear all at once. This is what is meant here by *semblance*. Some of those senses have a power to return, without which there are no memories, no contemplations, no dreams. Others are more opaque and the stuff of matter: dense packages that block lines of sight, obstacles that interrupt paths, portend collisions, and may even inflict wounds that, regardless of how slight or overwhelming, permit no going back.

Anthropological studies have grown increasingly sensitive to how violence takes on many guises, to the point that there would seem no time or place wholly free from its multiple threats and historical sedimentations. According to a critical consensus, so-called eras of peace offer no certain reprieve from fears of physical predation and at the very least occlude structural forms of violence that maintain social hierarchies and gendered modes of class and racial exploitation. Exposure to killing and perceptions of insecurity vary as do their intensities and always unequal distributions. Risks to life might in some respects even get measurably worse after an official end to a militarized conflict or simply acquire different manifestations, as scholars of contemporary Guatemala have noted.[36] Nor is military conflict actually required for killing to become widespread, such as in Honduras, where US imperialism and unrelenting neoliberal value extraction would create opportunities for transnational cartels to seize the ranks of *maras*, thereby putting shocking figures of alienated urban youth, and the fear they inspired, to work in ongoing criminal rackets.[37] While the risks of physical predation in Peru following the defeat of Shining Path have not remained the same, much less intensified, the era of aftermath has carried forward notable features of the former conflict. Perhaps postwar in Peru, as Isaías Rojas-Perez suggests, has introduced a new national order founded upon a "paradoxical temporality" of multiple pasts.[38] Perhaps some of those pasts, as he describes, are deliberately closed off or "finished" through practices of impunity and amnesia. Others, all the while, may well insist into the present by repeating wartime figures and fears of "terrorism," which serve to organize and to justify the violence of a postwar state regime.[39]

Thus, the passage from war to aftermath, when grasped as a movement of political time, has entailed no clean break. And yet if it is important to question the conceptual soundness of drawing any strict categorical separation between them, empirical distinctions are often more revealing. In the Upper Huallaga, the differences in routines, rhythms, and tones of ordinary life—when military strife was an ever-pressing possibility and those more recent states of affairs when such strife has figured nowhere on the immediate horizon—cannot be understated. The transformation in comportments, shared affects, and visibilities, while gradual, has been no less striking: a vivacious shift in direction, ethnographically evident. As I have tried to become sensitive to those changes, I have been reminded that the study of violence might be better approached obliquely and, moreover, from a philosophy of sense. In this regard, a basic insight, which I first came across when reading Henri Bergson, has informed my thinking.[40] Bergson observed, and maintained, that perception tends to have a strictly utilitarian character: turned toward the present and its immediate future horizons, it is poised less to acquire knowledge through contemplation than to prepare for action in a manner that can extract some advantage. There were several reasons why he made this claim in *Matter and Memory*, but a key motivation was that the setting of his inquiry was the human body, which he explained must continually look to the present for the twin needs of nourishment and repair. Attending to those two tasks was what located the body in time, providing the ground for habit and for a present-future perceptual orientation that strongly favored recollections that could demonstrate some resemblance to the situation at hand. Orientation, rotation, turning toward, direction: these are all similar expressions for naming a critical register of sense—one out of many. And within that broader, always plural field of sense, Bergson's notion of the body—deliberately abstract and, therefore, removed from any explicit social specification—was fundamental for what became an exquisitely nuanced and supple theorization of memory and perception. Here that notion contains valuable insights for thinking about temporal reference, or how material bodies become anchored in time, which for Bergson was what established "present" and "past" as fundamentally different in kind.[41] It also informs tasks of ethnographic inquiry, which rely on the researcher's own body as an indispensable notational device for sounding out recollections and for moving a little closer to empirical worlds.

Postwar, if thought of as responding to a new patterning of relations, necessarily introduces perceptual reorientations particular to the durations of the prevailing moment—a moment laden with strategic, existential constraints, which are inseparable from the demands of living and crafting livelihoods within particular, historical terrains. Political time, to the extent it expresses a concrete situation that continues to pass, presupposes its own present-future orientations, which are moving and ever undergoing shifts of tone, infinitesimal changes of shade.

In a photographic essay on the remains of German fortifications along the North Atlantic coast of France, Paul Virilio writes of the stark sensorial, atmospheric shifts entailed by the passage from mid-twentieth-century battlefields to their aftermaths.[42] Where French families resumed beachgoing lives amid the ruins, they largely ignored what had been the Atlantic Wall. Virilio warned of looming dangers brought on by what had irreparably changed: after that last war, the specter of total war had advanced by leaps and bounds. Not only would the power of projectiles forever more overwhelm the most secure of defenses, but rockets with lethal payloads could now without prior notice rain down on any point on the planet. The threat of devastating bursts of fire, which before would have arrived only from distant horizontal lines where sky meets the earth, had now moved directly overhead—a historic alteration he called "the vertical horizon." No place was safe, and no receding into the ground, no matter how deep, would be enough. Virilio's concern was with documenting the architectural frontiers and dystopian progress of military technologies. And yet when I succeed in separating the black-and-white photographs contained in his marvelous collection from the critical contrasts he draws in words, when I can look at the images and them alone, what I see across textured undulations of sands swallowing monolithic blocks are surface reliefs in so many hues of gray.

Every change of shade drags pasts with it to subsist alongside the present as an ever-growing field of oblivion. Prehistories of war hide in that opaque, to commingle with other pasts. From there they threaten, always threaten, to intrude once again into the tissues of unfolding events. The conflict in the Upper Huallaga happened hardly thirty to forty years later. Compared with the war Virilio described, it transpired at a minimal threshold of intensity and with tech that was low and on occasion ridiculously outmoded. Even so, on this other side of the earth, and as if another world, the Upper Huallaga was at times considered in all of Peru the most terrifying place to go.

Bergson offered critical observations for weighing how war might couple with forgetting: when he insisted that material bodies are precisely where present and past merge, without one ever becoming reduced to the other; when he affirmed that the past does not follow the present but coheres with it, if in ways that remain obscure. These are tenets to be aware of or to *generally* keep in mind. Their stress is thus conceptual rather than empirical. Ethnographic inquiry could take on a more specific and rather different charge: to hold the empirical close by devoting the preponderance of efforts to the description of traces grasped from lived presents, as they pass and find a place in ever-new constellations of time. Describing those traces has pointed me to the surfaces and surface reliefs of Huallaga terrains whose vital currents I could always sense but not really see or adequately take in.

Part of territory is feeling not necessarily stuck but moving in place. In conversation with a ferry operator whom I name Tina, a cement room sounds and resounds the hollows, now going back in time (where one cannot return: Bijao), now going over there (where one should not travel:

Magdalena), going not in body but through the partial images she and others share, images that "gratify," through what Maurice Blanchot described as their conventional mode, because they facilitate a transport across great distances without hazarding exposure to the elements.[43]

The word *image* can designate many things. I have a predilection for notions or conceptions that stress not mediation but distance, texture, material, and movement. Bergson notably refused to accept a difference in kind between image and matter, which had the effect of removing reality as the criterion for distinguishing and judging between them. For Bergson, images do not circulate between other terms, because everything of the material world is image already. Everything material is image and images are what enter into relation, determined by the kinds of movement they transmit to each other. What circulates primarily is movement itself; everything moves and is in movement. By refusing an image/matter opposition, Bergson in effect pulls the theory of sense, memory, and perception away from mimesis and guides it toward topography. Sometimes images are translucid and, like Epicurean simulacra, give not a copy of the matter perceived but its surface: a surface that has texture and color but no depth. Sometimes, however, images are less transparent. They mark out areas of opacity precisely where the transmission of movements hits an impasse. Bergson calls these areas "zones of indetermination." The class of images that give rise to them, he says, are special, calling them "bodies." They are special because they do not have to react automatically to the solicitations of the movements they receive. They can wait. Waiting injects uncertainty. While deciding how to act, they can draw on memory, contracting from the past in order to craft a present response.

Bernard Cache takes up Bergson's theory of image and perception, moving them, even more explicitly, in a topographic direction.[44] He finds in physical geography a principle that ruptures scale. Geography, landscapes, and their reliefs are what no frame can enclose and no box can shut out. Yet far more than exterior surroundings that establish a setting—for a factory, let's say, or for a house (like Virilio, Cache's concerns are architectural)—geography is an absolute outside running through the surfaces of all things. From the most distant horizon to whatever is at the tip of one's fingers, geography traces a line of what is external through everything in between: those mountain passes, that lake, this city, the run-down church on the streets below, these living quarters up high, her desk over there, here a chair, and hovering nearby the stain of coffee on a mug now empty.

Moving toward topography, Cache looks for intervals as landscapes butt up against and run through the "artworks" of built environments. Espousing an architectural practice based in the invention of different kinds of frames, he draws on the probability theory of Eugène Dupréel, a Belgian philosopher and sociologist whose philosophical project aligned closely with the vitalism of Bergson.[45] Dupréel affirmed that relations of cause and effect could never eliminate indeterminacy, because between them, there would always be a gap—marked off by the surrounding conditions, which he called "frames of probability." What transpired in that gap could not be known in advance; otherwise, the effect would already be identical to the cause. Cache carries Dupréel's insights over to architecture to claim that every sort of construction introduces frames into geographic terrains, where they not only orient perception but re-create material conditions that render events more predictable. A roof overhead brings shade and a likelihood of staying dry in event of rain. A roof does not determine what happens underneath it or foretell when leaks might spring. As for the Huallaga, the question of gaps in valley landscapes and the "artworks" of built environments will return in the pages to come: first, through close attention to everyday techniques for crossing the river; and later, through reflections on the territorial effects of counterinsurgency forts.

Intervals are implicitly unruly: they escape the calculations of probability, even the most creative ways that probability may get framed. In this sense they are opaque: they do not hand themselves over entirely to prevision. Echoing Bergson, but also pushing further, Cache explains that a body appears "wherever there is an indetermination with respect to a milieu, wherever something that is localized escapes global conditions"—by which he means laws of cause and effect and to which we might add the rules and returns of war.[46] "Thus there are bodies in rivers where unpredictable whirlpools form."[47] Such bodies are striking, he says, for the intervals they create, introducing uncertainty and chance into chains of cause and effect so that aleatory aspects of life can arise and, perhaps, take hold.

The aspirations of this book send me toward actual terrains of postwar and seemingly toward something Bergson gave a name but did not go to lengths to explain: "concrete extensity."[48] As a notion, concrete extensity gestures toward what words like *relief* or *terrain* might wish to approximate. Others instead might speak of *rubble* marking stark contrasts with *ruins*,[49] while drawing attention to what wrought devastation and what may endure through it.[50] Or else, they might underscore the vivacities that matter and materials disclose as rights of their own.[51] Others still could insist on the political implications and capacities therein, for acknowledging divergent orientations where incommensurate worlds overlap.[52] The work undertaken here is less about advocating for any particular concept—*legal topography*, *semblance*, or *political time*—than for rendering proximities through descriptions, which are never pure but always mixed with different sorts of remove.

If perception takes place in the thing perceived, as Bergson's famous thesis would have it, then in that spirit this book reaches toward people and places that do not always respond readily or fully to their solicitation. Such solicitations might be questions both well and clumsily posed. They might be glances or visitations or even silences, shared and not, and in ways that can confound. In reacting, the people and places of my fieldwork return "images" that are more than what they might ever represent. Some images are transparent. Others carve out regions that interrupt all light. I am interested in that opacity, as an aspect of all material bodies. How it sometimes takes shape in the silences that accompany routine ways of speaking, but also in little wounds from the past that do not sound off in any conventional sense but insist nonetheless in every passing present. On occasion, I will call these other images *bultos*. They are what the war in its wake left strewn in and around the river to go largely unseen but sometimes to be felt. Opaque as the densest of matters, bultos suggest *something* that one might sense, or in perceiving register, but without getting any good, clear, or certain reading before it slips away, leaving nothing but a waning charge. One of the circumstances I track in this book is how solicitation and response change with shifts in political time but also in the legal relations that acquire their specificity only with regard to moving terrains.

The sheer accumulation of temporal distance from war has material effects. Those effects can manifest, and sometimes do, in conversation— and then as symptoms—in the patterned ways the wartime past gets referenced and becomes recognized. Perhaps too, at the precise points where breaks in those same patterns emerge. Sometimes the prior war circulates as a generalizing abstraction—as something clearly identified and presumably held in common: *tú sabes, el terrorismo*, as if to say "of course, we all know what that was like." Whether eliciting a silent nod or conjuring instead scenes for competing views, such generalizing fig- ures explicitly mark off an area and an era of history, which separates the war as past and can on occasion screen it off from further inquiry. Even among those who have most generously contributed their own recollec- tions and reflections to my research, I have seen how the specificity and vividness of their narrated accounts have waned and deteriorated in the accumulation of years, even as the constraints on speaking have loosened considerably. And this has happened right as fieldwork photography has felt lighter and increasingly feasible. If the implications of this are mixed and not altogether apparent, they are irreducible to loss. As such, they do not alter the crucial ethnographic task of remaining sensitive to what returns alongside what does not.

If telling history could also be a reading of political time, then the increase in temporal distance does not in itself justify laying all stress on the indelible lines of chronological reckoning, where each and every event can be dated according to its moment of actualization and has no trouble falling into its own allotted place. Directional sequences of time, understood as ordinary and indeed ordinating lines, seem indispensable to historical narration. How to get by without alluding to the 1970s or to the early and late 1980s as situationally distinct and other to the early or late 1990s or to the year 2000, 2002, or 2012? And yet anchoring events as so many beads on a thread is but one possible reading of time. And the problem here is not the exclusion of other reckonings but how sequential ordering can insinuate itself as an inherent background against which everything presumably happens. Sequence insinuates itself into the crafting of relationships between times: from a "here, now"—time of reading and of an audience that listens—to a "there" time back then to what happened. Sequence, as an irreversible, logical-temporal ordering has legal implications too, which establish the ground of point and counterpoint that can then allow for asserting what is a violation and what is a justified response. In the history of Peru's internal war, how many times did the army justify the extreme violence of its tactics as a legitimate coercion because exercised in reaction to a prior disturbance by those who had started "it"?—the "it" being armed insurrection launched by Shining Path. Insurgency, no less than counterinsurgency, thrives on point and counterpoint. To belabor the negative requires ordination too: a sequencing of time, without which there could be neither law nor its ironic inversion.

As a flat, backdrop mode of reckoning, sequence remains detached from events and the places they haunt. Would moving closer then to the reliefs of those places not give time a more topographical rendering, one that could disclose perspectives while remaining open to every possible sense, to every possible trajectory, reversible and irrevocable? Michel Serres proposed that a cloth handkerchief would be far superior to the arrow as a model for imagining and thinking about time:[53] pliable enough to accommodate the obviousness of extreme distance (the corners of the cloth when completely unfolded) together with the obtuse proximities that occasionally connect moments chronologically far-flung (the same corners touching when the cloth has been folded). This model is topological, which means it does not grapple with the historical matters, materials, or surface variations of geographic places. And though Serres underscores its resemblance to the sense of time as weather, the model of the handkerchief leaves out what hovers above. Political time meets actual terrains precisely in the precipitation of atmospheres, which can be sensed only up close, in the vicinities of events and the fleeting alliances that obtain between earth and sky. Such is the charge of ethnography and, more so, ethnographic composition, which thrives only by refusing to get a step up on the world.

Fieldwork presupposes choosing a region and following the slants of perspectives that region makes available. Ethnographic writing can endeavor to render those slants at once generative and compositional. Ethnographic writing can also strive to constellate the fragments fieldwork gathers without assuring their adherence to a transcending totality or even advocating for their truth value. Instead, as a compositional gesture, ethnography can privilege description understood less as thick than as vivid, moving, eventful, and ever pushing toward what might be felt but is seldom seen. Pushing toward the opaque is a push toward material things and toward tale with its vitalities and fascinations, and beyond, to where the setting stirs, shifting now to the fore, now to the back, from side to side. Vibrancies, fascinations, settings, leaving debates for later or for others perhaps. To craft vibrancies that might *true* at singular moments in time with the material densities of a place is something different from securing the truth value of proper reference. Here argument earns a minor role lest it siphon off critical resources from rendering that place and the infinitesimal shades of its presents as they pass. And all the more so with fieldwork in the vicinity of prohibition-laden worlds, such as those of the Upper Huallaga.

Where prohibition conspicuously seeps as if into everything, obstacles, uncertainties, apparent failures, and even exhaustions of body and *ánimo* become generative features of the setting. So too threats of legal jeopardy, whether expressed as an ever-actualizing predation, an engrossing imagination, or a lived air. As much as I shy from converting written compositions into vehicles solely for delivering arguments, I am no less wary of the seductions of access where things illicit are concerned. In part because what one cannot, and should not, bring into view may be more pressing that what one can. In gathering and then sounding out fieldwork materials, I have discovered how important it is to acknowledge what circulates as screens. Major ones in this book are *narco*; *Sendero*; *ejército*; and *policía*. They do name something—collectively recognized entities and institutions—yet here they remain largely unexplored. To a great extent this has been by choice, since getting close to any one of them would have placed significant strain on all other relationships, with the threat of devastating effects for those I have depended on and learned from during many visits to the Huallaga. People, of course, speak to me about those groups knowingly, sharing specific details of their encounters.

They also speak obliquely, by way of indirection. Because they might have been someone else in another time. Because they might be weighing risks that are emerging only now or that persist from before into the present. Sometimes ethnographic writing benefits from a little indirection or from moving laterally as a means for appreciating the opacities of empirical worlds. Such appreciation passes as well over to the photographs and videos from my fieldwork, where depictions of past violence are nowhere to be seen and where nothing unambiguously points to them. If images of that past persist even there, and I am certain they do, then it is at best as an ocular oblivion flickering at the edges of the frame, lingering as a latent visuality. All the while, images that can be neither filmed nor photographically taken remain, latent or concealed and inseparable somehow, in the very places the war once thrived.

Fieldwork in the Huallaga has taught me to be concerned less with who people are and were than with what they have hovered close to. Ethnographic inquiry for me has increasingly turned toward weighing and describing vicinities of the people I spend time with. Not who Tina or Reynaldo or Mauro or Chara were and are but where they have lingered—in tension with what I have sensed and with what they and others have told but also kept silent. Rather than scrutinize for reference—weighing the proprieties of claims made on any specific state of affairs—I prefer to leave truth in abeyance and strive instead for a certain truing to the terrain.

Proper reference is where speech and image are given no choice but to put forward a legal face. By the late 1990s, once its military prowess had been vastly diminished, the Huallaga Shining Path increasingly favored low-risk propaganda actions that could be carried out at night: painting graffiti and placing small red hammer and sickle flags along either side of the Marginal Highway. State forces responded by removing, marring, destroying those signs but also by intervening in the spaces that opened up between Maoist inscriptions and their reading, intent on turning them against the insurgency. A journalist from Tocache told me how constrained he felt when reporting on Shining Path actions. He could not call the red pieces of cloth "flags"; they would have to be described as "rags." Otherwise, he could be charged with "apologizing for the crime of terrorism"—a legal threat, promising a lengthy prison sentence.[54]

One way of eluding an overly dogmatic anchorage of reference—where those flags must be rags or where all loggers are politically suspect—is to reach instead toward terrain, striving to true to what happens there: taking notice of the many versions that circulate about the very same events, even when told by the same person at different moments. If every version counts, then hearing each one means letting all the terms switch places with one another. And holding on to that insight is to linger as long as possible with ethnographic description and to err in favor of semblance. Described relationally, *in favor of semblance* is to remain open to how hostility and hospitality intertwine in shifting configurations, which depend on, and in so doing express, the specific, intensive constraints of the moment no less than of the territories to be crossed.

Political time meets terrain. And curiously, fortuitously, some of the most influential models of memory and forgetting are topological schema: Bergson's cone but also Freud's mystic writing pad, which closely resembles Nietzsche's own dual-level formulation.[55] Marc Augé described how the seas of forgetting crash against the hardened mainland coasts of memory, continually reshaping their contours.[56] A metaphor to be sure but perhaps pointing to something more. Oblivion in Augé's rendering appears as an impersonal, propagating force, a rising tide, pressing without moral valence, obliging to seek ever-higher ground by dint of its sheer accumulation. The Huallaga, meanwhile, is a river that, thanks to a moving mesh of tributaries, partitions lands that seem impossibly far from the closest of seas. And yet like all bodies of water, the Huallaga has a surface that shimmers, revealing trace after trace, holding long not to any single one.

Recollection is always selection. To remember always runs up against the empirical limits of a lived present moment. Something has to give. Something must be left out. Far too much: in order to live in this here and now rather than in some other. To examine the deep past, Augé notes, requires forgetting pasts chronologically closer in time—an observation I did not begin to comprehend until, when in the midst of writing about Tina, Reynaldo, and others, I found myself forced to contend with the intermediate pasts that had to be stepped over or momentarily disregarded simply to have a chance to draw other, older things back to seemingly more tangible shores. Pasts that accumulate in between are also why the specificity and vividness of stories told about the war seem to decay when explicit prohibitions on speaking no longer obtain. And so, to err in favor of semblance is not to overlook empirical constraints but to explore the legal orientations and atmospheres of political time, while remaining open to the concrete extensities of terrain: an absolute outside running through the surfaces of all things.

My hope for this book is to move—with an assist from these topological schema—toward a sensorially rich topographic grasp of a postwar setting: toward residues left as a semblance in and accruing to the banks of a river in continual movement and transformation; toward the matter and matters of expression of places where political time redraws how earth might reach toward the skies. Bergson maintained that the past cannot be destroyed. Neither does it simply precede the present but establishes instead the ground and general field through which all presents pass. If chronology is not the only way to situate, recall, but also forget, even turn oblivious to that past, why must a straight arrow be privileged? Why not describe images and how they move as matter intersecting with sensations: percolating up and down, filtering back and forth, through strata of time, living and acting, untethered to sequence, much less to any one reading, as images in dreams so often do.

precipitating surfaces

After the downpour: long boats began departing again, ferrying passengers and their things from the left bank over to Nuevo Progreso. The lull in movement had lasted an hour. All river traffic at a standstill, as *mototaxistas* ducked under the brightly colored awnings of their machines. Furling plastic sheeting down and over handlebars to protect against the press of wet air, they straddled their engines, welcoming travelers to take cover on the passenger bench. Others had to seek refuge farther away: beneath a palm leaf roof of a lone kiosk on this side of the river, an open-air stand where a woman sold drinks and served food she prepared each morning before crossing the water. Her kiosk was where I found shelter too upon reaching the shore from the inland village of Paraíso. From the top of the bank where the dirt road abruptly stopped, I cut across faint paths, splaying every which way over the bare, treeless shore, and made for the kiosk. Parking my bike below the eaves, I stepped inside to join the crowd just as the rain turned severe.

But now, the heaviest showers had subsided. The movement from shore to shore had picked up again. After the downpour: first one canoe, a second, then a third. So after stowing my camera and wiping water off the seat, I walked my motorcycle toward the river's edge. All the *boteros* who had waited out the rain on this side had by now passed over to town, but it wasn't long before I saw Reynaldo pulling his corrugated-metal canoe up alongside the shore with another ferryman following close behind.

"Progreso?" he asks, waiving me aboard. "No, no," he instructs. "Leave the bike there," as he hops onto the shore. Taking hold of the handlebars, he struggles for a moment as if expecting the bike to be lighter, easier to maneuver, but he quickly adjusts his footing and is soon pushing

FIGURE 2.1. la banda, Nuevo Progreso

the motorbike over to the side of the boat. Pausing there, Reynaldo seems to be gauging how he wants to get it in, but when I ask if I can lend a hand, he urges me again to step aboard and instead calls the other botero over to help.

So, what I do is watch as they lift the front wheel up and over the side of the canoe and then push the chassis onto the edge, where they let it rest for a second to catch a breath. Now that it's halfway in, they push the bike back and forth, using its brute weight to build momentum, until in a final heave they raise the rear wheel up and over to set it down onto the metal floor. Reynaldo jumps in, rolls the bike toward the center of the canoe, and putting down the kickstand, parks it just long enough for me to hop back on and keep it steady.

Boat operators seldom cross the river with fewer than four fare-paying passengers. I am the first and, as yet, only one. So, in the mist we wait: me sitting on the bike and Reynaldo walking up and down the length of the canoe with what is a noticeable wobble in his step. I ask if he is hurt.

His right leg, he says. Ever since he woke this morning, it's been bother-
ing him, a sharp pain shooting up all the way to his hip. Despite that, here
he is out on the river loading cargo on and off his boat in between bursts
of rain. The image of him deadlifting my motorcycle with his feet sinking
into the wet earth takes on another sense now that I know he is injured.

Waiting for passengers, five minutes elapse, then ten, before a three-
wheel mototaxi from Paraíso rolls down the bank. Some teenagers jump
out, two boy-girl couples, lugging small rucksacks and talking animatedly
among themselves. As they board, Reynaldo quickly steps out to untie the
rope. The mototaxi, meanwhile, moves over to a different boat, which a
moment before had come aground and which unlike Reynaldo's has a wide,
flat, open bow designed to allow the loading of three- and four-wheel vehicles. Seeing the taxi preparing to drive onto the other craft, one of the
teenagers says something about having forgotten to ask for their change,
and suddenly they are getting out en masse, walking over to talk to the
taxi driver. But instead of getting their money and returning—a task that

FIGURE 2.2. work shoes

did not require all of them to leave anyhow, much less take their bags with them—they step onto the other boat, apparently deciding they will ride it to the other side.

Reynaldo, realizing he is losing his passengers, calls over to the fer-ryman, who had not only started up the engine but was already inching his boat away from the shore. It's not your turn, Reynaldo tells him. But the other man, who though middle-aged looked not only a good twenty years younger but taller, thicker, and more imposing than Reynaldo, re-buffed him in a parting shot before pivoting his boat around and heading back to Progreso. I cannot make out what the man said. I grasp only a demeaning tone. And yet against this minor everyday injustice, Reynaldo appeared not merely unprepared but resigned and ultimately at a loss for words. For he said nothing more, delivering not even an insult in return, as the other man pressed his craft on toward the center of the river, steal-ing away with fares that might have belonged to another.

Reynaldo limped back toward the stern to tend to the motor. As he passed by, a slight trembling in his lower lip caught my eye. In the place of words he had chosen not to speak or simply could not muster, something else—an uncontrollable quiver—appeared at the edge of his mouth. A tremor that moved through his lip. He knew his canoe could not accommodate the mototaxi, and I am sure he suspected the passengers left as soon as they saw a chance to catch a ride for free (mototaxistas pay a flat fee to cross whether they have passengers or not). But this time I ask him nothing. A dagger of pain shoots up whenever he puts weight on his right leg. The tremor that courses through his lip, though, is a different kind of sting.

precipitations

Within local history, this river is a deeply storied terrain. And yet for a region of Peru long animated by Maoist insurgency, state repression, and the cocaine trade, braving the Huallaga's currents has a history all its own—one hardly indifferent to prior events of political violence. Here, now, and in the wake of that turbulent past, the ostensibly ordinary times of postwar move through the seemingly precarious coordinations of human bodies, road vehicles, and watercraft that make crossing the Huallaga River possible today. Here—where there are no bridges—sensations, bodily habits, and objects large and small combine to overcome the river's obstructive force: less by assembling a durable edifice that would permanently connect one bank to the other than by precipitating sporadic surfaces through the staggered movements of material things. If such movements rely on a certain day-in and day-out vigilance and care by people known as *balseros* and *boteros*, they also raise questions about the extent to which shifts in political time may inflect the very material things upon which such surfaces depend, affecting how they enter and withdraw from visibility—even as they remain silent with regard to the broader historical trajectories they inevitably express. This is to say that the sensory and material tetherings that enable everyday passage commingle—in the very act of traversing the river—with the war's aftermath: an era in which the insurgency is no more.

Photographs and videos I have gathered during fieldwork intimate the sensorial and material life of postwar river crossings and something of their social worlds, where operators of canoes and barges make a livelihood from ferrying between the Huallaga's shores. Then and now those who offer passage across the river have been known as *vaderos*, and the service they provide *el vado*. In standard Spanish *el vado* names less a practice than a topos. Following from the Latin *vadum* it refers to a shallow place in a body of churning water: a shoal, a ford, from where it is possible to stand and from there attempt to cross. In the Upper Huallaga el vado as both place *and* practice cannot be easily separated from the territorial significance that the valley's main river acquired throughout the years of conflict. The Huallaga River became an intensely charged political-legal boundary that placed right bank towns like Nuevo Progreso and Aucayacu—as administrative islands of the Peruvian state—in spatial opposition to the remote rural expanses of the left bank, where Shining Path held greatest sway and where the cocaine trade could operate with minimal interference from the police. El vado thus bears upon that prior time, through the ways its everyday practice expresses ongoing shifts in territory, at a moment of postwar when the state is extending its infrastructural reach into the countryside.

Political eras acquire territorial attributes through the ways empirical relations entwine with the topographic specificities of physical landscapes, shaping and directing movements of people and things. In the Upper Huallaga, the passing of the war has radically reconfigured the social connectivities that sanction human circulations in and across the valley's rural expanses. And yet el vado, a practice of rural transit well predating the onset of political violence, has remained a steadfast feature of rural life, proximate to and intimately involved with the valley's riverine terrains—the legal relations that have settled within them, the events that continue to pulse them—subject always to material conditions those terrains interpose. This situates el vado at the juncture of distinct political times, territorial formations, and the river's own thrust, making it a privileged vantage point from which to weigh how the past, with all the extremities of what happened before, insists in the ever-passing present.

intervals

Across this region roads, streams, and trails descend to meet the mighty Huallaga. Those who travel by land encounter there a moving mass of

FIGURE 2.3. "el puerto," Nuevo Progreso

water, which blocks their path in one decisive horizontal cut. Here political terrors of another time have fallen away. Human corpses no longer roil in eddies, no longer mix with surface debris. Hostile territories wait not on the other side. All there is, is this thick, turning expanse. Against it barge and canoe operators perform vital labors of translation. Drawing on an array of tetherings, bodily adjustments, and artful positionings of matter, they piece together a hard, buoyant surface with which to ply the ever-moving currents. The intermittent ground they improvise is patchy as if by design, because every time a canoe or barge pulls in to shore, a material gap between muddy bank and boat tenaciously appears. Since this interval constantly varies with the river's own displacements, it must be resolved each time anew to secure the loading of mototaxis, cars, pickups, cargo trucks, and other road machines even before crossing to the other side. To do so, ferry people (mostly men but women too) rely on a series of background things, which hover between quasi–raw materials and tools. Wood planks and poles, iron rods, shovels but also chains and rope—dropped casually inside longboats, atop barges, and along shores, but always close enough to grab when needed.

The purpose and utility of some of these things are immediately evident. Ropes and chains, tied to cement and wood posts or to metal rods sunk deep into the earthen bank, keep watercraft of all kinds from drifting downstream. A sawed-off pole thrust into shallow riverbeds holds a canoe steady against the currents. With an elongated *tangana* boat operators push away from shore and navigate their way in and out of port.

Other things, though, look less like tools than discarded objects. These bear general names that obscure a secret utility known only to those who

FIGURE 2.4. planks and chocks and wedges and rods

position them. "Each little piece of wood has its function," one barge operator assures me. Each one has a specific use covered over by its generic grouping as a block (*taco*) or wedge (*cuña*)—ever at the ready when ferrymen contend with that seemingly most minor of gaps: the one that always opens between bank and boat.

This first step of passage repeats in miniature the broader transposition from one shore to the next, so it receives the brunt of their attentions. Foot passengers can be oblivious: traversing the gap takes but a brief moment, overcome no sooner than they hop on or off again. It is rather with road machines that the interval between boat and shore veers prominently into view.

Precarity intensifies with increases in mass and density. I am reminded of this whenever I cross the Huallaga with a motorcycle, which suddenly becomes heavy and unwieldy upon coming to a full stop. Transferring it into a canoe invariably feels awkward. The fear of slipping and falling forever haunts: whether finding an elusive footing when raising the dead weight up and over the edge, or whether navigating a thin wood plank that boteros sometimes set down as an impromptu ramp—a smooth surface on which to roll the motorcycle aboard. Either way the maneuver requires strength, sometimes luck, but all the more so technique, which I seldom have sufficient opportunity to acquire. For it is technique that grapples with the interval and the opaqueness that necessarily persists within it.

As the material manifestation of a restive, intractable geography, the distance between bank and boat relentlessly shifts—widening, narrowing—forcing ferrymen to figure out optimal angles of approach. Hardly inconsequential too is the concrete form of the craft. Canoes with bows that rise up and taper to a point must pull up alongside the shore when moving heavy objects on and off. Flat, open bows of more recent longboat models, however, permit operators to slant and sometimes even drive straight into the shore, greatly enhancing the speed and ease of loading and unloading. This makes me wonder why open bows have only lately begun to proliferate. A minor reorientation of postwar, perhaps, now that the territorial prohibitions, which once tensed movements between left bank and right, have all but dissipated? One no longer thinks twice about crossing to the other side. Such changes in political time course through the landscapes of this river and through the material things scattered there. They run along registers that do not always coincide with the visibilities available to vaderos, or else they simply may not fall within the purview of their expertise.

On this afternoon Reynaldo spares me the sensation of precariousness. Or rather that sensation is displaced onto the act of watching him, with help from another ferryman, heave my bike up and in. And because here, on this side, boats pull less into than on top of the shore, which slopes ever so gradually toward the river before meeting it one on one. And so, there is no place to lay down a plank. The work is all lift: black lace-up shoes and plastic *chancletas* or sandals sink into the damp, silty earth. And seeing this only sharpens the admiration I feel for the vaderos who enable these vulnerable, if ever-so-basic, material translations. Inseparable from technique, though, are the bodies that make such translations possible, bodies that wear, slow, and eventually break down.

Reynaldo has spent forty years and more out on this river. I think about what his body tolerates. I think too about the durations that persist in trained hands, hips, and feet—his and those of others—but also in the blocks, wedges, and rods picked up and repositioned in order to convey people from one shore to the next. I wonder how their trajectories interweave with other sorts of time and weather: of war and postwar, but of agricultural booms as well—here most blatantly coca, along with the cacao that would later pretend to supplant it, both finding ways to collapse without much regard for legalities. The durations themselves, coursing through so many material bodies and things, do not say. They are as if mute, and when people refer to them, they seem to do so only indirectly—unless specifically asked, and even then what people describe frequently amounts to little more than a gesture.

A lip trembles what it cannot say. And in this place known for pasts of historical extremes a welcome boredom has settled in. Many from here call that "good." Fierce prohibitions on speaking are no longer in force. And yet their disappearance has unleashed no drive to talk about what before could not be widely shared. And the stories people do tell, to my ear at least, have little of the luster, richness of detail, and urgency of ten, fifteen years ago. People seem to have other concerns.

I too can be a stranger now without menace. I can wait here, photograph, and film. I can watch the ferrymen. This is new. I can take in and be receptive to different details and to different kinds of tone as never before. In so doing I find that what pulls at me more and more are their ordinary days. Not the highs and not the lows but what transpires in between, moving for so many years in ways I could not see, below clouds towering majestic.

the receding

Two years later, the tremor of a bad encounter endures. Separated from Reynaldo's lip it persists but with me, held in the image I recall of that moment. Two years later I return to this town where the season is the same: heavy rains have subsided, to become intermittent and on occasion to surprise. I find Reynaldo no more at the river but stuck at home.

It's been three months since he was let go. A new *patrón,* man of wealth, bought one of the town's two fluvial transportation businesses and then decided Reynaldo was too slow and inefficient to continue operating company boats. Reynaldo worries aloud about finding work, and at the same time, he insists on telling me about each of the personal economic catastrophes that brought him to this point. Telling me takes hours, and it should: it's his life history, or at least a version of it, the one that ends up with him out of work, stuck at home, and stir-crazy. Afterward, when I ask if first thing tomorrow he will accompany me to the river, he doesn't mull it over.

Next morning, we find the town's port exactly where I left it two years ago. At Nuevo Progreso the river has largely held course. From here, the hilly cordillera on the other side rises up in the distance to mark off the horizon. From out there, the land rushes toward us, down and ever more down, until reaching the Huallaga. The terrain flows, as it were, from high to low, in a smooth, continuous slope. Up close though, it is the banks where variation turns unpredictable as the direct effect of the moving currents and the ways they rise and fall. Day in, day out, the shores never stop shifting, such that everything of importance for crossing must begin there. And it is the ferry people who contend and pay close attention, so no one else be concerned. The riverbanks are what vary, expressing the change that only a select few ever grasp.

FIGURE 2.5. untitled

But noticing this takes time. At first, I do not think to look. My attention is drawn to something no longer there. The wood boats: Where have they gone? The ferrymen, Reynaldo tells me, are all using metal, not only the corrugated steel I had seen before but also a smooth alloy they call *acerado*. Reynaldo points now to where a boat maker has set up shop not far from the port and later takes me over to see the assistants at work.

Many of the longboats used as ferries here have rectangular bows to pull directly into the shore and, thus, facilitate loading and unloading of wheeled vehicles. Again, this reorientation is not new, and yet the design appears to have taken over, displacing not only older materials and forms of construction—the plank (*enfalcado*) and the single-trunk dugout (*fundición*)—but also the bodily techniques that ferrymen had long relied on to operate them. And increasingly, longboats have roofing as well. Passengers demand that, I'm told—willing no more to be exposed to the harsh rays of the sun.

Where have all the wooden boats gone? This becomes the question I ask of every vadero I meet going forward. And again and again I am told

FIGURE 2.6. transfers

they are disappearing. But maybe, "if you go to Puerto Huicte." "No, en Huicte ya no hay," another says. "Go to Tipishca! In Tipishca, *there* you can still find them."

In this regional history of transit materials, the dugouts and plank boats in which I had crossed the river in years past seem to be receding from view. They are disappearing as the speed boats once did back in the late 1980s: those lightweight aluminum phantoms of another time moving passengers and their suitcases of money in and out of Paraíso faster than the police or anyone else could follow. Those were the *chalupas* another longtime ferryman tells me, adding that he had operated one as well, when he was the botero *de confianza* for a drug trader who trusted him to move sacks of dollars to a former hideout downstream. What he called chalupas, others called *deslizadores*, and if they had little steering wheels instead of hand-operated outboard motors, some would call them *yates* (yachts)—tongue in cheek, no doubt, but affirming still a desire to wander in worlds of the filthy rich, which maybe, just maybe, were not altogether out of reach. Back then, the port was far busier and the boteros numbered somewhere in the upper forties, far more than the fifteen or so

FIGURE 2.7. boat making, Nuevo Progreso

who work between the shores today. When the frenetic pace of the drug trade moved elsewhere, dugouts and plank canoes remained to move an ever-dwindling number of passengers between the banks.

But now ferrymen cross the water in boats no longer made of wood. The vaderos I ask about this tend to stress the distinctive advantages of metal alloy. They remark too that the hard woods required to build sturdy longboats had become increasingly scarce and thus, expensive—direct consequence of extensive logging in the left bank: an extractive economy that took off in the late 1990s and early 2000s, twilight years of the war. The hardwoods—caobas, moenas, and tornillos—are all gone, which is why I'm told the dugouts have become increasingly rare. Small canoes of plank and tar do still abound in the *peque peques* that fishers navigate across the Huallaga and upstream into adjoining tributaries, but at Nuevo Progreso there is not a single enfalcado still in operation for ferrying passengers and their things. That is not to say wood has disappeared from the practice of el vado—only certain kinds and forms. Wood itself retains a crucial role in longboats and in barges too. Boteros and balseros rely on planks to create smooth planes—as flooring, ramps, and passenger

FIGURE 2.8. metal, open bow; plank or *enfalcado*;
dugout or *fundición*

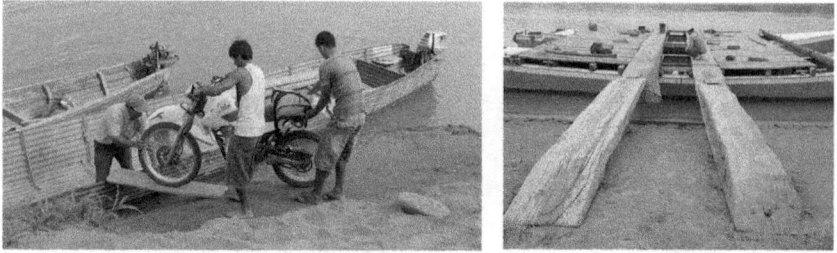

FIGURE 2.9. from *tabla* to *tablón*

seats but also to level out those abrupt, uneven points of contact where the bow comes to a rest against the earthy shore.

la tabla es todo

The disappearance of wood canoes caught my attention. Inquiring about their absence helped me notice something else: how much wood there still was in different cuts, shapes, and sizes and how much those pieces contributed to performing critical tasks within el vado—of precipitating smooth surfaces to fill in and bridge the gaps that open up between bank and boat, not only of long canoes but barges too. Of all those cuts, shapes, and sizes, the most obvious and widespread was *la tabla*.

Vital for moving motorcycles and other vehicles into and out of the craft, a *tabla* or wood plank ties over the interval. Between boat and bank, it's an ever-ready flat surface making material translations possible. For foot traffic and in-line wheels a single tabla becomes a ramp. Multiply by two, increase thickness, and double-axle vehicles can move on and off. We go from *this*—canoe—to *this*—barge—for ferrying cars and trucks (see figure 2.9).

The jump from canoe to barge does not merely express a difference in magnitude of what can be transported. The jump from one craft to the other is what tablas themselves enable. A barge is but two or more longboats connected by a series of wood planks thrown on top. In the Huallaga, such joining tends to be permanent. Once assembled, a barge is not broken down into its component parts until it is taken out of operation for repairs or relocation by land to a different port, river, or region of the country. And yet in Nuevo Progreso hitching

FIGURE 2.10. sculpted shores

together several canoes to move pickups and larger trucks was once a regular part of being a botero. In the 1980s, I am told, ferrymen would gather anywhere from two to five wood canoes—depending on the size and weight of the vehicle, the aluminum chalupas or speed boats being useless for the task—and attach them with large, thick planks (*tablones*) before making the journey to Megote, the port on the left side of the river. After offloading their cargo, the boteros would disassemble the barge and return to work as individual canoe operators.

In the 1980s Megote was two kilometers from Progreso and tucked well out of view of the town's port. Now all boats make a three-minute jaunt to the opposite shore, which this season is in full sight but several hundred meters away. As the Huallaga moves and travels, so do its shores. Thus, all the ferrymen's labors must refer back to the river itself and how its currents continually reshape the shoreline, whether through flood, through retreat, or by simply holding course. And what the river disrupts of the shore, the ferrymen attempt to sculpt anew into smooth gradients—here on the Nuevo Progreso side there is a separate earthen ramp for each boat, and every botero has a small shovel with which he tends to the earth whenever waiting for passengers.

On both sides there is also a permanent two-plank ramp that juts out over the water, marking the point where the barge pulls in to dock. Perhaps is it here that shoreline variations become most explicit, through the balseros' careful adjustments, raising up and then setting down the tablones to match to the level of the barge as affected by the weight of its cargo. Here too is where "each little piece of wood has its function."

But maybe all this—I mean el vado as practice and technique as well as the care with which boteros and balseros attend to the ever-moving banks—will end and perhaps soon. For rumors of a bridge to come have taken on definitive contours ever since July 2015, when in a surprise helicopter visit to the nearby hamlet of Yanajanca, President Humala "lifted" the state of emergency over the Upper Huallaga Valley. Declaring the thirty-year-old counterinsurgency effort a success, he announced that his government would now build a bridge to connect these very shores. If those plans were to be enacted, as eventually they were, the tabla might indeed become everything—but only if "everything" meant seizing from el vado the single *formal* element that here has visibly spanned time and terrain.

For what formally links canoe to barge to bridge is the smooth line of the plank. Along its unidirectional vector the artful precipitations of sporadic surfaces in constant touch with a restive river geography are raised up and funneled into a fixed, enduring platform. As architectural intervention a bridge injects a frame of probability into the landscape far different from what the ferry people now provide.[1] The bridge is a monumental incarnation of the tabla—no longer wood but a permanent edifice tethered by cables into cement foundations. And yet once the bridge is built, what happens to the social and sensorial life of the port and to the livelihoods of men and women for whom that life is still crucial? What becomes of the paths boteros trace as they crisscross the water's surface when replaced by a wide line that hangs strong and supple overhead? And what too of the interval that is the river itself, when those smaller variable gaps between boat and bank have withdrawn from the setting and are mostly forgotten?

FIGURE 2.11. moving elsewhere . . .

This is how ferry crossings bear upon political time: through layers of history manifesting in the sensory and material tetherings that impel rural transit still, persisting, falling out of practice, receding from view, disappearing less than moving elsewhere, tucked perhaps not so far away. El vado lattices history, interweaving layer upon layer of distinct sorts of time: what this matter pulses, that memory selects from pasts turning ever-more distant and opaque. Across those layers, planks of wood repeat. They return in a series that might get sketched out as a vectorial progression—from dugout to enfalcado, from balsa to bridge—or they might get drawn into the knots of something more elaborate. El vado as practice is what vaderos continually "craft": the bodily techniques they quietly accumulate and will in time suffer, the fragmentary surfaces they help precipitate all the while. Their craft brings visibilities: a particular perspective on use and utility, a specific orientation toward the world as it renders a world of its own. El vado endures through the war, through its aftermaths and prehistories, through the ways war's coming and going drastically reorient sense and sensibilities, through differential gravities and buoyancies, through claims on bodies and the relations they sustain. Where war moves, so do centers of threat with lopsided effects: what some will experience as dispelling a crushing weight sends others for a headlong plunge.

Rural transit corresponds with regional variations in political time, which in turn cannot be severed from local variations in territory. Transportation infrastructures old and new not only become ensnared in the periods and contingencies of state governance. They have repercussions for the sense and value of the implements and techniques that enable displacements between town and country. What part of such things insists irrespective of era and territorial regime? A wood plank is rudimentary for the way it repeats—visibly spanning time and terrain.

A president visits a village that was once a formidable place, at least in the stories people told lately: the last known residence of Artemio— the ultimate, now captured, leader of the Huallaga faction of Shining Path. A president arrives to cancel the perennial state of emergency that had long underscored the Upper Huallaga's condition as a frontier internal to the nation. Declaring war "over" has fiscal, fiduciary, and territorial implications: a new order of reciprocities between state and province. Remaining military forts will be shuttered. A bridge will be built. What once towered intense at the tops of hills gets exchanged for narrow horizontal platforms raised up and over moving currents. So what, if such landscape interventions facilitate an oblivion of what happened before? So what, if their reorientations of terrain, their pivoting of sense and perspective, motivate a forgetting? If they efface materials upon which memories would have otherwise attached, what then? And where does that leave the ways of the ferry? Does the coming of a bridge close out el vado as a practice—to be positioned as a bridge's prehistory, shunted into its shadows? Does the bridge's coming permanently banish the singular worlds that el vado animates and sustains in a particular place? What then of the bridge that later fails, falls, gets destroyed—as during the war when several small bridges over Huallaga tributaries were severely damaged by Shining Path dynamite? What then, when el vado returns, to go forward and backward, back and forth, filling gaps between shores once again?

Perhaps the most that can be said *in general* and *for sure* is that what translates movements between river and road becomes implicated in shifts of political time. El vado and the bridge offer two different kinds of surface work and two distinct ways of contending with a turbulent interval. El vado crisscrosses materials to precipitate a buoyant surface that rides, cuts across a churning flow. A bridge lifts a hard, continuous surface up and away, suspending it at a certain safe distance from the roiling below.

taco, cuña, tablón

Huallaga transit histories intimate themselves in fragments—in the material things and implements left about the embarkments of ports and boat landings, but sometimes too in casual talk I strike up with boteros and balseros. These brief exchanges can spark longer conversations on board moored canoes and barges, or else at a nearby kiosk where vaderos kill time waiting their turn, for passengers and cargo to show, or simply to catch their breath. Occasionally, these discussions get more involved, wandering into their reminiscences of what happened not so long ago, and lead to invitations to drop by their homes on their days off so we might continue or else to look up siblings and relatives who have moved to other towns.

Through the war and into the early years of its aftermath, the Huallaga River remained a highly charged tract: the scene of silent exertions, of guarded glances, and sometimes stinging jokes—where the air could grow dense, intolerably so, to the point where a small gesture of kindness might startle. What I have experienced on the river's banks and in the moments of crossing sticks with me, as do the stories told by others—a contact that resonates and runs deep, because of what I found along and across these shores so many times before: a force that greeted by turning away, that unsettled my every attempt to look about or glance toward the other side. Yet what I encountered at the port of Nuevo Progreso, beginning in 2013, was a different sort of stirring, unlike prior visits there, and until then, anywhere else on the Huallaga: a singularly buoyant, cheerful tone, a movement, a social life of distinctive vibrance. There secret forces no longer hovered behind, vigilant, threatening, ready to burst into view—that, or simply no one seemed to care. Something had slipped, and it was hard not to be impressed, not to be taken by a certain awe. When I returned two years later, a similar vibrance accrued to these shores still, but then I learned of the bridge, and it was impossible not to sense a different sort of disquiet. Impossible not to wonder too what would happen to this vital terrain, to the social worlds and to these shores and to what made them so recently feel, if only to me, somehow incomparable to all those years prior, when the war had pressed so much closer. At that point everything I saw and documented drifted within a new threshold and the shadows it cast, as if to say *all this*—together with the lives and livelihoods of balseros and boteros—will recede soon enough.

Most days during my visits to Nuevo Progreso in 2015 I would find Lobo out on the barge, working alongside his assistant. Though every now and then he would be operating a metal longboat by himself, covering a shift for his brother or for his father, both of whom worked as boteros at the port. Friends had told me that Lobo's father was among the vaderos who had worked in Nuevo Progreso the longest— a man of great experience, they said, and what stories he must have to share. But with him I would have little luck. He assented to having me photograph him on his boat, and I later give him copies. Yet when I asked about his experiences in el vado and what he has seen change over the years, Lobo's father looked at me askance. How different from his sons, who were all smiles and cheer, always angling for the next wisecrack. More than once I tried, and each time he gently rebuffed my entreaties, only to allude with cryptic gestures to a possible trans- action: the words I imagined he might have for money he imagined I must possess. His refusals, with their airs of intrigue, felt familiar, if redolent of another time not long ago when strangers merited distrust and speaking with them in public best avoided. So rather than press, I would look elsewhere. Other vaderos were far more accommodating, including some of his generation.

I could look elsewhere, because Huallaga transit histories subsist in innumerable threads. Some I pulled on at a remove from the Huallaga River. Such were my conversations with Hugo Taboada, a veteran driver of the Comité de Autos Número Uno in Tingo María. For over thirty years, Hugo shuttled passengers in his dark four-door sedan to Aucayacu, Tocache, and back again, even during the most turbulent stretches of the war.

I have known Hugo since the late 1990s when our paths would regularly cross in Tingo María, Aucayacu, or on the Marginal Highway, always with an exchange of waves or conversation in passing. We had friends in common, and through them I came to know two of his grown children, both then in their early to mid-twenties and, like their father, working for the same comité de autos: son Mitchel, who raced from town to town in a white station wagon, and daughter Pilar, the comité's secretary, who kept a running log of drivers as they departed for a run and then marked them down once again upon their return. Back then, whenever I made a day trip to Tingo María to go to the bank or buy supplies, I would leave my motorbike and helmet in Pilar's care, as well as any other packages I might be carrying.

Years later, long after moving to Lima where she now lives with her husband and two children, Pilar would help me with my research. She would transcribe the interviews I was recording with Huallaga transportistas. Through her close exposure to those fieldwork materials, Pilar would frequently ask questions, make suggestions, and tell anecdotes, sharing her rich knowledge of the region. Once after I told her about a visit I made in 2011 to a left bank farm near the village of Venenillo, Pilar reminded me that she had spent her early childhood close by in the hamlet of La Roca, before the war forced her family to withdraw to the relative safety of Tingo María.

La Roca sits on the right side of the Huallaga River across the water from Venenillo, which was and still is the first of a handful of small left bank settler communities scattered along the extended floodplain known as the Bolsón Cuchara. Pilar also told me then something I had never known: beginning in the late 1950s and thus long before becoming a *chofer* with the comité, her father had worked as a vadero, first from the village of Mercedes de Locro and a decade later from La Roca, ferrying passengers and their cargo between left bank and right. Pilar encouraged me to speak with him to learn more about Venenillo and the history of that area. And so, on my subsequent trips to the region over the next few years, I would make a point of stopping by her parents' family home in Tingo María.

On my visits to see him, I found Hugo visibly older and increasingly frail. Problems with his health had forced Hugo to take a prolonged leave of absence from the comité, but that did not stop him from welcoming me in. Hugo liked to talk politics and had an appreciation for local history. Perhaps because of that he took an interest in my work. Whenever he had a chance, he would introduce me to friends, telling them that I had experienced the Marginal Highway firsthand during the most tumultuous years of political violence. An overstatement to be sure, but not without some basis as my travels had overlapped with the tail end of the army's counterinsurgency campaigns. That I was willing to travel alone on a motorbike back then was something that Hugo held in high regard. And around that perception of a certain point in common, a connection emerged and with it a warmth of disposition. Hugo said he wanted to help and obviously prepared for my visits, often sifting through old local newspaper clippings ahead of time in search of something new to share. One conversation easily spun into another. Hours flew by until we found ourselves having to say good-bye, but already looking forward to next time. These visits went on year after year, every time I could return to the Huallaga Valley.

During one of our later conversations, I showed Hugo a selection of the photographs and videos I had been taking at the ports of Aucayacu and Nuevo Progreso. Among the images I shared from my laptop screen were a good many close-ups of wedges, blocks, boards, and timbers. I told Hugo I was keen to learn more about vadero equipment and techniques and wanted to hear his thoughts. What to make of these wood pieces scattered about? I wondered too about the tension between their rudimentary character and the tremendous consequence they acquired in the context of river crossings, where the only thing keeping a truck from rolling off into the water might conceivably be a wedge, well lodged and timely placed.

Four years had now passed since Pilar had suggested I pay him a visit. Hugo had still not gone back to work, and though he kept close tabs on comité affairs and internal politics, he was essentially retired. Glancing at the images as they moved across the screen, Hugo explained that the first balsa ferries sprung up in direct response to the need to find an easy, reliable way to convey large vehicles. But I did not expect him to tell me that the very techniques I was documenting in photographs and videos were what he, his brother Alquiles, and his compadre Mashico had discovered in the mid-1970s, working as vaderos just west of Tingo María on the road to Monzón. A surge in the Huallaga River had knocked down a bridge near the village of Bella, creating an instant opportunity for ferry operators. Hugo was one of twenty vaderos who relocated to the site, staying there four years until the bridge could be rebuilt.

Hugo insisted they were only experimenting, seeing what might work. "We needed to ferry vehicles . . . and so we came up with a way of using tablones." By joining two longboats together with flat timbers, he said, they could transport small cars and pickup trucks. Larger trucks too, if they simply increased the size and number of wood boats. As far as Hugo knew, no one else was doing that back then, and it was clear that the thought they might have been the originators pleased him. Yet barely had they started to hone their technique when construction on the bridge neared completion. Hugo and the other vaderos found themselves out of work. "So, my compadre and my brother and the rest of us, we all left for elsewhere," each one headed to different points north along the Huallaga, taking with them their intimate knowledge of how to move people, vehicles, and freight wherever a road arrives at a river and finds there no bridge.

Rafts had long been a common, if dangerous, means of navigating the Huallaga River. By fastening several logs of a topa tree (balsa; *Ochroma pyramidale*) together, they served to connect the region to the entire Amazon Basin through the Huallaga River's eventual confluence with the Marañón. Unlike el vado, journeys by raft moved not from one bank to the other but according to the course and material thrust of the river. Whether upstream by paddle and oar or downstream by the pulse of the Huallaga, rafts traveled *in line* with the same moving vector so they assumed a different relation to the river and to its currents. Not to say rafts could not be repurposed to ferry people and light loads from side to side. Sometimes they were—but mainly on smaller streams. To accommodate heavy freight—cars and all the more so trucks—required a more robust structure than a raft of mere tethered logs, lest it begin to list, drop its cargo, sink.

The construction of the Marginal Highway in the mid- to late 1960s ended the reliance of rafts as a mode of long-distance transit but not el vado as profession and practice. To the contrary, el vado acquired heightened importance on account of the government colonization programs, which accompanied the new road.[2] The agrarian reforms of the 1960s and 1970s appropriated land along both sides of the Huallaga River, redistributing it to anyone willing to permanently settle in the valley. The main transportation route into and out of the valley became the Marginal Highway. However, the new road, which ran beside the river—on the right bank up to Tocache and from there along the left bank until Pizana and then back over again until Punta Arenas—rarely provided access to the other side. Most bridges built along the Marginal Highway were small. They raised the road over minor tributaries but left long stretches of the Huallaga River without permanent crossings. Even with the completion of a large suspension bridge over the Huallaga at Tocache in the late 1970s, a 170-kilometer expanse remained along the southward route—all the way to Tingo María.[3] Meanwhile, the largest tracts made available through the agrarian reforms were to be found on the left bank. People who claimed them and set up farms required a way to move back and forth across the river as well as reliable access to markets. Much of the war to come would happen in the protracted gaps between bridges over the Huallaga River, that is, in the very domain where vaderos delivered a vital service.

In Hugo's telling, the eventual repair of a bridge near the village of Bella cost the vaderos their jobs, sending them north toward a zone of new colonization. The reestablishment of a land route previously severed by the river's own movements in turn displaced a tightknit world of friends, many related by bonds of kinship as well. That bridge's restoration also spread a novel method for moving cars and trucks throughout the Huallaga Valley, if not beyond. Hugo's brother Alquiles went to Uchiza, while Mashico, who Hugo said had become quite the specialist in building balsas, went to Tocache, where construction on the suspension bridge over the Huallaga was under way and where there would thus be a steady stream of equipment and supplies to ferry. Mashico stayed on at Tocache until the suspension bridge was finished. He then moved to the nearby port of Nueva Unión, where he built a balsa with four iron longboats capable of conveying large container trucks. Situated on the Huallaga River's left bank at the entrance to the village of Santa Lucía, the balsa at Nueva Unión would acquire strategic and logistical importance in the 1980s, providing an essential communications link to Uchiza, the lone major town of the Upper Huallaga not located on the route of the Marginal Highway. Santa Lucía was also home to a major palm oil processing plant and,[4] for a time, to a hardened outpost of the DEA, later handed over to the Peruvian police to act as its proxy in the US-financed war on drugs.

Hugo did not follow Mashico or Alquiles. He returned instead to La Roca, where he had been working for a number of years before he was in Bella, ever since community leaders across the river in Venenillo had asked his father to set up a ferry service in the mid-1960s. New settlers were arriving all the time, and since Venenillo was the point of entry and exit for the entire Bolsón Cuchara, there was urgent need for regular, reliable transportation. Hugo had moved to La Roca initially to give his father a hand, and together with another brother, Antonio, he eventually took charge of ferrying passengers. Together, Antonio and Hugo conveyed people and the goods they carried, leaving the task of moving bulkier cargos of local harvests to a separate group of vaderos. In La Roca, Hugo also met the woman with whom he formed a family. His new wife had several brothers, and in the coming years Hugo would call on them to help out on the river.

La Roca became the family home, and following his extended stint near Bella, Hugo went back there to stay. Again he would oversee the ferry service, though largely left day-to-day operations to Antonio and his brothers-in-law. Rather than work on the river himself, Hugo took jobs fixing outboard motors, which meant being on call and having to make day trips away from home. He also bought an automobile and began providing an independent car service to and from Tingo María along the Marginal Highway. Little by little, Hugo spent less and less actual time on the river. His daily rhythms increasingly followed the road and its winding path up and down the right bank, leaving him perhaps less tuned in to changing states of affairs in the Bolsón Cuchara. Because in 1983 when the Communist Party (which was how people referred to Sendero Luminoso back then) first made its presence known in the left bank, Hugo said it took him by complete surprise. For Hugo, their violence arrived as if out of nowhere, and a year later he abandoned La Roca, moving with his wife and their five young children to Tingo María. The start of the war snatched his family from a rural, riverine world, the only realm his children had known, thrusting them into a new, urban way of life. Hugo's own separation from the river's currents and shores was now complete. He left el vado behind and by joining the comité de autos, became fully reoriented toward the road, which was another world, all of its own.

tearing up

The morning I shared photographs and videos with Hugo, he had invited his brother-in-law Pedro to join our conversation over lunch. And as we waited for Pedro, Hugo remarked that all the longboats at Nuevo Progreso seemed to be made of metal, offering too that they were metal because hardwoods had become so scarce. I told him about the bridge project announced by President Humala. And I told him, that no, they have not started laying the foundation. Not yet. Well, Hugo said, once work gets started, the vaderos will have at least two years to continue working. Hugo leaned here on his authority: *Esa es cosa de un par de años.* Maybe even a few more. Construction rarely stays on schedule.

Pedro soon arrived to take a seat beside Hugo on the couch. Suddenly, I found myself in the company of two veteran transportistas, reminiscing about episodes from their pasts swept along by the war. Pedro had worked for Hugo as a botero in La Roca, but he did not follow him to Tingo María with the onset of the conflict. He stayed on to persist with el vado for a decade and more, well into the mid-1990s.

To persist with el vado, to and from Venenillo in those years, was to persist with the insurgency, and Pedro spoke at length about the advent of Shining Path in the Upper Huallaga: naming names, places, and dates with a precision that evinced a finely tuned understanding of local histories. Sendero graffiti first appeared, he said, on houses along the Marginal Highway, north of Aucayacu and near the village of Pucayacu—which was not far from the Party's first base in the region, the hamlet of Gosen as early as 1979. That is, Shining Path started out on the right bank of the Huallaga. But within two years its operatives had crossed the river and begun to establish a nascent, clandestine presence in the Bolsón Cuchara. From the village of Corvina, a Party apparatus slowly took hold before expanding to nearby hamlets.

In the midst of these changes, the atmosphere of rural communities Pedro had known for many years began to grow heavy, slowly, palpably turning a little bit hostile. You had to be more guarded and careful to think ahead of time of the impression you might make on others. If people did not like how you glanced at them, they might say you were the enemy. Hate and envy were the crux of the problem, affirmed Pedro, without saying where the negative sentiments came from and without putting blame squarely on Sendero.

The insurgency would reveal its intentions little by little, but Pedro recalled one date he considered decisive: March 3, 1983, when Sendero killed five longtime residents of Venenillo. Those were the first executions, but not until the following year did a stronger and increasingly confident Sendero assert its will. That was when, he said, the situation really started to shift. Hugo had already moved to Tingo María by then, so he did not directly experience what Pedro called "the intensification," much less the specific ways it affected el vado.[5]

Pedro felt the transformation most directly in the orders received from local Party leaders in La Roca. By five in the afternoon he had to cross the river and dock his boat on the left bank at Venenillo. After that Pedro could not leave without permission. Concentrating all vaderos before nightfall kept them on hand whenever the senderistas had a mission and required river transport. Pedro had to remain on call, ready with his canoe at the port.

"¡Bote al otro lado!" With Sendero "everything was controlled," Pedro said. "One was no longer the owner of anything: not your farm, not your children, not your wife, not your belongings, nothing. You had nothing at your own disposal, not even your time, because as soon as they told you something, you had to go. You could not even take off a day to work on your farm. Each and every day you had to go over here and go over there. They would say, "First the Party, then you can attend to your own things." Of course, tending to what the Party demanded left little or no time to spare. And you could not complain or refuse because "they would kill you right there . . . or if not at that very moment, then later at a people's trial."

"Ya no hay salida para nadie" was the rule after 5:00 p.m. After five no one leaves, and the justification they gave was always the same: If, when crossing to the other side, you run into the army or the police, you will be on your own. "And they will kill you," they would say, "either that, or we will." Above all, Party leaders prohibited vaderos from giving passage to *la represión*: the security forces of the Peruvian state. But complying with that most cardinal of Sendero rules, Pedro quickly learned, was nearly impossible. For the police would show up at the shores of La Roca and finding him there, they would put him in a bind. They would say, "Compadre, guess what? We know about you. You give rides to the people over there, to Sendero. So, give us a ride too." Their words appealed to his sense of fairness and hospitality even as they enclosed a threat. For the police were armed, and Pedro was not. So, what else could he do but wave them aboard with an "okay, let's go"? Encounters with military patrols would unfold along similar lines, becoming typical: a genre in its own right.

Sendero's command over Venenillo would last a decade, until the army moved in and set up a permanent counterinsurgency fort. When that happened, political control over el vado changed hands. Pedro still had to bring his boat there to dock before dark, but now, fearing the wrath and reprisals of Sendero, he had no choice but to sleep at the fort for his own protection.

Pedro recounted these patterns: what the war's factions imposed on him and other vaderos. All the while he underscored that el vado is a *public* service, which regardless of the season has a constancy and a permanence simply not required when your boat is just for yourself. In the Huallaga Valley ferries customarily operate under concession from the nearest municipal government, precisely the sort of civil regulatory authority that withered and withdrew during the war. Here though, Pedro referred more broadly to a keen appreciation that el vado was a service provided to all, without distinction, and that becoming a vadero brought with it a sense of responsibility and a commitment to be at the ready to ensure safe passage. With the coming of war, demands for that constancy and permanence intensified severalfold, until Pedro found himself all but stuck at the river's banks. "Every day from six in the morning to six in the afternoon. Even when I was sick, I did not leave. Not Saturdays, not Sundays, not even holidays." Until late in the day he worked, and by the time Pedro went home, he was utterly spent.

Hugo, who sat next to Pedro throughout, closely weighed his every word, echoing in tones of agreement, occasionally stopping him to insist on some minor correction, called this state of affairs of being stuck at water's edge "a prison." Pedro did not disagree but laid stress somewhere else. There was no escaping the cargo and lifting; there was always another sack of potatoes to load and unload. This comment made me realize that our conversation so far had dwelled little on what vaderos actually did and still do to enable crossings over the Huallaga River. So, I asked about the equipment boteros relied on when practicing el vado. Here Pedro emphasized again that having a canoe for one's own personal use differed in significant ways from el vado as a profession. If you are going to take the boat out only occasionally, once every week or two, every month, there is very little you need in terms of equipment. Just your paddle, Hugo laughed, and your long pole or tangana! But Pedro did not make light, he clarified, his voice remaining steady and serious: you must have a boat . . . a motor, a paddle, a tangana . . . but also a motorist who knows the river and an assistant to help with the lifting. You must have a board as well—your *tablita* for groceries, merchandise, sacks of potatoes, motorcycles too.

Back then motorbikes tended toward the small—125cc mostly, now and again a 185. Even so, you could not load it on and off by yourself.

If you did not have an assistant, you would ask the owner to pitch in, and together you would lift the front wheel up and inside the canoe, followed by the back. Here Hugo interjected with some old-school advice: you have to load it from the side, not the bow, and once it's aboard, you must know how to align and accommodate it. And, back to Pedro, completing the thought: you'd be on your way! Though everything always worked better if you could pull the side of the boat right up to the shore. With the canoe flush against the bank, he said, loading and unloading were much easier, but if a gap remained, you'd put down a tablita.

Every botero must carry a *tablero*, Pedro explained. To roll the motorcycle into the boat, and then, reaching the other shore, to roll it out again. And every botero carries his tablita to ensure the cargo does not get soaked, because *el agua lagrimea*: water gets in, runs everywhere, which is why you place a wood board at the bottom of the boat. For the purpose of conveying passengers, a tablero is not needed every time; that depends on the shore. Yet since there will always be someone who is bringing things, merchandise too, it becomes critical equipment, something a botero must have on hand. For water always waters, always tears up, precipitates, shedding tears that tear away the dry. And so la tablita lifts; la tablita separates—keeping cargo above and water with its dampness down low.

This was what Pedro confirmed: la tabla introduced a smooth, stable surface, held in place just long enough to fill the interval, to guide safe passage, and to ward off falls. La tabla resolved differences in height, unfolding from the material variability of a river's banks and from the tendency of water to tear up and spread, always in search of a lower point. La tabla so that people and their things might move from this side to that, undisturbed by the material force of the Huallaga's currents.

in shivers

Pedro has errands in town and takes leave from us immediately after lunch. In his absence Hugo and I return to the couch and continue our talk. At some point Hugo comes back around to my photographs of wedges, blocks, and boards, picking up again where we first began: "These are small things," he said. "So simple at first glance, you could even say of no importance. But if you look at them from the point of view of what they're for, their importance is enormous." Something apparently negligible expresses outsized worth, going unheeded, misread even, if not approached, he suggested, from the angle of their proper utility and purpose—as if sense, visibility, and value would lean on one another in mutual support.

Hugo says he understands my curiosity.

Here are things so small but upon them depends a world. Here is something minor at the crux of the monumental.

Hugo reaffirms my fascination. Something in these material things shimmers, stirs, creates eddies: so obvious, so utterly basic, yet he has no more words at the ready. We have reached an end before something, the opaqueness of a mass blocking our way. That we can pursue this no further, Hugo seems to signal when he answers my initial question by effectively restating it.

And so our conversation heads now in another direction, as if before these wedges, blocks, and boards, there was nothing more to see or say.

Later I will wonder whether pushing further into the opaqueness that made us pause would not demand a more intimate examination of the photographs themselves. Looking at them carefully could perhaps offer a means of gaining proximity to what they portray, which would presuppose asking, of course, how these images and the material things they depict intricately bear upon one another. For Hugo, a proper appreciation of the implements of el vado entailed recognizing their use-value from the perspective of ferry operators themselves. On that critical assertion, he rested all explanation, and there was no more headway to be made, at least not then and apparently not together.

But what if pushing further into what repelled our inquiry required separating out all that rotates on use? Assuming of course there were a pushing further and that utility did not have an absolute controlling stake in what might be perceived in any particular present. Could one then ask whose utility shapes what comes into view? Might one ask as well if the contours of the useful could be closely traced and enough so as to grasp precisely which side pivots to match interest with what interests? Would that tracing also reveal perhaps what becomes obvious in any encounter? For if utility guides perception, must it do so with such a heavy hand and to such an extent that—in turning solely to that side of the thing perceived, which interest singles out—a shroud is thereby cast over each and every other aspect of that thing in its very multiplicity? That would be to say that the obvious is essentially reductive and results from a framing that privileges what has been precatalogued for use. Moreover, if the contours of the useful are always molded by the specific circumstances determining what in any particular moment is deemed convenient, sensible, even advantageous, that would seem to imply as well that utility as such cannot be detached from political time or the broader states of affairs it intones.

Throughout the modern history of the Huallaga Valley, the basic need to cross the river has endured, spanning multiple eras, amid sharp swings in intensity. And yet the social institutions and technical means for satisfying that need—el vado and los vaderos—find themselves forever turned toward the ever-changing press of the moment. As they face that present, pushing headlong into its ever-fleeting cusp, boteros and balseros drag with them the material residues and affective weight of the past. And yet, through it all, el vado persists into the aftermaths of a brutal stretch and as new political circumstances never cease to unfold.

El vado persists, bringing different eras into proximity right where time meets terrain, now with its own future in doubt.

The point when my conversation with Hugo could go no further seemed to open onto a larger task: listening for, drawing out, the temporal constellations that insisted through el vado as social institution and technical means for crossing the Huallaga River. If that task sent me again and again back to the photographs, perhaps it was because returning to them and getting involved with their details would create opportunities to start over—in hopes of discovering, if not a way around the impasse, then at least a different sort of proximity. And yet maybe, what Hugo alluded to without ever saying so explicitly was that returning to the details required a respect and a special sensitivity toward utility itself so as to take a step closer to what utility cloaks and sets at a remove.

Ethnography, by seeking out the rhythms and multiple aspects that hover *over* use, that rise *behind* use, that disappear *in* use, by reaching toward what appears when something falls *in* and *out* of use, might do more than affirm a descriptive purpose. And it might expand that purpose to reveal the contours of the obvious and the specific ways those contours carry on the tones and exigencies of a prevailing political era.

Here there were photographs to describe. Approaching them ethnographically entailed retracing the lines of the empirical but not merely to render what was already given. Tracing those lines again involved moving toward the limits of what the empirical made evident but only as a means toward preparing a new ground, where what was not yet discernible, not yet intelligible, not yet readable in their image, might be composed. Redoubling the lines of the empirical meant starting anew, by turning in toward the obvious and by bending with it, so that the very act of seeking out the expedient could hold open the possibility of happening upon what was less primed for use. To find in that return and to draw off from it something more multiple, more vibrant, more unexpected, ethnographic description might bring forth what did not yet exist.

The subject matter of the photographs I shared with Hugo were the tools and quasi-tools that made up the everyday repertoire of el vado. What drew me to them were those things that seemed to fall in and out of use, but also in and out of view, through their intermittent flickering: from debris to equipment and from equipment to debris. I wondered what that flickering expressed about the material dimensions of territory, about the anticipatory boundaries shaping where might one safely go, depending on the place. I wondered no less about what it could disclose about shifts in political time and how they continued reworking common sense about what was advantageous, here in the very moment photographs were taken.

Examining the images again, I realized how much they seemed to hold my gaze. The things and implements were certainly striking of their own accord. And yet in the movement between photographic image and the materials portrayed I could sense a certain tension. If textures, colors, weight, and densities of the things depicted were what communicated impenetrability, then perhaps the impasse was marked off by the photographic frame, leaving the problem to reside completely on the side of

FIGURE 2.12. twilight crossing

matter itself: with how matter stimulates and generates affects, as Bergson once claimed,[6] with how it produces fascination by blocking, refusing to yield, to what would take hold of it. In so doing matter commanded attention; it called for effort and demanded involvement.

These, however, were not material things themselves but images of them. Still, I felt no less commanded. And yet to begin to think with these photographs seemed to demand something more than an additional or even a sustained effort: a greater and more varied connection than looking alone might provide. So I tried describing them in writing. And as I tried, little by little, I came to think of description as a method for forcing sight, a method that retraces the lines of the empirical in anticipation of what cannot be grasped: beyond opaqueness, beyond a tremor, toward something not quite discernible behind use. Perhaps ethnographic description could be where writing becomes composition in the offhand chance that in drawing out something new, it might actually create.

Operators of barges from the port of Nuevo Progreso, such as the one shown here and in the coming pages, create sporadic surfaces that come into direct contact with the Huallaga and ride its currents from

FIGURE 2.13. toothed contours, splinters, and splits

side to side. They do so with the help of simple instruments and bits of matter transformed into ephemeral equipment, which lay about in shivers when not in use. There are two spots where tools and quasi-tools of balseros tend to fall: atop the barge's wooden platform and underneath the twin timber beam ramps that jut out over the water. Those beams bear the load of trucks when they move on and off the barge. They are thus the heaviest equipment of this simple machine for bringing the horizontal vector of ferry passage in line with the river's intermittent swells and declines. The human operators are what reach for this block or that wedge in the midst of raising and lowering the beams onto and then off the raft, making them perhaps the most critical pieces of all.

Shooting askance into the center of this next photograph (figure 2.13), two large overlying beams tend now to the right. They hang dense, inches above the platform, mass and gravity visually evident, as they wait to be lowered for the next truck or left behind as the raft pulls off to answer a call from the other bank. Their front edges or *lips* carry marks of prior leveraging: stress fractures on the left crack a rounded arc, sketching out a small chunk about to break away, the beginnings of a more profound splitting right down the middle. Across this same plank, and in striking distance of the barge, a rope slithers up from the graveled soil to lie in loops and bunched-up curves, as if still holding on to residual motions of its last release from a balsero's hand.

Tucked just below these hanging beams, the barge floor spreads across the photograph's lower half: a stable ground fashioned by anchoring together different sizes of lumber. Small boards, separated by thin dark crevices, run crossways up and down either side of two vertebrating planks, spaced apart to receive the wheels of heavy vehicles. Atop the platform are smaller, fragmentary bits of wood—close and at the ready. A diminutive block rests contained within smoothed perpendicular angles, as if inert. Four wedges surround it, relaying movement in toothed contours, splinters, and splits.

These minor pieces give the setting a certain workshop air in their casual mix of improv and the purposiveness of craft. Dirt particles, wood dust, and minute splinters cover the barge floor, yet as debris seem less foreign than pertinent to the tasks at hand. And all these wood forms bear traces from use, augmenting exterior textures that up close look like so many orographic maps, even as they reveal tendencies of interior configuration. Unlike the hard edges of timber-mill cuts, these crackings, splinterings, crumblings all happen in line with the grain. In decomposition they reiterate prior vectors of growth, retracing past steps as they bend out toward other horizons.

Strikingly continuous is the graduation of tones in all but the uppermost band of the photograph. An earthen bank, strewn with clods, stones, and gravel, pulls balsero implements and structures into a single reciprocal topography of ashen browns. Tawny bone. Sienna. Umber. Even the lone metal rod—straight, hollow, with tip slightly squashed—repeats these same hues as it juts into the lower left corner. Like other balsero tools, swept up in a flurry of activity whenever there is cargo to take on or off, this lever quickly recedes into the wood platform, becoming yet another background thing once the barge departs.

And now again, in the words of a balsero: each little piece of wood has its function (figure 2.14).

FIGURE 2.14. a secret utility

FIGURE 2.15. dual vectors

And now again, a balsa ramp appears, an architectural intervention in the landscape (figure 2.15). Two timber beams stretching out straight, flat, over the water. Arrayed side by side to express the dual, ambivalent vector of el vado: transmitting and receiving movements. The nearest beam protrudes toward the middle of the river, manifesting the powers of perspective. Suspended over the water, its blunt end holds steady in the sky, amid clouds and just above hills that frame the town of Nuevo Progreso on the other bank. The end of the farthest beam actually touches those hills, accentuating the ridgeline as it repeats the river's course in parallel and at higher elevation. Up close: a rocky shoreline snakes wave-like from the fore, undulating up as it retreats, passing a rope that dangles down from the far-right beam to pull together, from another angle and along a separate path, distinct features of the place: a sliver of pale sky, a distant bluff fading to haze in an abrupt downward slope, a dark slice of opposing shore, crossing now the moving water before reaching damp silt and stones where it tucks itself from view.

I learn from Pilar, in back-and-forth messages, with long waits as she finds time to consult with her father, that the large timbers for ramps and barges must be made from a single piece of hardwood. Otherwise they break under the weight of road vehicles. Traditionally, they have been crafted from the trunk of the chamisa tree, which these days is almost impossible to find.

Here each of the ramp's twin timbers rests upon a single column of stacked wood. A mass shouldered by careful arrangements of small blocks, sawed-off planks, and stumps. To be precise, both columns begin with a thick wood brick to create a base upon rocky soil. Then on top of that initial foundation, a large round trunk section is set, followed by three ascending pieces: a short wide plank, a medium-sized block, and a much smaller brick to top off the stack. This final piece is the only chunk of wood that comes into direct contact with the horizontal beam, and yet all receive the downward thrust of the beam's formidable weight. The columns tilt inward. The more distant of the two, sitting awkward, as if in danger of buckling.

Note the movement. The many lines for eyes to unthinkingly follow. Note the gap navigated here between arriving barge and stone-strewn bank: how its watery surface shimmers dark reflections of the twin

FIGURE 2.16. coupling planks and timbers

overhanging timbers. Note the platform and how its thick planks extend out as much as a meter and more. Note how in their approach they must fit underneath the shoreside ramp, making it critical to ensure the columns are not stacked too close. And again, on the barge platform, see the damaged end of the right flat beam: a tearing, ripping away, traces perhaps of prior collisions and unguarded moments that might have preceded them.

So many directions for eyes to follow. The balsero tells me about a time he dropped a ramp timber on his thumb. How it puffed up this big—swelling like he had never seen. And all that pain. At home in repose for several months, he says; he could not work at all.

The twin platform planks are here closing in, pivoting now to couple up with the timbers hanging from the shore. And along one horizontal register, beams, bank, faraway horizon all run together to strike a contrast with four people in vertical stance: two on the barge, two on the shore, and between them a lone transitional figure—the balsero's assistant in curved pose, stretching to grab a rope. Moving back now to the deck, blocks, sloped boards, wedges, split logs, and wood chips lay scattered yet ready, several already gathered together to make a fulcrum.

FIGURE 2.17. pushing, coaxing into place

Balseros piece together materials as they transit between the river's shores. From particulars and particulates they craft temporary surfaces that express their own plural, ever-historical sense. Some of those senses can be sketched topologically as a spatial diagram: a line drawing of elegant slopes and spirals that could render with great precision how el vado in this place might operate in another. Topology in that regard would meet up and partially overlap with topography but without subsuming it. For who says topography should denote a metric of spatial homogeneities? Might it name instead something more akin to what Bergson called "concrete extensity": the indivisible multiplicities of materials and sensations in movement, with their folds and textures, buoyancies and weights, colors and opacities—as intimated to some extent by these photographs? The singular verve of such aspects and details of empirical worlds are what ethnographic writing might attempt to describe on the way toward something else not yet seen.

Longboats tethered together make a barge. Here their tapered points shoot out to the right, a three-pronged fork turned up and floating on the water. Dual timber beams draw the barge into a stone-embedded, sandy-gray expanse. In an image that turns on counter-poised angles, the balsero plants bare feet upon the left plank, leaning in now to lodge a metal lever underneath the right plank, pushing, coaxing it into place. The larger of two white trucks appears to slope with him, off kilter, while in front of the other truck, a man watches, arms crossed, leaning forward slightly as if a compositional response to the balsero at work.

Getting closer to things in their concrete extensity suggests getting closer to how those things happen, to the encounters they take part in and rever-berate *topographically*. For where political time meets terrain, moments from vastly different eras might reveal some unforeseen proximity. Here deep crevices run up the middle of the flat timbers. To their outer tips thin metal bars have been tacked to hold them together and attenuate further breakage. Next to their mass and density, the balsero's feet look terribly exposed. In the absence of clothing that would provide partial protection, what are already trying tasks demand all the more care, attention, and skill.

Every night el balsero I've called Lobo sleeps in the former outpost of the Peruvian police—a bare multistory, cinder-block structure facing the river, two blocks from the port. He tells me that townspeople who later took up residence in this vacant dilapidated building would hear noises at night, which they feared were wandering souls of policemen killed in Shining Path attacks. Lobo tells me this late one afternoon upon finding me at a kiosk overlooking the Huallaga. Pulling up a seat, this balsero swears that ever since moving into that discreet ruin of local war history, he has neither heard nor feared any such thing. But just in case, Lobo says, sending me a wry smile, he has installed electrical wiring and lights in all the rooms. He keeps the master switch right by his bed. Any strange sound after dark, he flips that switch.

The balsero's smirk lingers with me, along its playful assurance about violent times withdrawn to a comfortable distance. I think about his elec-trical lights, which at the touch of a finger displace the night but never definitively dispel the shadows of the wartime past. Events transpired in that place, where the balsero now sleeps, drag into the ever-passing present, apparently powerless to act but resounding nonetheless in their

FIGURE 2.18. again and off again, the pallet platform

proximity to the port. These are some of the relations—material, social, historical, temporal—that animate crossings on the Huallaga River. These are some sites of fleeting but rarely indifferent face-to-face encounters, where a war, though no longer unfolding, hovers near the ordinary work of rural transit. What happens on and in between the river's banks, now largely free of the trepidations and threats that formerly could stop one in their tracks, still offers up a measure of what binds friends to acquaintances, kin to strangers, and neighbors to enemies. From those encounters a local scene emerges, revealing its contours and limits.

It's been claimed that "a place changes in quality according to the facility with which it can be crossed."[7] If so, then how has the relative ease and unease of movement across the Huallaga Valley corresponded with recent shifts in political time? How has rural transit expressed variations in territory that accompanied not only a counterinsurgency war but its aftermaths, where the building of roads and bridges reworks landscapes and reroutes local itineraries?

The "quality" of a place is a casual way of saying its semblance: where matter, sensation, and image intersect. Here shifts in political time find expression in the airs that merge with embankments, continually remodeled by a river's moving currents. Here territory happens, when skies reach down to take hold of damp earth, even as clouds appear to draw off imaginations, sending them elsewhere to divert a gaze momentarily from the scene. Matter, sensation, and image intersect in photographs and videos of the port of Nuevo Progreso and the boat landing on the opposite bank. They reveal the debris, tools, and techniques of el vado, around which cluster other images, stories, histories, and times—a plurality that does not privilege any single perspective.

For if there is never a here without a drifting elsewhere—in distraction, in daydream, in sleep—the reference anchoring any point of view can always be loosened, made to float, or released from sequence. That's why getting closer by way of description hardly need collapse the differential workings of material distance into a presence imagined as unitary, univocal, or definitive. Indeed, political time meets terrain whenever two, three, four eras and more enter into constellation to be held together less by mimetic recognition than an intense charge of secret topographic proximities, briefly disclosed and barely heeded. Just as analogy does not render concrete extensity any more than it can do justice to material vicinity, getting closer by way of description sometimes calls for taking stock of historical airs that move in and around things. Ethnographic writing calls sometimes too for tracing out distinct expressions of distance: between visits to the same place; between acquaintances fleeting and enduring; between close-ups and landscapes. Wherever pulsings of difference draw out a remoteness to become a tangible expanse.

Postwar conjoins different times. It partitions past from present by reorienting perceptions toward what is newly expedient, reliable, and useful. In the Upper Huallaga its prolonged stretch overlaps with a longer history of el vado. Boteros and balseros weave a lattice with common materials, simple tools, and carefully honed techniques, on top of currents, up and down a moving course, between points where roads end and begin again, between shores where bridges might fall and in the lull until they might be restored. With the changes postwar brings is el vado to be overrun or merely displaced? Will el vado merely persist or will it do more, by continuing to stitch the very intervals of war and aftermath together, folding one back and forth into always yet another back and forth? Will it do more, alongside tending to that ever-pressing immediate need to ferry people, their vehicles, goods, and so many other things to the other side?

Something stirs in the simplicities of materials that await a botero's or balsero's reach. In the quasi-tools of boards, blocks, and wedges. In the round poles, long and short. In the extended rectangular stakes, where one end tapers to a flat point.

In these simplicities, a swirl, so subtle. A churning discrete in these scatterings. Metal rods of a pair, the thick one and the thin. That short-handled hoe. And in shivers broken off from something larger, so many splinters and splinterings, thin and sharp, strewn atop and alongside straight-line planks, some with edges now chipped. An eddying just beyond the twilight of a glimpse, where crestings of water become notchings of wood. Here colors muddy in sands of ashen beige, in raw-umbered silts, in rusts and burnt siennas where metal and timber cross, in the pitch of crevices grown opaque.

Through careful placements and well-timed lodgings balseros move people, vehicles, and cargo on and off pallet platforms, composed in twin timbers and surrounded by perpendicular boards. By angling and lever-aging metal bars, by gripping, prying, and pressing, by leaning in now to bring the entire weight of their bodies to bear. With quick blows of a pickax they clear small stones so a ramp timber can settle flat. Grabbing and positioning a chock, they stabilize motions, keeping a truck at rest.

To sustain these temporary grounds in displacements to and fro, they draw on the planked, the sectioned, and the slabbed. They appeal to stack-ings of sawed-off boards, blocks, and stumps. They depend on tether-ings and bindings of ropes and chains but also on long slender branches plunged deep—makeshift moorings in waterlogged banks.

And amid it all, so many implicating lines: the creases, the ridges, the folds, the wrinkles, the grains of wood moving diagonal, splinter-ing horizonal, bending now toward a single, vertical stream. Only to be washed out in the glares of midday, ricocheting off the water: blinding, burning, forcing eyes askance. And later to be hidden with the gloaming that will arrive to cool, dim, fold everything in shadow. Through it all, the currents, waxing and wandering, rising, then receding. Through it all, el vado upright between two waters—the river and the clouds. El vado oblong between two earths—the left shore and the right where vaderos quietly tend to intervals and intercalary spaces that continually crop up between boat and bank. In their movements back and forth vaderos precipitate surfaces solid underfoot, capable of carrying heavy loads yet ever fleeting even as they fill in and bridge the gaps.

through the hollows

The words Tina shares draw forth an imaging, a reaching out from the here of our nascent acquaintance, spanning the distance, out there, to the wheres of what happened. From her stories, a picturing laden with charge and yet always vague. Conveying only the slimmest of details, it prompts a waiting, sets in motion an anticipation of other, more substantial, fragments to come. In fits and starts that effort of imaging, reaching, anticipating constellates multiple thens with our ever-passing present, where Mauro sits wooden, receding to the farthest edges of our conversation, sometimes leaving us all alone.

And through her words spread so many implicating lines, not only of male siblings gone or of their mother, heartbroken, expiring little by little, but of Tina's own grown daughters with boyfriends becoming sons-in-law: elder children of her first and second partners, about whom almost nothing is ever said. The policeman that left for Lima. Or the other that Mauro says was narco. Through her union with Wilson, who stayed on to make a home, she has a baby girl and two sons in their early teens already. And now on the years of those later children she leans to count back in time, chronologically anchoring for me the events she recounts.

Later too I will meet Chara and learn how close he hovers: as a farmhand or *jornalero*, as a stray taken in, perhaps as a *socio*. Theirs is *one* of ineffable bonds, tying the two to an earlier era, to her first years as a *vadera*, and to his—though she disclosed this only once and never mentioned it again—as a one-time village *miliciano*. They are practically family, and over this arrangement always on the verge of falling apart Wilson's irritation is palpable. Chara drinking . . . again. Chara growing surly . . . again. Chara nearly coming to blows . . . again. On and on, without end, resurfacing, then setting itself straight, for at least one more day until the next time beer gets passed around. What ties him and Tina to that earlier time such that their commitment might never waver? A little poison.

Venenillo. Where *it* was strong. Where Tina might never have gone if not approached by her brother, enticing her with opportunities. "I had two boats," and Grober said there was *chamba*. I could only wonder at the resilience of that justification—*chamba*, work: where all explanation comes to a full stop. Enough to send her into certain danger: Where *it* was strong. And where there was so much money. Tina admitted she was scared, told me that she hesitated, that she told her brother back then to just take the boats and work them himself, but no, Grober insisted, as their owner she had to be in charge, but he also made it seem somehow doable: *todo depende que sabemos trabajar y nos portamos bien.* Shaping their comportment into a straight arrow would give them a way to reckon, something solid to hold on to. Another time. So many other implicating lines.

Venenillo. Strong. A place under remarkable patterns. There, where other rules prevail, a certain unfathomable license. The column arrives. Every guerrillero gets to grab a girl. "Mami" has them ready: girls from all over. The rigid moral economy Sendero imposed elsewhere in the countryside was here somehow suspended. Venenillo, Tina explained, was "almost pueblo" with its urban air of bars, billiards, brothels. Never before had a place with but ten rustic huts seemed so colossal. Little poison. In this place there would be no *limpieza social*. "Almost pueblo." Eight stores with shelves overflowing in anticipation of the coming warrior concentration, of the parties, of the drinking, of the dancing, then left bare by the break of dawn when the column of a thousand men and more than a few young guerrilla women moved on.

Working that river, Tina charged a set price per head, ferrying people and their cargo to and fro: Venenillo, La Roca, sometimes Cocha. The real prospects came with what she called *las carreras especiales*. Short charter trips to move drugs or sacks of money up- or downstream were where the takings improved severalfold. Enough to stomach the day-to-day risk. Enough to get by, all the while, with an ear to the wind, waiting, waiting for the *toco-toco* of a helicopter approaching. Eerie was that cusp of not yet knowing, that pause when all came to a stop, right before the threshing became unbearably evident, right before the mad dash for cover, right before the heart-thumping *toco-toco toco-toco* flight, as far away as possible from bombs ready to drop.

But first, before Tina and her brother could even begin, permissions had to be secured. Everything had to be discussed with the Party ahead of time. Venenillo was Sendero's lair, said she, where *it* all began. Tina meant where the movement first took root in the Alto Huallaga. Venenillo was where not just anyone could go—"no se entraba por entrar"—much less arrive to set up shop, not without the Party's authorization. Grober knew this, because he had already been going there to buy raw cocaine like many of the other *traqueteros* from town, so he would make some preliminary inquiries. Then they could travel there together to talk with the *mando.* Grober would speak on her behalf and explain that it was their wish to work as vaderos with the Party's blessing and concession. At that point the Party, before giving its consent, would want to investigate Tina, follow her comings and goings, find out about her past and with whom she passed her days. At any rate there would be a certain lapse in time. Through it all, Grober would vouch for his sister, but if she ever deviated from the rules, it would be his head. Along with hers.

Maybe you won't believe me, she would say, but I worked in Venenillo for twelve years. Twelve years with my boat and my motor. Life there was money. In those days so . . . much . . . money. We'd do a run carrying drugs, just a little way round a curve, and two hundred dollars they would pay us. That's how it was, but you had to be super straight, because if you went crooked on them, they'd do it to you, then and there. And running through it all the ever-present danger of stupid mistakes: like the time Tina almost got killed because the guerrilla mixed her up with someone else, which was one story she never finished telling.

Grober's fate, however, was entwined with a different threat—one that showed itself the very first day he and Tina went to talk with the Sendero leader. Barely ten minutes after pulling her canoe into the port of Venenillo, after looking for but not finding him there, they ferried back over to the shores of La Roca, just in time for the police to stage a daylight raid. They grabbed Tina's brother, accused him of being a ter-ruco, and hauled him away.

Knowing where they were taking him, Tina went downstream by ca-noe a short distance to the village of Santa Lucía. Here, Tina explained, she had no friends, no acquaintances, no one to vouch for her, but in the intrepidness of youth Tina would not be deterred. She tied her boat to the shore and marched straight up the trail to the headquarters of the UMOPAR—a mobile rural unit of the national police, then Civil Guard, dedicated ostensibly to antinarcotics enforcement. Seeing a group of po-licemen standing out front, she approached, demanding to know "Who is the owner of this circus? I sure don't want to speak with the clown!" And how the policemen laughed as Tina pressed her case: "I must speak with the circus owner, and if I have to pay to get my brother back, I can do that too." An older officer appeared now in the doorway, started to-ward them, but Tina beat him to the draw: "Sir, we just arrived from Aucayacu, so why have you brought my brother here? What do you want? Be straight with me. Just tell me what you want."

"Pucha, qué brava, esa china," said the officer, as he tossed a vaguely malicious smile to the other policemen and to them alone, before turning to Tina: "No, señora. Don't worry señorita. We have simply summoned him for now."

"Well, if that's so," Tina replied, "what could you possibly have to talk with him about?" Her feign of impatience faltering slightly now— "We don't know this place"—at risk of falling into pleading tones—"We have come here in search of work, this morning for the very first time."

"Okay, señora, okay, don't get upset, señorita—the officer, teetering again between these two modes of address—not wanting to offend per-haps, but also as if married already or awaiting betrothal where the only social conditions he imagined she might fulfill—before throwing her a surprise: "You can take your brother."

And without as much as a warning, they let Grober go, all the while leaving a threat implicit then and there, and also in every version of the story she would share with me in the years to come. In all those tellings Tina and Grober walked back to the river, jumped into the boat, and motored home. Sometimes they headed the very next day to Venenillo to start work. Sometimes they had to wait a few days before receiving word from the Party, summoning them to talk with the mando, so they could finalize the terms for purchasing and running the concession. Over the next several years Tina would work with her brother, ferrying people and their goods between La Roca, Cocha, and Venenillo, though on the particulars she was often hazy. Sometimes, she spoke as if she stayed close to home, leaving day-to-day operations largely to her brother. At other times, she said, they had worked hand in hand. Whether Tina's presence in el vado was constant or sporadic, they made money. Two canoes with outboard motors little by little became six, and Tina had designs on acquiring a whole fleet of boats and making a good living leasing them out to other boteros. But that was before the war started claiming her brothers, stealing this dream amid so many others.

Details were hazy, but ever perched above her work on the river was Venenillo in its days of glory. Pucha, Richard, that was *la muerte*. By which she meant something beyond compare. There were bars. There were billiard halls. There was prostitution, and all of it presided over by the terrucos. "I found out these things only when I started going to Venenillo." And there Tina could barely believe what she saw. The red flags hoisted up, all in a line. How the helicopter would come, tear up the place, bombarding everything in sight. How the guerrilla, or what everyone called *la columna*, would show up, throw parties, get drunk.

In the early-morning chill with a tape spooling between us, Tina told about the day she had just pulled in from La Roca. "I had gone over to the banda, and in the banda I was sitting under the flags flapping there, those red flags in the port. I was sitting near the road, which was wide with a discotheque, bars, and all that, and I was talking with my motorist, when I looked up and saw something like a thousand people. I lifted my head and saw what looked like the army; they were all dressed in green. As I've been telling you, I still did not have a handle on what that place was like. And I said to my motorist, pucha, Aníbal, the army! Where?!? he said, looking around. I said, we better run. No, that's not the army, he tells me, that's the guerrilla! They're arriving! Pucha, today there will parties, he said, getting all excited. Today . . . pucha, forget about it: people will be selling all night long. And sure enough, the next day, how the bodegas had been emptied out and how the owners had to replenish their stocks once again. Well, the guerrilla . . . a thousand men, men and women cleaned up, buying clothes, shoes, paying with dollars. . . . And they all had that money because they had been stealing along the way. They flat out robbed, holding up traqueteros at gunpoint, killing. So, they had all that money, and by the next day the stores had been emptied out and their owners would have to bring in boats. And pucha, that meant work for us too. Boats loaded with cargo. That was Venenillo."

Grober was not the first of her brothers the war stole, but in all the versions Tina told, his death seemed to bracket off her first five years as a Venenillo ferry operator. In the port of that left bank hamlet, Grober was killed—and in that initial telling and in it alone, strangled with the rope of one of Tina's very own boats. But what never varied in her accounts was that he lost his life at the hands of the police, the UMOPAR, stationed at Santa Lucía on the river's right bank—a headquarters that continues there to this day if under a different unit insignia and name, made ever conspicuous for many years by a checkpoint where traffic on both sides of the Marginal Highway had to stop.

After Grober's death, Tina let the Sendero leaders in Venenillo know she wished to hold on to the ferryboat concession, that she would take charge in her brother's place. But señora, they cautioned, if that's so, then you must be steadfast. Regardless of the things that happen here that you might not like. Well, if it's for work . . . , she assured them, if that's what the job demands, what else could she do? Thus began the second era of Tina's work as a vadera, providing passage to and from Venenillo, with the help of motor operators and assistants she personally contracted. Each morning they would set out from the right bank hamlet of La Cocha or later from La Roca, moving in between places where, as she liked to say, *las papas quemaban,* where the atmosphere of war crosscutting a thriving cocaine trade turned most intense. For twelve years, even as the army made its incursions on Venenillo and eventually installed a counterinsurgency fort there, Tina worked. The permanent presence of the army in Venenillo starkly refigured the terrain, and in Tina's telling it provided a coda of sorts to her time there—a twilight era as business fell off little by little, with fewer and fewer passengers crossing, with the short runs for cocaine traders becoming less and less frequent, until there was no longer any money to be made.

These things Tina told me the fourth time we met up, the year of our initial acquaintance: 2002. In that cement room, I did not yet know Chara or anything about him. I had no idea little poison was what had brought them close, there, where he lost a stepfather and she her eldest brother.

shades and the fury

These conversations all take place in quiet, back and forth, moving from opposite sides of the old wooden desk, where a small cassette player sits to record not just words but every bit of the surrounding hollow. In quiet we talk of what has happened, as a new tape spools round upon round, because across the room the metal rolling door stays shut, blocking out the lingering ears and harsh glares of the street. From out there, as if undeterred by this steel wall unfurled, only a jagged mishmash of sounds enters to become our background hum: the plug-plug of motorbikes, shifting gears, round the corner; the squeal of brakes as a pickup truck pulls to the curb; sidewalk chatter of schoolkids dragging feet, then quickening the pace, belting out to classmates, you better wait up. Nothing more gets in, nothing except slithers of light, stealing through a thin gap where metal sheeting meets hard, unfinished cement floor.

Every morning I arrive early and enter quickly through a small oblong door inset into those extended planks of steel. With the turn of a key, planks ripple, giving way, as the little door opens. Duck. Step inside. Shut out street. In one seamless motion until the whiff of damp gritty air stops me cold, seizing with the urge to back out and abandon this tiny front room of a residence converted into a local human rights office. Here the absence of friends and familiar faces touches in the dust that grates inside, tightening throat, making eyes well up and water. And yet there is nowhere else to go—not to do this work, not with the pace, concentration, and shelter it still demands. This place has been shuttered for months, its staff summoned to the city of Tingo María to run the temporary district headquarters of a national truth commission. And it's odd to return and not find them here—the handful of lawyers, teachers, and youthful volunteers, who through untold hours have hobbled this office together and kept it running these last few years. Perhaps the conflict—a ripple in planks of steel—though ostensibly over in the rest of the country, still presses too close here to conduct the national commission's day-to-day affairs in the open. Perhaps, in the greater anonymity afforded by the city, those who have testimonies to give—a tape spools round and round—would feel less exposed, more willing to come forward. Even so, there is something jarring in the thought that the staff of this local human rights office should be pulled away from where the war still touches deep—damp as a choking whiff. Odd too that as they leave, and thanks to that very same commission, I have been able to make a brief return, though with a different role from theirs—not to collect testimonies but to research a regional history of the conflict. What I have been doing in one way or another for some time already.

Most mornings the sun rises bright and hot. Yet within these walls a pleasant chill lingers until well past noon, giving me a few hours to receive visitors or review notes and write under a lone incandescent bulb, hanging dimly at the ends of wire that disappear into the ceiling. From that dark cobwebbed hole, a feeble dome of light falls freely before joining forces with a diffuse luminescence that enters though the small side window overlooking a neighbor's empty lot. Together, they push the shadows back toward the corners of the room and up onto pale green walls. From where I sit with pen and paper, the metal rolling door across the room offers the only access to the street. To leave it open invites more than scrutiny. People appear, seeking legal services, wanting to know the status of cases pending. A few clumsy attempts at fielding their questions sufficed to show how much I am out of my depth. Better not to disappoint. Better to work quietly here, fading as much as possible into the vacancy of this place.

But nothing would happen without Mauro, who shows up on the warm recommendation of lawyers called away. Smiling, insistent, hanging on a chance—a diffuse luminescence. Our most dependable volunteer, they assured. He will help you, put you in contact with people from the countryside. He will bring them to you here in the office so they can share what they know. A convenient setup to be sure yet so foreign to everything this place taught me only a few years before: about never appearing too curious, never probing beyond what was offered, never posing a question of any gravity, certainly not initially or even long after. And so, all this could not but feel rushed and almost wrong, a jagged mishmash of sounds, but I do not have time, not with this charge. Collect information, write quick, produce report. And to make that happen, there must be someone to connect me to the right people without delay, without inciting mistrust. For this place a near impossible task, but then Mauro appears day after day, rasping knuckles on a metal door, accompanied by a friend or a relative to speak with me, one at a time.

Most of those Mauro brings by are second-generation settlers. People whose parents arrived from elsewhere to claim tracts of land, sometimes upward of a hundred hectares and more, on the left bank of the Huallaga River. The era of agrarian reform, spanning the late 1950s into the early 1970s, is the background of most accounts I hear. Recalling that prior era is important, because without it what happened next would be terribly hard to follow. The valley's settler past is also Mauro's history, that of his parents and siblings, all of whom related in some way to each and every person he brings by. Those relations are in turn tied to specific places in the countryside. For while dozens of hamlets surround this right bank town, the histories of people I meet through Mauro are attached to select rural areas on the other side of the Huallaga River: whether immediately across the water, to the hamlets of San José, Primavera, and San Martín, or else farther north to the sector of Magdalena, which runs in parallel with the right bank village of Ramal de Aspuzana, just off the Marginal Highway.

One morning Mauro arrived with an elderly gentleman he introduced as an original colonist of La Morada. In this agrarian settler society, to be recognized as a *colono* still carried a palpable charge of respect. *Colonos* were the region's elders after all, but among them, those who had founded the hamlet of La Morada in the late 1950s held a special, undisputed prominence, as their endeavors were thought, at least in one dominant rendering of that history, to have provided the spark for waves of colonizations that soon followed.[1] And yet even before this man spoke a single word, his clothes conveyed a dignity and eloquence, less diminished than accentuated by how they underscored hard practicalities of rural life. The

black beat-up pair of Tigre-brand canvas tennis shoes, securing his footing through fields and trails in a land of frequent rain. The baseball cap
covering his head and partially shielding his face from the sun's punishing rays. The pale, threadbare-collar shirt he had tucked neatly into the
waistband of faded dark trousers and tied off with an old brown leather
belt. Even the small smudges of mud, picked up as he walked across town
this morning, held fast to the formalities of male attire from an earlier
age and, with them, expressed a certain humility of station.

From that station edged a voice of fact, stirring a steady telling of
things as they had happened, hewing close to the broad strokes of a sequential history I had heard time and again—when coca became the valley's lone agricultural concern, when Colombians appeared with sacks of
money and techniques for making cocaine, when Shining Path's armed
struggle swept up the countryside before pressing in on the towns. In between those strokes this man placed special stress on the ways the army
later imposed its will with methods of a magnitude that would outpace
the means of all others combined. For La Morada that will culminated
with a fury on a particular month and year—July 1989: when the army
bombed the village and burned down its dwellings in reprisal for a nearby ambush of soldiers. Warned ahead of time of impending destruction,
many of the hamlet's residents opted to flee, and for the good part of a
decade, he said, most did not return.

And yet, from what this gentleman shared, the villagers were not
caught completely off-guard. From their tensed relations with the counterinsurgency fort, newly installed across the river in Madre Mía, they had
already become acquainted with what the army was capable of. Indeed,
one of that fort's first commanders had been notoriously ruthless—taking many victims, among them the brother-in-law of this original colono,
murdered along with several other villagers after they filed a complaint
about military abuses. As was common then, none of the villagers knew
the captain's legal name, only the *chapa* or nickname people used to refer to, but not directly address, that terrible man: "Chisito"—in playful
allusion to a national brand of corn puffs, rhyming too with *rizito* or
little curl, perhaps for the reddish-blond whorls of the captain's closely
cropped hair.

In that some base commanders comported themselves in ways far crueler than others, there was nothing special. The gentleman mentioned this captain in particular, only because of the turn of fate through which his legal identity was unexpectedly revealed. The state of affairs, which made that disclosure possible, had transpired elsewhere and several years later when an elite group of army commandos carried out a surprise mission in the city of Lima that ended a four-month-long occupation of the Japanese ambassador's residence by MRTA guerrillas.[2] That 1996 army raid rescued seventy-two hostages, among them many high-profile officials and other dignitaries. It also left all fourteen insurgents dead, either killed in the shootout or summarily executed upon their surrender. Two army commandos were also lost and promptly hailed as national heroes. Photographic portraits of each man taken in military attire, and presumably under happier circumstances, quickly spread across all print and broadcast media. On the higher ranked of the two, journalists doted in particular: a colonel of surname Valer Sandoval. Just imagine, the gentleman from La Morada said, his surprise and that of other villagers' too at coming face-to-face with Chisito once again.

Here as elsewhere the war aggravated intractable problems of national belonging, which less dissipated than acquired new forms as overt fighting began to wane. In the Upper Huallaga, coming to the realization that the very same men who had directed indiscriminate killing might later be venerated as martyrs for the nation, even heroes to revere, was one specific way people, but especially those from the countryside, found themselves forced to hold together contrary sentiments. Such holding together, internalizing point and counterpoint without further ado, sometimes seemed like the unspoken price of admittance to a new political community. Protection and hostility were no less of a coin in the conflict's wake than they had been during the war. Nor was their dispersal any less uneven—as Shining Path actions grew less frequent, as counterinsurgency forts stopped sending out patrols, relaxed their checkpoints. Fury pervaded across heads and tails, leaving hospitality marooned on one side to bob up and down in a sea of forgetting.

In the postwar era, which histories of violence mattered nationally reiterated Lima's structural dominance. Even though it would be easy to demonstrate how pivotal the Huallaga region had been to Peru's economic survival during the 1980s and 1990s, to its geopolitical influence in the Americas, and to the Armed Forces' eventual defeat of Shining Path, the details on what had transpired in this valley drew little to no public concern in the nation's capital. As a rule, local histories of the conflict became selected for retelling only when circumstances on a national stage happened to spark a fleeting interest in the region. Chisito would remain a secret largely circumscribed to La Morada's small circle of older residents, as journalists never drew a connection between the commando hero and his prior deeds as counterinsurgency captain stationed at Madre Mía.

The national press and political parties would, however, take a far keener if short-lived interest in the army's wartime doings in Madre Mía when a former military officer, Ollanta Humala, launched his candidacy for the presidency of Peru in 2006. In that electoral context, there was an abrupt, solicitous urgency to discover past army transgressions. Suddenly, what base commanders had let happen, presided over, and possibly actively perpetrated in the Huallaga seemed scandalous, but only if it could be traced to Humala. Such concern pushed a dubious proposition that having actually committed atrocities would out of hand disqualify one for becoming the head of state—a premise that required in turns forgetting, ignoring, and deliberately keeping silent on how those same atrocities provided the historical foundations for the current political era.

For one electoral cycle, the newsworthiness of Humala's Huallaga tenure remained fierce,[3] all the while leaving unexplored the systemic character of the army's interventions in the region: how the counterinsurgency forts had transformed landscapes, recrafted territorial relations, and altered everyday movements across the valley's riverine terrains. Though the army had carried out sporadic operations against Shining Path in the Upper Huallaga since the mid-1980s, only when it began to establish a network of bases, as the centerpiece of a revamped counterinsurgency strategy introduced at the end of that decade, did the war's momentum begin to shift in its favor. Under a unified command called the Frente Huallaga, an old, terrible, system of images and procedures was renewed and made newly meticulous. From every counterinsurgency fort the army would send out patrols into nearby hamlets to abduct suspects back to the base for interrogation. Torture, ablations, and other disfigurements became common, along with rapes and executions, followed by clandestine burials or the dumping of bodies, often dismembered, into the river. One key feature of this "system" was the constant rotation of anonymous base commanders, whose periods and locales of service were as closely guarded as were their legal identities. As they always operated under pseudonyms, people knew them and could recall them only by their local nicknames, making it nearly impossible to pin them down as someone specific in a particular locale and moment in time. And without that, there could be little chance of subsequent legal redress. The army's entire strategy was already in place by the time Humala served as the base commander at Madre Mía in the early 1990s.

I found it curious then, and a symptom of something somehow significant, that prior to Humala's candidacy I had never come across any notable reference to him in the Huallaga: not in the many local tellings of war history heard during stints of fieldwork between 1995 and 2005, not in any published news accounts from the years he would have been at Madre Mía. No one mentioned Humala among the base commanders who had been especially brutal,[4] and as best I could tell, he had been but a minor figure in the far larger constellation of the army's "pacification" enterprise.[5] And yet with his rise as a leader of national politics, vying for the presidency, losing in 2006, then finding success on a second try in 2011, the telling of regional history migrated to a different star, retroactively shifting the constellation.[6] A new, emerging political time exerted force upon the past through how prior events came to be imbued with a collective importance they might never have received at the moment of their initial actualization. And locally no one seemed immune, judging from the influence Humala's political ascension later had on what people chose to recount and what they no longer seemed to remember.

widows
Another morning Mauro returned, this time with a stocky dark-haired woman of flirtatious smiles, who in strange, baby-voice tones told of her sorry fate in affairs of the heart. How her first three loves perished soon

after taking her as their bride. A first husband she met when just thirteen, still a child living alone with her father on their left bank Magdalena farm. Theirs was a humble life. Her father, a gregarious, kindhearted man, she said, used a rope to tie his pants up and never put on shoes: going barefoot, even when playing football, and what a mighty player he was. Despite limited means, as an original settler of that area, he had claimed a large stretch of land, where they grew plantains and many other staple crops. One day a group of Colombians approached, asking him to rent them a small portion of his farm. They had a problem: so much cocaine but no safe place to hold it while waiting for the next plane to ship it out. With her father a generous agreement was quickly reached. Never before had she seen that much money, and she would see much more. Soon, Colombians were dropping by all the time, and with a certain one, whom everyone called "Barba Roja," for the reddish hue of his facial hair, she became close. A year went by in love, until one day, when she was six-months' pregnant, he left for Colombia. That was all she knew, until much, much later: many years in fact before someone told her Barba Roja was dead, murdered perhaps. That was all she knew.

Love fared better, if only for a time, with a young Peruvian from the lowland city of Pucallpa, who worked for a patrón in Uchiza, purchasing raw cocaine from coca farmers. Her second husband stayed long enough for them to have a daughter and to form a home for her and her two children. All was well until Sendero began targeting people from the local *firmas*. The year was 1990, and the Party, determined to show the narcos who was who, imposed a temporary ban on all sales of cocaine.[7] In a demonstration of seriousness, one morning the dead bodies of a score of traqueteros, more than she could remember, appeared outside town, beginning at a small bridge and then continuing on down the road. When she first heard the news early that day, she already had a bad feeling. Her husband had not come home the night before and just before dawn, her son had woken abruptly, gone to her, and announced: "My father is dead." Under a mango tree near the village of Cotomonillo she found the body of her husband, stripped of his watch, bracelet, ring, and shoes. They had left him in nothing more than undergarments, hands tied, with a sign nearby: *así mueren los compradores de droga*.[8] Later she learned he had forty thousand dollars on him at the time of his death. But, along with his motorcycle, that large sum was gone.

Everything looked as if Sendero had killed him, yet she told me that made no sense because with the Party he stayed on exceedingly good terms. Through one of his contacts, the Party had purchased weapons; also, handy as he was with needle and thread, more than one gunshot wound had he sutured at their request. None of this squared, and that made her uneasy. She wanted to know. The late 1980s and early 1990s were other times, an era when the guerrilla was close: people recognized them and often had means to approach, ask a question, make a request. She wanted to know, and so, after attending to the wake and to the burial, she went to the village of Pueblo Nuevo and sought out an important Shining Path leader, with whom she was familiar, familiar enough to be on a first-name basis: Ormeño. Why would the Party kill her husband, she asked? Ormeño did not know what to tell her but promised to inquire. A few days later, he gave her this answer: that the death had not been their doing. Friends of her husband had taken advantage of the night, when other traqueteros were being killed, to shoot him and steal his money. We know who they are, Ormeño said, and can kill them if you wish, but she insisted, no: killing them would not bring him back.

Having lost for the second time a husband, she told me that she suddenly had no way to fend for herself or for her two young children. So, to Lima she took them in search of work. For six months she cleaned the house of a German family in the influential residential district of Miraflores, before taking a job at a Chinese restaurant closer to the center of Lima. Working at that restaurant she met a doctor, and once again there was love. And once again bad luck persisted. About a year after they became a steady couple, her new partner perished in a car accident. Heading north on the Pan-American Highway during a weekend excursion with his parents, a single blow to the head and he was gone—which was why, she said, with a quip of a laugh that people called her *la viuda negra*. Black widow—bringing death to every man who dare love her.

And yet for this region and for that time hers was an ordinary life, unfolding like that of so many others who came of age in the movement of a cocaine boom rendered inextricable from a people's war. For with the lone exception of her union with the doctor, which gave her a daughter—born following his fatal accident and soon after she returned with her other kids to this Huallaga town—most everything she recounted about her personal life seemed deeply intertwined with that intense history of conflict, with its desires so visceral and imaginations vertiginous. Like so many others, proximity to events of risk and ungraspable magnitude gave her stories a special weight and allure.

A long stretch passed, she said, before she found a new partner, her fourth. This time, it seemed that a fateful pattern had been broken. Finally, her circumstances had been set aright. He was supporting them, putting in a hard day's work "en la chacra," while she lived with her three, and eventually four, children in town. What she did not say, not then, was that his work on the farm was intimately tied to the Party. Now in 2002, and less than ever, one's ongoing relations with Sendero could not be acknowledged. What we did not know then was that he too, in but a few years, would suffer catastrophe, not lethal like her other loves but life-devastating to be sure. Enough to tear them apart and hold them separate. His social death would keep her ensnared and forever talking up the hope, no matter how implausible, that any day now his legal problems would get sorted out and that the government would let him return home to her and the kids.

the fording

Then one day there was Tina, whom I also met thanks to Mauro, but out of all those he brought by, she was the only one preceded by a certain notoriety. I had been hearing about Tina's family, or rather about her brothers, ever since my initial visit to this town seven years before. In local renderings of conflict history, those brothers—ever numerous and running as if in a pack[9]—always seemed to arise whenever talk turned to la Urbana—a semi-clandestine cell of Shining Path, which during the latter half of the 1980s, gathered fame for the havoc it sowed through the unscrupulous enforcement of insurgent law. Townspeople I knew would go on and on about the terrors of la Urbana, with those male siblings deeply entwined in a historical moment, which in chronological terms was but a brief, almost negligible, sliver of time. What struck me about Tina during our early meetings though was something else—her gift as a storyteller and the darkly charged atmosphere pervading her words. A vivacity that was hers and something else altogether, impelling images, which because partial and practically vacant, seemed to invite me to imagine and, in so doing, silently fill in the gaps.

Like the gentleman from La Morada, Tina was close to the local histories I had hoped to learn, and, like la viuda negra, she was far more enmeshed in them than most. No one in this town, she claimed, had lost more family to the war, and that was where Tina began, with the killing of six brothers. Across the hollows of this cement room, she drew a line going back in time. She did not rehash local versions I might recognize. She proceeded as if I were unaware of those dominant tellings, framing things instead directly counter to their prevailing sense. Hardly ruthless, her brothers had been unwitting victims to a caprice of events, carried off in the fury of those years. She spoke in words that were sure and fell into a familiar place as a tale told many times before.

The sense of Tina I retain from that first conversation—fifteen years ago and more—still lingers strong. An impression that haunts resilient, sketching scenes that often blur when I try to hold them. The waiting, the reaching, with Tina, hovering close to the history of lands running up and down either side of the river, a story she traces back to her father, long since passed and whose death she never cast as tragic. Elsewhere catastrophe insisted: into his male offspring, where the costs of war arrived for Tina's family, taking six of the ten sons her father had named after himself, every brother given exactly the same name and distinguished solely by sequential distance from the founder, el Primero—crazy man, my father—which is to say, distinguished solely by order of birth. Segundo, Tercero, Cuarto, Quinto, Sexto, Séptimo . . . how else to tell them apart? And then, later, how the killing would crosscut that ordinal series, picking and plucking in ways not altogether random.

Tina spoke that day, and all of a sudden, she was a Lady of Sorrows, telling of incalculable loss. She explained to me the fate of each brother in the order in which it happened and by whose hand. Describing too what that did to those spared. To Tina's mother consumed first by grief and then by diabetes. To the rest of the family too: so helpless as the demise of one son followed upon the next in quick succession. Six times. The waiting. The reaching. One dagger after another plunged into suffering hearts: this one by the police, that one by Sendero, and the remaining four killed or disappeared by the army. The rending circumstances of their abrupt passing was a murky region with the power to hold face-to-face encounters in thrall. It was a power Tina clearly knew how to wield, judging from the fathomless intensity it injected into our first acquaintance and that very first conversation. Those losses were where she abruptly went. And I would later suspect that this was something she had learned: a power to draw on as occasions demanded, a power with which to transfix speech. Eventually, I would come to suspect that for Tina the sorrows she led with at our first encounter were but one intermittent place within an extraordinarily spirited, and rugged, life. For when, time after time, those sorrows did return, I would see her shake them off and push herself away, from where they haunted, gaining traction now, picking up thrust, heading elsewhere, moving away once again.

Yet Tina's brothers were only the most obvious thread of her entanglements with the war. Other threads were many. Some I would come to grasp only much later, like the connection she acquired by marriage, through Wilson, to a municipal mayor that Shining Path had forewarned and then assassinated. That had happened in the late 1980s, when la Urbana was tightening its hold on the town. The mayor was Wilson's father, yet no one in Tina's family ever said to me what role, if any, her own siblings might have played. Even Wilson, who rarely lacked for words, had little to tell about the exact details of his father's death, offering up a glimpse of haze before steering the conversation elsewhere.

All of Tina's connections to the war were regions of the past that insisted, some more than others, into our unfolding presents. Too much to share in any one sitting, as each one demanded an extended conversation all of its own. Most of Tina's proximities to the conflict stemmed, however, less from other people than from the daily movements that had placed her directly on the river, straddling the topographic threshold connecting town with country—the political frontier upon which pivoted the coca/cocaine economy and with it the war. This too I would only come to learn in time.

the hollows

The weight and breadth of events, transpired during the conflict and carried on somehow in its wakes, could feel massive in that cement room: far too much to digest, far too tangled to bestow any one definitive sense. Elsewhere in Peru, before the impossibility of telling whole what the war had brought to pass, emblematic cases and other generalizing contractions were tasked to speak for, and sometimes over, mute expanses of histories too immense to grasp.[10] But what if those histories could not be approached as typifying cases but only along singular happenings that persisted by affirming their own partial and, therefore constrained, view? And what if, from each of those events, more and more pathways opened up, so much so that at best but *a few* could be steadfastly followed? Sometimes those few might converge at a narrow crossroads, only to branch out all over again. If one were to give that crossroads a name here, she might be called Tina.

She who draws lines through the hollows.

Since the early 1980s Tina had been the owner and operator of canoes, transiting freight along the Huallaga from left bank farms to markets both close and far away. She had also administered a *servicio de vado* or ferry service between the right bank village of La Roca and the left bank hamlet of Venenillo, even as the worst violence came to a head. Venenillo was an early Sendero stronghold and cocaine trading post, doing a brisk business that drew people from all around. Eventually that stream of passengers thinned to a trickle, and when it did, she withdrew to Aucayacu, where she continued on as a botera, working now at the town's main port.

A decade later when Tina and I met for the first time, she was wondering whether to finally give up her boats and the life of working the river. She was wondering whether to reclaim the left bank farm in Magdalena, an area long under Shining Path rule, which she had inherited from her now deceased father. Many families living in the countryside had been forced to flee when the army carried out large-scale counterinsurgency operations during the early to mid-1990s. But with the reduction in intensity and then virtual cessation of those operations in recent years, Tina said, the Party had begun quietly reorganizing, choosing Magdalena for its relative remoteness. Hoping to assert control anew over the area, Sendero required a population, so they were asking families, including those who had lived there before, to return. Tina worried that if she did not show up soon, she might lose any claim on her father's land to people with no prior ties to the area. Land for loyalty, support, and silence: that was the exchange. If only the army would set up a base there, she said. Sendero would move elsewhere, and then returning would be far more feasible. But living out there on the farm alone, without the army nearby, she would have to answer to the Party and assume all the risks that entailed.

Tina said she was waiting to see what would happen. She complained about being displaced from the countryside, that she and her family were now practically living in a condition of exile. Even so, I doubted she had any intention of abandoning the town that was her home in favor of the farm at some future point. What Tina aimed for, as did anyone who wished to make a living in agriculture on the Huallaga's left bank, was a durable, ongoing connection to the roads and markets on the opposite side. For that a residence in town was, if not indispensable, then advantageous and certainly critical to the decision Tina was now weighing—a choice that would shift her away from her life as a botera, tucking that era behind her as *the past*, all the while opening up a horizon that she wagered could be secured only by making an effective claim on what had been her father's farm.

As I listened to her then, the hours moved fast. From the tight enclosure of this office temporarily shuttered, she animated scene after scene from that place way over there, out of reach but not so far that one could not trace the distance. And in listening to Tina tell what happened, my imagination would race with her *out there*, to where I knew I could not now go and to where many who did would find making a life all but impossible. The impossibility of being *out there* in any good way—Venenillo long ago, recently Bijao, now and for quite a few years still to come, Magdalena—seemed to be one point of what Tina wished to share. And so, between here and there, the hollow, this cement cavern. The rattling of a rolling metal door. The shooting across the room of each acceleration of every motor on the street. And amid the silence that inhabited the intervals between passing bikes and trucks, whatever sounded, sounded deep and vacant, mixing with all I did and do not know, with all that has happened since, mixing with the place from where I now jump.

    the waiting.

    the reaching.

    the hollows.

    And this: the beginning of conversations that would grow on and off over several days, resuming again in the years to come.

the trench

Shego tells me he knows something about asphalt. That jammed into his lower back is a bit of road history. All because his friend, the one steering the motorbike as Shego looked on from behind, forgot the trench.

This is how Shego described that night:

A band was going to play in Tingo María and it was late, but we decided, Why not? Let's just go. The kid insisted on driving. I never thought it could happen, because how many times had we made the trip? He knew all the trenches, the big ones, medium ones, the small ones too. With earth the edges had been filled in, so you knew how to approach, how to cross. So how could he forget?

The bike was a Honda 250, which has great pickup, because before the trench there was a bridge that had been knocked down. But the river was shallow and there the bridge had simply dropped down on top . . . and so we zipped right over. Once across, instead of slowing, the kid leaned on the accelerator. He forgot. I tell him, "Hey, the trench!"

That was all I had time to say . . . and then *choom*—I felt it: we crashed into the other side of the trench. It's like I'm telling you. It was large enough to crash into and sink. And that's where I messed up my back.

At the time it only hurt for a week. Fifteen days it may have bothered me. Then I forgot about it. Where I felt it again was six years later when I started driving a mototaxi. I felt the pain in my back concentrating there near the waist. So, I went to get x-rays and learned I have three deviated vertebrae. Three lumbar vertebrae out of place. And *that* is the memory I have of the trenches the guerrilla dug.

Shego tells me these things on one of my visits to see him at his one-story cement house in Aucayacu—a block from the malecón and from the town's main port on the Huallaga River. The rainy season was well under way, and on that damp, almost misty evening, we talked in an interior room, dark except for a soft glow, filtering in from the kitchen through a sheer curtain draped over an adjoining doorway. Shego sat down in an old hammock and offered me a place at the couch. We had avoided the main living room, I assumed, because there the front door and windows opened out to the street from where we could be overheard by neighbors or by passersby who might linger at the cement sidewalk bordering the house. Such precautions were still a habitual part of living in town. To dispense with them would have felt uncomfortable, even though we were only talking about the road.

The night we spoke about the trenches, nearly ten years had elapsed since Shego's accident. The ditches themselves had only recently been repaired, but when traveling the road, it was possible to perceive their shadowy traces in the smooth lumps and grooves that marked, if faintly, the reconditioned asphalt. This was a notable change from the mid-1990s when I first visited the Huallaga. By then all the bridges had been replaced or refitted, and yet the hard surface of the highway was still furrowed by shallow ditches that violently punctuated the journey, jarring travelers and taking vehicles apart, piece by piece. Spaced in a pattern far too regular to be potholes, these were deliberate marks, though at first, I had no idea about their origins. Every time I made the short trip between Tingo María and Aucayacu, no one, while in transit at least, would say a thing about them. With continued maintenance and repair, those material traces would slowly vanish over time. Effaced from the present, they left behind a troubling history nonetheless, the particulars of which for many, in the late 1990s, still seemed risky to bring up in public.

In this chapter Shining Path's disruption of the Marginal Highway insists as the bodily echoes that returned in what Shego called "the memory" of his collision with the largest of the trenches. Through that wound Shego would tell about acts of sabotage, carried out during a series of armed strikes (*paros armados*) in the late 1980s—attacks that seemed to disclose something critical about the complex roles public works could play in mediating the political attachments of the populations of the Huallaga, when conceived as peripheral to the nation as a whole. Impairing the Marginal Highway's physical surface revealed something general too about the deeply entwined material and allegorical force of *frontier roads* that derived, at least in part, from the inscriptive power of highway building through which nation-states mark and, in so doing, attempt to territorially incorporate the physical landscapes of hinterland regions. Frontier roads in this way can serve as a means for extending an already existing legal order, even when from the perspective of the places they physically traverse they actually entail the arrival of new law.

Frontier roads found law where they can be performatively figured as somehow originary. Only then, and as "first roads," can the land appropriations they set in motion succeed in projecting a sedentary *nomos*, a new territorial order that reorients the movement of populations, all the while giving topographic expression to the very legal relations that would entangle and bind them. Rural highways often draw allegorical support from narratives and image worlds that might appear to fuse with the actual substance of roads through a temporizing process of animation. This is akin to what Penny Harvey and Hannah Knox have called *infrastructural enchantment*:[1] a horizon of modernity presaging a release from social ills through a series of promises that endure in spite of actualizations partial, lopsided, or aborted. Harvey and Knox identify "speed and connectivity," "political freedom," and "economic prosperity" as having particular salience in Peru. Infrastructural enchantment in their reading names the surprising capacity of roads to "retain a generic social promise, even in the face of specific circumstances in which they are acknowledged as having failed to deliver."[2]

If the social promise of infrastructure in the 1980s-era Huallaga clearly ran up against the countervailing fury of a Maoist people's war, the broader history of the Marginal Highway suggests the extent to which material terrains affect legal relations. And so, this chapter dwells with how the Marginal Highway came to frame those relations while giving specific attention to the degree to which their legal tone and weight depended on the sense of the road's surface. That sense inevitably shifted when the road was physically altered in ways that refunctioned it. Digging trenches into the asphalt cover recast the Marginal Highway's promissory horizons by turning the materiality of the road against its original intended and locally accepted purpose. By making the surface jut abruptly *into* the sensory experience of travelers, digging trenches brought the road's political significance to the fore, rendering it intimate through the bodies they impressed, and all the while magnifying the highway's presence *as an image* inseparable from the region's present-future bearings.

Wartime struggles for political sovereignty in the Alto Huallaga rearranged everyday mobility. They also inflected local experiences of time. A brief historical recounting of the road's ostensible beginnings in the 1960s suggests, however, that Shining Path sabotage was no mere military operation (though it was that as well) but rather a turn of events that struck at the heart of what makes transit infrastructure a *public* work. The Marginal Highway would become a primary locale of the insurgent-counterinsurgent war, where violent episodes of the conflict threatened and occasionally manifested as datable actualizations in time and space. It was also the material pivot and anchor point for starkly different versions of modernity—each one crafting its own attendant "people."

Public works, if they can capture and breathe life into situational collectives, are fundamentally works *on a public*: a power that Shining Path guerrillas tapped into when they recruited rural communities and travelers into blocking and later excavating the road. Then, there was the aftermath with the road's asphalt top now furrowed. Drivers and passengers were suddenly left to contend with abrupt intervals that punctuated the experience of passage—intervals that had to be rendered transitable through well-timed maneuvers or through careful, makeshift placements of surface connectors, such as wood planks.

Sabotaging a hinterland road might well be a potent means for undermining the territorial appropriations of a state that rules from afar. Its impacts, however, on the affective attachments of local populations— to one political force rather than to another—are anything but certain.

Careful attention to affects and affectations is crucial for grasping the legal and topographic complexities of a nation-state frontier. That attention here, in these pages, refers back as well to Shego's wound and how through it the wake of Peru's internal war became his own private, deeply embodied affair. For the Marginal Highway was one place during the war and its aftermaths where the conflict unfolded on an affective plane: at times traceable to the asphalt cover (marred and subsequently repaired) and at others dispersed across opaque, indiscernible regions of individual bodies and subjectivities swept up by events and pressured into taking all sides at once.

first roads

To one day open the tropical heart of South America to agrarian settlement—such was the idea relentlessly espoused by Fernando Belaúnde Terry, two-time president of Peru and architect of the dubious claim that one road might integrate an entire continent. For Belaúnde, the construction of the highway presupposed *Peru's Own Conquest*—such was the eventual English name of the book he published in 1959 while a mere presidential hopeful.[3] A literal rendering of the original Spanish title—"The Conquest of Peru by the Peruvian People"—more explicitly conveys, however, his dark insinuation that conquering a nation would be good and cause for celebration if a country's own people merely took the task upon themselves.

North to Caracas, south to Asunción, under the sign of the liberator Simón Bolívar, Belaúnde called this future road la Carretera "Bolivariana" Marginal de la Selva. Peru's portion would extend over one thousand five hundred kilometers through the country's high forest (*selva alta*) to someday form a network with east-west "penetration" routes connecting the Pacific coast and highlands with the country's lowland frontier. With the United States offering political and some economic backing, Bolivia, Colombia, Ecuador, and Venezuela would embark on versions of their own. In Peru, however, the international dimensions of the project were soon to be forgotten, and what Belaúnde proclaimed "the work of our time" became known simply as la Marginal.

Roads should do more than merely join one place with another; they should open up new agricultural lands. That was the core of what

Belaúnde claimed was his own *filosofía vial*—a program for asserting the territorializing force of frontier roads. In many speeches on the subject, first as politician and then as head of state, Belaúnde cast the country's eastern territories as unoccupied expanse, frontier roads figured as instruments of Civilization itself, equated with imperial engineering feats of Incas and Romans in the tradition of the mestizo chronicler Garcilaso de la Vega. High on grandeur but never without a certain feigned naïveté, Belaúnde borrowed freely from foreign tales of settler destiny and domination: of "red skin paths" giving way to covered-wagon trails where the Union Pacific Railroad and the "incorporation of the American West" merged into one.[4] The ever-expanding extension of nation into its outer reaches could be read, he once suggested, as an ontogenesis of the road itself, which "like childhood, has the virtue of getting stronger and growing." The narrow *trocha* (trail), he said, was the road's infancy and had "the virtue of opening up a region and consolidating its economy before justifying an effort by the country to rebuild the route."[5] In adolescence would come the *camino afirmado* (gravel road), but only later, presumably once the frontier economy had proved itself, would the road attain maturity and receive a smooth dark cap of pitch.

If the Marginal Highway, in Belaúnde's writing and speeches, became an allegorical figure of one well-worn version of modernity and national progress, perhaps frontier roads require rhetorical infusions to render them as original events. And though it is nearly impossible to separate a highway as a material thing from the claims made about it, first roads would seem to derive allegorical strength precisely from the tension of matter and narration, which while inextricably intertwined can become provocatively mismatched when viewed from afar. In part this is the discrepancy that may crop up between physical landscapes and the cartographic depictions that would smooth away their singular features. It can also manifest through political distance, and the overconfident legibility that administrative centers sometimes assume toward their peripheries,[6] such as when frontier roads may well appear on the books, only to exist actually in diminished form or even in a terminal state of deferred completion.[7] That is, where they do not vanish altogether—a recurrent problem in tropical climes.[8] These problems of representational fit have a potential to incite, but they operate on a level other than that of the material force of first roads themselves, which inscribe a particular orientation upon the land. The ecological impact of that inscription is especially striking in cloud forests, where the introduction of modern roads so often sets in motion a cascading series of detrimental effects, from invasive human migration to extermination of native fauna to relentless logging, which conspire together to permanently alter the land.

In terms of material force, the event character of a first road stems from a presumed impossibility of returning to pre-road times. Path dependency of frontier highways is such that to speak of a before and after of the road is to refer to radically different spatial and ecological configurations. First roads threaten to irreversibly transfigure tropical landscapes. Less overt, if still far-reaching, are their political and legal consequences.

Carl Schmitt's writings on the spatial dimensions of law offer preliminary insight into these ramifications, which is to say, into the concrete "order and orientation" inaugurated by frontier roads. Schmitt explored the topographic aspects of law through the Greek concept *nomos*, which he defined as a first measure of earth that establishes a legal regime. "The *nomos*," he wrote, "by which a tribe, a retinue or a people becomes settled, i.e. by which it becomes historically situated and turns a part of the earth's surface into the force-field of a particular order, becomes visible in the appropriation of land and in the founding of a city or colony."[9] Without dwelling on the full range of events and choices such foundings often entail,[10] in this passage Schmitt sets forth several key, interrelated elements: the *investment* of an exterior segment of earth with a palpable, historically specific charge; the *visibilization* of an emerging social order; both preceded by an initial *seizure* of land. If all three elements are arguably features of highway construction in formerly road-less domains, then from this particular reading of *nomos*, it is but a small step to assert the law-manifesting force of first roads—here specifically of the Marginal Highway in the context of a modern hinterland settlement project. For beyond the profound impact the building of la Marginal would have on the natural landscape of the Huallaga Valley, the highway drew the region's legal topographies away from the river and rearticulated them in favor of the Peruvian state by serving now and into the foreseeable future as the primary axis of its territorializing power. The road was in that sense an originary mark—"a first measure"—from which the state's claim over the land issued forth.

The complex constellation of material and affective relations that frontier roads inaugurate could be approached conceptually as the introduction of a "state space," though perhaps at the cost of according less importance to their event character and legal implications.[11] Henri Lefebvre suggested that transit infrastructure is one active and ongoing means through which "the State binds itself to space,"[12] producing national territory from physical terrains "mapped, modified, transformed by the networks, circuits and flows." Lefebvre also stressed that, as a region of state control, national territory acquires an "optical and visual" character.[13] In this regard both Lefebvre and Schmitt underscore the importance of visuality. And their otherwise distinctive spatial theories—Lefebvre's more elaborate, inspired too by very different political affinities and sensibilities[14]—nonetheless, intersect in shared emphases on the seizure, dividing up, and infrastructural alteration of physical landscapes.

Attention to other genealogies of *nomos* keep the discussion of frontier roads more strictly attuned to juridical registers while expanding beyond—and not necessarily overturning—Schmitt's explicit formulations. Gilles Deleuze opposed what he called a "sedentary *nomos*" of walls and enclosures to nomadic movements that neither divide nor allocate land but instead spread across an open terrain.[15] As a concept that will reappear in Deleuze's later work with Felix Guattari on territory-as-transformation,[16] nomadic *nomos* sketches relationships between law and terrain not in terms of rightful apportionment but as intensive distributions in space. With respect to frontier highways, *nomos* as nomadic can turn inquiry toward how they incite, inflect, and transform travel. And yet, what moves on a road, and how, does so according to the material conditions of its exterior cover.[17] Through those movements, road surfaces express an order and orientation—a plural sense—that become tangible through sensorial contact. Events that physically alter the sense of those surfaces thus interweave law as a "sedentary *nomos*" of emplaced works (walls, fences, but also property markers and roads) with a more *nomadic* conception of displacements and distributions. Focusing on the ordering and orientations of the surfaces of roads, together with the affects and sensations they elicit, thus serves to sound out their topographic weight, all the while underscoring the multiplicity of relations that roads as physical things select for and sustain.

Elsewhere I have examined how Shining Path insurgents and Peruvian state forces asserted claims of territorial sovereignty by intervening upon the Marginal Highway's material surface.[18] Here in approaching that same history of conflict again, I privilege the temporal dimensions of first roads—as territorializing events that reconfigure physical terrains, infusing them with legal force while creating a material platform for other "surface events" to come. Narrative accounts of the construction of the Marginal Highway, and of the events that because of its construction later unfolded, can be read as framing devices for grasping regional shifts in political time. Yet, as the echoes of Shego's wound show, such shifts presuppose a subterranean work of remembrance and oblivion, which sometimes pulls the historical sedimentations of road events into visibility and sometimes pulls them away.

perpendicular cuts

The size of the trenches dug into the highway, Shego said, averaged a half-meter wide and a meter deep. Some were larger, reaching two meters down and another three or four across. In all there were scores of them, along those sixty kilometers of paved road. The one where Shego and his friend had crashed lay just beyond the bridge at the village of Anda. It was a vast five to six meters wide and deep enough to stand up in without being able to peer over the edge. The oblong cuts began at the Tulumayo River and continued in uneven groups to a small village twenty kilometers past the town of Aucayacu. The asphalt hardtop ended there, and with it the trenches, while the highway proceeded as a compact dirt road. Within each group of ditches, the cuts were spaced every ten or twenty meters. Shego surmised the physical dimensions and distribution of the grooves were a good indication of the number of people who had taken part in the work, which is to say, of the strength and size of the teams Shining Path had managed to organize at any particular place. Bigger, deeper, and close together: more workers on hand. Shallow, thin, and far apart: less people to draw from.

As occurred with many of those whom I became close to in Huallaga towns, I met Shego through what felt like an arbitrary string of relationships, which later proved to be less random than first imagined. One friend would take me to see a relative, a neighbor, or a former classmate, who then would become a friendly acquaintance. Much would have to happen, however, before we would strike up a conversation of any consequence. People did not speak openly with those they did not know. Not in the late 1990s, when I got to know Shego. Spies and snitches lurked everywhere, occasionally in the flesh though far more frequently in the mind, and because of that, confidences were rarely extended unless you had already ceased to be a stranger. Such transformations took a long while and some luck. Above all, you could not be in a hurry or give the impression that you were anxious to know something.

A mutual friend I'll call Lucio first put us in touch, telling me beforehand that Shego had once worked for a successful drug trader, so he could tell me anything I cared to know about the cocaine economy and its local history. And yet, despite giving Shego numerous opportunities, he never spoke in any detail about his former life. No, no, never for a narco, he claimed. His boss owned a motorcycle resale business, and it was Shego's job to buy bikes at a Honda dealership in Tingo María and then take them up the road to sell in Tocache—which in the 1980s just happened to be one of the most important regional markets of the cocaine boom. Shego said he made good money and left it at that, never saying anything about his employer, how long he had worked for him, or when he had stopped.

The motorcycle business may have been an attempt to lead me astray. I was more inclined to see in Shego's dissembling a shard of truth. He was telling me the camouflage they had used to cover their tracks back then. This was not uncommon. I was often introduced to someone because of a unique experience or expertise they were known or believed to have, only to intuit that it was not something they wished to reveal. People might share an anecdote or speak in vague terms about an event but would carefully steer away from details that might pinpoint their own participation. Such avoidances could give their narratives about the past a thin and tenuous quality with gaps that were impossible to fill.

I never doubted that Shego's crash on the highway had taken place in the way he said it had. I did wonder if the reason he gave for the trip was not a convenient invention. Were they going to see a show, or had perhaps more serious business put them on the highway that night? Shego never told me the name of the person who drove the motorbike into the trench. What I do know is that not pushing for particulars became one of the crucial understandings of our friendship and to a great extent made it possible.

Reticent as Shego was to talk about his own personal connections with the drug trade, that did not stop him from encouraging me to visit. He had time on his hands. Excruciating pain from the injured vertebrae had long since forced him to give up driving the mototaxi. More recently, it had gotten worse and was keeping him from helping out his dad and his brothers at the family carpentry shop. Bored, worried, and a little bummed out, Shego was spending more and more time at home. So he'd tell me to come by. I'd pick up a large bottle of cola and a few small packs of saltine crackers and show up on his doorstep, usually in the afternoon, occasionally at night. We would talk for an hour, maybe two, and at some point Shego would ask me to lend him my motorcycle so he could take his wife and their young daughter out for a Saturday-evening spin. Such was the basic structure of reciprocity that got hashed out as if on its own: soda, crackers, a motorcycle on a few hours' loan, and the avoidance of overly probing questions about his own past.

wilderness to wilderness

Just as time may have its arrows, so too roads sometimes appear to unfurl as if effortlessly across the land. Thirty years before the trenches dug under Shining Path command had been finally repaired, initial construction on la Marginal began as little more than a spur off the Central Highway east of Tingo María, moving north along the Huallaga River. Road-building crews advanced toward the town of Tocache, where they would eventually meet up with another group that descended south from the Mayo River Basin. Following immediately behind, other workers measured plots for the settlers who would later arrive. That was in the mid-1960s, twenty-five years after the Central Highway had become a first road in its own right—when it was extended from Tingo María, then a mere trading post at the base of the Central Andes, to the lowland town of Pucallpa on the Ucayali River—to establish a reliable overland route between Lima and a navigable tributary of the Amazon. In each case the building of ostensibly original roads implied a land appropriation: the imposition of a new spatial order and an expansion of state power discursively expressed through a civilizing motif of Progress premised upon the domination of an untamed, unexploited wilderness. And while road construction of both the Central and Marginal Highways served as a primary division of earth from which cadastral measurements would be taken, prior to the conversion of forestland into farming plots, agricultural productivity would be the celebrated rationale of la Marginal.

Agrarian reform was the watchword of 1960s Peru, a time of escalating unrest in the highlands. And though Belaúnde as a presidential candidate had promised a legislative remedy, once in office he discovered he was politically unable to confront the power of landed elites, much less radically transform land tenure inequities at their source.[19] So while peasant communities staged dramatic occupations of sierra haciendas and clashed with police, Belaúnde championed the expansion of the "agricultural frontier": eastward migration into the tropical forests as a relatively painless alternative.

During his first government, the state-sponsored colonization project running north of Tingo María to the Huallaga River town of Tocache became a showcase presentation of the economic and social benefits of the new highway. The effort to convert the valley into a settler region would, Belaúnde assured, make the Huallaga the future breadbasket of the nation. And on the weight of that promise many families emigrated from adjoining highlands and lowlands—among them Shego's parents, who staked hopes on the offer of free land, ultimately building a homestead of their own near the village of Pacae.

President Belaúnde had more trouble convincing one of his most powerful constituencies that a jungle road would ever be a panacea for the county's problems. A group of nationalist reform-minded military officers, fearing Peru would be immersed in widespread civil strife if a sweeping, far more ambitious, program of land redistribution were not promptly implemented, ousted him from power in 1968. Under Armed Forces rule the national scope of the Marginal Highway was drastically scaled back. Yet in the Huallaga and Mayo basins, construction did not stop. The settlement effort begun under Belaúnde was renamed the Tingo María–Tocache–Campanilla colonization project and expanded along a two-hundred-kilometer stretch of the new and as yet unpaved road. Even when an internal countercoup in 1975 replaced the nationalist military leadership with a pro-US faction, improvements on the highway proceeded. A large suspension bridge that carried the road over the Huallaga River into the town of Tocache was completed in 1979, a year before Peru returned to civilian rule with the election of Belaúnde to a new term.

By then the idea of transforming the Upper Huallaga Valley into a bountiful heartland for the production of agricultural foodstuffs had run into serious trouble. Cooperatives created during the first military government were mired in debt, while smaller-scale farmers struggled to find viable markets for the cash crops of maize, rice, soybeans, and tropical fruits promoted by government bureaucrats. Against this background of state-sponsored frustration, an agricultural dilemma of a different ilk surfaced. For it was not that agrarian ways had failed to take to the Huallaga. They had done so all too well, though with an agriculture of the "wrong" sort, which was rapidly converting the region into a center of coca leaf cultivation for the international trade in illicit cocaine. Unlike crops destined for the food and livestock industries, coca and its narcotic derivatives did not depend on the road. Raw cocaine made its way to Colombia with the help of trails, rivers, and makeshift landing strips.

Over the next fifteen years, this cocaine boom came to dominate the economic, political, and social life of the valley. As it did, the names Tingo María, Tocache, and Campanilla, along with those of other Huallaga towns and villages, would at different times ring synonymous with the drug trade—but also with Shining Path. By the early 1980s the Maoist insurgency had quietly arrived to organize rural settlers (now coca farmers) in exchange for protecting them and their harvests from the police and from the ruthless tumble of the cocaine economy. Their arrival coincided with the last major improvement the Marginal Highway would receive in the Huallaga for many years to come, when a sixty-kilometer section north of Tingo María was paved with a layer of asphalt. The road, if only over this short stretch, had "come of age," and just as a need had arisen for the antinarcotics police based in Tingo María to make regular raids on Huallaga villages and farms. Along the smoothed hardened surface police trucks would speed on their way to confiscate coca, to raze fields, and to extort money, if it came to that.

"Wilderness" had returned to the Upper Huallaga under a new guise, one that was hardly stateless and that brought with it all the bad aspects of state rule and few of the good. It is in that context—of the road's intimate association with Belaúnde, of the police's predatory turn on the very people the state had promised a better way of life, and of the highway's status as a first road imposing a specific spatial order—that Shining Path's fixation on la Marginal can be grasped as more than a mere tactic of guerrilla warfare.

echoes

In certain respects, the intention to mar the Marginal Highway's material surface and to fell bridges, which ferried the road over rivers, corresponded to a more generalized national strategy and practice of damaging Peru's essential infrastructure.[20] As such it joined a list of Shining Path acts of sabotage, among them knocking down high-voltage wires, sacking agricultural development projects, as well as burning road-building and other government property. Combined with the targeted assassination of public functionaries, these actions sought to undercut the Peruvian state's ability to govern and administer basic services, while heightening an already acute economic crisis. On a national level Shining Path ostensibly hoped to push everyday living conditions to an appalling state so that a tipping point might be reached and the country's majority population, historically marginalized, economically impoverished, and now increasingly desperate, would toss their fortunes in with the Maoists. If the long-term aim of revolutionary violence were to force the flip of an imaginary switch, thereby reversing the tilt of mass allegiance, their tactics could be thought of as a mode of social engineering and statecraft. Certainly too, there is a deeper question about the contexts under which destruction might begin to look like the initial stages of creation. If acts of violence could actually transform perspectives, even collective frames of mind, their supposed efficacy would, nonetheless, seem quite fragile, given how easily attempts to deliver a message through brute force can slip and take on the sheen of a destruction devoid of all sense.

The attacks on the Marginal Highway might be situated within the larger patterns of what Shining Path considered armed actions of a people's war. Yet it can also get lost there if what distinguished specific episodes from others is blurred. This risk accompanies interpretations of any historical event. And yet the danger seems greater with events of violence, especially during periods of protracted strife, when actions might take on an ahistorical quality—through the repetition of the same names and, superficially, the same stories—a process in which language itself becomes complicit. Abstract terms, such as *war*, *peace*, or *crisis*, mark off durations, but they also shape expectations of what will and will not happen within them. They offer a certain commonsensical self-evidence, but where they strip events of their uniqueness, they become less portals that invite further consideration than walls blocking the possibility of extended inquiry.

Old friends I have in Peru will speak of the years of political violence, of the 1980s and 1990s, as a previous time, separate and distinct from their own living present. Some from the Huallaga call those years, extending for them somewhat longer, "the era of terrorism" (*la época del terrorismo*), while others there refer simply to "the social movement" (*el movimiento social*), which are no doubt two distinctly valenced ways of recognizing a past while setting it at a distance. Clearly, all who lived during the war and experienced it up close know an awful lot about what transpired. All the same, no continuous thread runs from what happens to what becomes widely known and then, from there, on to what might stand in for the totality of a local, much less national, social experience. Contingent processes of selection and exclusion always intervene. Some versions achieve power over others. Certain aspects are grouped into broader phenomena, while less assimilable facets get lopped off as jagged edges resistant to the direction of pressing moment and its dominant modes of framing.

However, in spite of who and what gets counted and remembered, history sediments. Regardless of whether residues of the past find voice in explicit representations and even as they do, history sediments—beyond all efforts, personal and collective, to constitute events in thought or through language. Here I am reminded of something Reinhardt Koselleck stressed: that history must never be reduced to its linguistic articulations.[21] And yet perhaps it could even be said that all historical interpretations, whether cast as *sources* or ennobled as *analyses*, become attached to what they refer. They too are sediments through which the past insists: an afterlife that retroactively gives a narrative body to events. In this regard, a road can become an apt figure for training attention on the material traces of history: to the ways those fragments are effaced and reworked but also to the events selected for and against, forgotten and then rediscovered in another political time.

But to which events do I refer? Is it to the road built into a natural setting where there was none before? Is it to the Maoist assault on the Huallaga Valley's only highway infrastructure? Or is it to an episode that happened as a result of those attacks? I would want to say it is all of the above, and more. I would want to say too that a first road is a highly absorbent phenomenon—a wave that projects a thin serpentine ribbon upon which other things happen that then *sink* into the very life of the road.

So my question is not simply which event, but at which level to approach, and also whether choosing one does not require crosscutting all of them at the same time.

That said, by moving through distinct historical registers,[22] what I would wish most to grasp are the material echoes of the interruption of an asphalt surface. Sometimes those echoes manifested as abrupt jolts that rattled passengers again and again as they were hurled toward their destinations. Sometimes they were the front-end alignment of a car so out of whack the driver had to keep the steering wheel turned hard right just to stay on a straight segment of road. Sometimes they would return suddenly as a debilitating lower-back pain. Such echoes were concrete traces that indexed larger episodes. Whether up front or hidden between the lines, most of all, they were the privileged ground upon which narratives would fasten.

agreements

From the hammock, his face barely visible, Shego spoke, telling me that in recent days he had been feeling the trenches more intensely. Their return had resurfaced not only the accident itself but those earlier episodes and larger contexts that had made it possible. The road had been restored. Still, Shego's back was smarting, and the reemergence of that injury, long dormant, traced a line to the accident and through it to the paros armados—the armed strikes of Shining Path.

Being from the town, Shego said he had not participated in the strikes, nor had he even once been on the highway when they had taken place. Nonetheless, I asked him if the people who had done the actual digging had been coerced. "Obviously," he said, going on to assure me that no one, not the townspeople, not those who lived and worked on area farms, had supported attacking the highway. To the contrary, they had cursed and complained bitterly, he explained, shifting his voice to convey the fuming exasperation of "the people":

> "What are we going to do? Walk?
> How are we going to get our crops to market?
> And if we have an accident? How are we ever going to get to the hospital in time?"[23]

By way of this performance of reported speech, Shego sought to clear any confusion or misconception on my part before distilling it all down to his main point: "There was no agreement [*acuerdo*]. Or I should say, it was not appreciated [*no era apreciado*]."

When I pressed him on this, Shego backtracked a step, conceding that the farmers had in fact supported sabotaging the highway. But *only*—he insisted—because they were compelled. "They never appreciated the destruction of bridges, the blocking of roads, the digging of trenches. Never, never, never."

Shego was adamant about the absolute opposition to damaging the road, but I wondered how he could be so sure about the sentiments of the rural population. We were talking about the mid- to late 1980s after all. By the end of the decade Shining Path would gather such force that the idea that taking power was within reach would seem almost plausible, no matter how far-fetched that very notion would appear only several years later. In very few places did Shining Path achieve the kind of sweeping dominance it came to enjoy in the Upper Huallaga country-side, an ascendancy that at least one respected political analyst in Lima described as effectively hegemonic.[24] Given Shining Path's momentum in the Huallaga—and imagining how that must have animated expectations back then—made it difficult for me to accept that at least some, if not many, of those who lived in rural areas had not willingly taken part in the attacks on the highway.

Shego was a sensitive, astute observer of local politics, and so I took seriously his point of view. Yet considering the stark social, economic, but also political divides that separated urban from rural spheres, I was generally dubious when townspeople tried to speak for the current de-sires, expectations, or needs of those who lived in the countryside. To do so from a distance of ten years hence, when so much had changed in between, seemed all the more imprudent.

The Upper Huallaga Valley, over the previous two decades, had un-dergone radical shifts in political climate and regime. In the 1980s the valley's main towns had lived under a constant threat of siege from rural areas where Shining Path had organized communities into its war ma-chine. By the end of the decade and into the early 1990s, the Peruvian Army would reverse the direction of fire with a counterinsurgency strategy that converted the countryside into the principal theater of the war. That extended campaign destroyed much of Shining Path's military capacity and greatly diminished its organizational prowess in the Huallaga, if not its influence. Through the multiple upheavals of the conflict, collective al-legiances could not possibly have remained constant, much less uniformly dispersed across the town-country rift. To the contrary, collective attach-ments were battered, fragmented, and unsure. That they could appear otherwise suggested a reading of the past overwhelmed by the current political moment where, in the towns at least, the army had broadly suc-ceeded in imposing its version of order.

And despite the vehemence of his claim that no one, outside Sendero Luminoso, had ever been in favor of damaging the highway, Shego for-mulated his point in a way that intimated the dicey ideological ground on which the road's destruction moved. The slipperiness of that setting revealed itself in the logical progression of three statements: first, there was no agreement; second, it was preferable to say it was not appreciated; and finally, if farmers and their families had supported it, they did so only under duress. Through this sequence of ideas Shego implicitly negotiated a complex set of historical imperatives that had shaped the local calculus of political belonging (and exclusion) in the Huallaga.

This negotiation played out foremost in Shego's choice of words. For between disagreement and a lack of appreciation there was a semantic distinction that made subtle reference to questions of deep historical relevance. Shining Path, when it first arrived in the Huallaga countryside, had demanded that all living and working in rural areas declare their loyalty to the Party. Compliance effectively enlisted one in their armed struggle. The everyday expression used to communicate the affirmation of one's alignment with the Party and its aims was *estar de acuerdo* (to be in agreement). This phrase articulated in ordinary language the categorical difference between friend and enemy that established one's place vis-à-vis the political and moral community of Shining Path. Anyone in the countryside who was not willing to demonstrate allegiance through a binding statement or act of agreement was forced—under threat of death—to leave and never come back, effectively abandoning not only all land and property to the guerrilla but even the possibility of doing commerce in rural areas. Banishment from the countryside was no small prohibition, considering the dominant economy (cocaine) happened in the interface of town and country.

Thus, in the matter of deciphering degrees of support for Shining Path actions, the phrase *de acuerdo* was laden with consequence. Farmers could not express overt disagreement without marking themselves as enemies of the Party. That in itself was sufficient reason for Shego to prefer a word both more nuanced and less complicit with the local Shining Path lexicon. As opposed to *disagreement*, actively not appreciating (or feeling an absence of "gratitude") conveyed displeasure in a more polite or honorific mode—one that did not entail a "crisis of belonging" with respect to Shining Path community.

Yet in his handling of the question of coercion, Shego also inherently navigated the present criteria of inclusion in the Peruvian state, or to be more precise, the specific discursive terms under which the rural population could "return" to the symbolic fold of the nation. The notion that the rural populace had been forced from the very beginning to do the guerrilla's bidding gained currency in the late 1990s among townspeople (in contrast, that is, to the long-standing claim that people who lived in the countryside were the guerrilla and inseparable from them). Speaking about the war, they increasingly commented that rural people had been obligated and had no choice other than to go along. Though this had basis in actual historical conditions, the presumption of a formerly coerced participation in Shining Path became one of the logical mechanisms through which the rural class, once the backbone of regional Shining Path strength, could find a place in the postwar nation.[25] The explanation that rural people had been compelled moved seamlessly with the direction of the times of waning conflict, so it made a kind of pragmatic sense.

Treating consent as if it could be completely divorced from (or was even antithetical to) coercion had advantages. It sidestepped the thorny ambiguities that accompanied questions of political allegiance and attachment, just as it assumed Shining Path could be easily separated from "the people," regardless of where in the valley they happened to live. This was another problem with abstract terms—here designating collective entities, whether "the state" or "the Party," which in the act of naming constellations and relations of social groups occluded what made them intricate, entangled, and often coterminous with one's past and even ongoing everyday lives. In Shego's case the logic of coerced involvement together with the clean lines of conceptual division between collective bodies permitted him to hold Shining Path responsible for attacking the road (and by extension for setting in play the events that would injure his back) while bearing no grudge against those who had actually dug the trenches.

Nonetheless, I sensed that Shego's emphatic response alluded to a profound phenomenon. The highway articulated the liaison between "people" and "state" in a way that gave what was otherwise an abstract relation a most concrete point of reference. In these new and emergent times of fading war, to be a "friend" to the Peruvian state and thus a good citizen of the nation required being now (and having always been) against the destruction of the road. In his remarks, Shego had channeled that imperative.

public works

Still I would later wonder: Should some special resonance be accorded the sabotage of a road, more so than any other public work? More than a power station? More than a dam?[26] Surely, any attempt to argue in favor of one over another would have to weigh relative degrees of utility: who and how many depended upon them and for what—which specific publics each work at once engendered and served. The attempt to grasp the differences between these infrastructural publics would also have to attend to the kinds of routines each work made possible and precluded. There would have to be some effort to consider their aesthetic qualities, their hold on the imagination no less than the moral sentiments they aroused, which no doubt figured strongly in the social and affective impact of their ruin. Regarding affective impressions in particular, something more would seem to be involved than the mere fact and scale of destruction, since acts "of nature" often produce perceptual effects far different from those blatantly guided by human intention. Peru is a country with a long history of recurrent environmental disasters. Floods, earthquakes, mudslides every year inflict fierce damage on the country's precarious transportation network. And though such calamities often contain the hand of human agency, by virtue of prior decisions made and strategies employed for dwelling in and exploiting natural landscapes, this does not prevent the apprehension of these occurrences as contingent and somehow fortuitous. With sabotage, however, there is little left to accident: conscious, purposive, human involvement is all too clear.

Yet what exactly comes to the fore through such deliberate acts of violence? Events, large and small, have a deep connection to revelation—but less obviously to concealment. They seem to increase visibility, but foremost they channel and intensify attention: toward this, away from that. It might be asked then what sabotage exposes, and also occludes, about the specifically *public* character of the works destroyed? What do they reveal about the collectives that rely on them, and what kind of pressure does their impairment apply? If the imposition of physical deprivation, through a deliberate interruption of "basic services," is a fast and ready means by which a counterstate group can intervene in a collective imagination—hitting the material to shape the affective dimensions of life (those of belief, conviction, will)—is it not precisely how loss distributes unevenly that shows what makes a public to be never neutral or apolitical?

Shining Path sought to alter how Peru as a social totality could be imagined. Events of violence were its way of redirecting attention. Destroy a public work—work on a public, by intervening at a critical point where "the state" linked up with "society." Transit and other infrastructures were not only materially embedded into the daily life rhythms of the local and the national; they correlated with notions of modernity and the different horizons they traced of the future. In that regard, working on a public was no less a work on perceptions of time.

During the 1980s, which again were the ascendant years of its armed movement, Shining Path displayed an acute sense for political theater as an aesthetics of brute force. In the early days of the insurrection, its actions could be obscurely symbolic as in one oft-cited episode when dogs appeared at daybreak dangling dead from lampposts in Lima; placards tied to them cursed Chinese leader Deng Xiaoping,[27] whom the Shining Path considered a traitor of Mao's Cultural Revolution. In the ensuing years the gunning down of Party enemies in broad daylight would become common and increasingly familiar—a policeman doing his rounds, a municipal official on his way home, a labor or community activist who criticized or refused to join the people's war.[28] Such killings were rarely complete until a handwritten cardboard sign had been tossed on the dying body. "This is how miserable dogs die" was a frequent theme. Shining Path did not simply dehumanize its victims; it sought to reframe the boundaries of the human itself, tracing a dividing line between a dignified (human) life that deserved to live and a wretched (animal) life that merited being snuffed out. A new moral community in the making.

If a language of corpses occupied a privileged place within Shining Path's idiom of violence, it was merely one facet of a repertoire that involved the marking of surfaces together with the interruption of routines. Imagine Maoist slogans painted on every visible cement and wood facade. That's what happened along the Marginal Highway and in Huallaga hamlets and towns. As a schoolteacher from Aucayacu succinctly put it: "Sendero made this town its blackboard." Wherever you looked, no visual plane unbroken by Party words.

Elsewhere Shining Path used dynamite to bring down high-tension wires and disrupt the flow of electricity to Peru's major cities. Explosive charges detonated in the evening hours would cast entire urban communities into darkness and perhaps reveal on a nearby hilltop the blazing image of a hammer and sickle. A theatrics of reversal underlay the abrupt shifts from light to dark, from artificial daylight to the night of natural time. By disturbing people's lives at the most basic level of everyday urban habits, those attacks created a sensation of ever-increasing spatiotemporal encroachment, as the Maoists pressed their war along an imaginary country to city trajectory.

Through such intrusions—whether actualized or simply left in virtual form to ferment states of apprehension—Shining Path sought to impose its own time, which was simultaneously an effort to impress its own interpretation of history. The Party claimed that the semifeudal character of social relations in the Andean highlands, propped up by an endemically corrupt landowner bureaucratic state based in Lima, validated the turn to armed struggle. It was the only means for breaking through the country's entrenched structures of social injustice and for releasing the so-called rural masses from their condition of backwardness.

The Party's acute awareness of the importance of orienting perceptions of time could be evinced in the practice of memorializing the revolution as it unfolded: by crafting dates from events deemed momentous, such as the initiation of its armed struggle or the uprising and subsequent massacre of imprisoned party cadre at the El Frontón island penitentiary.[29] This commemorative calendar of the people's war was intended to clash with that of the Peruvian nation-state. Major dates from both became likely occasions for Maoist violence. Shining Path's work on time would, nonetheless, attain its most pointed and intense expression in the armed strikes or stoppages known as paros armados.[30]

While the Party had its own way of explaining the purpose and aims of the paros,[31] to grasp their temporal effects, it is helpful to think of how affecting movement across space could at once alter and create a sense of time. A paro began with a declaration: an announcement of when it would start and perhaps how long it would be in force. In this respect the paro might be thought of as a technique for shaping perceptions of time precisely by controlling space and saying what could happen on it. In brief: a spatial appropriation effected a capture of time. This quality of capture would manifest in everyday spoken language, as when people who were away from home and found themselves hindered from returning might say, *me agarró el paro* ("I got caught in the stoppage," or more literal, "the stoppage grabbed me"). They would say this just as they might speak of getting caught in or by a storm. The paro interrupted at the level of habit, where the living present subsisted as a structure of time, a second nature laminating but also pulsing through the material world. Yet to the degree it dislocated one mode of habit, the paro was no less the start of another. It opened up a new tract of time with its own distinctive horizons of possibility.

Though often discussed as an urban tactic, before Shining Path ever carried out its armed strikes in Peru's major metropolitan areas, it rehearsed them in the provinces: the southern highlands of Ayacucho as early as 1983,[32] and then the Upper Huallaga Valley from 1985 forward. In the Huallaga, however, more so than anywhere else, the paros were focused entirely on one road. This was due in large part to the Marginal Highway's quality as a first road and as the Peruvian state's main orienting vector into the valley. It also reflected how Shining Path insurrection overlapped with the historical arc of the Huallaga cocaine boom (1975–1995), producing a symbiosis of Maoist armed struggle and blossoming illicit frontier capitalism that would distinguish the regional Party from the movement nationally.

blocking

Shining Path called many paros in the Huallaga between 1985 and 1990, and with each one the Party grew more confident. A decade later I would hear that throughout that earlier period the stoppages were "honored to the letter." I would hear: "They were strong." I would hear: "Nothing circulated. People didn't go out." And in the main towns—Aucayacu, Nuevo Progreso, Uchiza, Tocache—that was true. Townspeople stayed inside their homes. The main markets would be shut down, store fronts closed, padlocks in place. Whatever happened, happened on the road, though at first only at night. For regardless of how weakened the Peruvian state had become, la Marginal remained its minimum territorial expression in the Huallaga—that originary mark of sedentary *nomos*, thin line of state space, symbol and matter kneaded together.

Armed strikes began with a mobilization of rural communities and could go on for several days (though some I spoke with insisted on a shorter, more precise duration: seventy-two hours, nothing more). Shining Path exerted political influence and control throughout the countryside, yet its strength concentrated in areas set off from the road, in the farming communities of the *bolsones*—most of which were situated on the left bank of the Huallaga River. Every time the Party carried out a paro, the inhabitants of each *bolsón*—men, women, and in some cases children—were formed into work crews and directed to descend upon the road. Thirty to forty armed members of Shining Path militias accompanied them, and along the way they called on all who lived in between to join in.

On "normal days," the road was where Shining Path could not operate unfettered in the daytime for fear of army patrols. Until 1989 the Peruvian military had only two permanent bases in the Upper Huallaga: a large contingent in the city of Tingo María and a small detachment in the town of Aucayacu. That is why the first paros began early in the evening—7:00 p.m. is the hour many recall—and why work went on until four in the morning, when there was little traffic and the labors could proceed under the shade of night. After that the armed militias and their work crews would pull back from the highway and recede into the *monte* (the bush). Once day broke, all would be silent on the road, now strewn with rocks and trees as if hit by a fierce overnight storm. The unusual scarcity of traffic made for a peculiar atmosphere, apparently calm yet tense. During the day the guerrilla might send out a spy or two to see what was happening on the highway. If the army was out and about, they might keep their force stowed away until dark. Otherwise, at strategic sites, a sharp turn perhaps around a rising bluff, they would resume their positions on the road, expectant, cautious, ever ready to fall back. Where features of the natural landscape provided cover, the guerrilla were better able to defend themselves in the event of a sudden encounter with government forces.

Reckoned chronologically, the Huallaga paros were an accumulating series. One piled onto the next, an ever-growing heap. In local recollections though, the specificities of dates and what happened in one as opposed to another blurred together. There were many of them, enough to lose track. Even so they came to be grouped into two ordinal kinds: the early ones that simply hindered travel on the road and those that followed and sought to damage the highway itself. These two ideal types of paros would in retrospect come to denote separate moments in the valley's relationship with Shining Path. For some, the passage from the first type to the next marked the beginning of a profound disillusionment with the Party and its armed struggle.

Of the strikes that merely obstructed the road, there were at least two. The first was in early January 1985. People who lived along the highway recall the knocks received at their front doors just after dusk. For those who went to answer, this is what they were told:

> Grab your tools and cut down trees.
> Drag large stones onto the road.
> Do everything to make transit impossible.

If you opened the door, you were recruited. No one I talked to ever admitted to refusing. Some did not answer the knocks in hopes the senderistas would think the house empty and go away.

The early paros had a discernibly festive air, and many who participated did so willingly. Some who took part later remarked on their enthusiastic spirit and intent. They remembered especially the communal pots set up on the road to serve food and drink to those who worked. In their recollections, those impromptu kitchens conveyed the high degree of coordination and collective effort that went into pulling off the strikes.

Still it was the armed militias assigned to each group that made sure everything went according to plan. At each point where crews were stationed, they watched over. They oversaw the progress of the work, they kept an eye out for the army and police, and they monitored who transited along the road. Each worksite was a checkpoint. Vehicles caught on the highway were forced to stop, and then they were painted with Party slogans. Those belonging to government agencies were burned.

Paros were days of judgment: special occasions of reckoning with Shining Path law. While they lasted, the insurgency would go to extra lengths to locate those considered potential enemies or who had run afoul of its rules. Militia members consulted a blacklist with the names of people wanted by the Party. Travelers deemed suspicious, suspected of being an undercover cop, a police informer, or a government bureaucrat were taken aside and tied up. If the captives were lucky—and such luck could come in different forms—they would be let go. If not, a *juicio popular* (people's trial) would be quickly arranged, after which the lifeless bodies of the accused would be displayed on the road.[33]

One man I met in what was a fleeting encounter claimed he had worked in each and every armed strike. We spoke for less than twenty minutes, and then he was gone. Though I never learned his name, I held on to his words for how they made me think. They were the kind of admission rarely voiced at the end of the 1990s. He told me the early armed strikes were "excellent" and that the very first one was a particularly "beautiful paro: pure tree trunk, no destruction of the road." He said this with a tone of wistful respect that communicated a sense of having been involved in something marvelous, something larger than life.

All that changed in mid-1987, he said, when the order came to dig up the highway and the Party began to blow up bridges. From that point forward everything Shining Path did was "by force." Farmers and their families began to abandon the countryside. Even the juicio popular was different: no pretense of consultation or coming to consensus—just the word of the Party imposed. Killing turned reckless, for its own sake, without justification of any kind. Shining Path, in other words, came to approximate the image that commonly circulated about the movement outside the Huallaga: as a kind of Khmer Rouge of the Andes, source of an absurdly brutal and senseless violence.[34] It is the dominant image many in Peru still have, and yet this man, who had more experience with the Party than most, implied something else altogether. He suggested that the so-called people's trials were not bad in themselves. They certainly did not diminish the festive tone of the early armed strikes. Instead he pointed to a time when the Party's use of force had enjoyed a high measure of legitimacy among the rural population: a golden age, as it were, of Shining Path law in the Huallaga.

If such a moment had once existed, in his version of events it ended with the destruction of the Marginal Highway. When that happened, time itself seemed to enter a retrograde mode or, as he phrased it, "Every day was like the crab: going backward."[35]

Whether a sensation of decline was how time came to be collectively experienced at the historical juncture of the highway's destruction, or whether this was merely one person's a posteriori interpretation, it is impossible to know. What is revealing, however, is the intimate relation the man drew between the perception of time and the changing valence of Maoist violence. If the lethal force of the Party appeared to have been stripped of its authoritative sheen, it did not for all that lose all sense. Rather as "raw" or "brute," Shining Path coercion had acquired a new orientation, that of a nonsensical gesture from which it was impossible to intuit coherent norms. What is it then about a frontier road, and moreover a first road, that could make its destruction the potent image and sign of a historic shift so momentous as to reverse, not just the character of violence but also the perception of temporal progress itself?

excavating

To reach full splendor, sovereignty—it would seem—must be performed in the light of day. It must achieve an appreciable duration too—something that did not happen until the third paro. That was when the destruction started, late one Tuesday, August 18, 1987, continuing through the next two days. Only then did the guerrilla withdraw, leaving behind three bridges—Pacae, Concha, and Pendencia—knocked down and the road itself marred with deep, repeating grooves.

Demolition began with an order. As during previous strikes, Shining Path communities on both banks of the Huallaga River were called upon "to work road" (a trabajar carretera).[36] Prepared ahead of time, villagers gathered picks, shovels, sledgehammers, chainsaws, and barretas (long iron bars used for making postholes). The militias led them group by group to their assigned sites. Some were deployed along the twenty-kilometer stretch north of Aucayacu up to the point where the asphalt stopped. The rest were stationed at worksites, beginning below the southernmost edge of Aucayacu and extending all the way to Tulumayo, where la Marginal merged with the Central Highway.

As before, those who lived alongside the road were pressed into service on the spur of the moment. Such was the fate of Lalo, a former coca farmer who lived in the village of Río Frío just south of the Aucayacu cemetery. "They indicated to us: dig here, here, here," he said, "and you had to do it. If the highway was in front of your house, that's where you had to dig. You had to bring your own tools, because they didn't give us anything." Lalo explained too that the blacktop was hard and repelled the metal blows of their tools. So kerosene was poured and set aflame. After burning for a while, the surface became pliable, easier to break up. The earth underneath was soft, and once the thin layer of tarmac had been removed, those who had no tools worked with their hands, clearing stones, as others dug around them.

Unlike earlier strikes, these "excavation paros" pushed more assuredly into daylight hours, taking advantage of daytime traffic to siphon off labor power from transportation workers and travelers who were interrupted mid-trip. When vehicles were stopped, drivers and passengers were asked to pitch in. They had to dig for several hours before they could resume their journey, this time on foot. The deep furrows made it impossible for vehicles to continue. Around trenches and downed bridges people could cross, but cars and buses were stranded.

Once the declared time was up, the guerrilla pulled back for good, and the people who lived far away from the road retired to their communities and homes. The paro was "over." For those who resided near the road, the dangers had less passed than shifted. Now it was the army's turn to venture out on the highway to assess the damage and begin the cleanup. Clearing the road was a concrete means of reasserting state authority, no matter how partial. Like Shining Path, the army also looked to the local population to do its "share," if not all, of the actual work—calling on them to prove their loyalty to the nation, punishing them for having damaged the road. These counter-roundups by the army would become a predictable feature of the immediate aftermath of every paro.

Excavation strikes etched the will of Shining Path into the matter of the road itself. In so doing, they transformed local perceptions of time in a way that simply blocking the highway never could. For even when an excavation strike was declared officially over, its effects lingered into the coming days, months, and years. Deep cuts into the asphalt could not be cleaned up as could rocks, brush, and trees. The difficulty lay in the material attributes of the surface. Whereas a dirt road could be quickly refilled and packed down, mending pavement required bringing in expensive machinery and people to run it. As long as Shining Path was strong enough to impede efforts to fix the road—and one of the insurgency's favorite targets for sabotage was road-building and maintenance equipment[37]—there would be no prompt return to its earlier condition. The Peruvian state could not quickly reverse the destruction, and until it erased the physical marks through which Shining Path appropriated the road, asphalt trenches and downed bridges would materially extend the interruptive force of the paro into an undefined future.

All the while for people living in the Upper Huallaga, extensive damage to the highway's surface and to its bridges seemed to increase physical distances—and with them their own sense of isolation and vulnerability—measured chronologically in the elongation of travel times along a road where violent events had become common. Whereas before the first excavation strike, the fifty-kilometer trip between Tingo María and Aucayacu took forty-five minutes by car, afterward the furrowed surface of the road impeded driving at high velocity. The time of travel multiplied severalfold—to nearly three hours. That is, three hours became the average travel time once passage had been restored, because in the days immediately following the strike, transit in and out of the valley was completely cut off. It took a while for those who regularly used the road—drivers of trucks, buses, cars, and motorcycles—to figure out how to navigate what had become a new, more challenging terrain. Makeshift solutions had to be found for each and every new obstacle and interruption along the course. Sometimes this meant filling in the edges of trenches to create enough firm ground to squeak by. Sometimes two planks of wood placed across ditches allowed drivers to line up the wheels of their vehicles and slip to the other side. Access was reestablished, though it remained precarious. Sometimes it was a matter of not forgetting where to swerve.

The deteriorated condition of the road created new transit opportunities. For a small fare, villagers who lived at those points along Huallaga tributaries where bridges had been downed began to convey people and vehicles on crude wood-pole rafts between interrupted sections of highway. They operated, some townspeople later told me, thanks to a concession from Shining Path—a rumor unconfirmed but circulating still in accounts of the war. Also, in the months that followed the first excavation strike, travel along the highway was so hazardous and difficult that operators of dugout and plank canoes, like Tina and Pedro, who normally ferried passengers and cargo from one bank of the Huallaga to the other, began providing commuter service to Tingo María. This in effect reintroduced a mode of long-distance river transit that had largely ceased to be economical in the late 1960s after the Marginal Highway had been built. With land transport thrown into disarray, boat operators rediscovered the old route and did well, if only for a short time, three months at most, before being pushed aside by the road once again.

Damage to the highway impacted not only the time but facility of travel: it was harder to move back and forth because the resistance of matter had increased. Refigured and refunctioned, the surface of the road was no longer smooth, making trips far more stressful on drivers, on passengers and cargo, and on the machines they all depended upon to ply the road. Along asphalted portions bad weather suddenly took a greater toll on travel. When it rained, streams where bridges had been felled would rise, impeding crossings for days at a time. And then, on a more minor register, when the weather was dry, the road became dusty—so much so it was as if the road had never been paved at all. The significance of dust lies here in how an asphalt road may "lift" or "liberate" one from dirt, a property asphalt shares with industrial materials used to build homes— iron, glass, brick, and cement—and which in Peru are known revealingly as *material noble*: for their durability, smoothness and for the way, far more than adobe or wood plank, they provide a certain separation from the tiny, pervasive, free-moving particles of earth. Where those "modern" materials are read as signaling and even standing in for an ever-forward progress toward greater physical comfort and well-being, their destruction can be experienced as a reversal of fortunes, sending one reeling back in time.

understanding

So why, I asked Shego, did the guerrilla knock down bridges and dig up asphalt? He explained that Shining Path insisted everything built by the Peruvian government had to be demolished. "We must destroy the old state," he said—intoning now the voice, or his rendition at least, of the local Shining Path—"in order to build the new state." He meant the future, revolutionary rule of Shining Path. "That was their policy . . . that the so-called bourgeois state had to be destroyed."

Repeating Party slogans was a common way I had heard people both in the towns and in the countryside account for Shining Path actions. In part this reflected the movement's own dependence on catchphrases to communicate its motives and acts, yet it also pointed to the curious way in which slogans themselves could double as both explanation and directive. Considering the high costs incurred by those who dared to disagree with the Party, understanding Shining Path intentions may have often been simply a matter of assimilating its commands. Communication reduced to slogan leaves few options beyond agreeing, differing, or keeping one's mouth shut.

Shego assured me he had talked to his share of senderistas. He was familiar with how they thought, even if these days many townspeople claimed that back then no one knew who they were. Not true, Shego said, "because we all lived mixed together. You knew who they were." Shego prided himself on having evaded recruitment by the young men in his neighborhood who had joined the Party, and he told me an anecdote or two concerning how he had deftly and most politely circumvented their entreaties. Proximity to members of Shining Path gave Shego insight into Party motives. Still it begged the question of how Shining Path could have been so clearly separated when living and blending in with everyone else.

The idea of destroying the road, Shego said, was to impede the transportation of farm products from the provinces to the country's large population centers. Shego called the destruction "a pretty silly idea," but that was the objective: to keep crops produced in the Huallaga from reaching the cities on Peru's coast and, in that way, to put them on the brink of starvation. This explanation in effect faithfully articulated Party rhetoric. However, it treated the Upper Huallaga as an agrarian region like any other and ignored the valley's unique agricultural and character position vis-à-vis the rest of the country. It also overstated the importance of the Marginal Highway for the regional economy back then.

If it was certainly true that at the time of our conversations—the late 1990s—Huallaga farmers depended on road infrastructure to get their legal harvests, of mostly papaya, rice, and plantains, to market, such was not the case in the 1980s and early 1990s, when coca monopolized agricultural production. During those years, coca itself rarely left the valley without first being converted into cocaine paste. It was then shipped less west, and by land, toward Lima and other costal markets than northeast to Colombia in small planes. This is to say that during the cocaine boom—and unlike the years of its immediate aftermath when legal crops became increasingly dominant—the economic viability of local agriculture did not depend on the road. To the contrary, the highway, at least in a pristine or well-maintained condition, arguably had a negative effect on the regional economy, since it permitted the rapid entry of antinarcotics police and coca-eradication crews into the valley, where they destroyed cultivations, confiscated chemical inputs and reserves of raw cocaine, and generally harassed the lower rungs of the trade. At a time when the Peruvian military had few helicopters, the highway also facilitated army counterinsurgency operations, which were a primary concern for Shining Path.

Shego knew this as well as anyone, and yet he underscored the short-sightedness of sabotaging the highway by stressing the road was something everyone held in common. La Marginal, whose value all reasonable people ostensibly agreed upon, served to commensurate differences across a delicate and thorny social landscape. Pointing to the road became a means of asserting an understanding across social distance, while placing the Maoist insurrection on the wrong side of historical progress. Shego was not alone. Retrospective explanations often overlooked, or conveniently forgot, what different stakes and interests there had been in the outcome of Sendero's armed struggle, and not only between urban and rural folk but also within farming communities, down to the level of individual subjectivity where competing affects fought for ground.

surface and depth

If a modern highway can be thought of as a particular kind of machine—with different functions depending on how the matter of the surface itself is configured—then in a strictly material sense, digging trenches less destroyed the Marginal Highway than altered its outer surface. Furrows did not ruin the road as much as eliminate the quality of exterior smoothness that permitted efficient and even displacement across space. Once the ditches had been dug, the character and experience of movement were transformed: it was no longer possible simply to coast along; the route demanded careful navigation at very low speeds. The highway was still there, but it did not perform as originally intended or as the people who depended on it had come to expect. This loss of functionality made the Marginal Highway appear to be less a road, or rather, less than it *should* have been. By diminishing the promise it held for those who used it, reconfiguring the highway's surface radically altered the road's existence as an ideal entity.

If disrupting movement on the road recrafted perceptions of time, the effects of digging trenches differed from those of downing bridges. Transit necessarily came to a full stop wherever bridges had been felled; they were the points of the most severe interruption. Meanwhile, ditches, but only after they had been provisionally repaired, merely slowed traffic down. Unlike attacks on bridges, they could also be dug at any point along the blacktop to achieve their purpose. They impacted movement less through site specificity than frequency, which materially imposed a low limit on velocity, much as speed bumps do, though by reverse technique: cutting away matter as opposed to adding it to the surface. Felling bridges affected particular places on the road, whereas trenches, as a continuous series, interrupted the road as a full body—as an elongated place in its own right.

Attacks on highway infrastructure allowed Shining Path to appropriate the space of the road and exercise greater control over it. The road still "worked" but toward new and different ends. To say the road had been refunctioned for war would be true but one-sided. For prior to the excavation strikes the highway had worked all too well for one of the warring factions—the security forces of the Peruvian state. Furrowing pavement and felling bridges gave Shining Path tactical advantages. Compelling traffic to slow down made surveillance easier and took away the motorized advantage of the state. The police and army could no longer launch surprise raids using the main and only road. The trenches facilitated guerrilla ambushes on army and police patrols and provided convenient places to bury explosive devices. Damaged bridges became virtual checkpoints, places where Party supporters, sympathizers, or members could police the local population and keep watch for spies.

In this way Shining Path materially introduced a new spatial order in the service of its own law. It did so by disrupting the main vector along which the Peruvian state projected force into the valley—literally chopping up the physical terrain of the road and turning it to new ends. Furrows in the asphalt revealed the hidden depths of the highway. What was below and at the lower levels of the road's foundation, what had been covered up since it was first built, was brought to the top. Those depths became the new surface and with them a new situation.

Shego and I talked about how over time, as trenches were filled in with earth, they still registered a former history and its conditions. Even if you did not know, he said, why or what they were about, you knew all too well they were there. Everyone felt them when traveling on the road—until they were finally patched and smoothed over, more than ten years after first being dug. With repairs, the exposed breaks became depth once again, depth pushed down and disappeared.

Time has its arrows. They may spiral and loop. For Shego it was an old wound that brought him low, upsetting the smooth surface of his working habits. Suddenly, there was no easy gliding along; only the throbbing, material echoes of those earlier events: the trip to Tingo María, *interrupted*; the asphalt, *broken up*; movement on the road, *suspended*; and long before that, a road-less landscape, *recast by a first road*.

In this regard the history of the war had by no means passed. No matter how little Shego or others talked about it, and no matter what they explicitly said when they did, all that had happened continued to sediment into the passing present. Yet Shego did have me know that the injury's return was not without upside. Since he could not go to work in the mornings, nothing stopped him from going out to the river, late at night, with his mask, snorkel, and harpoon pistol. He was eager to tell about the *zúngaros* he would hunt. How the giant catfish liked to rest on the river floor, close to the shore. How they just hovered there, and since easy to spot, all he had to do was point his pistol and pull the trigger. One shot was enough.

"No, no." The shallow diving did not bother his back at all—because I did ask.

The hard part, he said, was hauling in the catch.

A dark stain leans in toward the right bank road. A vague oblong shape turns round upon its own darkness, moving to but never quite securing human form. And upon that stain, I see these words scrawled in paint— *Qué bajen todos hombre y mujer*: yellow waves on a sea of black, a static whirl, colors of the army at war. Step down into the lowest of the low, down to the source. Get out in descent. Come face-to-face with the founding.

We are locked in by the route, a straight shot; we are but separable elements hurling forward to the halt before that thick patch. We are locked in by the routine: we must step down one by one, to be checked and then maybe waved on, or maybe retained and sent headlong into pails of piss and crap. If so, does the fall end right there, or might there be some way to keep on falling, to go lower and lower, to escape the pull of gravity, to reach the other side of shit?

Locked in by the routine, no way to swerve, it is a straight shot to what's up ahead where that dark stain leans in, pointing now left, beyond the road and toward the river, where at an eddy's edge, bodies hover in silent heaps that in the aftermath can be sensed more than they can be seen and heard, more than stench might linger to saturate every direction at once, pointing left now with the war and to what remains opaque, to what moves in bulk, to what returns as bulto.

Bulto is a mass turning unruly, a storm that gathers at the thresholds and edges of bodies, where the incorporeal blurs outlines, obscures features. Bultos are atmospheric disturbances where the cruel demise of some persists in a landscape of rivers. Where the turbulence of currents roils with the invisible dead of Peru's civil war and with other deaths remote from public reckoning, bultos interrupt as a presence, ever growing denser than what surrounds them, always hard to make out and impossible to confirm; they are what happen. Because out of the irreversibility of matter, something returns: bultos come back to transgress the boundaries of the incorporeal as a difference that constellates times, always leaning in, always leaning left.

This was the scene, now twenty years ago: I am riding in a rural car service, one of five passengers, heading out on the Marginal Highway. We

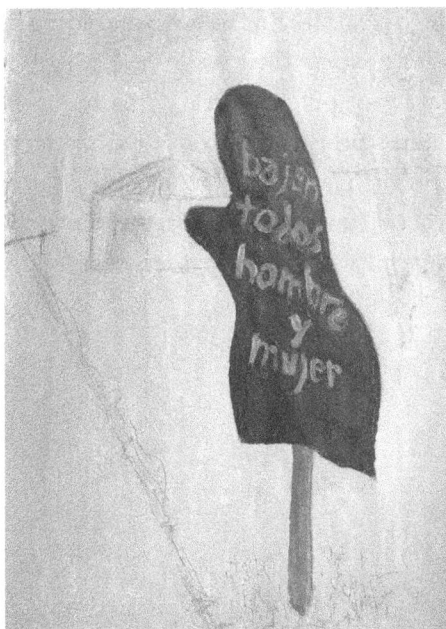

FIGURE F.I. painted sketch from field-work

stop at every checkpoint north of Tingo María; the next is the village of Anda: a little shack at the side of the road with a long cane pole dropped down to block our way. The base itself looms a good distance from the road; from the middle of a flat, grassy field it trades messages with the shack back and forth along a thin unpaved street. We must stop, and as the driver slows along that straight shot, there it is: that elongated sign, curve of yellow words snaking down dull black, stretching out, approaching human-size form. Outside the bases I have never seen anything like it, yet it does not last. Ten days later I pass through Anda again, and the black floating patch is gone. Twenty years ago, I would hear about how the army killed in mass, how the bases disposed of their victims, stuffing gunny sacks with chopped remains, tossing them into the Huallaga River so currents might carry them away. Here a black bulto hovers static, leaning left, several feet above the shoulder—in echo of that other time that prevailed then just a few years before—leaning in toward the road and beyond toward the river. If fortifications materially anticipate the impact of the projectiles they expect their walls to absorb, here army forts send projectiles the other way: out into rural expanses of the Huallaga Valley. From the bases bultos proliferate, to roil the countryside and to set all who would pass through on edge. Here a checkpoint sign appeared then quickly withdrew: ever since it has been returning to me, an ethnographic image flashing, intermittent, again and now again.

writing time as weather

Catching me on the street about to walk inside, Chara pulls up on his red Honda: "Let's go for a ride." Until now everything had passed through Tina, so this was unforeseen. I hop on. Chara accelerates, carrying us headlong toward the corner where he hangs a left. For several minutes we circle through cement streets with the sun bearing down, before he speaks again: "Should we get a beer?" Only a week before we were on this same bike, but traveling with Tina between us, crossing a different kind of terrain on the way to his farm.

What I know of Chara is his remoteness, his paucity of words, and the inconspicuous manner in which he observes those around him. There is a scowl he wears with a certain glower of his eyes, as if he is in a perpetual bad mood or just wants you to know he is a hard man. Then all of a sudden, his eyes may flicker as frown turns wry and he lets out a hearty laugh—*Ha-Ha-Ha*—which endears him to those who know him best. That laugh has force precisely because it punctuates the dark reserve that presides over his demeanor. And when he speaks, his words have a certain weight that has little to do with what he actually says and derives only in part from their infrequence. Their downward pull owes much to what others grasp of his particular proximity to a violent past he conveys through every step he takes.

What connects us is Tina. She is his *socia* or business partner and long-time friend. I only know Chara through my friendship with her. Tina is between us not wholly unlike she is between Chara and her husband, Wilson. Because while Chara lives in their house, the two men rarely speak to one another. Important decisions happen through her mediation and direction. In Tina the household finds its anchor as well as the pivot around which all relations turn.

Tina needles Chara by speaking to me *about him* in his presence. That Chara's body is making him pay for what he did the day before. "Hey, Charapa! Yesterday you were *cashpiadito*!" Tina makes fun of him with a directness no one else would dare, and Chara never protests. The theme is always the same: Chara's bouts of beer drinking, that getting shit-faced drunk is how he chooses to spend his days off. And whenever Chara wants a drink, she says, you can see that desire in his face. His mouth gets all crooked, his lip turns up this way, and down like that. She laughs. And through it all, Chara says nothing.

But when he's no longer in earshot, Tina tells me over and again that Chara is a beautiful person. For he is always there to help with her farm in Magdalena or whatever else needs to be done. It's only when he drinks. Then, haughty, rash, unpredictable, he becomes someone else. Then, she prefers he stay away.

Most of what I know of Chara I have learned over several trips to his farm in Venenillo. Last year was the second time and—speaking now from the hindsight of mid-2011—it happened like this: A three-wheel *motocar* let me off at the house on the malecón just past seven, where Tina and Chara were still getting ready, moving back and forth between the kitchen and bedrooms. So I waited for them in the front room, where I found the food and supplies that Tina and I had bought the night before scattered across a corner tabletop. A few minutes later she came in and set a small red overnight bag on the ground. She explained that Wilson was waiting for us at the farm: "He has gone ahead to feed the pigs."

She then begins to pack our supplies, one by one, into a pale green nylon sack. In this as in so many things Tina has her method and as always she refuses my help. Not wanting to sit, I walk around taking snapshots of the interior: a broken computer on a desk, four chairs lined up beneath a boarded window, a grade-school portrait of Tina's youngest daughter, framed and hung on a concrete wall. All the while I am poised in case Filimón, the family's frenetic coati, comes shooting across the floor. I've been wanting to get that picture since I arrived in town, but this morning the ever so nimble Filimón is nowhere to be found.

Chara's red Honda stands parked just inside the front door. With a few swift kicks he starts it up and just leaves the motor running until finally they say *it's time*. Chara rolls the bike out to the street and mounts it. We follow behind carrying the pale green sack, bulging and heavy now with supplies, which we lift on to the gas tank and into Chara's arms. To secure the unwieldy bundle, he opens a hole on either side. The nylon fabric is loose and easily gives way to his probing fingers. Tina then hands him a long, knitted cotton *pretina* or belt, which he threads first through the holes, then behind his neck, before tying it back down to the sack. This done, he grabs the bag firmly with both hands and adjusts it until finding the right balance. He then signals us to hop on. Tina first, and me behind her, and when we say we are ready, he eases us into motion.

As Chara weaves the bike down the town's cement streets, Tina and I, with backpacks and bags of our own, each try to find a comfortable equilibrium. Don't lean your foot on the exhaust, she cautions, telling me a few weeks ago she melted a new pair of rubber boots. The pipe grows hot fast. Place your feet beside mine, she says: on the footrests instead. But as much as I hold them there, with every bump in the road they slip off, and it seems easier simply to let them dangle.

Once we reach the highway, I can't help being impressed by how much this motorcycle has affected Tina's and Chara's movements between town and country. The first time I went to the farm, which was four years before this second trip, Tina; my wife, Angela; and I took a longer and more roundabout route: a taxi south to Tingo María, where we changed to another car that crossed the Huallaga River over the city bridge, before snaking along a dirt road up the left bank until we reached the village of Venenillo. Tina could only take us to Venenillo, she said then, because there the army maintained a counterinsurgency fort. Angela would be her *cuñada* or sister-in-law, with me, her gringo husband, tagging along.

Then we had met Chara at his farm. Because before he purchased the motorcycle—with earnings from his harvests of coca—an old mountain bike was all Chara had to get around. Either that or on foot were the only ways back to the river, and then on to the highway, where motorized transport could be caught. Before the Honda, moving back or forth took a whole morning or all afternoon, so Chara's trips to town were far less frequent, and he certainly had no way to give Tina a ride. On this second visit Tina figures she will tell Chara's neighbors or anyone who asks that I am her *compadre*: the future *padrino* for her youngest daughter, who next year will celebrate her fifteenth birthday. Today we will cross the river well above Tingo María and reach the farm in under an hour. In time, Tina says, for breakfast.

The road is amazingly smooth, and Chara, confident the sack will stay at rest on the tank, accelerates until we are racing down the pristine jet asphalt. This two-lane highway looks and feels brand-new though it was first built in the late 1960s. A road-building consortium recently finished a year-long stint of construction in which it dug out the worn, broken surface and rebuilt it again. Where before there weren't even shoulders, neat V-shaped cement ditches now frame it on either side. Sharp yellow and white lines guide traffic by day, while by night red reflectors grab the glare of headlights to trace forward a ghostly ribbon of lanes. The roadside has transformed, too, populated with signs where once there were almost none. Bright yellow diamonds with black lettering advise of upcoming curves. White on green rectangles announce remote hamlets and turnoffs onto formerly obscure rural trails.

The ordinariness of these details cloaks something remarkable. For many years one could pick up the lay of the land only gradually and with great effort, that is, by actually traveling to areas off the highway or, less directly, through the versions that cycled by hushed word of mouth, versions that often warned against traveling at all. Many villages were hidden from the highway, and one learned of them haphazardly and often without knowing exactly where they were. One would hear of them and know strangers were not welcome. But now an instant diagram unfolds, place-name by place-name, for anyone who takes the road. The signs give away freely what before was secret and say "you can go there" regardless of who you are. On *this* side of the river the fateful air that hovered over many Huallaga villages has waned, except perhaps in the memories of those still deeply marked by earlier times. On the *other* side roads are not paved and there are few signs.

As we cut along the highway, a light mist falls. The waves of tiny droplets feel cool on my face and coat everything: our clutching hands and clothes, all surfaces growing wet to the touch. "Just like Lima,"

Tina says, turning her head back toward me. And instinctively we look up at the sky, overcast with gray billowing clouds, for a sense of what is to come. "Will it rain?" I ask. But Tina shakes her head and insists that no, not a chance. It is the confident voice of one who knows. But as we move on and minutes pass, the mist only thickens. Clouds darken. Tina leans toward Chara, her voice now sounding concern: "It might rain." He nods but says nothing as he presses us forward into the wet air.

This was once the road where the Shining Path left corpses so often that to travel along it entailed confronting the dead. There was no way to avoid them. Using the road meant being exposed to a repeating presentation of putrefying remains. Their display became an idiom of violence—a visual language that crafted anticipations of immediate futures and of one's own place within them.[1] However, today there is nothing on or about the road that signals former histories of violence, much less the specific work that human corpses once performed. Today road travel traces horizons of expectation that promise possibilities far less intense and threatening.

At the village of Pueblo Nuevo, Chara barely slows as he hangs a right onto a well-packed dirt road. Suddenly we are being bounced around and Tina complains, demanding he knock it off. Chara just laughs, and if anything accelerates more down the straight two-hundred-yard stretch until the Huallaga comes into view. A murky green-gray expanse rippling under ashen skies. We have left the mist and the immediate threat of showers behind. Chara brakes to a halt. Tina and I hop off at the top of the bank as he coasts the bike down to one of two long, wooden canoes waiting at water's edge. This is Puerto La Roca. Here we cross for Venenillo.

Here dirt road meets river under a thick mat of clouds. Volvo trucks come to carry crates of bananas off to the highway and across the Andes. Farmers and farmhands arrive as they move back and forth from one side to the other. Beyond that little more than a name marks this place. Puerto La Roca is but one of many points of passage linking left bank with right. It is one of many sites where river, trails, and dirt roads come together. Here small movements and rhythms within moments of waiting create a sense of utter stillness, a stillness where the world of things sometimes takes on an extra charge. Within such moments a silence redoubles and there is a sense of air thickening, which might well be the shared, unspoken knowledge that illicit lifeways linger near. Or it might well be nothing at all.

Tina and I wait *our* turn, taking small steps down the bank as a boat operator and his teenage assistant help Chara lift the motorbike up and into a canoe painted deep cobalt-blue with thick bands of red and white. Once both wheels have been securely planted on the floor of the craft, Chara sits atop his bike again, leaning forward slightly, gripping the handlebars, looking proud. On a wooden plank behind him Tina finds a seat and motions for me to come on.

This is Puerto La Roca in year 2010: two lean-to shelters on a pale alluvium bank that descends abruptly into the water. On the other side there are no major towns, no regular police, and little institutional presence of the state, only tiny hamlets anchoring constellations of scattered farms. Here and there the Peruvian Army operates small counterinsurgency outposts.

Little over a decade ago the left bank was still the red side of the Huallaga River, and that made crossing not only politically significant but affectively charged. Crossing the river entailed going over to another world with its own regime of rules, with its own highly tensed fields of force. This river, the most prominent topographic feature of the valley, became a political boundary unmarked yet felt, a threshold that gave onto another legal order. To inquire how that happened is to ask about the means through which moral-political forces fuse with natural-historical landscapes to project an atmosphere—in this case, an atmosphere of threat that imposes lines and shapes movements.

What once made Puerto La Roca a remarkable point was its geographic location on the right bank roughly across the water from the sparsely populated villages of the Bolsón Cuchara. Throughout the 1980s and into the 1990s the Cuchara basin was a Shining Path stronghold, and as such it became a regular target of incursions by the Peruvian military and police. But unlike the army, which slaughtered en masse to provoke a generalized flight of all who lived on the left bank, Shining Path practiced a far more selective violence within its territorial zones. The Party killed just enough to control the contours of its civilian bases of support.

And yet over the last fifteen years there had been a widespread if uneven contraction of Shining Path influence. So much so that Tina and Wilson told me there was now only one place, Magdalena, also on the left bank and thirty kilometers north of the Cuchara basin. There, insurgents still controlled who came and went, and Tina and Wilson were able to say this because in Magdalena they have a farm. Today, however, we are headed to Venenillo, the entrance for the Cuchara, and where an army fort transforms the terrain as it guards against the unlikely return of Shining Path.

The boatman ferries us upriver for a good ten minutes before bringing the canoe alongside the shore. Tina and I step out onto the bank. As she waits there for Chara, I walk several yards to set the bags down on drier ground. I then turn around to take a few snapshots: of the boatman and his helper heaving the motorbike onto shore, but also of the lone remaining passenger—a man in an orange jersey and dark jeans who sits perched on the boat's edge, casually flipping the pages of a newspaper.

While I have this man in my frame, Chara rides by and up the bank. Tina follows behind on foot toward a dirt trail that disappears from view into a grassy thicket. After handing the boatman a ten-sol note, I pick up our bags and tread quickly in pursuit. Reaching the top of the bank, I see Chara and Tina paused before the high grasses as I start down the trail.

Half an hour after crossing the river we reached the farm, thanks to Chara, who deftly maneuvered us up muddy trails and over small streams, the largest of which came last. It was there that we had no choice but to traverse on foot, with Chara insisting on pushing the bike alone against the current through the rocky muck that lay beneath. Up the other bank a path led us through an intimate forest of cacao and fruit trees until we reached a small clearing. To the far left of what was a dirt patio, Chara's wood-slat cabin came into view, and through the doorway we could see Tina's husband, Wilson, at the table, sharpening a machete, oblivious to our approach. As we walked toward him, Wilson looked up, welcomed us with a smirk, and then met us at the door, machete hanging loosely at his side.

Forget pleasantries. Tina's first question was "The chickens"?

Wilson deadpanned: "They're not here."

Alarm flashed over Tina's expression, spreading to her shoulders on its way down her arms, only to dissipate when a wry smile on Wilson's face made her realize he was pulling her leg.

Visibly reassured, Tina turned to me and explained: the eighteen chickens they brought to the farm a month ago had dwindled already to twelve. What they didn't know for sure was what had happened. This much they assumed: while the six chickens might have been plucked from the air by birds of prey, most likely they had been stolen by human hands. Such was the beginning of a refrain I would hear throughout the rest of the trip about the petty thefts and even armed robberies to which they and other farmers were continually exposed. These days having property stolen was *the* concern.

The most recent incident at the farm involved the disappearance of a large plastic tub filled to the brim with harvested cacao: a batch of white fleshy seeds Wilson had removed from their pods and left outside the cabin when he returned to town. Thefts of cacao seemed all the more cruel, because the crop was supposed to be their future. Coca had been what Chara and Tina grew here, that is, until last month, May 2010, when a police-escorted eradication crew arrived and razed their coca plants to the ground. From all sides the same worry pressed down upon area farmers: how to hold on to the fruits of their labor? Later that day Tina would confide something else that had happened that previous month: a close friend of Chara's had been gunned down by two men just so they could steal from him several kilos of raw cocaine.

Tina and I set down our bags on the long table inside, as Chara parked the red Honda across the room along a clothesline sagging with old work shirts and trousers. He then headed out to inspect the cacao groves, leaving Tina to take charge of the kitchen. Turning to stoke the fire, Tina asked her husband to sit down and talk with me while she prepared breakfast. "Tell him about your story," she said, and that was enough for Wilson to settle into something much broader: a long, hour and a half talk about the history of the region, beginning decades before the highway was built, when the valley was a refuge, he said, for dissidents of the political left. He told of the era of absentee landlords and the times of agrarian reform and the process of land titling that began with the construction of the road—a process still in its infancy when Sendero appeared in the early 1980s.

Wilson recalled that when Shining Path arrived to organize villages on the left bank of the river, Party leaders announced that any land deeds issued by the government were no longer valid. They promised, however, once their revolution had triumphed, there would be plenty of land to go around. Until then, Sendero would decide who could stay and harvest, and how much. In essence, the Party claimed the underlying title of all arable land and thereby forced all farmers into a relationship of subjection. Access to land depended on maintaining a (good) relationship with local Party leaders.

In years past Wilson had stressed to me that Shining Path should not be viewed as an utterly negative movement. I remember one such instance in particular from four years before: we were sitting at a table in his home when he began to speak of the curious legal situation that, on account of Sendero, prevailed at their farm in Magdalena. I remember that he prefaced his comments most carefully with the insistence that everything has a good side as well as a bad. "Out there on the highway," he said, "there are robberies and rapes." But in Magdalena, there is none of that. "It's different." Over there, other rules are in force. "One cannot just enter." One can't just walk in, Wilson said, and there was no need to explain. Sendero law meant boundaries to free circulation, but also a space imagined as sheltered from "common" robbery and at least one form of sexual violence. Such went the claim.

This morning at Chara's farm, however, now June 2010, Wilson could find no redeeming virtues and spoke only of Sendero's many flaws. Ever since Party leaders in Magdalena had banned him from entering the area again, his perspective had hardened. He could no longer go with Tina to their farm. And so exiled from that property, Wilson divided his time between the farm in Venenillo, where he tended the chickens and pigs, and the house he shared with Tina in the town of Aucayacu.

Stung by this most recent of harms at Shining Path hands, Wilson was now thoroughly dismissive of everything the insurgency had ever been. Nonetheless, he liked to talk about Sendero. About the many conversations he had had with Party leaders over the years: about their ways and the reasons why their revolution had failed.

Wilson described this political history as a matter of fact, in a voice, slow, steady, and calm, always drawing as needed on stories and anecdotes from his former days as a river canoe operator, when he ferried people and cargoes of raw cocaine up and down the Huallaga and Magdalena Rivers. Like all boat operators of those times, now decades ago, the Party kept him under watch and continually on call. At any moment he and his boat might be commandeered and sent on commissions. Wilson recalled working all night to pass people back and forth when the guerrillas staged armed stop- pages on the Marginal Highway. He recalled too the ill-fated 1989 attack on the Madre Mía army fort, when he transported combatants toward the scene of the battle and then back to the other side with so many dead and wounded in tow. Wilson said the toll on the Party from that single fight—in losses of seasoned fighters and damage to morale—became a turning point in the war. Or so one veteran guerrilla combatant later confided to him. The soldiers, secure in their underground bunkers, "won" without firing a shot, as various groups of senderistas converged upon the fort from different locales. Confused about who was who in the dark of night, the guerrillas opened fire on each another into the early-morning hours, until they had decimated their own ranks. This was the moment of historical revelation that Wilson fore- grounded to explain how the storm of people's war had hurtled off course.

In our conversations Wilson echoed many things I had heard about Shining Path rule during the heights of its power. He said that to reside in rural villages, which were recast as People's Committees as early as 1982, was to live subjected to the demands of a Maoist-inspired armed struggle. There, it was forbidden to espouse other political doctrines or to do anything that might betray the revolution. Mobility in and out of areas of insurgent control was severely curtailed. One could not enter or leave without permis- sion. Power ostensibly belonged to "the people"; yet Wilson insisted that lo- cal Party delegates exercised a vertical, despotic control.

Attracted by an ascendant cocaine boom, the insurgency's political in- frastructure and influence spread quickly throughout the countryside of the Upper Huallaga Valley. Within a few years all farmland upon which the co- caine trade depended came under Party dominion. Anyone who wished to grow coca had to express support for the insurgency and its armed struggle.

Wilson could talk for hours. Yet he was quick to admit that his under- standing of Shining Path was that of an outsider. The one you must speak to is Charapa, but Tina says, "No." He won't speak about that, meaning he would not speak with me.

For Chara is aloof, almost mysterious, in a manner I have come to appreciate. I figure it is less important to learn what he experienced than to reflect on the distances he draws and see what happens next. I figure this since fieldwork for me tends to thrive most through the unexpectedness of encounters, that is, if I manage to draw on their power to jolt and inspire thought. I find that even though fieldwork encounters are fleeting, their ephemerality does not prevent them from delivering strong, if not the strongest of, impressions. The fleeting is what vanishes but often not without leaving behind dense condensations or residual images. Rarely offering clear lines, those images evoke a permanence through the persistence with which they recur *anew*—in thought, in reminiscence. That recurrence is often what impels me to write.

Late that same morning I come upon Wilson and Tina clearing the flat field of what were once thriving bushes of coca. I watch how they fill their arms with long bare branches and dirt-caked roots and then deposit them in a pile at the edge of the field. I see this is something I can do, and so I go to give them a hand. A month has now elapsed since an eradication crew set up camp in Venenillo and then went farm by farm, manually ripping up all the coca they could find. Today we deal with the remains, walking to and fro across this patch of pale yellow earth, carrying the dead branches left in their wake. Here I will spend the hottest hours of the day with Wilson, preparing the soil, before planting small stalks of yuca in row upon row.

Just beyond this parched plot the ground turns a vibrant green as short grasses run the distance to forest backdrop, through a patchwork of flourishing cacao trees. Those trees, they are what cushioned the blow, Tina tells me, saying it's a good thing Chara took her advice last year and switched half of his land over to cacao. Otherwise it would have been a total loss. When I was here the first time, four years ago, there was no cacao, and across this same flat field the delicate leafy branches of young coca bushes spread forward in straight neat rows toward the forest and up to the base of a rising mound. "Everyone" was growing coca back then.

The beginning of the mound marked the limit of Chara's land, and on that trip I recall he spent most of his time walking about, strapped to a backpack fumigator, spraying the grounds. On the morning of the second day of our brief visit, Tina took Angela and me through the field and up to meet her friend Óscar, who had his own farm at the top of the hill.

We found him picking coca with the help of a man roughly Óscar's middling age and a boy in his early teens. The sun was burning high in the sky, and Tina called on him to sit with us in the cool shade outside a one-room cabin next to the field. "Vamos a bolear," she said. Óscar came right over and passed around a small plastic bag of leaves. As each of us took a few, Tina introduced her friends. But it was the two of them who quickly fell into intense conversation, as Angela and I listened on, and as the leaves, softened by spit, slowly nestled between lower gum and cheek.

Óscar shared his concerns: pending travels, a shipment needing to go out, but also a brother's problems with the law, his recent arrest and looming court appearance. As he talked, Tina began drawing leaves from the plastic bag, one by one until she had six that met her unspoken criteria. Taking them between her palms she blew on them lightly and murmured soft words, before tossing them on the ground. That trip . . . don't do it now. Wait until the week after, she advised. Then she pointed to the leaves showing Óscar where obstacles cropped up early but how afterward the road cleared. On a second throw Tina saw complications. The brother's legal situation wouldn't be resolved soon, but in the end the judge, she said, would rule in his favor.

But that was four years ago and Óscar is now long gone. Tina tells me he abandoned his farm well before the helicopters came and workers ripped everyone's coca up by the roots. She insists she had seen Óscar's demise in the leaves and that everything the coca had told her had come to pass. He was scamming his neighbors, she said, accepting their coca and later refusing to pay. She warned him of a fall approaching if he didn't stop what she called his *pendejadas*. And then, someone tipped off the police. They came, confiscated his *merca*, all his money too. Óscar escaped. But without any capital to start over again and with no one in Venenillo willing to do business with him anyhow, he had no choice but to withdraw to his hometown in the highlands.

There it was in the leaves, she said. All of it happened. His brother even got out of jail.

Coca eradication teams drop from the sky and work under armed police escort. They move fast with digging tools that reach down, grab the roots, and then drag them aboveground. I've heard they can clear a hectare in an hour flat. But it's difficult going and dangerous too. Farmers leave booby traps, and Shining Path fighters may take potshots from a distance or even confront them up close, which is what happened late last April. Near the hamlet of Alto Corvina, a few kilometers north of Chara's farm, Sendero staged an ambush that killed a policeman and two workers.

Tina traces the loss of their coca to the ambush. She claims the eradication teams had no plans on coming to Venenillo, at least not anytime soon, but that the attack pissed them off. So they decided to retaliate by destroying all the coca they could find. The ambush had intensified a storm that six weeks later was still under way. The police, meanwhile, zeroed in on Alto Corvina itself: they set fourteen dwellings ablaze and tortured three villagers before hauling them off to a base in Tingo María. That according to human rights groups. The police brushed off their reports.

Tina didn't mention reprisals by the police per se but did say of Chara that he was on the farm in the first days of May when he heard the helicopters approach. A profound sadness overcame him, she explained, and he couldn't bear to stick around and watch. So he left. Tina didn't tell me where to or how, but I imagined Chara getting on his red Honda again and riding off deep into the left bank as far as there were roads.

In early May, when the eradication workers came through, in their haste they missed a handful of plants, which had blended in with the trees at the margins of the field. This morning immediately after breakfast, Tina went to pick the remaining leaves. She then brought them to Chara's cabin and spread them out on the dirt patio. As she laid the last of her coca down to dry, Tina reminisced about how the leaves used to overflow the flat ground come harvest time, every three months. There never was enough room.

And now all that's left is this little island of mute green leaves set in the earthen yard upon an old black tarp.

Throughout that month of June 2010, eradication teams were destroying coca fields south of Aucayacu, the last leg I was told of a several-month campaign.

Farmers were devastated by the loss of their crops, but this time there were no demonstrations: no roadblocks, no strikes. The local cocalero movement had ebbed to its lowest point in a decade. And in the days leading up to my trip to Venenillo, teams were finishing off the hamlets of Angashyacu and Pacae, the final stop apparently before leaving the Huallaga.

The police declare they are surpassing their annual goal. Even so, word is everyone is planting coca again. Everyone also says it will be a year before production comes back strong.

Three months after this second trip, I call Tina now by phone and from Florida. She tells me she is growing coca. Not in Venenillo, where the eradication teams could easily return, but on her land in Magdalena, where the police rarely enter. What she does not say, since we are on the phone and she knows I understand, is that the police don't enter because in the Huallaga Magdalena is one of the few places where Shining Path has anything approximating territorial control.

Nine months pass, it's another year, I am visiting again, and once more Tina says she cannot take me to Magdalena. Wilson wonders aloud: Why not? Yet Tina insists: No and no, and so, back we go to Venenillo. To reach Chara's farm we take the highway once again south for half an hour before crossing over to the left bank. A long canoe with a small outboard motor ferries us to the other side. Chara pushes the motorbike across a shore of sand and stone, up to the nearest trail, as she and I follow behind.

The Huallaga flows in intricate braids, and when rains come for days on end, the river becomes a formidable liquid mass that overruns and redraws territories. The path to the village of Venenillo, and beyond it to the farm, changes with the river's ever-shifting course, year after year.

The long canoe pulls away from the shore. We ride with our backs to the Huallaga along a trail well-worn and hedged by tall grasses. We ride over a ground that grows increasingly uneven. Small pools of water cut up the path and conceal the sharp rocks, sticks, or deep holes that may lie beneath. Tina fears a fall. She says she and I must hop off so Chara can continue alone along the main trail. The bike is his, and, besides, for him walking more than brief stretches quickly turns cumbersome. Tina leads me along a shortcut.

We meet up with Chara again outside the village and ride in together, passing the army fort, en route to the farm where we spend the night.

If the left bank of the Huallaga River was for many years the red side—the political territory of Shining Path—Venenillo was an original epicenter of Maoist influence in the region. The name of the village carried a viscerally imposing charge for most anyone who did not have the Party's permission to enter, though in the years to come there would be many other such places. Even now there are still a few. Today, however, Venenillo is a village whose name conveys at best a hollowed-out intensity. Chara is tied to that place not only because of the farm. In Venenillo he was born and raised, and on account of that he was pressed into the people's war when Shining Path arrived in the early 1980s. When I first met him, Tina whispered to me that Chara had been in the guerrilla, where he had been known and appreciated for his skill as a crack shot. She also told me the story, one version that is, of his wound, which is the reason he finds it difficult to walk. Tina said he was badly injured—surely she had said injured in a firefight with the army, but just that once and then never again—an event that irrupted into his life and precipitated unforeseen betrayals. Because once it was apparent that the severity of his injury would prevent him from returning to the long marches of the guerrilla, the Party abandoned him. They did not contribute to his treatment or do anything to help him recover. It was there that Tina located the origins of Chara's eventual disillusionment with Shining Path— the moment *their* revolution left *him* behind.

Chara does not invite questions about the past. I sense that any query at all could risk breaking off what little proximity I have to him. He knows of my wish to learn about the political and social history of the region. He has seen me talk at length with Tina and Wilson. But I sense his deep reticence, and taking my cues from him, I am careful not to ask.

Of Chara's parents I have learned little. I have heard him speak only of a stepfather and how he was killed. Tina says his mother died of cancer. I do not know how long ago. But when she passed away, she left her land outside

Venenillo to her two sons, who promptly divided it into separate farms. The stepfather is buried on what is now Chara's property. I know this because Tina has shown me the burial site. It is covered with *yacusisa*, which is the only thing that indicates the spot. She tells me: this delicate green fern has but one medicinal use. It cures infants of *mal aire* (malevolent air) and *susto* (fright), afflictions provoked by the spirits of the dead.

The stepfather's grave ties Chara's moving present to the political history of the region, not unlike the injury to his leg, except that the latter he takes with him wherever he goes. Of the two, Chara's injury has a far more active life. For while the burial site is left unattended, Tina cares for his wound whenever Chara reinjures it—especially when he gets drunk and then crashes or simply falls from his motorbike. But also when quite sober he loses control while driving across the uneven terrain between river and farm.

I have seen his wound, or at least one of its localizations, but only once and then only in a flash. We were on our way to the river, when Chara halted and pulled up his trouser leg so that Tina could give it a massage. The wound was on the inside of his left calf: a small sinkhole-like depression with tight striating lines splaying outward. A churning eddy in miniature, captured at full stop.

The next morning we return to the river, always the river, on our way back to town. Again, we begin on motorcycle. Again, Tina and I hop off once we have passed the village. Again, she guides me along a bending footpath—one we have never taken before. She says it will lead us to the shore. Soon we come to a stream bed where a long finger-shaped pool of water, accumulated from the rains of the last few days, sits absolutely still across our path. Tina instructs: this was once the channel along which the long canoes would travel to and from the port of the Venenillo. Over there, beneath that hill there was a powerful eddy, she says, ever tricky to navigate. That was during the years she worked as a botera running drug couriers and their merchandise between village and town. That was when Venenillo was a place of openly illicit, if strictly controlled, commerce, and when Shining Path decided who could come and who could go. There its delegates operated a Party scale on which the traqueteros would weigh the balls of raw cocaine they purchased from local farmers.

Of that earlier political history, little to nothing does the landscape now disclose. What traces remain—whether visible still or available solely through their disappearance—become legible only in what is spoken about times past. Without Tina, I would see nothing at all. For the flow of the river has long since shifted. It has moved away from the village, and that is why Venenillo now lies a full hour on foot from the closest access by water. Today, instead of a port, the village has the small army garrison that we must slip by on our way to and from the farm. As Tina and I clear the tall grasses, an immense sandy floodplain opens before us. In the distance, Chara rests atop the red motorcycle, waiting at the river's edge for us to catch up.

That was one week ago and now Chara drives me to the Recreo la Roca in Aucayacu, an outdoor lounge perched high above a small river—the town's namesake—next to the wood and metal bridge that hangs over the water as it empties into the Huallaga. We take a seat at one of several tables set beneath cabana-style shelters. A young woman in shorts and flip-flops walks over to take our order. Holding eye contact with us, she wipes off the table in long, deliberately extended motions, before swiveling about suddenly and strolling back to the bar with a slightly pronounced, almost coy, gait. The Recreo is a "family place," at least during meals and during daytime hours on holidays, but in between it serves only beer, and that is when the young women employed there become a crucial part of the business and its allure. Male clients stick around, drink more. Not "bar girls" per se but invoking that line of potential, while leaving the path of where things might lead ever ambiguous. She and others like her make the Recreo the place it is, if only for the men who come and use their image as a trigger to imagine possibilities for other times and places.

It's 2:00 p.m. and the middle of the week. The Recreo is quiet and empty, except for us and for two men sitting and drinking at another table. Somewhere sounds of *cumbia* play on a radio. Today is June 23. Tomorrow is a major regional holiday, but on this hot afternoon the airs of festival have not yet begun to stir.

The young woman returns with two tall bottles of pilsner. One after another we pour the rounds, and suddenly, Chara is of a different mood. Amiable as I have never seen him before. Without prompting he begins talking. You realize that with *los tíos* (the uncles), he says, in indirect reference to Shining Path, there was too much coercion. I never spoke against them or against anything they did. And that's the reason I survived.

Yet Chara does not dwell on this; he moves abruptly instead to how the Peruvian Army murdered his stepfather. I interrupt: "That was . . . *when?*" "1985 . . . No. 1986," he says. A friend of his stepdad, a woman, operated a stand in the village port. One morning she asked him to come keep an eye on her kiosk. So the stepfather went, but to his misfortune that very day a group of soldiers appeared out of the blue and opened fire, killing everyone who was there at the port. The power and sheer quantity of the bullets, Chara explained, disfigured the bodies of the victims. And after their firing stopped, the soldiers gathered the corpses and placed them one after another in a row.

Upon learning of their stepfather's demise, Chara and his brother felt obliged to go recover the body, but the thought of the soldiers still nearby held them in check. The dilemma, Chara tells me, was less the actual danger than an overwhelming fright. To counter that fear, they gathered with several friends around a bottle of cane alcohol. They took swig after swig until they found the collective courage to venture out to the port. When they arrived, soldiers were still there, but under the protective cover of their drunken stupor they walked straight past them and over to the bodies. Finding the stepfather, they hoisted him into a hammock and carried him, with their friends' help, back to the farm.

That night they buried him in the spot where yacusisa ferns now grow.

Chara waves at a young guy who is driving by on a motorbike in the direction of the bridge, motions vigorously for him to join us. Chara says, "This is my friend!" and tells me too that his father owns a local *hospedaje*. Seeing him sit down at our table, the young woman emerges again and starts toward us only to stop and turn around when Chara holds up two fingers. A moment later she returns with the beers, collects our empty bottles, and wipes down the table. As she withdraws, the friend follows her with a casual glance.

Increasingly animated, Chara speaks, telling us that living in Venenillo, he always steered clear of problems. "My only vice is that I'm a *gilero*—a ladies' man," he says, shooting his friend a grin and the friend—who owes their acquaintance to occasions Chara has taken a sweetheart to his father's hostel—beams a complicitous smile. But in those days, Chara explains, he was still with his wife, and if he had acted on his inclinations, the Party would have killed him for adultery.

Of course, he says, that was before my injury. And how did that happen? I ask. *Trampero*—animal trap. His answer was not one I expected, though it was easy to appreciate the usefulness of an explanation that drained the wound of overt political significance.

The injury was the beginning of his troubles, Chara says. The recovery lasted fourteen, largely bedridden, months. He could not work or provide for his family, and soon his young wife began to grow distant. She would go to the closest city, Tingo María, with her girlfriends, who took her to discos and to parties. Chara tells us his friends and his neighbors realized his wife was cheating on him. "Everyone" in Venenillo knew, but no one said a word . . . at least, not to him. And yet in his story there was a different sort of silence, a logical hole I did not think about until later. For if "everyone knew," why did the community not act and punish his wife for her infidelity in the name of Shining Path?

Such holes were common in accounts of those who had been personally lured into the conflict, to the extent the political times of a postwar now demanded an extremely selective disclosure of what had happened. That Chara did not draw attention to this gap or to others, much less attempt to address uncertainties they raised, did not surprise me. Nor would I have pressed him in any case. We were just having a few beers on a Wednesday, early afternoon, where, regardless of what he related or what he concealed, the anonymous past would tug *through his words* and in so doing participate in the present.

The possibility of sensing how that impersonal force weighed in what he said promised less a revelation than an opportunity to gauge distances. For the "back then" of events that marked Chara today in the present sign of his limp was another political time, just as the then and the now of the other side of the Huallaga were a world apart, entangled between the river's natural history and the mutations of political territory.

The young woman returns again to collect the bottles. "Two more?" Chara asks us. Sure, the friend says. And once she withdraws, I wonder aloud if there are rooms behind the Recreo. "Private rooms?" Chara asks. "Here? Unlikely," he says, shaking his head. "But you know what? There used to be a place in town years ago: El Bar Tiburón."

"The Tiburón had private rooms with beds in the back. The owner was blind. He had a curious habit. Whenever a patron followed one of the women who worked at his bar into a back room and closed the door behind them, the blind man would grab a guitar, which he kept on the floor propped up against a wall. He'd start playing. He'd play and he'd keep strumming the strings until the couple reappeared. Only once they sat down at their table again, would he stop. And only then would he return the guitar to its place against the wall."

FIGURE 6.1 *el vado*, 2013

stranger terrain

With a wave of his hand, the ferryman calls me over to a rusting, corrugated canoe that had just now pulled up alongside the dark sands of the shore. Though he had never before singled me out for conversation, I had seen this ferryman many times. In previous years he had taken me across the river, more than once. And he also figured in photographs, from my earlier trips, always wearing the same red cap. Still, we had never really spoken, and I did not know him beyond the briefest of introductions my friend Melissa had made in passing, when I returned only a few days before to Nuevo Progreso—the small town on the Huallaga River they both call home. In that fleeting moment of presentation, as he was arriving from the other side and as I was waiting to board someone else's boat, I handed him a few printed snapshots in which his red cap made him easy to spot. Today, it is on the shore opposite the town where this ferryman finds me walking and taking photographs at the water's edge, and where, a few yards behind me, mototaxi drivers lounge, ever ready to retrieve passengers and convey them to the village of Paraíso or to other nearby hamlets on the Huallaga's left bank. The ferryman sees me, and, with a wave, he initiates an encounter I do not expect.

More surprising is the ease with which he talks to me *out here* for all to see. Surprising, because I am foreign to this place, but also because I had grown accustomed to receiving from the boteros or vaderos a treatment that in years past could be markedly terse, cold, and occasionally mocking. River crossings were, not so long ago, some of the most intensely scrutinized places in this valley. Not only was everything one said and did on display, but one felt actively watched. So, the ferryman's openness felt somehow significant—as if in his talking to me here and now

FIGURE 6.2. intervals

there might be some crucial hint of more fundamental alterations in the region's political climate.

Such changes have unfolded gradually in this ongoing period of postwar: an aftermath in which lingering threats of a formerly powerful Maoist insurgency have slowly waned until seemingly they are no more. The era of political violence is overtly *over*. Yet it coexists with the passing present, if in ways not immediately evident. So much so that on my return trips I end up looking for everyday traces where these transformations find subtle expression.

The year is 2013, and the month now July, but only later will it occur to me that if this ferryman had not appeared repeatedly in my fieldwork pictures,[1] and each time with his red cap, I might never have come to know him. And yet there was something more: an undeniable lightness I perceived that day in the simplest of his gestures and that seemed to extend as if *through him* to the river crossing itself—a levity that elsewhere, in other circumstances, might not have merited remark, if not for what it threw into relief. Gone were the silent, penetrating stares that once conveyed an ambiguous mix of forces, borne of adversarial state projects, which had turned these turbulent waters into a political threshold separating territorial zones. Now those forces felt curiously absent. In their place a distinct sort of buoyancy was palpable—a different kind of charge, at once matter-of-fact and hospitable—and not only from this one man. For in the coming days I would notice unmistakable courtesy from most all of the ferrymen who facilitated passage in barges and canoes. That unexpected kindness made me wonder if a considerable change in the atmospherics of everyday sociality (especially toward those who were visibly strangers) did not reflect corresponding modifications in time.

That is, shifts in *political time*, by which I mean the possibilities *for* political community and the attributes of what counts *as* political community not only have temporal characteristics but acquire temporal designations, which implicitly mix memory and forgetting. Designations of time fluctuate above all in the trend from war to postwar—an ideal line to be sure, but not without concrete particulars corresponding to it, which scatter along a corporeal register and from which other incorporeal things may emanate.[2] For now the movements of people between towns, like Nuevo Progreso, and the countryside, where one finds Paraíso and other hamlets, are patently different. Road building, though once expressly forbidden by Sendero, has during the last ten years been widespread across the immense plains of the river's left bank. Dirt roads, as if in testament to the insurgency's passing, increasingly stitch the region's hamlets into an ever-expanding rural transportation network. Cell-phone towers have followed and even eclipsed transit routes in offering coverage to rural areas that before seemed unfathomably distant. The national government, meanwhile, is said to envision a future where bridges will multiply across the entire Huallaga River; construction on the first of a promised many has already been completed just north of the village of Madre Mía. Still, in most places where road traffic meets the river, canoes and barges provide the only means for movement between earth and water.

These changes have run apace with others I have noticed. Since at least 2005, there has been a steady easing of what might be called a "law of silence":[3] people seem much less guarded and anxious to speak in public.

FIGURE 6.3. *gorra roja*

And yet when Huallaga residents refer to the war era, they do so in increasingly perfunctory and abstract terms. The generality with which they discuss those earlier times is compounded by the ever-growing remoteness of those who took active part in the conflict and who now are either dead, forgotten, or simply in some unknown elsewhere. Finally, there is an apparent falling away of spatial prohibitions revealed in the gestures, words, and tones of everyday sociality, in the places where one hears it is now safe to go, and less tangibly, but perhaps more momentous, in new ways of seeing and even visually documenting the river and its rural expanses, which simply did not seem possible but a few years ago.

Still and moving images from my fieldwork highlight the material techniques, socialities, and forms of labor that enable Huallaga River crossings today. In so doing they reveal a socially dense, tactile space. But they evoke other images too, conveyed in rumor and stories charged with personal memory as well as in dreams of sleep and waking hours. The distinct manners in which images have emerged during fieldwork, and become integral to it, make me wonder about the relationships that arise between them. I am concerned first of all with how *nonphotographic* images sometimes bring the Huallaga's wartime past into intimate proximity with its postwar present. I am also concerned with how fieldwork photographs and videos might contribute to ethnographically rendering the aftermaths of war, and differently too, where that proximity is taken into account.

Images played a transformative role in the creation and maintenance of spatial interdictions throughout the war and its immediate wake. Foregrounding that role makes it possible to show how *one kind of image work*—which circulated primarily in verbal accounts of spectacular killings and deterred travel across the region's rural expanses—formerly dissuaded another, *that of photography*. Attention to the changing relations between these two distinct kinds of image work offers one vector for grasping how landscapes express movements of political time. In the Upper Huallaga those landscapes continue to resonate a history of spatial interdictions—ostensibly no longer in force, yet imparting, sometimes still, a disquieting semblance to the terrain.

Given that ethnographers have long grappled with how perception becomes intertwined with visual technologies,[4] it is perhaps worth considering the extent to which their entangled relations could become territorially significant and, as such, useful for gauging how natural historical landscapes manifest political time. If ethnography can be paraphrased as an activity that receives, generates, and elaborates images—from bodily impressions, dreams, stories, historical memories, and, of course, through technologies of visual reproduction—then one way of discriminating between these different image manifestations is by following the distinctive manner in which they draw limits and even assure their own separation from empirical encounters, albeit enfolded within the promise of facilitating greater approximation. During my early fieldwork in the Huallaga Valley attempts to take photographs always seemed to run up against interdictions. Reflecting on the image-conjuring qualities of those prohibitions here suggests a means for exploring how territory and image converge in the problem of distance.

Photographic still and moving pictures are distinctive for how they impose strict visual frames. Here one might consider that such pictures share with acts of remembrance a certain labor of selection, always, necessarily, predicated on what they leave out. And yet perhaps it is the strictness of the frame that differentiates photographic recall—constituting, as Susan Sontag suggests, an "invitation to pay attention."[5] If so, then what visual frames exclude can offer insights for relaying through writing how the material traces of war linger on into its aftermath. Careful attention to what fieldwork photographs and videos circumscribe, rather than what they explicitly depict, can also serve to draw out the latent visuality of a more turbulent, seemingly absent, past. Such latency is disclosed when nonphotographic images—as if solicited by dint of their very exclusion from what can be photographically documented—come to the fore to express prior histories and events. In this manner fieldwork photographs and videos create possibilities for sounding out other species of images.[6] Describing their attributes here entails assessing the specific distances each species conveys. For it is through the intervals they introduce and communicate that images become vital for understanding the material force of the past as it inheres in postwar landscapes.

In the Huallaga few things condensed more vividly the former era of political violence than the figure of the unwelcome stranger and, its close relative, the soplón or snitch. Images of the swift, often brutal, death that awaited outsiders "who just showed up" and how those images drew limits of where it was once advisable to travel became both a basis for spatial interdictions and for the ways in which prohibitions themselves might take hold of the imagination.

In times of war the social category of *stranger* always risks getting muddled with that of *enemy*. Strangers were once unwelcome in the Huallaga because of the strategic role policing secrets played for Shining Path in its attempts to assert control over rural territories and populations, but also for farming communities themselves, which regardless of their actual support for the insurgency, depended as did area towns on the cocaine trade for their economic well-being. Strangers might reveal secrets if they were allowed to leave. So, there was uncertainty, which could become quite intense. The dangers of revelation were, of course, not restricted to those who arrived from elsewhere. Anyone who lived in a rural community could be accused of being a snitch—by a local leader of the insurgency, if not by neighbors or even family—and against that charge there was no sure defense. Throughout the valley, photographic equipment came to be closely associated with spying and the ever-present danger of being so accused. Carrying a camera accentuated personal risk.

If ethnographic fieldwork and photography coincide in the temporality of the encounter,[7] then that creates opportunities to consider moments when taking photographs requires navigating fields of threat and the uncertainties threat would seem to presuppose. Uncertainty itself might well be a general condition of all encounters.[8] And yet the repertoire of probabilities lording over what could foreseeably happen bears the stamp of prevailing political situations. That is why subsequent changes in stranger sociality offer a separate vector (overlapping with the comparison of species of images with regard to distance) for tracking the movement from war to postwar. To convey a more concrete sense of the magnitude of those transformations, I later draw on the verbal accounts that two grade-school teachers shared with me of their first trips and their first-time arrivals, in the early 1990s, to left bank hamlets across the river from Nuevo Progreso. Their stories offer rich material for examining the conditions and dangers of strangerhood during the war. They also reveal the extent to which stranger encounters would transform as the military defeat of Shining Path gave way to a wholly new political time when the possibilities for the use of visual technologies would also confront far fewer constraints. Such changes set in relief how Huallaga River crossings continue to be a crucial place where wartimes past and their aftermaths palpably intersect. They also suggest that the broader field of image making might be inextricable from spatial interdictions and the ways they mark off territory.

semblance

On its northeastward push from the central highlands toward the tropical lowlands of Peru, the Huallaga River partitions what over the last forty years has been one of the country's most important centers of illicit cocaine production. Through this valley—where the ferryman in the red cap lives and works—the river moves without reprieve, manifesting a material force that pulls in tow whatever it can. That roaming line continually eats away at its own borders and in moments of catastrophic swell can tear off chunks of earth, sending fields and roads downstream. When that happens, the river may abruptly alter course, abandoning the boat landings or "ports" that previously occupied its edges.

Even in moments of calm, the Huallaga is a liquid barrier to be reckoned with. To those who move on land, it demands coming to a full stop or at minimum obliges a downshift of speed. Yet as a material obstacle the river also draws legal boundaries. Some are mundanely bureaucratic, such as where it retraces the borders of Peru's regional jurisdictions. Throughout the war, however, the river separated political domains far more hostile: on the left bank, the most enduring of insurgent territories; on the right, areas of greater state control. The river's shores became highly surveilled spaces. The fluvial currents that ran between them served for many years too as a dumpsite for victims of the violence—a burial practice that reiterated the boundary time and again and made *simply* crossing the river a charged political act. Back then, it was the boteros who daily navigated this political-legal threshold but also who specialized, some claim, in the labor of watching and taking note of all that passed from one side to the other. Though, it's best to add, that if you ask ferrymen about that prior sentry work today, most say they did no such thing. Shuttling between the river's shores, they were caught between antagonistic political forces and could little afford to throw their lot in with one out of fear for what the other might do.

The details of what *really* happened back then, even those disclosed through stories that people told and sometimes tell again, are at best unconfirmed. Harder to grasp still is what remains from the times of war in the present day—ethnographic sensibility, imagination, and presentiment offer perhaps the only way. Sensibility, imagination, and presentiment—so often relegated to aesthetics—are underappreciated registers of legal phenomena and territoriality. They also provide one important means for tracking how the wartime past persists and accrues to local terrains as an evasive *semblance*: hovering over, behind, and alongside the postwar present. My attempts to register that semblance continue to play out here in the intersections of matter, sensation, and image. Mindful that aftermaths of armed conflicts entail perceptual reorientations, I suggest that it is *in* those intersections—which sometimes facilitate a turning away from the past and at other times bring echoes of war-era events, predicaments, to the fore—and perhaps *only* there, that the historicity of spatial prohibitions can be traced. Getting at their historicity is what continually returns me to the problem of images: what appears in them patently or else reveals itself behind and alongside them, whether rising up in an occasional flash or enduring, somehow, as a barely audible rustling. This is why my reflections take initial bearings from the insights of the writer-philosopher Maurice Blanchot.

In his theorization of images Blanchot accorded a central place to distance.[9] He also attributed a prominent role to the human corpse, which, he claimed, operates as the image's inextricable foil. Corpses, with their tendency toward leaky decomposition that renders a once living body unrecognizable, seem to demand a prompt social response. They also mark the very spots where death has transpired. For Blanchot, they are exemplar of an unruly base materiality—unruly because it subverts idealism, which, he contended, not only structures categorical thinking but provides a commonplace version of the image as that which transparently grasps things and events in order to return them as mere form, a point I will return to shortly. For now perhaps it suffices to note that in the anthropological literature on death,[10] including contexts of war,[11] how closely incorporeal forms, whether rendered as souls, evil spirits, or benevolent ancestors, correspond with transformations in the base materiality of corpses.

The modern history of the Huallaga has profound connections with bad death—due in part to how insurgent and counterinsurgent forces drew political boundaries through the creation and display of mutilated human remains. Elsewhere I have explored how corpses, thanks to their ability to mark off and animate visceral limits to the human, can become a material force in contesting but also reaffirming political order.[12] In the Upper Huallaga the strategic use of human corpses introduced spatial interdictions, which altered the sensorial charge and perception of specific locales. In so doing they transformed everyday socialities—recrafting shared notions about who could move safely across the region and how.

What I have not previously considered is the degree to which maintaining those prohibitions depended upon a specific "visual economy"—in the sense Deborah Poole has employed the term to describe the systematicity with which images are produced, circulate, and gather value.[13] War here brought with it a particular economy of vision—one that generated images powerful enough to stop *some* people in their tracks or to persuade them to forgo plans to travel. Operating as if at a remove, and yet always rushing in from across a palpable expanse to land blows with the viscerality of a bodily contact, these images were—to borrow Kathleen Stewart's fortuitous phrasing—"arresting" through the various ways they seized, battered, and jammed "the senses with a negating, yet mesmerizing, force."[14] In the Huallaga at war the senses could often get battered and jammed, and yet the negating force of prohibitions on movement did not impose a simple "no." They added obstacles that reconfigured the terrain: akin to how field fortifications complicate an enemy's approach, heightening trepidations and bodily risks.

Images that announced spatial interdictions frequently had the material residues of bad death as their ultimate, if not explicit, referent.[15] Significantly, those images circulated *without* the aid of photographic technologies. Throughout the 1980s and 1990s, while photography was not expressly forbidden, an atmosphere of heightened threat enveloped the practice of taking snapshots. Not only was the sight of cameras uncommon, but the region was inhospitable for journalists. As a result, prior to the mid-1990s, photographic representations of war—as it specifically transpired there—seldom found their way into the national public sphere.[16] Conversely, within the confines of the valley, scenes of the conflict and related local happenings traveled widely, *not* along photographic or video registers but through rumor and stories shared quietly, withdrawn from public scrutiny. There, a rich image world unfurled to inform and inflect everyday good sense about permissible movements, while also animating contemporary and retrospective accounts of the events of the war.[17]

In the visual economy of that other time, spatial interdictions constrained photographs. One of the most striking and exhausting aspects of my early fieldwork (mid- to late 1990s) was the intense surveillance of public places: town squares, river crossings, and any point where rural roads merged with the region's lone trunk highway. Except for highly choreographed occasions where people wanted keepsake photographs—such as *quinceañera* parties or school parade competitions—visually representing public surroundings seemed ill-advised. Which is to say that beyond scripted, ceremonial events, I felt those constraints less as an outright ban than as a heavy unease about the advisability of using a camera. I still took many pictures, more than I would later recall. Constraints materialized instead through discomfiting pressures that less deterred than shaped the select moments, places, and subjects I felt I could photograph. In retrospect, those limitations seem symptomatic of local, historically specific territorializing practices, which impinged not only on the possibilities of visual representation but on perceiving, and taking in, the broader setting of the Huallaga's natural historical landscapes.

No doubt "territory is a way of seeing," as Andrea Brighenti persuasively suggests,[18] presupposing bodies that sense as they pass through lived terrains continually *coming to terms* with others. "Coming to terms" entails crafting affectively charged distances. Sometimes those distances are called "critical," as Gilles Deleuze and Felix Guattari do when they assert that territory is fashioned by drawing separations that become decisive, tensed, hazardous, and, as such, sensorially packed.[19] Sometimes instead those separations are considered *meaningful*, as Nancy Munn does, when she underscores that territory happens through processes of selection and elaboration in a "corporeal-sensual field of *significant* distances stretching out from the body in a particular stance or action at a given locale or as it moves through locales."[20] Either way territories emerge through bodily movements, bearings, and intimations.[21] Here: remaining in place with expressive gestures that mark off domains—"Don't anybody touch me; I growl if anyone enters my territory."[22] There: actively seeking out encounters or else avoiding them altogether with detours that as Munn says, "carve out a negative space."[23]

The distances and blockages that make territory unfold in perception, which never ceases to be perspectival. They appear through what tingles and brushes up against the skin. They manifest as sounds and odors drifting in from afar. They rise up as dense fields of force to repel and redirect glances. And yet, because contemporaneous to the political time of local states of affairs, territoriality spreads as a sensorial insistence—shaping degrees of alertness, soliciting specific postures, informing preparations for movement. As territory unfolds through perception, imagination is also where it takes root:[24] not abstractly but situated—historically and so-cially—in concrete relations and routines that form places through the im-ages they introduce into otherwise unbounded geographies. Accordingly, territories, as artful framings of the terrains that exceed them and can never be fully contained by them,[25] converge with image in the problem of distance, which becomes plural as the past enters into ever-new prox-imities with the present. For territories have afterlives, which hover in and around their former terrains as a *semblance*—sometimes felt, inter-mittently glimpsed, and even more rarely grasped.

other times

The ferryman in his red cap seems to seek more than passing conversation. For without prompting he mentions the violence of another era. Raising his arms to animate the scene, he recalls how explosions resounded—one, two, three: his right hand slapping briskly at the air—during Sendero's attacks on Nuevo Progreso. Then, just as quick, arms drop back to their side, as he switches to his own history and the many things he has seen and done. After all, he's been working as a boat operator since the 1960s. Well before the completion of the valley's first and only trunk road, he braved the river's tricky currents from Tocache to Aucayacu, sometimes as far south as La Roca. He shares too that he has three children now all grown—brimming with pride about the one who received a university degree. In the midst of telling me how that son landed a job at a credit as-sociation in an upriver town, it suddenly dawns on him that the place he has stationed his canoe is blocking the entrance of other ferrymen.

Worried he'll be a hindrance to the next botero wanting to unload onto the shore, he asks me to wait as he resituates his craft. Over there, he says, motioning to a spot several yards away, we can talk until it's his turn to take on passengers. In this way, I discern how, through mi-nor imperatives of proper boat positioning and through the schedule of turns that each operator should follow, ferrymen endow the river's edge with their own guidelines and routines—a scheme that reigns here today, where at other times, there were other coordinates and other rules, if of a wholly different magnitude.

The vadero hurries to dislodge the boat. I step back to give him space and pull out my camera to film his maneuver. I observe how he pushes at the bank with a long pole. Unsuccessful on first try, he gets out and the wood pole becomes a lever with which to pry his craft from the clutches of damp earth and restore it to the buoyant waters. As I record this man fluidly coordinate the movement of jumping back into the boat with the pole as his sole support, I admire his skill. And I wonder too how many of such small abilities are required not merely to survive but to eloquently traverse the precarities of his world? Dropping the pole on a long bench inside his craft, the man turns to the outboard motor and with a single pull *sets it humming*. The motor's force throws the boat forward. Its operator steers the craft upriver, momentarily tracing a small arc in the water and in so doing displaying the prolonged, narrow profile of the boat and, as its backdrop, the town of Progreso below a thick mat of clouds. This panoramic view unfolds by following the botero with the camera—until he parks his craft on the other side of someone else's canoe.

Later, upon looking at the film I made of this moment, I am impressed by how it manages to convey the crude appearances of these two craft: one made of soldered sheets of corrugated metal, the other fashioned from a thick trunk of tornillo (*Cedreinga catenaeformis*).[26] Not only do they express different construction techniques, but their materials carry the marks of their own temporal trajectories. If human gestures at this river crossing express changes in political climate, the iron and wood with which these boats are assembled affirm historical durations that persist without disclosing the events that left their traces upon them. And yet as mute witnesses to a history that cannot be directly read from them, they provoke in me the specter of their own passing—when government-promised bridges refigure this riverine landscape, effacing the material traces that now show but do not speak. For those bridges, before they arrive, and even if they never do, already announce an overcoming of the last significant barrier to making the Huallaga Valley a territory accessible from afar.[27]

In that regard "sensing" in this place with the social life that accrues to it *now* cannot be separated from image making—that is, from the figments the act of reading sensations provokes—raising in turn the question of where and how matter and sensation meet image: the very crux or problem of empiricism. But that also raises again the even more basic issue of what an image is *after all*. Here "image" covers a collection of things that are heterogeneous and, therefore, do not arise in the same fashion. And yet, since ethnographically they have become available and insisted in ways that I would not know how to name otherwise, I take their insistence seriously. *Image* as I use it arguably operates as a "badly analyzed composite"; it "arbitrarily groups things that differ in kind."[28] Ethnography, however, to the extent it relies on empirical encounters has little choice but to begin with composites poorly construed and for which more rigorous analysis awaits. My purpose is precisely to tease out how distinct sorts of images from fieldwork may vary with regard to distance, which is but one domain along which their own heterogeneity manifests and takes shape. So while I am aware that the sense and reference of the word *image* is not stable in anthropology,[29] much less uniform across other disciplines of study,[30] Blanchot's formulations resonate strongly with my own fieldwork experiences in ways that I can now describe.

the retrieve

Every image—if I can follow the sense Blanchot gave the concept—enters into a vital relation with what he referred to as a "fundamental" or unformed materiality.[31] And images hold that relation to the extent they appear to be "form without matter."[32] Or at least in one of their "versions," images are what exclude all materiality in order to conjure it back *as departed*. This is to say, for Blanchot, the image "continues to affirm things in their disappearance,"[33] offering up not an absent thing but the thing-as-absent.[34] In so doing, image produces distance. It marks off a limit at "the edge of the indefinite"—"that less than nothing that subsists when there is nothing"—thereby converting the absence of the disappeared thing into an interval.[35] But that is not all: "sometimes" the image creates an impression of control over what now stretches between—whenever it "speaks of the world" with a view toward utility and in an attempt to anchor the real.

Blanchot called this operation the image's "gratifying aspect" because it permits the fictitious, yet agreeable luxury of appreciating from a safe remove while simultaneously protecting the act of gazing from the "blind pressure" of distance.[36] Here, it is worth mentioning that a contemplation spared from the excessive disturbance, or disorienting noise, of distance itself could be construed as a basic attribute of spatial interdictions.

"Sometimes," Blanchot stressed, image is what follows from perception, from lived encounters—therein its relevance for ethnography. One paragraph from his text is especially revealing and deserves citing at length: "According to the ordinary analysis, the image is secondary to the object. It is what follows. We see, then we imagine. After the object comes the image."[37] Here Blanchot might well have been referring to empiricism, though note how the passage unfolds: "'After' means that the thing must first take itself off a ways in order to be grasped. But this remove is not the simple displacement of a moveable object which would nevertheless remain the same. Here the *distance is in the heart of the thing.* The thing was there; we grasped it in the vital movement of a comprehensive action—and lo, having become image, instantly it has become that which no one can grasp, the unreal, the impossible. It is not the same thing at a distance but the thing as distance . . . the return of what does not come back."[38]

His text continues, but I stop here to underscore that this analysis, or commonsense "version," of the image presupposes an empirical perspective turned toward an ever-passing present and toward what will soon, if not already, be past. In other words, this version assumes the same perceptual stance as ethnographic documentation—even where ethnography has as its chosen task to register the emergent. Rooted in empirical encounters, ethnography unavoidably draws its material from the formerly present, which is precisely "what does not come back" except (perhaps) as image.

In a manner of speaking, since the mid-1990s when I began my fieldwork, *images*, if that word can be given the broadest of scopes, are what I have gathered. The most notable stemmed from singular impressions produced by the events, lived or dreamed, of direct personal experience: my own, certainly, but more important, those conveyed by others. But images would also appear as verbal motifs recurring in the episodes of

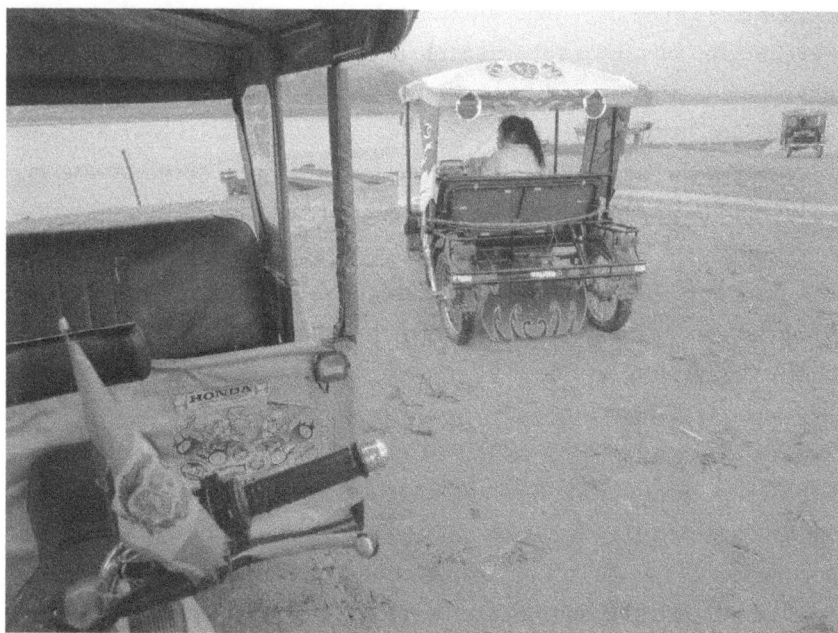

FIGURE 6.4. the wait: mototaxis

local history as residents narrated them to me. Or they might be the photographs I took—at first in 35mm film with an old manual SLR and, more recently, with digital cameras: each with their own divergent implications for the temporalities, creative potentials, and predicaments of fieldwork encounters. From the early photographs I scarcely attempted to write. Not so with verbal and perceptual images—which I prized for their power to linger and even haunt, so much so they became the spark and inspiration for almost every word I rendered.

If the temporalities of ethnographic encounters may be said to coincide with those immanent to photography, perhaps they do so in at least one respect: both link up lived, historical moments, which have quickly moved into the past, with future efforts of retrospective scrutiny. Those efforts may inform, but they can also unsettle as when something minor unexpectedly appears that impels the viewer beyond the frame. "Punctum" was what Roland Barthes called the unforeseen forcing exerted by a photographic detail that became somehow discomfiting, all the while demonstrating a certain "power of expansion."[39] Encounters of ethnographic fieldwork and of photography potentially share a similar power to amplify across time—permitting retroactive appraisals even as they reaffirm distance through the guise of bringing close what has already departed.

Barthes observed as well that what a photograph gives is the assurance of a "that-has-been." While images in general enable the reemergence of what does not or cannot return, photography adds a verifying stamp: it assures that what appears in the frame is a trace of something actually once there. Unassailable historical *proof* of a prior encounter was, for Barthes, photography's magic and what distinguished it from all previous image-making techniques.[40] Extending that probatory promise to ethnographic fieldwork was one hope of early modern anthropology. The first anthropologists who attempted to do so would discover there were severe limitations to the truth values photography might reliably produce.[41] Yet for an ethnographic practice invested not in verification per se (even less in a positivistic collecting of "facts") and instead in the potential of images to animate writing, fieldwork photographs can open up other possibilities. They can acutely foreground the material, sensorial, and temporal dimensions that infuse ethnographic encounters,[42] even as they mark off distance from them.[43] They can orient questions too, asking what insists from the past that was not visible before? Or else: What new intervals can photographs now draw in ways that differ from those that unfold from other sorts of images?[44]

One might also wonder if dwelling on photography's material constraints—its strict "co-natural" adhesion to a physical referent[45]—could awaken prospects less for reversing than *de-ordinating* the empirical encounter-image relation so that the image (now in a different version) might precede or hover behind things. So that events themselves, as Blanchot suggested, might be lived *as image*: if not sweeping one up in what he called an "undetermined milieu of fascination," then at least rendering what is taken for "the real," increasingly expansive and porous.[46] For that to happen, the anchorage points of sequential time would have to loosen and begin to slide, no longer moving in a unidirectional arrow but overlapping to become more obviously material and more undeniably topographic.

Profound shifts in the Huallaga's political states of affairs have pushed me to ask how verbal, perceptual, and dreamy images from earlier stints of fieldwork could be coupled with the rural transit scenes I have documented in recent years through photography and video recordings: scenes originating in and belonging to very different ethnographic presents of postwar. Above all, I am intrigued by the generative capacity of these contemporary transit pictures to direct attention not solely to what appears *within* the borders of the image but also to what invests, escapes, or even hovers behind the explicit visuality delimited by the frame. In the era of postconflict, what exceeds and does not immediately appear in the frame can become tangibly patent.[47] The absence of what once dominated everyday concerns is felt. I have felt it, even as dreadful images circulate occasionally still, in musings and stories shared from those other times.

Certainly from the point of view of ethnographic writing, I continually find myself *situated* in the "aftermath" Blanchot describes. I find myself "affirm[ing] things in their disappearance," ever attentive to "the return of what does not come back," always contending with distinct manifestations of distance—even when those distances do not orient my gaze toward the past. What I recognize too, what surprises me, nonetheless, is that the different images I accumulated have always been, or at least until recently, affected by, and even entangled with, the interdictions that previously animated rural areas. All the more striking is the possibility that those images in their various forms became enmeshed with territory *on account of the image-making qualities of prohibitions themselves* as well as the power of those same prohibitions to captivate the minds of those they have claimed. For while legal phenomena operate across multiple registers, one understudied domain where they intervene and work is the imagination, especially where it blurs with sensibility and turns visceral. This is perhaps why *the Law*—if always a social production and as such "for all"—exists singularly for each and every one, but most pressingly at moments when existential decisions must be mulled about how to respond best to the barriers prohibitions impose.

My focus is thus less on how images themselves circulate than on how they intervene territorially and thereby "move" in an intransitive sense[48]—through their reception and in ways that inflect the mobility and immobility of people and their things. Though I have chosen to examine the Huallaga as one critical site that became infused with spatial interdictions during prior times of political violence, the river was hardly the only such locale. There were certain hamlets on either side whose names seemed to inspire an incomparable sense of unease among those who lived in the valley but who did not specifically dwell in those places. "Árabe," "Santa Marta," "Culebra," "Alto Pacae," "Paraíso," but many others as well, resounded images of extreme danger. Simply saying them aloud could provoke a shudder. They also became a dark content that spread dread or haunted the silent dreamy musings of town dwellers, when some pressing errand forced them travel. And yet their notoriety was not invariable: names of places to where one should never go continually changed, varying with the circumstances and territorial distributions of the insurgent-counterinsurgent war.

receding thunder

His craft resituated a little farther down the shore, the ferryman invites me aboard, offering a seat near the prow, which points inland now toward a small road leading toward Paraíso, the main settlement on this side of the river. Not long ago its residents renamed their community "Nuevo Paraíso," expressing in this way a collective desire to mark a separation from events that once made their village notorious. The people living there today say they are all newcomers, that those who resided during the times of violence are no more. From that other era, they insist, hardly anyone remains.

Throughout the 1980s, Paraíso was an enclave of the illicit drug trade with several local landing strips where dollars, from Colombia, and cocaine base, from the Huallaga, regularly changed hands. In that era Paraíso joined the towns of Uchiza and Tocache to form a territorial triangle, interconnecting the three most significant markets for cocaine transactions—all within what was then the largest coca-growing zone of the country (if not the world). It was another era when the ferrymen of Progreso plied the river's currents in speedboats, conveying passengers with small briefcases of cash always in a hurry to cross to the other side or to be taken on longer trips up- and downstream.

It was another time when the *gatilleros* (triggermen) guarded the port of Megote—the place where the river met the unpaved road to Paraíso. They awaited all who attempted to enter the village, letting the well-known pass but stopping anyone unfamiliar, threatening to leave them then and there without life. Indeed, the ferrymen now make this point with a laugh, saying that if I had dared to cross the river back then, *los gatilleros me hubieran dejado como abono* (that with my body they would have fertilized the ground). *He-he.* On strangers pressed the peril of sudden transformation into corpse—but only for those with no one from the place to vouch for them. This is to say that what made one unwelcome was not the fact of being from somewhere else, which was already the condition of most everyone who came to Paraíso: the *mafiosos* of the cocaine trade (Peruvian, Colombian, and Brazilian); the youthful male and female combatants who appeared whenever a large senderista guerrilla column came through; young women from all over Peru who worked in the bars, discos, and brothels that, for a time, gave rural Paraíso an unmistakable urban feel. Even residents who had preceded the prosperous times of cocaine were themselves migrants with at most ten years living in the hamlet. The critical point was less one's provenance than the relations that could be counted on there, and in a pinch.

The gatilleros, however, did not last. When the epicenter of the cocaine economy fragmented toward the end of the decade and the bulk of the trade moved north, east, and south, they followed. What remained in Paraíso was the political control of Sendero, and on account of that, one former resident once told me, for most of the 1990s the village and nearby hamlets were condemned to a miserable silence.

But in 2013—I am told Paraíso has become "Nuevo," that its community now projects toward horizons not only different but distinctly auspicious. Meanwhile, from here, the port of Megote is no longer visible. With the passage of time the river has altered its course, pulling these shores toward Progreso, leaving Megote ever more distant from its waters. Now in this place it is mototaxi drivers who await anyone wishing to enter Paraíso, and these days *entrar* communicates none of the heightened charge—rousing, oppressive—it carried in years past.

Here and now: at the base of the road an open wall shelter awaits. Inside this kiosk fashioned with timber and bamboo poles, palm leaves, and plastic sheeting, a woman sells food and drink. Mototaxi operators gather there between shifts and during the occasional thundershower to talk, make jokes, grab something to eat. A whiteboard hangs at eye level, listing names and nicknames of drivers according to their positions in the queue. What's novel too is that everyone has a cell phone: travelers, transportistas, the woman who tends to her stand.

If building new roads and bridges could ever safeguard the region from a future resurgence of Sendero—as the infrastructural rhetoric of the national government widely proclaims—people who live and work in the countryside insist cell phones are what really have made a difference. Never again can the guerrilla show up at one of the area hamlets to gather villagers for a meeting or to carry out an execution. Someone would promptly tip off the police. Yet no one mentions that many cell phones can take pictures, and the widespread introduction of that capability seems a no less crucial factor. So much so that to move about rural areas with a camera feels surprisingly relaxed. The absence of that weight is as astonishing as it is new.

During the years of the conflict, crossing from one bank to the other inevitably triggered questions about intentions, allegiances. Now those times have chronologically receded. Evidence of their demise is sensed in the absence of explicit prohibitions that once encumbered everyday passage. It is also demonstrated in the extension of state space into previously remote expanses on both sides of the river, not only through transportation works and telecommunications but land titling, health clinics, and the occasional police station—as if new infrastructures provided a ready strategy for postwar forgetting. Rural roads, moreover, have become *public* in a new yet most particular sense: for most strangers it has become feasible to travel upon them without taking precautions. Precisely for those from other places, who have no ties to the cocaine trade or to the insurgency, passage in the Huallaga countryside has become *thinkable*, whereas before it gave rise to trepidation and distress.

glass of water

In the late 1990s I often traveled between towns along the valley's main trunk highway, on public transportation and then on motorbike. Local friends warned me to take special care when veering off onto trails leading to outlying hamlets. Unless accompanied by someone from the specific village I wished to visit, they said I should stay out of rural areas. As an agrarian region, the Huallaga countryside loomed large over the towns: there, turned away from the highway, coca fields covered hillsides with maceration pits hidden nearby; there, Sendero had its local origins, organizationally persisting into the present day. But here I was told to stick to the road, to keep myself at a distance, which meant missing out precisely on places that seemed most relevant. Few locales *at that time* mixed historical significance with politically remoteness quite so intensely as Paraíso—such was its storied life.[49] But I did not know anyone there, and to show up on my own would have been at least unwise, if not a hazardous thing to do.

Traveling the highway by motorbike, I always carried a camera in my bags. I would pull it out only if I stopped along an unpopulated stretch of road because, before actually using the camera, risk accrued to being seen with it: at the sight of the camera people might conclude I was a snitch. Fear made taking pictures incredibly awkward—as if an air of imprudence, less spoken than presupposed, infused that simple act. And these were already times of diminished danger.

For although the Upper Huallaga had been one of the final fronts of the armed conflict, by the late 1990s the era of extreme violence had waned. Militarily, Shining Path had suffered an unequivocal defeat and in that regard the war was "over." Yet violence stemming from the conflict had not altogether stopped. The insurgency—though rag-tag and but a faint shadow of its former strength—remained active, ambushing government patrols on occasion and halting traffic on the main road. Even well into the new decade, Sendero would continue to wield a palpable influence and sometimes direct control in patches and pockets of the countryside—nowhere more than on the left bank of the river below Paraíso. Though shrinking with every passing year, the insurgency would take final refuge in an ever-dwindling number of left bank communities, until it all (seemingly) ended with the arrest of Artemio—the Huallaga faction's leader—in early 2012.

Ten years before that pivotal capture, in 2002, I had my first chance to visit Paraíso when I returned to the Upper Huallaga as a researcher and consultant with the Peruvian Truth and Reconciliation Commission. I traveled to Paraíso with two journalists and residents of Tocache who were intent on shooting a short video exposé on the arrival of "peace" to the village. Through them I met the local mayor and thus was able to visit a couple of times more that year. The commission had asked me to gather local accounts of the war. The mayor kindly narrated the village's history in broad outlines punctuated by major events of the conflict. It felt scripted, and all of the main characters had long since departed.[50] Finding anyone who admitted to having lived through those decisive events proved exceedingly difficult. In fact, beyond the mayor and his family, few longtime residents said much of anything in public. Polite but firm: they would not be seen talking at length about events that had nourished Paraíso's dark fame. Their reticence was familiar—not unlike what I had experienced in Huallaga towns, where at least secluded spaces could be found. But here in the hamlet itself, there was nowhere to speak without feeling intensely watched and heard.

Much of what I learned about Paraíso that year was shared by former residents who spoke with me not in the village but in nearby towns: Nuevo Progreso and Tocache. One was a teacher who had moved to Paraíso in the 1990s to work at the village's primary school. The ostentatious mafias were already gone by then, and in their wake Paraíso, she said, had become a desert. She described what happened the day she arrived for her new job. From her hometown of Tocache she traveled early one morning with her infant daughter by car to the port of Nuevo Progreso. A boat ferried them across the river, but when they stepped off at Puerto Megote, she discovered there was no motorized transport to Paraíso, so they had to proceed on foot: beneath the hot midday sun, carrying her daughter, and lugging a tote bag with their clothes.

Scattered along that dirt road, small wood-slat dwellings appeared, here and there, but with front doors and windows tightly shut. Whenever she approached a dwelling to ask how far they still had go for Paraíso, anyone who answered claimed not to know. And when she pleaded for a glass of water to quench her baby's thirst, they replied they had none to share—a rejection that left her feeling anxious and, more than that, perplexed.

After a brutal hour and a half and with her baby daughter dehydrated and hungry, the teacher finally reached Paraíso, but only to discover that no one would come forth to welcome them, much less offer assistance. Instead, she found that the villagers kept their distance, gazing at the newly arrived with an uncommon distrust. Their reticence to extend even the most basic hospitality stunned her, and that shock felt like the hook of her story, as she told it to me, a shudder reverberating through the image of the glass of water refused. She had entered a realm where she had no moral entitlements. There, she and her daughter would be no one's guests, underscoring an old anthropological insight that the laws of hospitality are often but "the reciprocal of the laws of strangerhood."[51] However, the image itself was what carried the affective charge of rejection. It did so by bringing to the fore an intersection of matter and sensation—whether the burning rays of the sun, whether dry mouths and exhausted limbs, or whether the longed-for materials that might provide satisfaction to an infant girl's fragile body and to her mother's own peace of mind.

In those years simply traveling to rural communities on the Huallaga's left bank could incite extreme suspicion. If one did not have previous ties to lean on, even places geographically close could feel unfathomably remote. Hard glares accompanied a stranger's arrival, but those looks were but preamble to the grilling that might then follow: Why have you entered? Who are you seeking? Who can vouch for you? About unknown persons hovered cutting questions, all ultimately distilled to a single one: ¿No será soplón?

Rural schoolteachers were prototypical strangers in the sense they came not only from elsewhere but often from the city and hence were accustomed to the lifeways of urban places. And one complaint I heard was that the Ministry of Education had regularly sent them to Shining Path areas of the Huallaga countryside—as if there, no war were ongoing—and where on account of their condition as employees of the Peruvian state, and thus as ostensible agents of the insurgency's sworn enemy, suspicions could accrue to them all the more. Perhaps that fear was overblown, considering that elsewhere Sendero had treated the public education system as a privileged field for clandestine recruitment and political indoctrination—not only in universities but in primary and secondary schools too, where they found support among some teachers, especially in the southern Andes.[52] In retrospect and from a later, wholly different political time, perhaps it was better not to say anything that might reveal one's prior sympathies for an insurgency now defeated. And yet back then, infiltration went both ways: lands on the left bank opposite Nuevo Progreso were a Shining Path domain, at a moment when in the Huallaga getting killed for "just showing up" was more than mere refrain. Given those circumstances, would it have crossed the schoolteacher's mind to pack a camera in her tote, much less pull it out for all to see?

fragile claims

In the history of the Upper Huallaga, expressions of territory have been intimately linked to the entrance, incorporation, and expulsion of outsiders—a condition inseparable from the region's overlapping constitution as a zone of internal migration and a state frontier. As a migratory destination, throughout the twentieth century Peruvians from other parts of the country have continually arrived seeking work and, at least temporary, residence. As a state frontier, the region has provided cover for various illegalities, among them, an illicit cocaine trade (1950–the present), a Maoist insurrection (1980–2012), and the extrajudicial ways the Peruvian Armed Forces and police have interacted with them. Since each of these activities depended on secrecy, but also on sustained relations with centers of power situated outside the region, during the tensed era of the war, how to receive and respond to strangers became a critical question that vexed everyday life. Indeed, a prohibition on snitches, widespread then, revolved around how to distinguish between friend and enemy, which entailed too how to sort through so many potentials for disguise. This was the predicament strangers heightened: dangerous, because they represented an unknown,[53] and within that unknown the possibility of hostile intentions.[54]

As a routinized episode, the spectacular killing of informers engendered images—captivating and repellent—that marked off local terrains by announcing a limit event in the personal destinies of those so accused. Stories that relayed those images, whether as news or as common sense repeated in the years to come, often began with the arrival of a stranger. The images did the work of keeping people away. Those who chose to disregard those images by entering areas where no one knew them were put on notice all the same.

If the stranger, as Meyer Fortes insisted, is at root a jural-political category,[55] then the reception and treatment of strangers are an important site for tracking modifications in political time. As political situations change, then so too must relations of sociality that modulate stranger status. Who can be received as guest? Who must be turned away? In these questions, strangerhood is inseparable from the decisions demanded by hospitality. They are also where the roles of host and guest take on a territorial dimension[56]—at that point where place and law concretely intertwine in quotidian life. Today the countryside is where I can easily travel, which also means it has become far less permeable and welcoming to strangers of other kinds and other social features, who for now are far more effectively proscribed and surveilled by the Peruvian state (i.e., those working with and for Shining Path or those overly careless about their own involvement in the cocaine trade). This current state of affairs is what schematically defines the Upper Huallaga as a postwar landscape—where suddenly there is an abundance and wide circulation of cell phones and other small, personal audiovisual recording devices.

In the early 1990s, however, and in the decade before it, the suspicion that greeted schoolteachers in some rural areas could be overwhelming. At least at first. For despite her unwelcome reception, the teacher, whom I later met and spoke with in Tocache, persevered, making a place for herself and her daughter that endured nearly eight years—for Paraíso, not the most notorious stretch of the war, but certainly one of the worst. During that stretch, she was not the only teacher to arrive. Some came and promptly abandoned their posts. Others left just as soon as their first contract was up. A select few stayed on as permanent appointees: among them, a man I met there in 2012.

The extended story of how he ended up moving to the area, thanks to his unexpected assignment to a tiny hamlet just past the port of Megote on the road to Paraíso, can take hours to tell. The first version he shared with me is quite compact, and that is the one I repeat here. The year was 1992, and living in northern Peru at that time, he did not yet know anything about the place. But to get there, he had to reach the other side of the river, which is what brought him to Nuevo Progreso. People at the town's port, upon seeing he was not only a stranger but preparing to cross, urged, even begged him: Do *not* go to Paraíso. *Ahí te van a matar.* They will kill you. But he refused to turn back; he had come so far and instead boarded a small canoe over to the left bank. After a short walk along the dirt road he found the hamlet and immediately went to the schoolhouse, where parents of his future students greeted him warmly with none of the mistrust that the other teacher had experienced along this same road only two years before.[57] The problem he would soon confront was another: by taking up residence in the village, he fell under the watchful gaze of Sendero—which, when speaking with me, he would always categorically separate from the local population. The insurgency, he said, suspected he was not a teacher. Though he had grown up in the coastal city of Trujillo, from his facial features—hazel eyes framed by a light-colored complexion—they doubted he was Peruvian. And to them, his tall, thick build seemed far more suitable for a different sort of occupation. Because of their suspicions, a threat hovered very near. Two weeks later they offered a demonstration of the actual risks he faced.

It was Mother's Day, and to celebrate, the school threw an evening party for the students and their families. People really got caught up in the fun, he said, between the music and the dancing, the food and drinks going round, when someone noticed that an armed group of young men and women had circled the schoolhouse. At first the group held their distance and merely watched over the celebration without moving closer. One of the parents pulled him aside and said not to worry: *no pasará nada*, nothing would come of it. So like everyone else, he just kept dancing, until the armed group moved in, turned off the music, and announced to all present that they were needed to conduct a juicio popular—a people's trial.

Only then did the teacher realize the senderistas had a prisoner: a man with his hands tied behind his back and whom he recognized as the father of four children who attended the school. The senderistas accused the man of being a soplón. His crime? Having crossed the river to Nuevo Progreso and supposedly informed the army about the insurgency's activities. The wife of the accused and his four children were there as well, having arrived earlier that evening for the celebration. Now, they implored, through streaming tears: *please*, do not kill him. The accused also implored, insisting the charges were false—but the senderistas held firm: his only hope was to acknowledge what he had done. The Party was understanding. If he confessed, they would release him, under the condition he leave the community that night and never return.

Hearing this, the man confessed to what he had not done, figuring it was his only out. He then asked that they pardon him, but the senderistas refused. Snitching, they said, was an unforgivable offense. Then they shot him in the head. The impact of the bullet sent flesh and blood flying in every direction, small bits of the man's head hitting people close and far, some splattering, the teacher said, across one of his trouser legs. A dead silence followed until the insurgents turned the music back on and ordered everyone to dance. And so they danced, as the senderistas watched, and they danced as the senderistas withdrew, and they kept on dancing a little while longer until the danger seemed to have passed. The gathering then broke up, and everyone, visibly shaken, retired to their homes for the night.

Although this appalling episode had happened years ago, the teacher insisted that his memories of it were as clear as if no time had passed. Stories of juicios populares populate many local renderings of the war in the Upper Huallaga and in other regions of Peru. Yet here, in his own account, what condensed the terrible event—*for me*, and at that moment his audience of one—was the image of his trouser leg. In an instant, and in the most crude of ways, a gunshot had connected his own life trajectory with that of a man whose personal destiny had come to a stop, when suspicions of having passed information—from one side of the river to the other—had thickened from accusation to full confession.

But what struck me most was *where* he conveyed this episode that shared key features with so many others from the war. The place was the village of Paraíso late one afternoon, a moment when we were but recent acquaintances. Seeing me walking up the outdoor staircase of a lodging house, where I rented a room just off the main road, the teacher pulled up on a motorbike and called out. I met him at the base of the stairs, and there we convened for a brief conversation in which he confided what I would have never expected right then and there. The night before he had attended a meeting of the town's road maintenance committee, where the mayor had introduced me and given me a chance to talk about my interest in the region's history through the lens of rural transportation. Now, finding me again a mere stone's throw from the street, the schoolteacher assured he had much to tell.

Ten years before no one in the village had dared to share anything of the sort. A year later, and a full year after the teacher disclosed this clear, most enduring memory, I would learn that such stories could now be openly told, even out on the banks of the river.

One basic effect of the earlier prohibitions on snitching was to limit who could enter but also leave the countryside—and in some cases Huallaga towns. To the extent those limits conditioned people's movements, they formed part of the spatial interdictions that imbued the valley's physical terrains and that asserted visceral pressures on the imagination. Spatial interdictions communicated grim images for thought: they *worked* by transmitting and interposing shared schemas of distance, which warded off encounters. While emerging from diverse, concrete practices that were hardly restricted to killing events but drew on their threat nonetheless—such as checkpoints and roadblocks, nighttime curfews imposed by the Peruvian Army in the towns, or the notebook ledgers local Sendero leaders used to document, monitor, and control the movements of hamlet residents—the intensity of interdictions was such that the idea of transgressing them could induce nightmares, vertigo, and over time profound fatigue. In this manner they touched mental life in ways that oriented behavior and became an implicit presupposition of everyday routines in rural areas and in the towns they surrounded.

Images of violent death animated spatial interdictions. They precipitated a heavy sense of foreboding as well as positive acts of avoidance. They discouraged practices of visual reproduction as well. Where those images halted, postponed, or at least inflected the movements of people, while adding a palpable burden to them, they were almost always combined with admonitions—the likes of "Do not go to Paraíso"—delivered in unequivocal tones that seemed to close off other possibilities. Though such images, and the warnings that constellated around them, were meant for some strangers, they tarried in the imaginations of nearly all. And yet here I have relayed personal accounts of two schoolteachers who were not deterred. Their tales begin with a disregard for spatial interdictions—unwittingly in the first, fully cognizant in the second. Both tales unfold through the act of recounting how an interval of terrain that prohibitions should rightly have kept intact, out of bounds, was traversed. Both stories suggest, moreover, that interdictions themselves, even those most forcefully announced, do not dispel the porosity, the ambiguity, of encounters, which, despite the probabilities that might haunt them, are and must be singular every time—and for each and every one. Therein their uncertainty, and what denies to prohibitions anything more than a frail claim to predict what will transpire.

all quiet, the disquiet

Seated before the ferryman I cannot help sensing how much the atmosphere has shifted. Other apprehensions predominate now, which the ferryman underscores by lamenting his meager earnings—a condition he blames on not having a boat of his own. Of the fares he charges, he keeps a third, so that if by day's end he has collected fifty soles, he pockets but seventeen when he heads home. The rest he hands over to his boss, who owns this craft plus another. Not always were his economic circumstances so troubled. The ferryman tells me that, during the 1980s, he had a large tract of farmland where he grew coca and dreamed of reaping a small fortune. Until one rainy season: the river's mighty currents ripped away twenty hectares, converting the remaining ten into swamp. To the loss of that tract of land, almost thirty years ago, he attributes his eventual, present fate as an impoverished ferryman—crossing, day after day, the same roaming, watery line, once laden with interdictions, now largely spent.

As he tells me this, I am reminded that prohibitions have a historicity of their own. A realization that becomes evident when I return to places where they formerly held sway, but also when in the act of writing and from a retrospective gaze, I appreciate fieldwork experiences that overlapped with that other era. In such moments, what is striking is the strong, prolonged decline in the affective intensities of spatial interdictions. At the same time, such transformations must be highly complex: not a linear deterioration but involving at minimum a refocusing on other targets. Certainly, their histories are far more entangled than I have managed to convey. Other, more precise, versions could be rendered, much like the personal histories people have shared with me.

Indeed, when I see him again, the ferryman will offer a fuller account of his own economic demise, far more elaborate than in this initial conversation. He will reveal that he lost not one parcel, but two. Where he cultivated coca was actually in the hills on the left bank and thus too high to succumb to seasonal floods. There was a second parcel, though, on the plains of the right bank—less suited for coca but ideal for plantains and rice because flat and close to the water. Both were taken from him, but by different catastrophes, one quickly followed by the next. His land on the left bank was in the hills controlled by Sendero. One day local Party leaders delivered an ultimatum. He had to choose between his parcel of coca and living in town. No longer could he do both or be allowed to travel back and forth. But when he told them he could not abandon his house in Nuevo Progreso, where his children lived and attended school, they gave his land to someone else and forbade him from returning—a simple gesture that effectively locked him out of the cocaine economy and dashed the dreams it had sustained. Then came the rains, and the swollen river stole off with the other farm.

While we talk, I take this photograph (figure 6.5) as well as several others, but soon his turn in the queue of boteros comes around. So he gives me his cell-phone number, saying I should call him to arrange a visit to his house. This agreed, I step out of the canoe. Four passengers board and find places to sit. Standing now on the shore, I hold my gaze firmly on the boat as the man in the red cap ferries back over to Nuevo Progreso.

Years before, the rural expanses of the Upper Huallaga not only seemed to have eyes, but they also repelled the gazes of many who arrived from outside. That strong rebuff, capable of arresting perception, fed on prohibitions that preoccupied travel along rural routes but also permeated names of specific hamlets in ways that made them ever so remote. One

FIGURE 6.5. the wait: between passengers

place where those prohibitions acquired an especially marked topographic expression was the Huallaga River—during the war but also bleeding as well into its immediate aftermath—another historical period to be sure. Another era too in terms of image-making technologies and their spread.

If a time of postwar entails the introduction of new everyday habits, it implies no less an extraordinary effort to separate from a (now) "former" state of affairs by pivoting collective attention toward other temporal horizons. In Peru the introduction of new infrastructures into rural areas has been treated as a self-evident means for imagining the Huallaga's future as having decisively departed from the times of conflict. And yet within that postwar imperative of turning away—formidable labor of erecting screens to block off the pressures of that past—*images* are given tasks that are different, though arguably no less vital than during the years of armed conflict.

From these shores an affective turbulence has now withdrawn. Still, a semblance of disquiet remains—perhaps to ensure that absence does not

lend itself to something all the more unsettling. Too much has surely happened for those events to simply vanish, leaving nothing of consequence
behind. All the while in the place of that former turbulence, images old
and new do circulate. Some are photographic, taken now in locales that
would not have been advisable before. Others of times past rise up from
stories or appear in dreams of day and night to hover near or even behind
everyday things, places, and encounters. Hardly seen but sometimes felt,
this semblance—surrounding, suffusing—presses in on what photographs
and videos might frame today of the terrain.

FIGURE 7.1. Madre Mía

between twilights

What happens when rustic army forts are positioned on the highest of hills to become architectural machines for the systematic capture, not only of terrain but of so many people stopped and forcibly taken inside? What happens *to* those forts once the war that called them forth is supposedly over? Do they merely enfold back into the obscure interiors of the state? Or do they linger around the lands they lorded over? And if so, what then?

This chapter reaches toward the complex histories of counterinsurgency bases in the Upper Huallaga Valley. A line drawing at best, it reflects on the resilience of the place or topos of the bases in the wake of the political, social, and territorial transformations they wrought. Across this region's rolling tropical landscape frontier outposts once appeared in an uneven, accreting movement that could be described as the material unfolding or *despliegue* of political emergency.[1] The eventual withdrawal of those same bases—their furling up or *repliegue* from the eastern slopes of the central Peruvian Andes—can likewise be read as a return to more normative times of state legality. And yet the temporalities in play here are deceptively elaborate and cannot be precisely rendered in chronological terms. It is helpful, nonetheless, to bear in mind once again that, while nationally the era of political violence is commonly said to span two decades, from 1980 to 2000, in some rural areas, especially those with historical connections to the cocaine trade, the insurgent-counterinsurgent conflict and the emergency status it conferred persisted far longer.[2]

In the Upper Huallaga, the official declaration to permanently lift the figure of legal exception did not come until 2015, at least a decade after the retracting movement of repliegue had already begun—all the while amid certain minor lateral transpositions through which, every now and then, a new base would be placed in an ever-more-remote region, previously considered undisputed territory of the guerrilla. Therein the difficulties in crafting an unmuddied chronological picture, and therein and perhaps more so my questions.

Once not pressingly visible in the landscape, have the bases simply gone, or have they merely receded from view as their effects nestle deep into the setting? This is to ask if during the folding back period of repliegue the times of the earlier despliegue persist and, if so, how? It is to ask as well about the *despliegue por venir*—about the next time and the ways it secretly animates the horizons of the aftermath. For what if that "next time" is already operating now and always was? These questions beg to be asked even if the responses seem wholly inadequate.

For when frontier forts are physically dismantled, or even if they operate still but in a reclusive mode that no longer intervenes overtly in local affairs, their wartime fury endures across multiple registers.[3] Stories of the conflict are one of those registers. In oral accounts of what happened, the bases return, this time as a rhetorical topos (which is a "doubling up" as it were of place) to preoccupy and hold critical positions. Indeed, without the bases to act as narrative location and prop, many stories of the conflict simply could not be told. Those stories are vital for offsetting the tendency to forget what actually established the *prehistoric* ground upon which everyday life and sociality would subsequently move during eras of postwar. And in turn without those stories it would be difficult to grasp exactly how that foundation came about.

This is a first, essential point.

A second is not to overlook the heavens.

Or more precise still, not to disregard that peculiar sky-ground alliance, distinguishing each and every new political situation, where the earth races out along an ever-receding horizon to meet the yonder:

where time becomes weather,

where helicopters first appear to sound off in distant thunder.

Stories run counter to a visual oblivion engendered by the repliegue itself through the shuttering of most bases and before that through the gradual cessation of daily surveillance and interruption of human movements across the valley. Visual oblivion arrives from other sources too: in a refurbished trunk highway and a vast expansion of rural roads where Shining Path once banned any kind of transit construction. These infrastructural works for mobility either efface the material traces of the war or reroute the itineraries of people away from sites where events of its violence had transpired. The repopulation of the countryside has also facilitated the quiet withdrawal of the bases—where "new people" now live who can claim to know nothing of what happened before. Among them are older residents who have learned how in their return to the land to be no less recent, no less contemporary, by carefully camouflaging earlier political sympathies and affiliations. Like any other political time, postconflict brings its own imperatives, and foremost is the demand that some must continually perform the labor of blending into the surroundings—they must merge with the place, crafting a new reciprocal topography: where many a moth disappears into bark, where so many butterflies become leaves.[4]

Another point, now obvious, bears repeating: the despliegue/repliegue of counterinsurgency bases had and has a direct relation to "political emergency," which is to say, to recurring situations of legal crisis for the Peruvian state, during which relations of power between the national government and the people it rules and claims to represent become uncertain and profoundly unsettled. Thus, despliegue and repliegue designate shifts between distinct categories of political-legal time. They mark out a conceptual register of ideal situations that lord over and largely render opaque far more multiple, local events—each with their own variations of affective intensity and material encumbrance. For to unfurl and furl back again is less a simple switch than a massive reorientation. Considering what the bases made possible, could they now *not haunt* the lands and populations they once recast? If so, where is that haunting and how do its traces manifest?

Though the war has ended, it is hardly over. Here I follow counterinsurgency bases from the prior era of despliegue through the entanglements of a specific thread. I reflect on the sorts of encounters army forts prompted for local transportistas—drivers of cars and operators of canoes—as they conveyed passengers on roads and rivers of the Upper Huallaga: transportistas who later shared their accounts with me. I weave their stories with reflections from my own experiences of the region, early on with the bases still pressing firmly on the social routines and atmospheres of ordinary life and then later with their near disappearance: a series of fieldwork visits and stays since the mid-1990s that remain for me convoluted. They are a winding constellation of temporal lines that reweave themselves retrospectively again and again into my own writing of events.

tanqueado

My reflections take a lateral entry. They begin, not with the bases, and not yet with transit operators, but with an improbable encounter in the city of Tingo María on a rainy Monday evening over twenty years ago. I had just finished dinner with Yéssica, a young woman and cocaine trader whose acquaintance I had made only a few months before. Our first meeting was in Lima and had led to a series of weekly conversations during which she revealed something of her life. Yéssica described how she, as a teenager in the Upper Huallaga town of Nuevo Progreso, learned the local ways of the drug trade before going on to become a traquetera who regularly moved cocaine from central Peru to Colombia via Iquitos. In those early conversations she also shared her own intimate knowledge of recent Huallaga history—though it was a version focused on illicit transactions and transshipments, turning on run-ins with police far more than with the army. Counterinsurgency bases barely figured in her renderings of regional history, perhaps because when the heady momentum of the cocaine trade began to abandon Tocache and Uchiza in the late 1980s, she followed it to Aguaytía, which is to say, Yéssica left the Upper Huallaga as the army was unfurling its bases across the land.[5]

Now in Tingo María our paths were overlapping much closer to her actual place of work. With Yéssica everything was secretive, always touch and go—our plans for dinner seemed off until three and a half hours later, and after many calls from a street payphone, she answered her cell: finally free, she promised to swing around to pick me up in a mototaxi. And soon we were en route to a chifa called El Pato Donald. In Tingo Yéssica seemed different: more at ease than in Lima, far more confident, moving in a world where she knew exactly what she needed to do. Clearly, something was in the offing, but Yéssica let on nothing—except to say that our dinner that night and but a few hours early tomorrow were the only times she could spare. So over plates of arroz chaufa and a large bottle of Inca Cola, we talked of paying a morning visit to the *curandero* she would contract to protect her on her upcoming trip. Leaving the restaurant with the nighttime sky threatening another downpour, I was about to say good-bye when Yéssica said no. First, I should come to her hotel. There was someone I had to meet.

A few blocks away we walked up a flight of stairs to the reception of a hotel with the bleak air of rundown accommodations. Several doors into the main corridor Yéssica stopped at a room. The door opened and inside we found her "prima" Elisa and a young man called "Walter," whom I presumed was Yéssica's partner or someone she had hired to assist her with an impending shipment. I did not know which, and I did not ask. Yéssica introduced me as someone studying the history of the region, calling me a "writer of books"—to my surprise and embarrassment, since I had never written even one.

Turning to Walter, she said, tell him about your time in the army. And Walter complied, describing himself with a certain air of satisfaction as *ex fuerza especial*. He explained he had received his initial commando instruction in the highlands, which he later completed in Tingo María and Tarapoto before being dispatched to bases in Aucayacu, Ramal de Aspuzana, Madre Mía, and Tocache—places where the conflict with Sendero had been quite intense. Those were years, he said, when the government gave the army free rein (*carta blanca*) to do what he called its "work." Here Yéssica injected: "Noooo . . . Tell him what you *did* to the terrorists." And Walter, point blank: "We carved them up! In the sierra they gave us dogs to train with, but here they gave us terrorists. Everyone had to cut."

If Walter were really telling it straight, he would have been no raw recruit, merely biding time until his term of obligatory service expired. But it was hard going. Near impossible to hold on to your sanity, which was why he claimed that in the Huallaga there wasn't a commando who did not resort to consuming drugs. Even so, Walter let me know that as fuerza especial, they were on top of the world: head and shoulders above everyone else. Above Shining Path to be sure. Very few terrorists, maybe two or three, ever defended their principles with conviction. The majority of them sang just like that (*cantaban al toque*).

And with the narcos, Walter laughed, with them he and other commandos did whatever they liked. If they needed transportation, they would just stop a *traqueta* and tell him to hand over his motorcycle.

"Is the tank full? Go fill it up. And bring it right back!"

Later, when the commandos returned the bike, and if they ever did, the drive train would be all torn up, but the traqueta could not say a word, much less do anything about it.

Again, Yéssica interjected, but now to shut down the conversation. It was late, she said; Walter had to leave before dawn. Yéssica, as best I could tell, had wanted him to tell me how the army treated people it accused of having ties to Sendero, and Walter had done that. So, we said farewells, and I did not see him again. Our brief encounter was improbable not only because I did not seek it out but because the social relationships that made my ongoing fieldwork possible generally demanded I keep my distance from the army. And yet, the meeting with Walter was not altogether unfamiliar. It shared crucial traits with others I had had in towns and villages north of Tingo: I would meet someone barely in passing, and at the urging of a friend held in common that person would reveal a remarkable fragment of local history, only for our paths to promptly diverge and never coincide again.

Here the army's violence—the live dismembering of people they captured—was not that fragment. Walter merely confirmed what I had heard many times from others—albeit not from someone who claimed to have participated directly. No: what Walter revealed was something else—something that immediately struck me as having special significance, even if in that moment I did not know what to make of it. Never before had anyone underscored so vividly the important role that confiscating vehicles had played in the army's occupation of the region, and certainly not in a way I would not forget, which is what made our conversation feel somehow extraordinary.

la llave

Some fragments from fieldwork become images that not only linger but insist. Perhaps it was how the former soldier channeled a sense of holding overwhelming power when describing his interactions with people dedicated to the cocaine trade. Maybe it was the certain glee he expressed when telling me about how he and his commando mates would take away the very things narcos and traqueteros most cherished and flaunted—their cars and motorcycles—ordering them about, treating them with disregard, and in so doing demonstrating to them their subordinate place in a reigning local hierarchy. All these years later, this fragment—*¿Está tanqueado? Llévalo a tanquear y tráemela*—is what persists most from our ever-so-brief conversation.

I return to it now because it brings forth the territorial transformations precipitated by the arrival of counterinsurgency bases. For the power to seize mobility reveals something vital about how those bases extended their reach far beyond their own physical structures in ways that reshaped the local lived terrains of the valley. They did so not only (or perhaps not mainly) through the detention and killing of suspected insurgents but through far more widespread captures of time and movement. For during the most intense years of the unfurling it was less the *extrema*—the army's terror images and procedures[6]—than what transpired around them, and what took distance from them, that became intrinsic to everyday life in the Huallaga.

At least that is my working hunch.

The conversation with Walter provides the spark for this inquiry but only to pivot quickly away from those who worked in the cocaine economy. For they were well used to losing their cars and bikes, and not only to the army. In communities north of Tingo María it is the stuff of local legend that in the 1970s, when police stopped a wealthy drug trader in town or out on the highway, he would resolve his "legal problem" by handing over the keys of the car he was driving. Such appropriations were hardly novel, but with the installation of army bases they did more than spread. They acquired new targets.

Hugo Taboada, the veteran driver of the Comité de Autos Número

Uno in Tingo María, explains. Over twenty-five years making daily runs up and down the Marginal Highway—to Aucayacu, Nuevo Progreso, as far as Tocache, and then back again—no matter how bad things got, Hugo was undeterred. Then and now, dealing with the police and their checkpoints has been a basic part of the job of all comité drivers. They are experts at navigating the *coimas* (bribes), petty extortions, and other low-grade disturbances that inevitably crop up. Sure, Hugo told me, the police would sometimes ask drivers to loan them their vehicles, but they never pressured them physically. Soldiers, though, were quick to assert their will: punching, kicking until the driver abandoned the vehicle, ordering anyone else sitting inside to step out and take their belongings with them.

In the early 1990s soldiers confiscated cars and pickup trucks from Aucayacu all the way to Tocache—Hugo had no direct knowledge of locales farther north—whenever the army was about to commence a major operation in the countryside—which back then seemed to happen just about every day. A sergeant would show up at the comité's Aucayacu office and point to any sedan parked out front: "Whose car is this? The captain needs the car. The key?"

Such questions lunged toward the tenderest of spots. And to any owner who refused, Hugo recalled one sergeant's cynical retort: *ay, que valiente eres*—"Oh, a courageous one, are you?!"—before sending soldiers over to pummel the driver with rifle butts. On top of that, they took the car. Then came the wait, the driver out of work, making no money, two, three days, until the soldiers brought his vehicle back: dented, the engine or suspension damaged, and without a drop of gas.

The practice of seizing cars and pickups became routine, Hugo said, but it was a matter of timing whether it happened to you or not. Sometimes you would arrive in town and the other comité drivers would tell you, *pucha*, they just drove off with four of our cars! That was how it was. Every base demanded vehicles, but the base in Aucayacu did it most of all.

Soldiers also closed the Marginal Highway for hours on end. They would stop the first car to arrive and tell its driver to park the vehicle perpendicular to oncoming traffic. The one and only justification they gave: *hay operativo*—the army out on patrol in close pursuit of the terrucos. And here Hugo echoed something I had heard others affirm: Ollanta

Humala was known in particular for his frequent closings of the highway near the base at Madre Mía. His soldiers would say, "hay operativo." Local residents would explain: soldiers halted traffic whenever the road was needed as a landing strip for drug planes. No choice but to wait—and if any driver got upset about it, the soldiers would drag him up the long stairs to "the garrison of Capitan Carlos" (who, of course, no one knew was Humala, much less that he would become president of Peru).[7]

Highway closures, vehicle seizures, but also checkpoints all became procedural appendages of the military base system—each one precipitating genres of encounter, by which I mean typical solicitations and event horizons that repatterned ordinary life. Those genres expressed frames of probability that the bases created through the specific ways they punctuated but also pulsed local experiences of time and movement.[8] With the unfurling of the bases, the circumstances through which one might meet soldiers vastly multiplied. And yet each individual encounter had its own singular rhythms that filled and sometimes overran the frame. For while frames of probability introduce intervals into a more expansive milieu, what transpires within them is never certain. This is to say, encounters, no matter how strictly drawn, remain porous—permeable to unforeseen angles of escape.

the glare

Frontier forts were island seeds of the Peruvian state, each one an apparatus for founding new law. Threaded together, they formed an archipelago interconnected by radio waves and by the helicopters that periodically swooped in (from Tingo María). Threaded together, they projected a supple mesh that rearranged the valley by laying claim to the land and (potentially) to everything that moved on and with it.

In the Upper Huallaga the army base network did not unfold all at once. Aucayacu was an early precursor (1984), followed four and five years later by the towns of Uchiza, Tocache, and Nuevo Progreso with right bank villages north of Tingo María strategically filled in here and there all the way to Juanjuí.[9] The army took up positions at the limit points of the valley's physical terrain. They perched their forts high on hills that abutted the Marginal Highway—and sometimes the very sites from which

Sendero had ambushed army patrols. They took the heights,[10] but they also made their presence felt down low where flows gathered: in major towns along the Huallaga River and, above all, in ports where ferrymen provided access with long canoes to the river's left bank, then the heart of Shining Path territories. Yet no matter their position, the bases imposed distances, which stretched between extrema separating terminal points, the seed of state power sweeping up every person who fell under its sway from the highest of the high, to the lowest of the low.

This is how foundations are made, and perhaps why army forts and garrisons are very basic places indeed—back to the Romans on the way to long before that.

Encounters with soldiers, however, unfolded less at a remove than in face-to-face proximity, creating moments when distances from the base could collapse, through one's capture and violent introjection into the nearest fort.

Here I cannot dwell on architecture or on what specific internal configurations these sites of incorporation actually had. Beyond a handful of brief visits, I spent little time on the inside. And while aspects of those interiors do come across in stories I have been told, those stories are not among the ones I share here. Nevertheless, the extremes that happened inside and behind the walls of individual installations were crucial to the gravitational shifts the army fort system unleashed: effects that circulated beyond any specific locale they occupied, effects that filled in the expanses created by the bases themselves.

Many of those effects were perceptual. As they alighted upon the heights, the forts did not just punctuate the landscape; they reoriented vision. They reasserted their presence too through all manner of soundings off: from inside their walls—with random shots fired and nighttime chants; from without—through cadenced songs of soldiers trotting through town and along the highway. But the most widespread effects happened through the ways the bases refigured local experiences of time and terrain: interrupting the movements of people between the towns but also to and from the countryside. For every base reposed in close proximity to rivers and roads where the army established sentry stations for watching, marking, and seizing whatever approached. By day soldiers halted traffic, required identification, asked about destinations and reasons for travel. Checkpoints forced a stopping, imposed a waiting, and then, for most, obliged the resumption of movement. In so doing, they released affects that were palpable yet specific to the era through the peculiar ways they commingled the hospitable and the hostile. Although *crossings* with soldiers might be low key and were sometimes even cordial, during the despliegue the threat of being detained always lingered near.[11]

Along the Huallaga River's right bank, the army often positioned its hilltop forts in such a way that they came into view only from certain angles. When stopped on the road below, travelers could look up at the bases, but doing so often required twisting around and craning upward at a steep angle to catch but a partial and wary glimpse. There, perched on the hilltop, set at a remove, hovering, waiting: a shimmer.

The blinding glares of territory—coming face-to-face with balls of fire, doubling up every now and then with the oppressive, piercing rays of the Huallaga sun.

And in that simple act of looking but also in refusing to look a charged distance opened up. In the craning to see no less than in the turning away, the base reached down to touch each and every person passing by. This was the delay checkpoints created: time to weigh the chances of being suddenly grabbed, dragged up the stairs, and forever removed from sight.

The army erected signs outside the walls of the base and sometimes etched into the surrounding setting. They displayed military iconography. Pithy phrases also called out: "We are watching you." "We are at war." "The order is attack." Visible solely in daytime hours and impossible to ignore, but everyone seemingly doing just that as if appearing curious were not a good idea. But what a strange pairing—that provocation to glance up, or over, mixed with the implicit dissuasion on any kind of sustained gaze. Taking photographs of military sites was prohibited, but where would the line for permissible looking be drawn? Maybe not prudent to ask, maybe better to just pass through. A different predicament faced those residing nearby. They had to live with the bases in peripheral view and ever in earshot of the rumors that swirled about what happened over there on the hill or across the field hidden behind its walls.

Frontier forts created routine anticipations, coaxed along by the signs

FIGURE 7.2. Puente Honoris

and by all the murmurs of what happened inside. Knowing the places where soldiers often waited—on roads, town streets, and ports—provided a thin outer layer of certainty: a frame. With such knowledge those places might be evaded altogether. Transportistas, however, were mostly locked in by the rhythms and itineraries of their trade and by the roads and watercourses they could not alter. They had no choice but to meet encounters head-on,[12] living in expectation of the coming interruption but also in apprehension of what might go awry—which is what transportistas faced when the army seized their vehicles, putting livelihoods and sometimes their lives, at risk—all for a job, of course, but more than that to ensure the ordinary persistence of a *public service* throughout the war.

la hembrita

Working as a botero, "I had many close scrapes with the army," Wilson explained one evening while sitting inside his home near Malecón Huallaga. It all started in the late 1980s, following the Shining Path's nighttime assault against the fort at Madre Mía—until then the largest insurgent operation and arguably, for the Party, the most disastrous of the war. That attack, in the rendering Wilson shared, revealed just how much the logistics of the insurgency depended on the ferrymen they recruited or pressed into service. Because, after that, the army began to restrict the movements of canoe operators throughout the valley, taking special interest, he said, in the boteros of Magdalena—killing them one by one.

Wilson counted himself among the lucky few who had managed to escape, and that evening, as we relaxed after dinner with his wife, Tina, he shared a fragment of all that had transpired. Wilson spoke of the war, as Tina and I listened along, his voice firm as it crossed the soft rumble of cricket and cicada songs droning in from outside—now and then cut through by the occasional mototaxi, running up and down streets, both distant and close, maybe honking a horn. Wilson spoke amid the interruption of nearby conversations that bounced off the surrounding bare cement walls but also as their two grown sons arrived one by one, each time prompting Tina to get up from her chair and follow them into the kitchen, asking, one by one, what she might give them to eat.

Speaking of the war, Wilson told me that the left bank region of Magdalena emerged early on as one of Shining Path's key areas of rural support. Indeed, it was among the strongest in the countryside. There, combatants would gather to prepare armed attacks, including that singular, fateful operation against Madre Mía. In Magdalena, Wilson kept land where he grew coca. Since the beginning of the decade he had also worked his canoe, alongside a dozen or more ferrymen who offered transportation to an ever-expanding community of settlers, thriving then thanks to the newfound promise of cocaine. Every day Wilson would make the two-hour trip from the farms and settlements along the Magdalena River to the small village of Ramal de Aspuzana on the right bank shores of the Huallaga. Back and forth Wilson moved people and cargo every day throughout the 1980s, until the military got wise.

Figuring that Ramal, for its strategic location—roughly across the water from Magdalena but also just down the road from Madre Mía—was the lifeline through which Sendero received provisions and funneled combatants,[13] the army set up a forward detachment next to the village port. Suddenly any botero departing from Ramal had to contend with a round-the-clock presence of soldiers, who monitored all traffic moving from one side to the other. Transferring provisions to the left bank was prohibited. No longer in the broad light of day could anyone drive up with supplies and load them onto boats. Though, as Wilson soon discovered, canoes originating from points elsewhere along the Huallaga River faced less scrutiny, thereby offering a ready means of slipping by the blockade. And so, Wilson made decent money, at least for a short time, ferrying provisions to Magdalena from his home town of Aucayacu, which lay between an hour and two upstream from Ramal—depending on the weather and on the direction one traveled.

On those trips Wilson mostly avoided Ramal. And yet on occasion, when running low on fuel perhaps, he had no choice but to dock. Even so, the soldiers, all in their late teens, or at least looking the part of barely becoming men, could usually be convinced. After all, they were only there to fulfill their compulsory service. So, if he just placed "a little something," a coin, in their hands "with a *vete nomás*, they would let me pass."

Wilson insisted the food he transported was not for the guerrilla but for "*la masa* . . . I mean, the people." Upon this crucial, and for him, obvious distinction, Wilson justified his actions: he relied on the very categorical difference the army had moved to obliterate. Such conceptual work did not happen on its own. Before the Peruvian government declared a state of emergency in the Huallaga specifically related to the armed conflict,[14] Shining Path had sought, through the categorical presuppositions of a people's war, to vastly reduce the distance between the Party and rural communities. Here Wilson had invoked the word *masa*—before correcting himself, substituting the more ordinary and politically unmarked *la gente*. And there was a reason for that: *masa* reiterated Sendero's own manner of designating local populations it aspired to incorporate into the armed struggle. In response: that left bank residents should flee their farms, should move stateside across the river, or else should go farther still and quit the Huallaga altogether had long been core words of counsel the army dispensed.

Question and answer, friend and enemy, because all who decided to remain on their farms threw their lot and ultimate fate in with the guerrilla to become there indistinguishable.

One day an army captain stationed in Ramal received a tip about a botero running supplies to Magdalena. He told his soldiers to be on the lookout, and the next time Wilson pulled into port, they were waiting.

Here, as elsewhere, Wilson's telling of his travels and encounters carried few to no sensorial details—which made me wonder about the sun's scorching rays that day: bearing down with unforgiving glares, forcing eyes askance, sinking into every patch of skin exposed. Parching. Curing. Turning hard. Or perhaps the day awoke instead with skies clouded over, with winds shifting slowly, bringing on fleeting breezes, cool and damp: portents of showers closing in, on a course ever churning forward, *closing in*, on the Huallaga's sway, back and forth, rebounding again against the banks, in countless swirls and eddies, that Wilson skirted across, that Wilson scattered, each time he angled the canoe's thin bow deftly toward the shore.

"They grabbed me and carried me off," Wilson said, as the patter of Tina's flip-flops traced an audible path behind us from the kitchen and out toward the street. "They told me . . . ," his voice shifting now to convey the soldiers' own words. Curt and punchy: "The captain wants to talk with you . . . but right now, he's away." And with that they escorted him the short distance to their headquarters, telling him he would have to wait inside for the captain's return.

Wilson found himself detained, his boat impounded.

"What they didn't mention," he explained, "was that they had already received the order to unload: 'because *that boat*—his voice inflecting theirs once again—is for *los tíos*.'"

They meant for *the uncles* and for *the aunts*, which is to say, for Shining Path.

Inside the headquarters a lieutenant directed the soldiers to bind Wilson's hands. He then walked over, shoved Wilson onto the floor, and seemed about ready to rough him up when a female voice called from across the room:

"Lieutenant . . . *What are you doing* to my uncle?"

The lieutenant paused and looked up. Wilson followed his gaze across the room over to a young woman, whom Wilson immediately recognized. His niece she was not but someone he had once gotten out of a pinch, giving her a ride from left bank to right. And there she was again, sitting now, in the captain's office.

"They were going to kill me," Wilson said, and as if to emphasize what was for him a foregone conclusion: "They had bound my hands."

The woman walked now over to the lieutenant. And with Wilson still there on the ground, she sent him a little gesture. A discrete wave, Wilson said, just for him—but without his hands what kind of signal could he possibly return?

"This is your uncle?" the lieutenant asked.

"Yes," she said, in a voice that Wilson intoned through words of his own: soft, calm, deliberate, firm.

"Well, the captain has ordered us to detain him."

"But he is not detained," she countered. "He is tied up. Tell me, why have you tied his hands?"

"That was the order, and we have followed it."

"Okay, then, where is your captain?

When the lieutenant replied "Madre Mía," she asked him to radio the base, which the lieutenant did but only to learn that the captain was already on his way. A moment later the captain walked in, and the young woman turned to face him.

"Look over here," she said. "You know what? Just as you order your soldiers, I am giving *you* an order: Untie him."

Here, Wilson, perhaps to ensure I was not getting lost in his tale, paused to interject: "It was because she was *su hembrita*"—what else could account for the way she spoke and for the hold her words seemed to have on the captain.

For there she stood, adamant: "I am ordering you, and if you don't release him, I will report you. . . . Why are they torturing my uncle?"

And the captain, "He is transporting supplies."

"But those supplies," she insisted: are for *la masa*"—there it was again: *la masa*, a word for and from another time. She meant they were not for Sendero. "I know about these things. Release him."

To Wilson's surprise the captain relented, telling a soldier to untie his hands. Suddenly he was free to go. The woman accompanied Wilson outside all the way to the shore, where he discovered his boat was empty. Pointing at the canoe, Wilson casually remarked that all his cargo had been removed. And for the captain's friend, who for purposes of the moment remained Wilson's niece, that was more than enough. "Load up that boat!" she said, and the soldiers rushed to restore what they had undone.

Once the cargo had been loaded and accounted for, Wilson stepped onboard and walked back to the motor. As he reached down to give it pull, the woman called out, loud enough for everyone to hear: "Okay, uncle, *saludos a mi tía*"—send regards to my aunt.

Wilson started up the motor, and with a wave of farewell, he edged back from the shore before turning the bow around to head not toward the other side, and the mouth of the Magdalena, but downstream, back home to Aucayacu.

Wilson said he had met that woman only once before, in a moment, for her, of extreme distress, desperate to leave the left bank. He knew no details, only that she had a falling out with one of the local groups who stockpiled unrefined cocaine nearby: "They had thrown her out, so I gave her a ride. I took her to Ramal."

On the second and last time their paths crossed, Wilson said, he did not know for sure, but from the way the woman ordered the captain about, he could only surmise she was his lover. How she dispensed commands, Wilson laughed, as if she were in charge. And thanks to that, she had saved his life.

Wilson offered no physical description. Yet his telling sketched an image of her all the same—an image that pivots on the phrase *su hembrita*, repeated in my thoughts every time I return to this story. *Hembra* is "woman" but with an accent placed on all aspects carnal—here in the diminutive, *hembrita*, so a term of endearment but also figuratively, if not literally, petite in stature. And from what had transpired, she was a woman clearly savvy and ever so strong. That she not only had a hold on the captain but could appropriate the force of the army, channeling its authority through words of her own design—seemed nothing less than remarkable. She moved diagonally, and all the more astonishing, since the very first impression Wilson had of her, which he shared only at the end of his tale, portrayed the woman in a far more vulnerable light.

"She had worked with *la firma, caleta, ya*. I do not know what the dispute was about. I do not know the owner of the stash." Wilson said there was disagreement, without needing to make explicit the peril. "He had kicked her out, and I happened to be passing by. She called out to me, crying, asked me to take her to Ramal. 'I have no money right now,' she explained, 'but I will pay you as soon as I can.'"

"Don't worry about *that*." Wilson assured, urging her aboard and saying—"Let's just *go*"—as he spirited her from that place.

"And so . . . how should I phrase it?" Wilson wondered aloud, for my benefit now, as if wanting to bring the story to a close: "*A service*: that's what a botero provides. And it's like you get rewarded for it later. Because if I had not met that woman, she wouldn't have known me either, and nobody would have intervened. . . . They already had me, and with all those provisions. They had me tagged as a supplier. And *for that*, they would have broken me into pieces. They would have sent me to the base."

They would have sent Wilson to the base. And in that fatality, there was an unwavering orientation, a destination prefigured that resisted teasing apart—a destiny that could not be altered, much less reversed, not until, as if out of nowhere, a young woman appeared.

The detachment at Ramal was a physical extension of the counterinsurgency base system. A tendril reaching out from beyond fort walls to enforce prohibitions on movement, to lay in wait in ways that that tensed everyday time, exposing all that passed to the same disjunctive: friend or enemy? The sharpest of questions, Elías Canetti affirmed, is where "only one or other of the two simplest answers is possible: yes or no."[15] And the army's insistence on this basic conundrum of the political drew a frame of encounter, which was no less the extension of the base, in the sense that it set forth a very limited range of generic possibilities. Yet where something arrived out of nowhere to breach that frame and throw the genre of anticipations on its head, the encounter turned remarkable, becoming an event from which one might later craft a tale.

The interference of the young woman underscores the porousness of every encounter. Though far closer to the specific circumstances Wilson relayed, it was through holes of the mesh, through gaps in the work of nets of the base system itself that she had moved. Those holes were not expected, though what she did unfolded in the light of day, happening right there for most all to see.

A net works only if it lets something pass through.

She was *local* to the extent she expressed prior attachments in the vicinity of left bank places and their people. And because of those ties and the intimate awareness they afforded, she *knew* "about such things." She *knew* where to separate civilian from combatant but also how to insist with an elective affinity for *la masa*. By stepping in to protect, she *knew* when to refuse the disjunctive question of the political.

darkness approaching

Whether along the road or inside the ports, checkpoints supplied daytime encounters with a setting that traced a direct line to the base. Yet when the army occupied Huallaga towns and villages, it also imposed curfews that partitioned off the night. Curfews expressed political emergency through a general command not to go outside after dark. Curfews turned night into that duration when soldiers—withdrawn to the protective walls of the bases and fortified sentry posts—would fire at will on anyone or anything moving on the streets, roads, trails, rivers, and streams. If in the constrained common sense of the emergency only "terrorists" moved about after dark, curfews did not merely oppose daylight hours to night; they hardened the partition of pendular time, already overlaid with a stark friend/enemy coupling—as if butterflies could be set off from moths.

At curfew the implicit question of the emergency restricted all movement to a standstill. For the arrival of night supplied the army a fixed answer that already preselected one side of the disjunctive: all that moves about outside is enemy, and whatever moves can be killed without regard. And yet suppressing one side of the question hardly settled matters. For everyone else it introduced new, if less favorable, choices: when coming upon soldiers at night, people could face them, flee, or take their chances playing dead, becoming, as it were, a still life—*una naturaleza muerta.* For the curfew commanded that all sense would hunker down, as if it were possible to drop ahead of each and every encounter all other referential anchors. As if the world could be flattened, turned monotone, as if transformations could ever be brought to a halt by threats of death. And these were but some of the specific ways curfews strained time, above all in the twilight as darkness approached.

In villages and towns that bordered the Huallaga, curfews extended to travel on the river—this much I have learned from boteros who worked in Nuevo Progreso, Ramal de Aspuzana, and Aucayacu. Don Florentín, an original colono of the community of Primavera across the water from Aucayacu, was a ferryman who belonged to one of the town's two canoe associations or comités during the years the army controlled the port. "We worked from six to six," he told me. "In the evening we handed over the key and the motor to the soldier on duty. . . . The operator and the passengers could still unload cargo, but until six the next morning not even permission could be asked to move the boat again."

Wilson, who himself never affiliated with the Aucayacu comités, said the army kept all boteros who lived in town under watch and on constant call. The base commander drew up a list of comité members and ordered them to report to the town plaza each Sunday morning for the flag-raising ceremony. Any time of day or night soldiers might appear at their homes unannounced, expecting to be conveyed up or down the river—which predictably set the ferrymen in the sights of Shining Path.

Elsewhere Huallaga boteros would confront something similar. Reynaldo, the now retired ferryman from Nuevo Progreso, confirmed that the army there not only enforced the same nighttime curfew but treated boteros with a heavy hand, insisting on controlling their movements, threatening to fire on any canoe traveling on the river at night. A ferryman working after six, the army claimed, must be transporting terrorists. "That's what they said . . . and that made people so scared they would not even walk about on the streets at night. Sometimes, if you had spent the day working on your farm, you might get delayed but rather than returning after curfew and facing the soldiers' questions—*¿Qué* *haces andando?*—one simply chose to hold off on returning to town until dawn."

entering twilight

Ferrying passengers was something Don Florentín did but sporadically, though that was long ago, and if I could read anything from the frailty of his elder years, gone were the days when he had the strength to work for others. Still, I had my chance to admire his hand as a balsero up close during one of several times Mauro took me to the farm. Pulling off the main road and along a footpath that snaked through a grove of cacao trees, we came to the Pucayacu, tributary of the nearby and ever-larger Huallaga. Mauro's home lay just beyond the moving currents. To reach it, we had to cross, but the only craft that could take us lay at rest on the other side. So, Mauro called out, once, then twice, until we heard a hoot in the distance, calling back and bringing a smile to Mauro's face. Moments later, his father appeared to send us a wave from the opposite bank before descending in small ginger steps toward the water's edge and onto a small wooden raft: four squat logs, gathered and tied. Picking up a bamboo tangana, ever so long and thin, he pushed against the bank, then against the river's still shallow floor, with quick, expert thrusts. The craft peeled off into the current and pivoted around. Don Florentín, heading now to meet us.

I call him Florentín, because his given name names a thriving. The family farm was where he explained about the wartime curfew the army had imposed on the Huallaga River at night, though initially I was hard-pressed to say exactly when he had told me. Surely it couldn't have been that same day in 2011 when, upon entering Primavera, I caught my first glimpse of the fort, sitting over there across a grassy low-cut field at a remove from the village dirt road. That time, when I could not *not* stop to steal a photograph: something appalling about the painted facade, making matters all too explicit, and hardly could I let *that* slip away without anything to show (see figure 7.3).

But now going back to my notes, I see it was almost eleven months later when he told me of his former life as an occasional botero.

I remember the two thatched-roof, open-air huts—each one set off but in clear view of each other—and how together they made a home for

FIGURE 7.3. Primavera

Mauro and his elderly parents. One hut rested upon a tawny gray earth, providing protective cover for the kitchen. The wood-plank floor of the other, where the family slept, rose a meter off the ground. At the edge of this second hut and sleeping quarters was where Don Florentín told me about how he had operated an outboard motor from time to time out of the port of Aucayacu. The motor, he said, was not his. For "to operate" is not to own but rather to work for another and with equipment someone else entrusted: the person who gave you the means and thus the opportunity to earn money, and for that you owed them.

Don Florentín worked as a botero by day and always along the same route. He would depart Aucayacu and cross over to *la banda* or opposite shore before heading downstream to the left bank villages of San José, San Martín, and after that, depending on his passengers, perhaps swing back to the right bank and farther down to Cotomonillo, before returning upstream to dock at the port of Aucayacu once again. The fare varied, he said, on distance: one sol to get dropped off at la banda; two to San José or San Martín de Pucate; two fifty for the entire one-way route to Cotomonillo.

At his farm we found ourselves returning to an earlier conversation, when Don Florentín had shared his version of how Sendero arrived in the 1980s to the Huallaga's left bank, moving hamlet by hamlet and ever farther north, until they reached Primavera. Like many other left bank communities, Primavera would be devastated during the military's 1994 Aries operations.[16] And for several long years after that, almost no one lived in the village, not until the late 1990s when people started to return. Soon the army would install there a fort out of concern Sendero appeared to be reorganizing, attempting to reassert influence over rural communities. As the first army base on the left bank directly across from the town of Aucayacu, it operated in a preventive capacity, since by then the insurgency no longer wielded sufficient influence or had the resources needed to train large numbers of combatants. That much I knew, and now Don Florentín, man of many eras, picked up the thread again about Sendero's early years, but this time to share how his children, who, like so many from other settler families, pushing into and beyond their teens, got pulled into the war—his daughter, among those who never made it back.

And in the midst of all that, Don Florentín jumped forward a decade in time to tell me about the evening he broke curfew on the Huallaga River, the same night that upon returning to the home they had kept in town—ever since the war had forced them, in heeding the army's counsel, to abandon the farm—he found his older son, the same son who had been missing for several years already, waiting to surprise him in the dark. Surprised too because on the way home a premonition had seeped into the words Florentín spoke in silence as he walked, moving back and forth between first and third versions of himself: *Capaz nuestro hijo va a aparecer hoy de noche, le digo . . . ¡No es posible! ¿Tal vez? me dice.* And turning now to our conversation, turning now to me, he explained: *medio así yo presiento.* And then, getting home, late as it was, from inside a voice called out that froze Florentín in his steps: *buenas noches papá.* It was a voice Florentín had not heard in two, almost three years.

Hearing that voice again, at first, I could not speak.

But then, after what seemed the longest time, finding his words, but still not able to see because of the dark, Don Florentín asked:

Who are you, son? Which of my sons are you: Mauro or Josué?

Josué papá. And he came to me. He gave me a hug, kissed me, and I began to cry.

It all started one afternoon, when at the closing stretch of a long shift, Don Florentín headed back to Aucayacu and pulled into the shore on what would have been his last run. The port was still under the control of the base:

"The army was there, the soldiers were still there, but right when I arrived, the son of the owner of the motor called to me: 'Brother, give me a ride.'"

Don Florentín had to say no—it was late, five-thirty already, time to hand the motor over to the army. He was in the midst of explaining when a soldier approached and point blank to Don Florentín echoed his words, "The motor stays put." Yes, replied Florentín, in agreement but also pushing, ever so gently, for some kind of exception: "We are talking about that just now. You see his father is the owner of the motor. He's the owner's son, and he wants me to take him downriver," but the soldier would have nothing of it. With every push by Don Florentín the soldier dug deeper into his "no" until a lieutenant walked over to ask what was up.

Turning quickly to face the superior officer, Don Florentín changed tack and requested permission to go out one last time. "I have a passenger here with a family member in Primavera who is gravely ill . . . his wife is sick." "Okay," the lieutenant said, "take him, but you must be back by six-thirty."

Ya mi teniente—Don Florentín said, as he rushed to embark, with the owner's son as the lone passenger, pushing his craft into the river before the official changed his mind.

Soon they were pulling into the port of San Martín, where the owner's son hopped out and disappeared from view. Don Florentín readied to turn around and head back up the Huallaga, when a teenage boy came up to the canoe.

"Señor Shapiama, Señor Shapiama, can you do me a favor?"

"What favor? I do not have time. I must get going."

Only when the boy said his father was drowning did Don Florentín pause and listen.

"A little animal has pulled him into the *palizada*."

The boy explained: His father had been fishing and was throwing a casting net from a raft when he caught a zúngaro—a goliath catfish. Thinking he had snared something small, he slowly began pulling in the net, but the zúngaro tugged back and with such force that it dragged him into the water. Everything happened so fast: the throw rope twisted around his right hand, such that when the Huallaga's currents carried the net and the zúngaro downriver, he got carried along with them all the way to a tiny island of accumulated branches and other woody debris. There, pressed against the palizada, the father managed to park himself and keep his head, if barely, above water. The zúngaro remained trapped in the net: pulling, threatening to drag him under.

Grasping the gravity of the situation, Don Florentín jumped onto the shore with a "let's go!" Along the water's edge he followed the boy, until he saw the father just as he had been described: in the water, arm caught in the net, pushed up against the palizada.

"I went into the water as far as I could," Don Florentín said to me, "feeling my way."

Soon he reached what he thought was a log under the surface. But when that log sent him a powerful kick, he realized he had found the tail of the zúngaro. "Bam, he hit me, just about knocking me over onto my back, but in that moment, right when he did that, I said to the father, "Pull the net." The net raised up. The zúngaro broke free and swam away.

"The man's hand was swollen. I separated him from the net." And Don Florentín, with a "ya amigo," was already spinning around to leave when the man wanted to know how much did he owe? "Not a thing," Don Florentín said—his mind was on the lieutenant and the order he had received. Getting back to town was now his only concern.

Running to his canoe, Don Florentín jumped in and pushed off from the shore, but when he tried to rev up the engine, "Pull, pull, pull . . . nothing. I had already drifted downriver almost to the point where I had untied the man, when finally, the motor started."

Upriver he headed once again with the time approaching seven o'clock. Drawing near the port of Aucayacu, someone, a soldier, fired a shot of warning, then another into the air, but Don Florentín simply pressed on.

As he pulled into the dock, a soldier ran over to the boat with a "Hey, carambas, what happened?" And in that moment too, the lieutenant walked over and, after sending the soldier back to his post, also wanted to know: "What in the world happened?"

"The motor broke down on me, and that's why I could not return any sooner."

"Well, okay," the lieutenant told him. "Get out of here but leave the boat right where it is."

"So, I left, and at that hour I went to my house. . . . I returned at that late hour, I entered into the room, I heard that voice, *buenas noches, papá* . . . and I just froze."

Simply telling this tale draws a thread from vast, far more entangled currents. Josué, waiting there in the dark, was already caught in the net, on a trajectory to the base, and in the weeks to come he would turn himself in: how else to secure the freedom of his mother, Don Florentín's wife, who the army held as his ransom? And how Mauro would follow, and how he would surely have died there too had not a niece, whom Don Florentín never named, placed her cunning at the service of his eventual release.

Mauro would never be the same, and only until very late in our acquaintance did I have any inkling of why he so often seemed a little off. Unlike so many others, he at least departed on his own two feet, even if he did not know when he walked out of the gate where he was, even if he could not recognize then his own mother's face.

"Which of my sons are you?"

Don Florentín still does not know exactly where Josué went from there or where he ended up.

And to push any further into the currents would only pull this thread in toward questions, honed too sharp and thrown all too frequently without care for what or how deep they cut.

The past spreads a field so thin lines can cast about to tether and then release moving presents: from the actual to the already anterior, then back again, weaving sky to earth in ever-new alliance.

Between twilights: an archipelago of dark condensations, marking off the intermittent force of intercalar terrains.

Here gaps sometimes matter, almost as much as or more than what they separate. For the stirrings they discharge and sustain, in the waiting, in anticipation of what might happen.

Intervals: for the secrets—they separate and murmur—always denser than the matter that surrounds them.

Intervals too, in the glares of territory: what really goes on over there, that row up at the base, towering above, all the while making its presence felt low, through the lowest of lows. The apex and the trench. Take it in, take it all in: the densities of depths without fathom.

Over there, across that field, where it happens, all so you might trace the distance, all so you might forget the difference between a moth and a butterfly. All so you wouldn't forget how from up there a messenger, carrying a note from the base commander himself, a note addressed only to you, running as fast as he can down the stairs, league after league, striving as he might yet never managing to make it past the grounds of the fort.

The eternal, the waiting, for the next time you get stopped at the checkpoint.

Always a next time, always a craning, reflecting, refracting: always a washing out, that thin line of water—*ir y venir*—between stones, the lattices and workings of nets.

Always a critical distance: the ball of fire high and resplendent, reaching, turning away all stares, always casting the longest of shadows between twilights.

By day, forts take up their positions overhead in line with the sun. Towering intermittent, with all those images, and with all the procedures to which they belong.

Bases reach down into the base, lowest of lows, ever founding new legal situations, new alliances of sky to earth where time is weather, in secret, thanks to their densities and to the opacities of so many bodies, weaving oblivions amid the irrepressible porosity of encounters.

Of butterflies never seen at dusk.

Of moths rushing toward the lights, turned on in the midst of night.

oblivious title

A bad feeling weighed on Tina as she stepped into the boat.[1] Only ten minutes before, she had noticed a canoe as it cut past the port heading fast upstream. And *Rayo*, the guy steering the outboard motor . . . not a pleasant character. *It's true*: he appeared to be alone, but put those two together—him going who knows where at *that* speed—well, she told herself, something's up. And it can't be good.

Standing on the bank of the Magdalena, tributary of the more mighty Huallaga River, Tina contemplated in silence as she waited for a ride to her farm. The achy tiredness in her limbs upon waking had all but dissipated when the mototaxi dropped her off at the port. Now that she had regained full command over her senses, she was guardedly optimistic: with any luck her body would not betray her later in the day.

As on most mornings several others gathered at the river's bank: people who had property near hers plus the boat operators with whom she stayed friendly. Today two strangers had arrived as well—men Tina called "engineers," looking nervous in the insignia vests and caps that marked them as state employees. Tina knew—from the rustle of conversation around the port—that they had come to measure the land, even before they approached to ask if she was traveling upriver.

Yes, she nodded: "Just wait. We can go together in the same boat." Hearing this, the men seemed visibly relieved. They had found someone from the place they could to talk to and who hopefully would guide them to their destination. Most of all they wanted to know how "the situation" was upstream. "Oh," Tina replied, "I'm sure you can imagine"—her evasiveness betraying how awkward *that question* sounded when asked by strangers and for everyone to hear. All the more so for at that moment Rayo sped by.

Watching him vanish around the bend, Tina thought to herself that the others must be hiding at the bottom of the canoe, but there was nothing she could do. She did not dare tip off the surveyors. Nor was there any time, because just then one of the operators hopped into his craft and called out to her: "Doña, let's go." So she boarded and took a seat, saying nothing when the surveyors followed her into the boat.

Tina knew in her heart as the canoe pulled from the shore that something was amiss. And sure enough, two, three, four bends from the port *it* happened. A group of men appeared on the far bank—Rayo among them—waving guns, calling out to the motorist—*¡Alto!* The boat operator complied, and as soon as the canoe touched shore, one of the armed men—short, thick-bodied, and noticeably older than the rest—ordered the passengers to get out. The surveyors went first, then Tina. After searching the men's pockets, he told them to lie face down on the bank. The surveyors dropped to the muddy earth, but Tina stayed put. "That means you too," the man demanded. "Why are you still standing?" Tina explained: she meant no disrespect, but it was unbecoming for a grown woman to lie down on the ground. As she spoke back to him, a grimace of annoyance spread across his face, yet *to her* the man said nothing more.

Instead he turned to the surveyors, warning them they were entering the area solely because he was allowing them to go and do their work. Tread carefully: he did not want to hear complaints about preferential treatments. He did not want to hear they had incited conflicts over land. To prevent such problems, he announced, his people would show them exactly where property lines should be drawn. One last thing: "You have not seen *Artemio*. If you later say you have met with him, keep in mind we know where you sleep. We know who your family is. You realize what I am telling you?"

Tina would later express to me her surprise. Despite having lived her entire life in the region and despite having known many members of Shining Path, never before had Tina come face-to-face with the elusive leader of its Huallaga faction.

Having delivered these instructions, Artemio let the three return to the canoe. As the boat pushed into the river's unflappable currents, no one dared look back as the senderistas faded from view. Nor did the surveyors say a word, though from their faces Tina could see they were shaken. So to break the silence, she reached over and touched the shoulder of one of the men, saying: "You must be scared . . . but do not worry. It will be okay. What's more, you are in luck. I know how to treat *susto* [fright]. Tonight if you come to my farm, I will cure you with a couple of eggs." At this the two men laughed, and Tina was happy to have at least helped cheer them up, even if they figured she was joking. The boat soon arrived at her farm, and as she got out, amid waves of good-bye, the surveyors promised to visit in the evening once they had completed their work for the day.

aftermaths

Tina's story about the day government surveyors entered a remote corner of the Huallaga, where Maoist insurgents still asserted territorial sovereignty, pulls a thread from an entangled history of violence and land as it permeates the legal registration of rural property in this region of Peru. That thread lends itself here to asking how rural titling could become an instrument of postwar oblivion—when particular claims to land, often based on illegal, sometimes violent appropriations, receive state authorization in disregard for the turbulent events from which they emerged. The name "Oblivious Title" gestures not toward an erasure of memory but to the ways that the formalization of rural property—as it lays a new ground of law atop gene-alogies of strife—cements over, and may even attempt to seal out, an un-settled, unsettling past. Land titles can be used in this manner since their conferral introduces a new partition in time.[2] They establish a hardened node of temporal reference back to which all future questions of legitimacy and legal validity are directed. In this respect, they may ignore preceding history—which is what in the aftermath of war invests them with a certain potential as administrative tools of forgetting.

As Tina's story unfolds over the pages to come, I recount how the mili-tarily defeated but nonetheless active Shining Path insurgency capitalized on a Peruvian government rural titling campaign. Hoping to secure farm-land for the postconflict futures of its members and local sympathizers, the insurgency lured the Peruvian government into validating property lines otherwise banned by national law. The means through which Shining Path accomplished that can be productively read as a form of counterfeiting.

Telling surveyors where they should draw the lines that divided land entailed an unauthorized capture of the state's prerogative to affirm the rights
of some against the competing claims of others. The status of that capture
was contingent, nevertheless, on movements of political time, because it
expressed changing relations of force within a specific state of affairs. Only
in defeat would the insurgents seek, albeit surreptitiously, the legal backing
of the Peruvian state; whereas before, when their rural dominance was not
yet on the wane, they could have simply imposed their own law.

In this chapter *political time* means the temporal attributes of political
communities (referring for the moment and for my purposes here strictly to
nation-states): how they figure and contest their own relation to presents,
pasts and futures—what must be recalled? what overlooked?—but also how
they contend with the passage of time itself. If the politics of nation-states
manifest what Koselleck called "temporal structures,"[3] others have noted
they express "characteristic amnesias," giving rise to narratives of national
identity.[4] Political time, nevertheless, passes—and in passing it "moves"
unevenly. Violent events and historical processes (such are armed conflicts
and other large-scale catastrophes) punctuate and often disrupt assertions
of sovereignty. And wherever the territorial coverage of sovereignty becomes
operationally discontinuous, political time moves unevenly all the more.

Variations in political time thus directly affect the administrative power
through which nation-states undergird legal property. Attention to that
administrative faculty, and specifically to what I would call its denotative,
signature function—orienting the material ways terrain is divided into
legally recognized property (via surveying, measuring, mapping, and issuing documents)—opens a rich conceptual domain for examining how
new rural land regimes create an infrastructural foundation for oblivion
in contexts of postconflict. That foundation emerges not with the explicit
purpose to suppress specific memories of what happened during an earlier, and violent, political time. For, again, oblivion does not presuppose
an erasure, much less the destruction of traces that give support to acts of
remembrance.[5] Instead, the signature function authorizes particular lines
of connection to the past, which safeguard new property while selectively
skirting associations that would animate alternate claims.[6]

In the Huallaga, the advent of postwar was at once postponed and prolonged, and that delay resulted, among other things, in a momentary overlapping of hostile property regimes. The passage away from times of war did not, however, simply alter the terms upon which claims to land could attain legitimacy. Rather, that temporal shift obscured significant traces of a former insurgent land order within a new government rural property registry. The transitory coincidence of insurgent and state re-gimes made that concealment possible. It also engendered opportunities for obtaining land titles that were *authentic yet false* to the extent that the holdings they guaranteed originated from seizures prohibited in the eyes of Peruvian law. In effect, the bestowal of new titles selectively suppressed a long history of conflicts over land. In so doing, it allowed those who had benefited from the insurgency's redistributions to achieve state recognition of private ownership. Recognition became *counterfeit*, I would suggest, where the bestowal of title presupposed a misappropriation of the state's sig-nature function and thus a deliberate usurpation of its denotational power to separate authorized from improper claims.[7] The power in question was the kind state institutions appear to assert when they pass administrative judgments on specific states of affairs, deciding therein how such affairs match up with or fulfill the claims made about them.

A discussion of falsification, nonetheless, need not focus on mimesis—how close a copy matches or interacts with an original. Stress can be placed, instead, on the achievement of an indiscernibility that enables public cir-culation of what is otherwise unsanctioned. Therein the importance of camouflage, that art of blending into surroundings by effacing external distinctions.[8] Counterfeiting depends upon certain camouflaging effects, which I underscore less as a mode of statecraft per se than as an exigency for securing property through the state on terms it would not openly condone.[9]

Here I explore a late episode of Shining Path's own falling apart. The specific story I relay happened in 2007, five years prior to the February 2012 capture of Artemio: nom de guerre of the man Peruvian news me-dia would describe as "the last historic leader" of Sendero Luminoso.[10] Artemio's capture, subsequent trial, and sentencing to life imprisonment became a new and latest marker of the movement's demise: a significant point in the aftermath of a counterinsurgency conflict now approaching twenty years. Indeed, postwar as a particular framing of political time is the broad theme of this chapter. My general concern is with the material constellations of memory and forgetting—manifesting in physical terrains,[11] but also bodies—that such aftermaths precipitate, and may even demand, as they differentially invest the stakes of what can and must not be publicly acknowledged. All of which brings me to the question: What happens to competing claims on rural land once war is deemed *over* in areas formerly under Shining Path control?

binding time

Postwar in Peru has a specificity inseparable not simply from what happened during the conflict but how the overt military phase came to a close. Unlike other guerrilla armies in Latin America, Sendero Luminoso never elicited even de facto recognition from the Peruvian state as an adversary to whom concessions would have to be made. The September 1992 surprise arrest of Abimael Guzmán—the Maoist Party's maximum leader—so decisively reversed the movement's fortunes that President Alberto Fujimori declared that victory over the insurgency was at hand. Yet if from a national perspective, the commencement of the postwar era must be located in some relation to the decade-long Fujimori regime, ascribing more than one beginning date is plausible. There is 1995, as a threshold year, when the Maoist movement arguably no longer had the operational capacity to pose a serious threat to national stability. Or else, there is the more commonly cited milestone event from 2000, when Fujimori fled the country amid his government's collapse: an event the Peruvian Truth and Reconciliation Commission would later take as the definitive transition from internal war.

Setting firm temporal boundaries on postwar is always politically fraught, and in Peru all the more so given the uneven geographic distribution of the conflict itself. State counterinsurgency relied on the carving up of national territory into emergency zones of legal exception, where indiscriminate mass violence could be dispensed against suspect populations at a remove from national scrutiny. Official disavowals of atrocities, threats of reprisals, and active shielding of military and police officers from criminal liability worked to keep significant sectors of national society either oblivious to the magnitude of the violence or complicit in staying silent. The profound social and physical distances that long separated Lima-centric mainstream society from remote rural areas greatly facilitated those labors of amnesia and oblivion, which did not abruptly end with the war but have repeated the violence of state denial in the aftermath.[12] Public secrecy within populations most affected by the conflict also shaped what might circulate across extended thresholds, setting rural community apart from national public spheres, as Olga González has carefully portrayed in her rich ethnography of the highland Ayacucho community of Sarhua.[13] No doubt deception courses through accounts and accountabilities of postwar,[14] above all, in former emergency zones where narratives told by communities may become keenly attuned to knowing what not to know about what had happened, whenever doing otherwise might undermine the possibilities for making a life in the present.[15]

Similar patterns prevailed in the Upper Huallaga, even if in vital respects, as I have mentioned before, especially in Chapter 1, the war unfolded differently there than in other areas of the country. The cocaine trade was the rural economy well into the late 1990s. The trade's illegality allowed Sendero to provide coca-growing communities with protection from the police, which in turn created openings for organizing rural hamlets politically with far greater success and for far longer than elsewhere in the country. War in the Upper Huallaga also differed in that the period of most intense violence—meted out during military operations of the Peruvian armed forces—arrived relatively late: half a decade and more after comparable counterinsurgency campaigns in the Peruvian highlands. Between 1992 and 1994 those operations targeted what was then the last major refuge of Shining Path, decimating the guerrilla army. Nevertheless, enough of the insurgency survived to exert a palpable presence in the countryside for years to come.[16] Consequently, the postwar era reached the Upper Huallaga with an appreciable delay, which kept the region out of sync with the political time of national society but also extended the length of the war's aftermath: namely, the specific and gradual ways life became reoriented, when it had to contend less and less with the intense press of military conflict and more and more with how the war by ending lingered on through traces that were often difficult to grasp.

Many of my conversations with Tina since we first met in 2002 have gravitated toward the farm she tends on what is left of her deceased father's land on the left bank, where for decades Sendero Luminoso imposed its own rules of land tenure. She tells of the lingering effects of seasonal floods and of the different crops to which she has tied her immediate fortunes. She comments on the day-to-day struggles required to pay back bank notes and keep transactions afloat—whether haggling with buyers or hiring help at critical junctures of the growing cycle just so she can ship harvests out and start all over again. Always building toward something, Tina explicitly sketches out a course for what remains of her economically productive years, even as she feels her own body breaking down under the onslaughts of a wasting disease. She plans with her children's futures in mind—teenagers with no desire to work in the fields within what had been a final guerrilla enclave. On one such visit to her home in mid-2012 the unexpected sale of a portion of her father's land, forcibly taken from her five years before, offered the occasion for her to return to the episode I recount here.

The day in 2007 Tina accompanied government surveyors up the Magdalena River, Sendero Luminoso was but a small, ragtag force—a radically diminished image of its former prowess in the Huallaga Valley. With the end of the insurgency in sight the group under Artemio's command had begun to compel farmers with holdings over twenty hectares to accept substantial reductions in their properties. While historically, this was only the latest of Shining Path redistributions, it would be a final one, undertaken in anticipation of the eventual disbanding of what few guerrilla fighters remained. In a sense it was Artemio's last chance to leave something concrete in the hands of his armed followers and collaborators. During the presidency of Alejandro Toledo (2001–2006), Artemio had repeatedly proposed peace talks to address the conflict's unresolved "social issues" and to negotiate the terms for demobilizing insurgent combatants. Toledo's government refused and pursued a strategy, followed by subsequent García and Humala administrations, that prioritized intelligence gathering and police operations to dismantle the Huallaga organization piece by piece.[17] Yet what distinguished this latest redistribution from those preceding it—and most important, how that redistribution bears upon the matter of counterfeiting and falsification—is that it coincided with the arrival of a national government campaign to provide free property titles to rural landholders.[18]

With that campaign the Peruvian state implicitly seized upon a moment of postconflict to overhaul its rural land registry and thereby potentiate a greater fungibility of real property, presumably in hopes of facilitating the expansion of agribusiness and, where possible, (trans)national concerns in mining, oil, and gas. I say presumably because the new rural titling registry was not rhetorically framed as an activity that corresponded with a period of aftermath, much less as a specific mechanism of transitional justice (such as truth commissions, criminal prosecutions, and reparations to affected communities and individuals). And yet, the war's retreat into a past, even as that past continued to insist within everyday presents, created conditions for the campaign to go forward, enabling it to serve as an activity at once appropriate to and generative of a new political era.

Where land claims depend upon state regimes to guarantee them, the political time of those regimes matters. Anthropologists who study contemporary and emergent forms of property note that abrupt changes in the temporal milieus of nation-states fundamentally alter ties between people and things.[19] In her study of decollectivization in Romania, Katherine Verdery identifies time not merely as a crucial dimension of property but as having provided a "critical link between the resources inherited from socialism and the possibility of postsocialist value creation."[20] Meanwhile, Catherine Alexander, drawing from her work on land privatization in postsocialist Kazakhstan, suggests the "temporal context of property relations" has direct bearing not only on specific kinds of rights people can claim to things but on the "credibility, and confidence in the source of legitimacy for upholding new property regimes."[21] The spectrum of relations that obtain between people and material things is by no means limited to those mediated through the nation-state—a point amply demonstrated by anthropological studies of sociality,[22] and of land tenure more specifically.[23] State regimes do, nonetheless, position themselves as final authority on the *propriety* and binding force of such relations. The notion of property often underscores the legal and moral implications of particular acts of seizure, occupation, and possession,[24] and it is no surprise that nation-states assert a widespread prerogative in determining their status. The exercise of that prerogative—what I understand to be the denotational power or signature faculty of state administration—is contingent on political conditions. Thus, attention to shifts in political time offer a means for weighing the legitimacy of specific appropriations and claims—here in reference to land—and even for acknowledging a broader field of attachments between people and things: those excluded by political and legal institutions or that manage to elude state recognition.

Sovereignty is fundamentally perspectival. It entails a cutting expressed through the violence of appropriations: theft for some can become gift for others. From the point of view of Peruvian state legality, Sendero land seizures in the countryside improperly articulated relations between people and things. Nonetheless, the future-oriented horizons of Maoist revolution did at one moment imbue insurgent appropriations with their own autonomous justification. Later, in the postwar era, if their political legitimacy could find no arbitrator other than the Peruvian state, the reason was that movements of political time had transformed the moral and legal character of property in land, including public claims that could be made to it.

In the Huallaga Valley, life projects and hopes that reliable access to farmland might sustain have also ridden atop the heady, threatening, and violent currents of political time. They have also been trapped or blocked by them. To grasp Sendero appropriations as proscribed without regard to transformations in political conditions, however, is to view them entirely under the sign of state legality with no remainder. One wonders what else they produced. One wonders: What kinds of predicaments or opportunities did they create and for whom? One wonders about their affective impact.

If dispossession is no less generative of relations than gift,[25] then both can provoke anxieties and forebodings, though of distinctive qualities and intensities. Property in land, but also constructions and other material things, all become powerful conduits for "politically and legally mediated affect."[26] State regimes legitimate property relations by positioning themselves as sole guarantor of proper possession for the present and into the future. The relative success of that positioning has widespread reverberations—through how those regimes threaten, reassure, and trace out lines of anticipation for the private claims and life projects they recognize, exclude, ignore, or persecute.

The war was militarily over in most of Peru by the mid-1990s. Yet in the Upper Huallaga the insurgents' rural dominance—which had long dissuaded the entrance of large, state-approved (i.e., legal) capital ventures—endured. And while the titling program (initiated elsewhere as early as 1995) presupposed a future for the region when insurgents would be no more, another decade would have to pass before Shining Path's influence on everyday rural life had waned enough to extend the program to most, but clearly not all, parts of the countryside. By 2007 a few islands of Sendero control still remained, as Tina's account shows. For when surveyors finally entered the area where she had her farm, armed senderistas would tell them where to draw lines, thereby revealing a situational meeting of land regimes: one in expansion, the other in swift decline.

defeated claims

It was late afternoon when Tina heard the sound of footsteps and voices approaching. Thinking the surveyors had decided to take her up on her invitation to visit, she smiled until she saw them with Rayo and a few *compañeros* leading the way. "We have come to measure the land," Rayo announced. "Since you have more than you need, you must give some back to the community." He then instructed the two surveyors to mark off a wide swath from each side of the farm, twenty hectares in all, leaving a middle patch undisturbed where Tina had her small cabin and fields of coca.

Tina had not seen this coming. Worst of all they planned to appropriate the portion she cared most about: a strip facing the water with banana and cacao trees. Tina protested it was unfair to seize areas she had worked terribly hard to clear. All of those hours. All that back-breaking effort. Rayo brushed her aside: "If you are not in agreement with the Party . . . with us who take care of you patrolling, always keeping watch so you can sleep at night, then you can leave."

Feeling her legs suddenly weaken, Tina slid to the ground. Tears now welling up in her eyes, she pleaded: "How can you take land from a woman? I am sick. I have diabetes. I work alone with no one to help me." But Rayo shook his head and, feigning impatience, said the decision had been made. He even refused to let her harvest whatever she could.

Within this turn of events the voice of Rayo crystallizes so much. There is a revolutionary idiom of redistribution: those who have more than they need must give back. There is a stark bargain of Hobbesian reciprocity: Tina's protection (and even peace of mind) in exchange for her obedience.

And there is as well a clear intimation of how sovereignty is fundamentally perspectival: those who patrol and police for the Party would be "terrorists" in the eyes of the Peruvian state; likewise, "armed robbery," what they seized and reassigned in the name of Party justice.

A year later, at a large ceremony in town on the right bank of the Huallaga River, a local Peruvian state representative presented Tina with a legal deed to her property: the middle portion surveyors had marked off that day. One of Rayo's close companions received title to the waterfront strip. And the deed to the portion from the other end of the farm was picked up by a villager sympathetic to the Party—someone whose name Tina never disclosed.

Tina insisted what happened to her was not exceptional. Indeed, I had been hearing coca farmers tell land redistribution stories for years, though shrouded in secrecy, rarely in detail. Then, I received from a woman who once had sizable holdings on the right side of the Huallaga River (but within an area that persisted until quite late under Shining Path influence) a detailed account that echoed Tina's story in several striking respects. This woman, a local merchant, had lost two-thirds of her then-untitled property: upward of thirty hectares split into two separate pieces. One parcel was given to armed members of Artemio's retinue and the other to sympathizers from a nearby hamlet. The transfer happened outside the confines of the government's free titling campaign. Instead, a private topographer handled the measurements with Artemio personally overseeing the process for which she was later given the tab and ordered to pay. The woman's story reiterated others in which the insurgent leader exerted direct influence on land redistribution. That Artemio's sway in such matters was imagined, at least by some, to have been extensive was also eloquently expressed by a former employee of the district Gobernación office. Telling of his own direct involvement in the titling process, the employee confided with a smirk how registry functionaries joked among themselves that the campaign had practically instituted Artemio's own agrarian reform. Though made in jest, the idea that new property titles might carry forward traces of an insurgent tenure regime in camouflaged form was hardly lost on those working in the program.

The two plots taken from Tina belonged to her father's original agrarian reform holdings—land she had reclaimed only a few years before. Unlike others, Tina had been fortunate to retain her father's property throughout the first decade of the conflict: she somehow managed to survive the everyday burdens of a Maoist people's war. When she eventually stopped going there, spending time there, it was not in response, she said, to any direct insurgent threat. The Party did not order her to give up the farm. She abandoned it of her own volition around 1994—a moment I knew to have coincided with the Peruvian army's brutal counterinsurgency operations on the left bank of the Huallaga River.[27] Tina withdrew to the safety of the town on the other side of the river, where she and her family kept a home.

When the army's operations finally ceased, the weakened insurgency attempted over the next half decade to rebuild its organization in the countryside. Needing a local population, Sendero selectively encouraged former residents to return to their farms. Tina learned of the Party's designs when people she knew from the left bank began dropping by the house to say her father's lands were waiting. She should go back lest Sendero give the farm to someone else.

Initially, Tina bided her time, continuing to earn a living as a boat operator on the Huallaga. Yet working day in, day out on the water, with the cold humidity that never seems to leave your bones, eventually takes a toll. So, after receiving assurances she was still welcome to return, Tina sold her boat and took up farming again. She planted coca to start but then branched out with other cash crops she hoped would someday spare her the downside of living with the fear of police arriving to rip up her fields. For the next few years Tina moved each week between town and country, working, as she said, to provide for her children's futures. Artemio's response to the arrival of the surveyors put those plans in jeopardy.

precarious disguise

Retelling Tina's story lets me emphasize that in 2007 the Sendero leader drew on what threat he still commanded to ensure the Maoist Party could speak through the government titling campaign. No doubt securing legal deeds for lands captured by unsanctioned means had monetary motivations. Once titles existed, rural real estate values would likely increase. The ground could be converted to currency, which leader and supporters might carry if forced to flee. The point I wish to make, though, moves in a different direction. Wherever the titling program overlooked tumultuous, ongoing histories of competing claims to land, it precipitated a state-driven form of forgetting since the very act of bestowing definitive ownership selected one group to the exclusion of all other possible claimants. Tina's case in this regard is complex: her claim was excluded, but only partially so, since she did receive a deed to a portion of what had been a more extensive terrain. What the program overlooked was the insurgent seizure of what else had been hers, while validating that seizure ex post facto with legal titles for those who benefited directly.

Oblivion here stems from a refusal to revisit the conflict and how its effects persist into the present. The state "forgets" what it refuses to recognize or actively denies. Indeed, a close reading of the program's procedural regulations would show that the titling campaign attempted to found a new year zero in the assignment of rural property. In that regard, my use of the notions of *forgetting* and *oblivion* overlaps with what Kregg Hetherington has called the "symbolic erasure" of claims that government surveying in rural Paraguay performs against groups who are not intended recipients of land reform (i.e., large property owners and indigenous communities).[28] There is one important difference: forgetting may well entail an erasure that does not destroy material traces, but it can also refer, as I do in this chapter, to a force of silencing, which inheres in Peru's postwar times. As such it is not only symbolic, or at least not primarily. In aftermaths of extended (counter)insurgency conflict, many unrecognized claims linger. From my fieldwork it would seem that rarely, in the Upper Huallaga, are they voiced *beyond* the sphere of rural hamlets. Forgetting, therefore, does not mean those claims do not exist. They simply do not circulate, much less regionally or even nationally. Oblivion names that condition of noncirculation that persists in that territorial beyond of claims held but not heard.

So, the assignment of rural property would begin again, as if from scratch. And yet, when the guerrilla movement tapped into the Peruvian state's administrative power, it did not merely alter who would receive property titles. It disguised the traces of its own land redistributions in a new rural property registry and even in the land deeds distributed by the state. The guerrillas' actions in effect heightened the ramifications of postwar oblivion by diminishing the legal grounds from which those who had lost their farms might present counterclaims. In so doing, they also cast special light on the way counterfeit things depend upon *the force* that underwrites legal signatures—by which I mean the denotational faculty of the state to authorize identifying marks as proper and valid.

Land clearly could not be falsified, only signatory marks that legitimated specific social ties to it. Such ties were precarious to the extent territory is never permanently fixed. The legal recognition of rural property is contingent, above all, on movements of political time and how they inflect the fortunes of the state. In the case of Tina, the lines surveyors drew to break up her farm did not speak for themselves. They relied on the undersigning authority of the Peruvian state that while operating at a remove invested their marks with an air of finality. What Sendero did was intervene in the distance that opened up between the survey lines and their legal ratification.

Here, it is worth noting Veena Das's observation, based on a Derridean reading of difference and iteration, that the state through its "technologies of writing . . . simultaneously institutes the possibility of forgery, imitation, and the mimetic performances of its power."[29] All legal signatures potentiate their own misappropriation—an insight widely elaborated upon in recent ethnographic explorations of state documents.[30] The advent of a rural titling campaign in Peru thus inevitably created novel opportunities for the fraudulent adjudication of property. My inquiry, however, dwells not with documents per se (electronic registries or paper deeds), or with the government-sponsored acts of surveying and mapping of territories per se, but with lived encounters on the land, namely, particular tracts bordering a riverine terrain in the prolonged transition from war to postwar. Those encounters reveal the molecular complexity of territorializing practices from which claims to property not only manifest but gain intensity. Claims manifest in the affects transmitted through the physical inscription and arrangement of material things. They accrue intensity in the tonalities of forces coursing through the gestures of social life. A command suddenly belts out *¡Alto!* A look of annoyance flashes across a face. The touching of a shoulder interrupts a fright-filled silence.

Mannerisms such as these introduce "critical distances" out of which territories begin to take shape.[31] Paying attention to them gives primacy to an aesthetic and material expressiveness that situates the analysis of property at the level of empirical encounters, confrontations, and avoidances. That is why I am intrigued by the prominent place Deleuze and Guattari (1998) accorded to the signature concept in their influential theory of territorial transformation.

What Deleuze and Guattari called "signatures" refers to a broader and more basic phenomena than the writing of one's personal name. They are "territorializing marks" that enable the constitution of new domains. In this sense signatures—understood as mannerisms that refigure distance—are inherently appropriative. Deleuze and Guattari described them as "qualities" and "matters of expression" in order to underscore their empirical but also aesthetic character.[32] Signatures have a vibrant materiality that is primary, not subsidiary, to territorial creation—of which property in land would be but one kind. Without a material, expressive mark (i.e., without a *signature* in Deleuze and Guattari's sense), there can be no territory. And yet a mark alone merely establishes a vector or "directional" claim. To territorialize, a signature must become "dimensional." It must endure, and it must achieve a palpable extension in space.[33] Curiously, this is precisely the promise of land titles: to secure the owner and screen off the threat of incursions and claims of others. Property titles promise to keep chaos at bay from a well-delimited terrain and for the foreseeable future.

Ethnographic attention to the mannerisms that pervade empirical encounters, confrontations, and avoidances can reveal the volatility of moments of territorial refashioning. Within those currents, which are immanent to everyday life, declaring possession is always an act of signing. Acknowledging this suggests that *legal signatures* (understood in the common language sense as that without which there could be no state-recognized legal property) should also be viewed as primarily appropriative. If so, then the categorical wall separating legal signatures from their falsification begins to collapse. Both assert possessory claims.

For that reason the counterfeit in this chapter refers not to the replica of an original but to the performance of a right—successful only where that performance achieves the backing of a legal seal: here a property title underwritten by the authority of a state, asserting in turn its own underlying right to the total expanse of national territory. A valid or legitimate title to rural property can thereby be imagined as a privileged subset within a wider field of claims—*all of them "fake" to begin with*—against which only some would secure a fitting, if precarious, disguise. The analysis of counterfeits, therefore, should unfold less by judging and denouncing imposters than by asking who temporarily succeeds in affirming their own particular will against other claimants. The role played by "the state" (understood here strictly as an administrative faculty) is that of selecting valid claimants from a broader field of mere pretenders or counterfeits.[34]

In this land surveying episode Sendero offered no alternative to the emerging property regime of the Peruvian state. Belligerents and their supporters vied no longer for revolution but for mastery over small, ever-dwindling returns. Yet the way insurgents capitalized on the titling campaign is revealing for how it resonates with a mode of counterfeiting that James Siegel in his study of Indonesian *palsu* calls the "real-but-false."[35] Siegel distinguishes this class of forgery from mere imitation in that it does not fake an authorizing signature or certification but instead uses an authentic one that has been secretly supplied by institutional "insiders"—for instance, when a consulate employee pilfers official seals, stamps, and documents, such as blank passport booklets, to produce papers that are "genuine-but-false."[36]

Counterfeiting in this instance turned on luring the Peruvian state into validating property lines otherwise banned by national law—to wit, lines that marked the violent seizures of an outlawed political force. Since the plausibility of a Shining Path revolution had faded, the insurgency's ability to impose its own legal signatures had dissipated. Therein the need to appropriate, albeit surreptitiously, the signature power of the state. What made it counterfeit was the unauthorized status of the capture, which is what brings notions of falsification and piracy into *conceptual proximity*. The "insiders" in this case were government surveyors who under duress provided the mark of verification in a region historically remote to the state, or at least to its protective and guaranteeing facade. Catching the sleight of hand required *empirical proximity* to mannerisms of everyday life and to the specific ways in which they conveyed territorial aspirations.

The efficacy of falsification in this case depended, moreover, upon a particular, if ultimately transient, constellation of forces. Through the demise of the insurgency's revolutionary promise, coupled with its lingering local influence, Shining Path would bring a mode of counterfeiting to bear. It would camouflage its seizures, precisely, where the legal signature of the Peruvian state converted land into property. How doing that could team up with forces of postwar forgetting is something to explore in the sections to come. First, though, I want to situate the surveyor's work and more so Tina's predicament within a larger regional history.

contracts and contemplations

In the Upper Huallaga innumerable dramas of land tenure have persisted under the threat of having the possibility of ownership stripped away. Indeed, the hope of obtaining indisputable claim to a farm of one's own has been a relatively stable horizon inhering throughout the region's modern times of conflict. One strategy for narrating that larger history is following people's struggles to secure enduring hold on arable land. People not unlike Tina.

Consider that during the 1960s and 1970s the valley was an agrarian reform zone populated by colonos—Tina's father among them—who with the Peruvian state's blessing and help arrived to appropriate vast areas of forest once claimed by absentee landlords. Consider too how to this day rural parts of the valley receive migrants who aspire to acquire farmland. The 1960s agrarian reform programs—first under President Belaúnde, then, greatly expanded, following the military coup of Juan Velasco Alvarado— promised parcels to anyone willing to take up farming or ranching in the region.[37] The process, nevertheless, for obtaining legal ownership to government-measured plots was not without hardship. The Ministry of Agriculture widely handed out provisional deeds, but as some still recall, many colonos took them to be proof of proprietorship. Others did not understand how to convert them into definitive titles or else never attended seriously enough to the bureaucratic steps for doing so. Perhaps since most, like Tina's father, were first-time homesteaders with no capital of their own, they were less able to meet the cash quotas required by the government. Regardless, many reform beneficiaries did pay and receive titles. Those who did not, no small number I am told, learned their temporary deeds afforded them negligible rights to land on which they had toiled and begun to make productive.

Expansion of coca cultivation in the mid-1970s transformed the

Huallaga not only into a monocrop economy but into Peru's production center for illicit cocaine. People from across the country relocated to the valley en masse to tap into the burgeoning illegal trade. The national government, suddenly less enthusiastic about migration to the region, adjusted its politics of land. Titling became a lure in the development arm of the coca eradication program.[38] The Peruvian state continued to formalize possession of agrarian reform parcels but solely for farmers who agreed to plant legal crops.[39] In the common sense of government policy, small-scale agricultural entrepreneurs should demonstrate proof of tenure before obtaining bank loans for seed, fertilizer, and other supplies. The broader intent, however, was to block state-guaranteed ownership to anyone growing coca, which by the early years of the 1980s was most everyone.

About that time Sendero Luminoso and its mode of revolutionary violence arrived. Rural areas turned hostile to employees of the state. Guerrillas attacked police patrols. They stymied construction of new roads: burned equipment, threatened workers. Hamlet by hamlet the Maoist Party extended its influence until it had effectively replaced the Peruvian state as holder of eminent domain over rural people and property alike.[40] The transformational aspirations of armed struggle grounded Shining Path's assertion of underlying title to the land—a claim whose guarantee ostensibly emanated from the movement of political time itself.

For the historical unfolding of modern revolution carried in the insurgents' view a legal prerogative of its own:[41] *a title* that validated—in anticipation as much as in retrospect—every act committed on the flight to inevitable victory: *La revolución se justifica.* This slogan would appear painted in red in public places and thoroughfares of the Upper Huallaga but also in the published declarations of that faction of the Party.[42] Belonging to a regional repertoire of Sendero speech, it was but a variation on Mao's *la rebelión se justifica* frequently cited in early documents of the Communist Party of Peru–Shining Path and in the pronouncements of the group's then undisputed leader Abimael Guzmán.[43] And so, if land surveyors ventured into rural areas and were summarily killed, well then . . . *la revolución se justifica.*

Interlocking time, land, and law, the notion of title condensed myriad phenomena across various scales of social and political life: the directed violence of collective transformation, the assertion of new eminent domain, and so many "private" claims of ownership. Stated differently, the possession of rural property in the Upper Huallaga collided with the lawmaking force of Maoist armed struggle that reassigned possessions precisely on account of the legal title of "legitimate revolution"[44]—a revolution that can be read, among other things, as a particular figuration of political time.

Affirming the legal authority of revolution was always a historically situated, time-sensitive speech act. Logically disputing its title required *simply* demonstrating the moment was not right. No wonder then that in Peru critics from across the political spectrum insisted Shining Path began its people's war at the wrong time: in 1980 as the country celebrated its first democratic elections in over a decade. They also observed that the group's characterization of rural property relations as "feudal" completely disregarded the sweeping changes of Velasco's reform. While regional studies of the insurgency have revealed a far more variegated picture,[45] Shining Path's insurrection was not the revolution many leftist activists and intellectuals once postulated as necessary to overcome the country's persistent socioeconomic inequalities. All the worse, the Party's willingness to kill anyone who disputed its authority—especially left-wing peasant and labor activists—seemed to resemble the acts of a ruthless organization.[46] Less acknowledged, though, was the extent to which armed revolutions often harbor a criminal, racketeering element. Combining legal and illegal tactics as a means for interrupting the ideological function of state legality has a deep history among clandestine political organizations of the radical left.[47] On that score, in the Upper Huallaga special circumstances prevailed. The illegal production of raw cocaine was by the late 1970s driving the regional economy in ways that strategically undermined the legitimacy of state law.[48] There, Sendero found a rural population that disregarded prohibitions against cocaine and was looking for protection from the police.

Shining Path was not the same in every region of the country, and as the war continued, different versions of the insurgency underwent significant changes. The name "Sendero Luminoso" designated different things depending on the historical moment and locale. Here that name indicates less a cohesive entity—though it is often spoken of in that way—than as a multilayered trajectory of events that became recognizable through the use of a relatively consistent repertoire of techniques for crafting alliances and asserting dominion.

Letters the Party anonymously delivered in Huallaga towns to political officials and the administrative heads of state agencies, advising them to resign, were one well-known technique. In the early to mid-1980s the movement's violence inspired such trepidation that many if not most government functionaries decided it best to abandon posts, withdrawing to the relative safety of cities. With the retreat of state authorities, farmers who had acquired land titles during the agrarian reform learned that in the eyes of the Party their property deeds were but words devoid of guarantee. Not to worry, Shining Path leaders assured, everyone would receive titles to land once the revolution had been won—a day just around the corner. Such was one promise of people's war.

Another notorious technique practiced in the countryside well into the 1990s were juicios populares.[49] The people's trials, whereby armed fighters gathered residents of rural communities to witness the execution of Party enemies and social misfits (adulterers, thieves, swindlers, drunks), became the event routine through which an order of insurgent land tenure first emerged. The juicio popular inaugurated a new social contract and with it an obligatory meditation: take in the act of killing, behold the remains, make a life-altering decision. Falling under the sway of the revolution entailed smaller contractions as well—a collection of new minor and not so minor habits—whether learning Party songs and slogans, figuring out how to stay awake during late-night meetings, shouldering the weight of myriad logistical tasks, receiving militia training, or acquiring a suspicious, honed perspicacity toward all strangers. Each habit presupposed in turn a perch from which to contemplate the passage of time and the possible futures that passage might trace out.

The earliest juicios predictably intervened in older histories of local disputes, becoming entangled with them. Yet at the same time, they introduced rural communities to Shining Path's program and to their own place within the armed struggle. For once the execution had been accomplished, residents who watched the killing or had been coerced into taking a more active part were often asked if they supported the Party's aspirations. This much I would hear again and again: anyone who failed to express agreement would be given twenty-four hours to abandon homes and fields with only what personal effects could be physically carried. Lands vacated by those who refused to join the insurrection were set aside as *chacras del pueblo* (people's farms or, more simply, community farms) administered by Party-appointed delegates. Abandoned fields were also handed to residents considered most supportive of the Party's cause. Thus, Shining Path not only supplanted the Peruvian state's authority for regulating ownership and use of rural property; it created a land distribution system of its own.[50] In this manner, the Party established control over coca fields and over a rural population weeded out and pressed into the people's war. Yet Sendero governance was not a purely top-down imposition. Day-to-day administration of Party rule was a community affair backed up by periodic visits from roving groups of insurgents. Shining Path may have arrived from elsewhere. Nonetheless, it became deeply entrenched in the place: through bonds of kinship, active participation in Party tasks, and a local sense, if not of purpose then of shared trajectory.

The extent of Shining Path control over arable land was largely ignored in government-level policy toward the region. Whereas elsewhere rural titling initiatives were occasionally carried out by the Peruvian Armed Forces in contexts of counterinsurgency,[51] in the Huallaga, land tenure questions were framed within government strategies for discouraging coca cultivation. Peruvian economist Hernando de Soto, who served briefly as special adviser to President Fujimori in the early 1990s—at the height of Shining Path power in the region—argued against withholding land rights, insisting the cocaine economy's dominance stemmed in part from the state's own marginalization of coca farmers. The remedy was to create a new land registry that no longer shunned but instead welcomed coca farmers by securing their rights as legitimate property owners so that over time, he predicted, they would become effective participants in non-coca-related agribusiness. While it is doubtful the Fujimori administration took de Soto's plan seriously,[52] political conditions prevailing in the countryside made introducing a new land registry impractical. For where Shining Path's influence was extensive, the state did not exercise sovereignty and could not have ensured the rights of anyone. What's more, as one analyst of the US Agency for International Development astutely observed at that time, issuing titles where Sendero forced out original tenants and replaced them with sympathizers would merely normalize insurgent redistributions of land and offend the "sense of justice" of all but Shining Path.[53]

For farmers, risk of losing access to land hardly ended after the first juicios populares. The threat endured throughout the times and ever-shifting territories of Sendero rule. Any accusation of asocial behavior, disloyalty, or assisting perceived enemies could precipitate exile from insurgent territories, that is, when it did not result in more lethal consequences. I have been told stories of local leaders who conspired to take away and redistribute plots according to their own, self-serving criteria: so-called *roba chacras* (farm grabbers). It was also common to hear how others (unnamed or indicated by a *chapa* [nickname] or a clandestine militant name) variously exploited Sendero law for "private" advantage. Such complaints formed a background clamor against which Huallaga residents often framed accounts of land politics, the echoes of which can be found in Tina's story, above all, in her negative portrayal of Rayo.

For the longest time, from the early 1980s into the waning years of the 1990s, people had to contend with the threat of being denied *any place* in the countryside. Many who abandoned farms—forced out by Sendero, in fear of the army's wrath or simply because they did not want their children to join the guerrilla—moved to nearby towns if they did not flee the region. They *urbanized* in the sense they became less involved in rural lifeways or else sought to preserve those ways as best they could by acquiring access to fields, close enough to work by day but not so far they would have trouble returning home by night. From the towns they grew accustomed to new rhythms and routines with very different demands. From the towns, they contemplated what had and could have been. Losing lands they had fought to clear and plant in order to create a future life trajectory often left a *vacío*, a hole, an uncertain longing. And that trajectory, though interrupted, remained on hold as years went by and they grew older—on hold so perhaps that same parcel of terrain could be taken up once again by their children. Waiting for times to change, fighting off the pressure to give up (forget): if all that yearning could be harnessed, one can imagine what a mighty force it would be.

fatigue

Access to farmland made particular kinds of life projects possible in the Upper Huallaga Valley. For two decades and more access hinged on the tenor of one's relationship to Shining Path. By 2007 what little remained of the insurgency could not block the Peruvian state from affirming eminent domain over the entire countryside. Just as significant as the loss of its military might, the movement no longer could make plausible claim to the lawmaking force of revolution and the legal signature its violence had previously animated. What the insurgency could do, for a limited period still and in a few ever-shrinking areas, was tap into the state's renewed assertion of underlying title to the land and parasitically turn that process of reclamation in its favor.

For Tina the legal deeds others received to the two portions cut from her father's original holdings were all too real. *Real* because publicly recognized and authorized by the Peruvian state. But also *false* because they were based on the concealment of their origin in an unsanctioned violence. While the specific circumstances leading to her loss of land were well-known at the level of the rural hamlet, they became much less apparent at a geographic and temporal remove—on the other side of the river and in the realm of the town, as well as after the fact. And yet no matter how concealed that violence was from afar, land titles obtained through Artemio's limited capture of the government registry program expressed an undeniable vitality—a vitality palpable in Tina's distress, palpable too in the confident tones that infused life plans others might trace out upon lands she considered hers.

Several months after Artemio's arrest in 2012 I visited Tina at her house in town. We sat outside on a long wooden bench. Before us ran the cement street that came to a stop at a grassy bluff above the Huallaga. While we talked, we looked out over the river toward the left bank's green hills rolling away under towering clouds.

Tina tells me she just returned from the nearby city of Tingo María. She had caught a car out of town early that morning, and when passing the hamlet of Santa Lucía, from the highway she could see coca eradication teams preparing to cross the river. She also tells me she is unbearably tired. Yesterday someone poisoned Manchi, her Siamese cat, and Britney Spears too, her teenage daughter's dog. Tina found them strewn at the edge of the cement street, foaming at the mouth. How her daughter cried over that little dog. How Tina went house by house talking to neighbors, but no one seemed to know or want to say anything about it.

I ask her if she will go to the farm this week. She says "no": her son's recent sickness has set back her plans, and she must stay in town to care for him until he is strong enough to return to his job in Lima. The farm is, nonetheless, in her thoughts, because she shares news that the strip along the water has now been sold. Last week she had a run-in with the man who bought the parcel. The owner, she tells me, who is originally from a northern region of Peru, recently moved to the area. As a new arrival he has no prior connection to the place or to its very specific relationship to Peru's recent history of conflict. Tina had hoped to convince him to pay compensation, at least for her crops, but instead an ugly confrontation ensued. She insisted she wasn't asking him to give back the land, but no matter, the man was rude. What did he care about her crops or whether the land had been hers once before? He had the title and good lawyers too. This week he will dig up the banana and cacao groves with a Caterpillar to make room for fields of rice.

Because of how he treated her, Tina is incensed. Now she is considering lodging a legal complaint. Though she needs more information and must weigh the risks. In telling me this, she falls back into the story of how she met two surveyors in the port at the edge of the Magdalena River. I ask, Did Sendero take the land because you refused Artemio's order to lie down on the ground? Tina isn't sure, but in her version of events, it is Rayo who is ultimately to blame for the initial loss of her land and its later sale.

At that moment we hear helicopters. Tina's son walks over and says, "Look! There are several flying over the left bank. They are heading *al fondo*, deep into the countryside." Tina explains: eradication teams have hundreds of workers who can manually shred a hectare of coca in no time at all. Especially since nowadays none of the coca plants are old. No longer do the bushes have thick trunks, which makes the work of ripping them up much easier.

Tina doesn't know whether to press her claim. The man has the legal deed after all. Against that what can she do? The only evidence in her favor is the provisional title the Ministry of Agriculture gave her father during the

1970s agrarian reform. But she doesn't have a copy. Perhaps if she travels to the nearby city of Huánuco, she can request one from the ministry. Even so, taking a case to court is expensive. It requires time and money she does not have, and doing that would surely earn her ill will in the community—the kind that not long ago would have gotten you killed. And so Tina seesaws back and forth: pursue her claim or desist?

Above all, it is in her own body where she feels the passage and press of time. From week to week her diabetes—a disease she attributes to her years working on the river but also to the shocks of the war—waxes and wanes. How to shoulder the fatigue? How to cope with the exhaustion as it comes in waves? Waves that punctuate and push her plans off track: of when she can enter the farm and when she must leave for the shelter of her home in town. Then there are the continual needs and the all-too-everyday crises of her children both grown and almost grown. It is their futures that worry her most. She is anxious her body will give out too soon, which is yet another way in which the aftermath of war manifests: in bodies, breaking down and still fragile after years of enduring the violence and threats of political unrest.

Tina tells me she can't believe hamlet leaders approved the sale, and behind her back no less. She says "everyone knows" what happened: those are *her lands* and Sendero, that Rayo, stole them. Knowing full well her lands had been seized—illegally from the perspective of the Peruvian state and then transferred to new owners under pretenses as false as they were falsified—her neighbors went ahead and made money at her expense. Thinking about litigation only increases Tina's sense of exhaustion. She doubts she can win, and she doubts she can muster the vitality required to press her claim to a successful end.

Tina had held out hope of recovering the land once most of the senderistas in the area had been captured. What she never anticipated was learning about its sale only after the fact. And I too was surprised at her predicament, and even more as I thought through its broader implications. For how could a new rural property registry secretly authenticate and thereby perpetuate an insurgent redistribution? Why would the Peruvian state endorse rural holdings that had originated in the unsanctioned violence of its internal enemy? What too of the oblivion imposed therein?

Oblivion: not because no one remembers, but because what circulates publicly as the state-recognized right to land skirts the entangled histories of how those rights have taken hold.

Only in mulling over these questions do I begin to appreciate how a land titling campaign could precipitate an infrastructural subsoil, as it were, of forgetting, by affirming property rights for some against the competing claims of others. What the particulars of Tina's predicament did was bring into starker relief the magnitude of that forgetting, giving material density to the war's effects *as a specific feature of postwar* itself. It suggested too how the temporal movement to an everyday less overtly marked by (counter)insurgency could magnify an oblivion effect filling the already deep chasm that separated national postconflict society from communities of the Huallaga countryside, where the war was more recent and its effects palpable still. For rural hamlets—as intimate realms where "everyone knows"—found themselves in the aftermath forced to adjudicate, far away from any court of Peruvian law, the many contingencies upon which conflicting property claims now turned.

oblivious deeds

New titles obscured the full range and history of social relations binding legal signatures to material things. They threatened to silence the multiplicity of prior and existing attachments to land. I wondered, though, what colored the legitimacy of these new legal deeds in the Huallaga and for whom? What traces of a former Sendero land order might they carry forward, and in so doing camouflage within an emerging status quo made official through the state's rural property registry? Recent ethnographic studies of land titling in Latin America—for example, Hetherington in Paraguay,[54] and Christopher Krupa in Ecuador[55]—have emphasized the infrastructural attributes of land registries and how they serve as a technology for targeting and enlisting specific publics or "communit[ies] of aspiration" into projects of state formation.[56] Krupa observes how cadastral reforms since the late twentieth century have responded to the global initiative of international development agencies seeking to formalize the property rights of marginalized rural populations. While that global effort conveys a general "mandate for state expansionism, extending the regulatory potency and administrative reach of the state into areas currently thought off its grid,"[57] Krupa specifies that it simultaneously promotes the decentralization of state bureaucracies in order to shore up local administrative control and facilitate tax collection. How, though, might cadastral renovation become a mechanism of forgetting by resetting the temporal calendar of legitimate claims? And to what extent might that oblivion animate what it excludes, sowing discord and future conflict?

Rural land registry reform has clearly been integral to a broader national politics of decentralization in Peru, which has transferred some authority and expertise from the central state to regional governments. Among my interlocutors, however, increased taxation has not been a concern they voice with regard to land titling. Anxieties seem to circulate instead around the present and future assurance of obtaining and holding on to land. Titles promise to secure that hold into the foreseeable future, so they are a strategic site for examining the time attributes of infrastructure that, as Hetherington explains, have been largely overlooked in scholarly studies that overwhelmingly privilege spatial features.[58] New titles in the Upper Huallaga manifested what Hetherington calls "infrastructural time": they resituated the place of rural property in the aftermath of war. They also induced an official oblivion with respect to the social connectivities state recognition selected against. Hetherington emphasizes what might be considered a general feature of infrastructures: they introduce specific rhythms and reorient temporal horizons. In this regard they create frames of probability, which are hardly restricted to material interventions in a landscape (buildings, walls, routes) but can be introduced through social practices, including bureaucratic procedures.

As I try to make sense of Tina's account and the ongoing history to which it belongs, the notion of a shadow realm of insurgent tenure persisting in times of postconflict looms large. Perhaps that idea is far-fetched, and admittedly I would be hard-pressed for now to provide extensive evidence of its effects. So in the absence of compelling proof, perhaps that idea can serve a heuristic purpose of foregrounding the afterlife of defeated claims more generally of all who lost land during the internal war and its immediate wake, together with the life plans those claims furtively held and may still keep.

Krupa notes that cadastral renovations promise historically marginalized—and what in the Upper Huallaga have been suspect and even persecuted—populations a new, ostensibly better, relation to the state. He astutely points out that unlike the peak period of Latin American agrarian reforms, the state in its contemporary neoliberal guise now gives away not land itself but legal recognition of one's right to hold land *as property*. A similar modulation in the type of state *gift* can be discerned in Peru. And yet what arguably conjoins distributions of land with their legal recognition as property, and potentially elides their difference, is the worry I often heard farmers express about attaining access to land, which would endure long enough for them to realize their own life plans.

Tina's story has allowed me to ask how property rights hinge on contingencies of political time. In contemporary Peru that means the place and non-place of armed revolution, certainly, but also the kinds of oblivion the prevailing era of postwar potentiates, and may well demand, now that Shining Path's influence in the Huallaga Valley has largely disappeared. What happens to land claims formerly blocked by the insurgency? What happens when they come up against the claims of those who received parcels and plots expropriated by Sendero that the Peruvian state later validated with legal deeds?

Safeguarding property is one crucial purpose of political community. Little use is having one's things if they can't be counted on from one moment to the next. Property in land, moreover, expresses an intensely material figuration of state legality through which the relative strength of claims over and under the earth are weighed. What hangs in the balance, among other outcomes, is the long-term viability of projects of self and familial transformation.

Given that the temporalities of state law are inextricably attached to the ever-shifting fortunes of political regimes, hopes for acquiring permanent title to property may haunt but cannot be definitively secured. This can be seen where the final remnants of a once-powerful insurgency converted some of its own land distributions into legal property—by capitalizing on a fleeting yet no less foundational moment when the Peruvian government reached out and took administrative hold of the countryside. In the context of that rural titling program, what was counterfeited—understood again not as the replica of an original but the performance of a right—was the proper character of claims to land: the social relationships that the state would guarantee through cadastral marks and (eventually) legal deeds. Grounded in movements of political time, the legal signature of the state promised durable possession for some while defeating the claims of others. What enabled the camouflaging effects of its falsification was an unauthorized capture, which—at a specific moment of postwar—served to extend, if surreptitiously, the protections of Peruvian law over precisely what that law should have proscribed.

All of this is to say that war does not end by ending. Its effects persist across material registers that when made visible belie the setting of firm temporal boundaries. Tina's body accumulates the wear, tear, and trauma of work amid the rise and fall of insurgency, threatening now to imperil the better life she desires for her children. The land itself accumulates the conflicts of neighbors and interlopers spurred on by the competing political projects that would animate them and from which they in turn seek their own "private" advantages. Most important, Tina's story shows how this aftermath of an extremely violent era (when Shining Path forced the Peruvian state to retreat from a region dominated by the cocaine economy) directly pivots on the secret interweaving of adversarial regimes of legal and illegal land titling. It shows how that very mixing circulates the war's legible and illegible traces into the present and future in ways that do not merely keep the past unsettled. They differentially invest the stakes of what can and must not be publicly acknowledged. In the wake of those stakes are land deeds that do not simply promise to secure property. They screen out the events that would throw their legal validity into doubt.

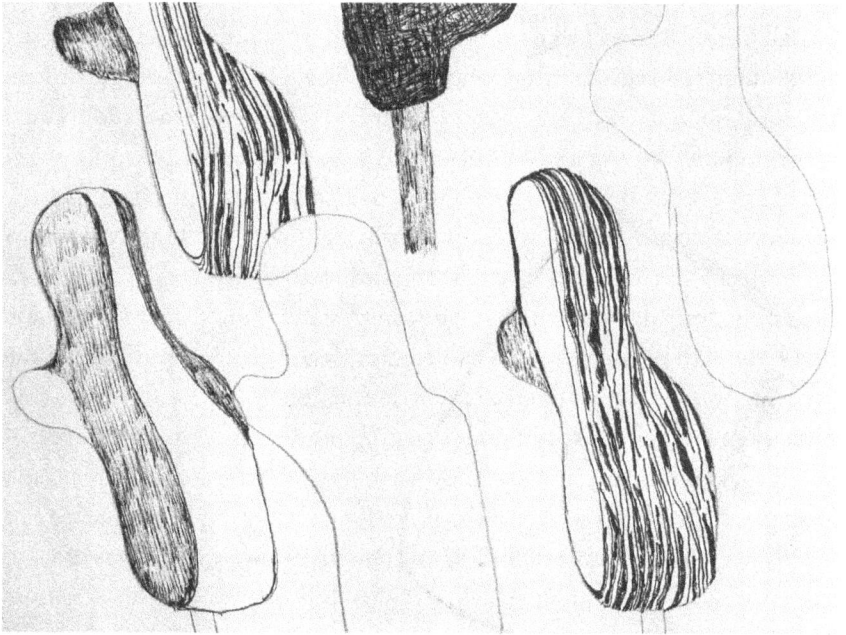

FIGURE 9.1. *bultos*, sketch from fieldwork

cloud to clod

How do images relate to intense materialities that move, sending other things reeling?

What to make of the ways that dreams, through their own peculiar modes of denotation, reach out to matter in its rawest manifestations?

Where to specify the precise points of contact that obtain between visceral remains of death and the recurrent images through which the dead return?

I ask Tina if her brother still visits her when she sleeps. It is the month of July 2013. We are sitting at her home in town along Malecón Huallaga. Not so much anymore, she says, though when he does, it is always as if he were alive. She sees him standing there in T-shirt and those running pants he so liked to wear. In dream Tina sees him as he was in life: tall and agile, cheerful and intrepid, for there was no terrain he would not dare cross on his motorbike. And when he got married, she tells me, he threw a narco-style wedding—*a lo grande*—because, narco he was, before Shining Path decided he would become one of theirs.

Tina explains that whenever she is staying at her farm in the deep beyond of the Huallaga's left bank and she begins to feel sad, she will go sit in front of his grave. And she will ask him: "Where are you? What are you doing?" And she does that, she says, in hopes he might see her. And sometimes she can feel him. Clear as day I can see him looking at me—even if that gaze of his, touching her there, at the grave, is always mute. The brother will speak to Tina but only in her sleep. And out of six brothers the war took, he is the only one who ever returns to her in dream, though now, he returns less and less, as that fateful day, twenty-four years ago, recedes ever further into the past, when his compañeros in arms shot him twice, before dumping his body, stripped of its life, into the river.

But wait, recently it happened again: he appeared to me. One night, once again, Tina was staying at the farm, and in her dream she went to see him at the grave and this time he seemed happy. Her brother told her, *Don't you worry. I live here now.* He laughed and then said, Go on back to the house!

And that was it. I woke with nothing but his image, that and knowing he was doing fine.

Two years pass. I am visiting Tina in town once again. We are sitting once again in the front room of the house along the malecón, when she mentions there is a mass grave on a plot in Magdalena where Chimbo her friend and occasional farmhand has been growing coca. The grave contains what's left of people Shining Path killed many years ago. She guesses something like sixteen or seventeen bodies must be buried there.

Tina tells me that roughly a decade before, around year 2005, and not long after she recovered what had originally been her father's agrarian reform homestead, a man she had hired to clear a field, on that very same plot, accidently disinterred the half-buried remains of two people. One body reeked of death no more, but the stench of the other continued strong. The hired hand kept on working, saying nothing of his discovery.

That same morning Tina was working too, but closer to the cabin, when she saw a thickset man she did not know crossing her land. He was wearing a T-shirt and black shorts. She called out to him, but he did not stop. So she started to follow, step after step, each one with greater urgency than the last, all in hopes of catching up. Sensing her pursuit, the man quickened his pace until he was running faster than she could manage and disappeared from view.

That very night Tina had a nightmare in which the same thickset man appeared to her. She did not recall much more, only that she woke screaming, startling her husband, Wilson, out of his own deep slumber. At breakfast the following morning, Tina and Wilson were talking about that nightmare when the farmhand arrived and, catching wind of their conversation, told them of finding two dead bodies the day before. Not once had it occurred to Tina that the thickset man could have been a wandering soul.

Soon after, Tina went to see the local political leader of Shining Path in

Magdalena. She went to inquire about the unmarked grave on her farm, but he rebuked her, telling Tina it was not her place to ask about such things. Even so, he did confirm that the Party had used those fields as a burial ground for the people they executed. That same place was precisely where about a year and a half ago—looking back from 2015, when Tina first told me, toward late 2013, which from the perspective of unfolding events surrounding her nightmare was a leap forward from times when Sendero still ruled the area to when they no longer did—Chimbo had cleared a plot to grow coca. Only that the plot Chimbo cleared no longer belonged to Tina but had been loaned by a neighbor, who held the lands bordering the north side of her farm and whose brother also held lands but bordering the south side of her farm; both of those tracts, north and south, just happened to be the same ones Shining Path had seized from Tina, excising them from her farm as it were, not long after she had reclaimed her father's homestead—a homestead that by right should really still be hers in its original, unbroken entirety, or such was the claim she refused to forget.

One afternoon in late 2013 Chimbo was working his parcel when a strange sensation hit him. The sheer strength of the feeling was so unnerving he dropped his tools and went to visit Tina at her cabin. Seeing Chimbo restless and unable to say or do anything that could calm him down, Tina urged him not to return to his plot but spend the night instead at her farm. She offered a hammock, and Chimbo agreed. That evening he went to sleep in the hammock, where he dreamed a terrible dream in which a thickset man came at him with a yelling that just would not stop.

In his waking hours Chimbo is quite the talker, always hunting for an audience of one or two he can hold in place. But it gets worse when something bothers him. There is no restraining the chatter. He cannot let it go. So he was telling anyone who would listen about that thickset man wailing from his dream, until someone proposed that to stop having nightmares, he should bite down on the sharp edge of a machete.

Chimbo followed the advice, and the thickset man never returned.

Here it is as if dreams draw close to the visceral, feeding off matter in its literal concreteness and in its most intense expressions. Where a

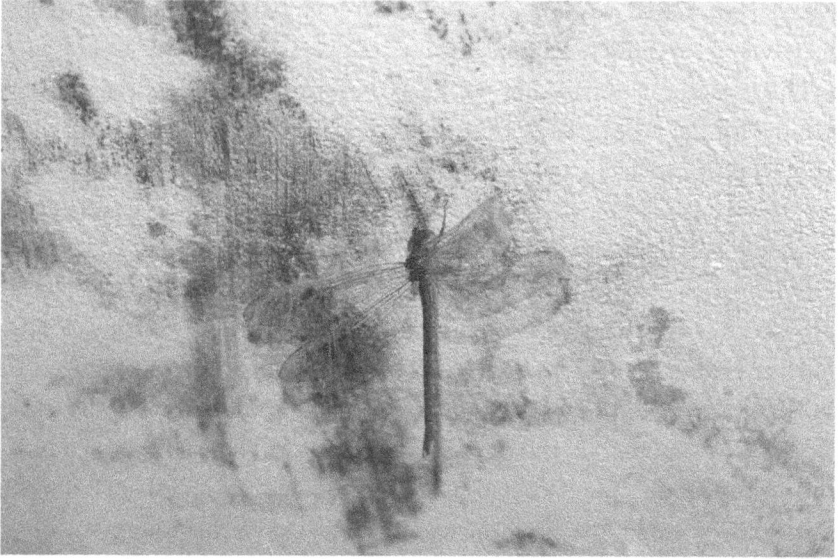

FIGURE 9.2. untitled

casual tilling turns up decomposing bodies. Where from the unsuspecting disturbance of soil at rest, dense apparitions come a hollering. Where sometimes to make the yelling go away, one must grind teeth into steel. Here dreams lean into the visceral as if to underscore a fundamental difference between senses reversible and those that will not return. For dreams form the closest of ties to those aspects of matter that cannot be undone and yet through dream somehow do return to unleash forces from other futures and other pasts.

Matter curves and folds but will not go back in time, which is the signature of its one-way irrevocable sense. And yet when matter turns intense, it all the more readily gives rise to images that can and will. For images have more play: they seesaw and ferry along a single thread, forward and backward, but only to launch elsewhere, becoming more multiple, becoming anything at all. Anything dream says. "Certain . . . always certain," yet "prior to any particular designation." Such is its denotational power: dream affirms and so it *just* is. Then dream affirms something else altogether different, and it also just *is*, without incongruity, without conflict. No contradiction to resolve, where something can always become something else.

All the while dream reaches toward places where things turn opaque, where all senses can and might be not just reversed but pushed further, sent headlong, tails spinning but only to pivot, thrusting now into new depths, below what was once all too apparent, creating there new surfaces. Dreams go lower than low to cut what tethers to gravity and to the grave. Lifting now into the air, dreams leap beyond reversals. Plucking from this direction and from that, dreams embrace direction *in-itself*. They embrace every direction, refusing to settle on one in particular. To prefer no single sense but to take them all up together is not only semblance but turbulence: that place from where bultos return.

In the late 1990s, friends in the Huallaga would sometimes share their dreams or those of their friends, dreams that carried with them histories of the war. And it is important to specify: I heard the dreams recounted, which is something quite different from waking from sleep having dreamt the dreams. Then, judging from the stories it was the army's killing that had left the deepest impressions, conveying images that lingered close, drifting in from that nearby past, another time altogether. There was that primary schoolteacher, my friend Mariela knew well, who had told her about a dream she had sometime in the early 1990s when the army was all fury. And how in that dream the schoolteacher's brother had appeared. How he had called out to her, "Come get me; the sun is burning my skin!" And when the schoolteacher came to and her brother was nowhere to be found anywhere in town, she went searching—together with her husband and several teachers from the school and two Catholic nuns from the local church. Like other families whose loved ones had disappeared, they knew where to go. At the edge of the Huallaga River they discovered him face down on the bank, but with his body still beneath the water except for part of his arm and his shoulder exposed to the sun's scorching rays, bearing signs that animals had already begun to feed.

Dreams recounted are never dreams themselves, only their approximation through story. Here those stories tell of a power of sensing across time, in the anticipations and in the aftermaths of something fateful. Dreams that ordinarily would be the least evidential here hover closest to what, for some, would be that most denotational of matters: a human corpse sliding toward decay. From cloud to clod to cloud again. Still I wonder, is it dream that privileges extremes—the highs and the lows, those pendular oppositions of life and death, day and night, waking and sleeping—or is it the telling of dream that only knows how to thrive where there is point and counterpoint, seeing and sawing, back and forth along a flat line?

Here a close brush with the remains of someone disturbs sleep.

Here which happens first is not determinate: the corpse or the image wandering from it.

Dream constellates different times without insisting on their direction or sequence.

For as rivers never cease to draw away from their own hidden sources, language bears witness too by setting at a remove what once were and therefore still are secretly conjoined. Cloud traces a lineage to rocks and hills, to heaps of dense, impenetrable things that if released from gravity might float toward the sky. Language, never ceasing to draw away from its sources, manifests secrets through condensations that would appear at first glance to evade the trouble of turbulence.

Yet who would confuse a pile of corpses with river eddies, with an enraged crowd, with a cyclone, much less a helicopter *toco toco*, closing in?

A month later I accompany Tina to her farm on the Magdalena River. Early in the morning we depart; an elderly mototaxi driver, Dante, appears at the door of her house to deliver us as far as Puerto Unión. Together we cross the Huallaga on a balsa that ferries us and our taxi to the other side. And now we are headed to Pavayacu on what is still a new rural road, when I tell Tina about the surprise visitor I had the night before. At my friends' house just off the plaza, I was getting ready for bed when, through a hole along the long edge of open bricks that connect the top of the wall with the roof, a dragonfly entered my room. I noticed the creature fluttering about, off-kilter, and when I drew closer to take a photo, I could see its body and the tips of its wings were covered in spiderwebs. Putting down the camera, I was surprised when I moved in

FIGURE 9.3. *chacra* supplies

close again that the dragonfly did not protest as I proceeded to remove the white cloudy mass.

The threads cling ever so tight to the wings that it is only with utmost delicacy that I can pull them away. One by one. With each soft pull the insect's thin elongated abdomen bends toward me under the stress, but all the while the dragonfly lets me work, does not get visibly unsettled, does not resist. After clearing away all the threads, again to my surprise the dragonfly does not leave but lingers on to spend the whole night with me there in the room. Only at the bluing of first morning's light will I watch it fly away.

When a dragonfly visits, Tina says, it's good luck, but it's not to share with others, because if you tell, then that luck is lost. What happened last night is for you, and for you alone; it's not something to be talked about. A long silence settles in the rest of the way, giving force to what feels like admonishment, and this is a place where close friends recount their dreams, where through telling they extend the circle of witnesses, in hopes perhaps of making it all the more real.

Reaching Pavayacu Dante takes us through the village and just beyond it to the river landing on the shores of the Magdalena, where we find Chara waiting in the boat to convey us to the farm. These are different times—for even five years ago, if political circumstances could have possibly allowed Tina to feel comfortable inviting me to her farm, there would have been no rural, left bank road running through Pavayacu to the river landing, and we would have had to travel instead by canoe up the Huallaga, past the right bank village of Ramal de Aspuzana, and farther still, to where the Magdalena releases its muddy flows. There, we would have crossed over and turned into the mouth of the Magdalena before heading upstream to reach the farm, just as Wilson had so often done in his former life as a botero.

Dante unloads our bags and supplies, setting our bultos on the ground. Wilson and Chara take charge of packing the things onto the boat. We do not tarry in the port. Chara operates the motor, snaking us between shores, bend after bend. Along the route lined with fronds of palm blocking any view of what lies behind, I take photographs of nothing on a journey that seems longer than I had recalled, for this time no passengers have come along, so this time there is no one to drop off at other farms along the way. Today, the boat lends but a private service, and as we travel in silence, the loss is palpable. There are no conversations among neighbors; there is nothing to share about the problems and novelties of the present day. No one complains about buyers of plantains and cacao. There is no scheduling done for the discreet shipment of coca packed into large sacks. No mention of petty disputes among neighbors or of early-teen girls who have run away from home. Chara is in no mood for making jokes, and he makes no allusions to earlier histories, makes no fun of the senderistas who now no longer control anything at all or give any cause for fright. Later, Tina will tell me that today they took on no freight.

Compared with my two earlier trips up the Magdalena two and three years ago, and how they had brimmed with the life of the place, today everything feels quiet, almost empty, until we arrive at Tina's farm and learn there is a problem. Chimbo has been booted from the plot of land where the current owner had loaned him fields to plant coca. The owner, whom I'll call Shanty, is one of a clan of siblings from the north coast, of whom I have met between three and four on my previous visits to

Magdalena. Tina says there is upward of nine altogether, but this brother had told Chimbo he could grow coca on that plot until he grew tired: in other words, just as long as he wished. In exchange Chimbo had worked as a hired hand on the man's farm for the last year and a half. But now Shanty says he is looking to sell his property, so Chimbo's chance is up. The horizon toward which he had invested so much sweat, attached so many hopes, has been closed.

Since yesterday Chimbo has been frantic, digging up and transferring his coca plants to a patch of land that Chara has helped him clear on the other side of Tina's farm. When we arrive, he insists on leading us then and there to the new plot so we can see for ourselves. And so we walk up from the river on a narrow path to the cabin, where we drop off our things, passing through the patio, where harvested leaves of coca are scattered to dry across a rusty sheet of tin roofing, heading now just beyond on another trail, tugged along by Chimbo's distress.

"Look at my little plants; look at my coca." The leaves are wilting, and the situation has left Chimbo utterly depressed. Tina tries her best to cheer him up, saying, Yes, the little leaves are going to fall off, but then they will spring forth again and stronger too. Don't worry, your plants are going to be okay.

But there is another problem. When Chimbo and Chara burned this thin strip of land at the edge of Tina's farm, they apparently breached an unmarked property line, and now the neighbor from the other side, Shanty's brother, whom I'll call Rober, arrives to complain. Tina goes out to talk with him, while Chara and Chimbo drift back toward the cabin, and I with them. From afar, we look on, as the conversation between Tina and Rober grows testy, quickly opening old wounds: of how Rayo at gunpoint and with the Party's authorization had seized two parcels from Tina, and before that, all Tina had sacrificed to recover her father's farm, how she faced off against Sendero, a woman all alone, staring down their threats. Though I must strain to hear, I can see the neighbor's hesitation, shifting his weight from left foot to right, clearly not wanting to follow her into a past he claimed not to share.

At best I catch fragments of their conversation slowly heating up, but enough to hear Tina falling back into the present, complaining that

Shanty has behaved poorly and asking why they are fighting over land. Rober answers her, but with words that seem cryptic, skirting the issue by circling back from a general point of view that "the people around us are who have to say whether we are good or bad."

And Tina emphatic, "Well, *I* never want to have problems with a neighbor."

With all the more reason, then, insists Rober, "We have to mark the property lines . . . to know where to work."

As if things were so simple, but I hear nothing more as their talk shifts toward a cooler, quieter path before reaching some sort of provisional accommodation, because soon Rober withdraws to his farm.

Tina walks back over to the cabin and begins unpacking the bags we brought from town. She lights a fire in the stove and, looking to prepare lunch, kills a hen for soup, because it's late morning already. And all the while I accompany her, lending a hand where she lets me, but mostly just listening to what she wants to share. How Chimbo's coca had been doing so well. How the leaves looked so pretty. How with that first harvest he would have finally pulled himself out of his mess. For if an arroba is selling for forty-five dollars, and if he was going to harvest eighty, well, that's money. Now, he will have to start over, Tina confides, saying too that what Shanty has done to Chimbo really bothers her. Just when things for Chimbo were starting to look up.

Tina tells me that the clan of nine brothers showed up in Magdalena when the price of farmland was extremely low. They arrived by way of the lieutenant governor of Tina's hamlet, and from him they secretly purchased the two parcels that Sendero had seized on the north and south ends of her farm. The Party gave the northside parcel to someone who later died of a tumor. That parcel is that one that Shanty currently owns. Meanwhile, Rober is the brother who several years ago threatened to mow down Tina's grove of cacao with a tractor to clear the land and plant rice. Over so many tellings, I lose track of how these parcels have changed hands. Only later does it dawn on me that the thickset man who once raged in Tina's and Chimbo's dreams is attached to the parcel that ended up as Shanty's property, the very plot that Chimbo had now abandoned, where Tina said there was a common grave, sixteen, seventeen bodies

FIGURE 9.4. the kitchen

buried, victims of Sendero's former rule. And now, pulling together disparate threads told to me at different moments over the years, I wonder if the location of that mass grave might have had something to do with which strips of land Sendero decided to excise from her farm.

Tina sets out bowls of hen soup on the table, calling us one by one: Wilson, Chimbo, Chara, and I to come sit down to eat. After lunch everyone heads out to the fields. The topic of conversation all afternoon and into the night will be the neighbors. What Shanty did to Chimbo. What Rober said today. Teasing out their implications. For Chimbo, Wilson, and Tina have words of advice: what he should do now, what he did well, and perhaps, where things went awry.

Night comes on fast, and as the sun drops beyond the forest, everyone gradually drifts back to the cabin. Chimbo rolls up a wheelbarrow filled with cacao. Wilson sits down beside it and begins to open the fruit, one by one, removing their fleshy seeds. As he fills one bucket and then two, I pull up a stool, and he talks to me about this latest conflict with the neighbors. His view: Shanty, watching Chimbo's coca beginning to flourish, decided to give him the boot to keep the plantings for himself.

Then, when Chimbo did the unexpected, dug up his coca and moved it to Tina's farm, the brother, Rober, invented a property line dispute.

Behind us, Tina is rekindling the fire to reheat the soup she will serve for dinner, when around dusk, Shanty comes walking along the trail at the edge of the farm. Crossing in front of the cabin, he does not once look over to where we are visibly seated. He does not send even a curt greeting our way. Tina takes notice and comments for only us to hear about how that strikes her as just strange.

Chara wanders off to set up a trap. Tonight he wants to hunt *picuro*, so we can eat bush meat tomorrow. Tina sets bowls on the table: first for Chimbo and then for me. The times I have been to the farm—this one but also to the *chacra* in Venenillo—Chara almost never has dinner. Tonight, after returning from readying the trap, he will retire to a rocker with a wad of coca, from the same leaves he had set out to dry earlier today, tucked inside his cheek, taking swigs from a potion concocted with the bark of a chuchuhuasi tree steeped in *aguardiente*.

While we are eating, it starts to pour outside. Wilson has already joined us at the table, and now Tina sits down too. I ask Chimbo about that time the thickset man appeared in his dreams, and he tells me that he had laid down in the hammock, gesturing to the one hung not far from the table. He had dozed off, when he felt a heavy jolt, as if someone were punching the ropes, and really strong: not once, but three, very deliberate, times . . . boom, boom, boom.

And in the midst of telling me this, the rain kept coming down harder and harder on the tin roof. Chimbo was sitting across from me, but with the racket of the downpour, I could barely make out what he was saying. Wilson then started on about that time he ran into two strangers, gringos he had never seen before. They cut straight through the farm heading toward the river but left no footprints on the ground, not even on the muddy bank of the boat landing, and it had just rained! Tina then mentioned that today Chara had found another grave, as the rain continued louder and louder until I could hear nothing else.

And tired of trying, and physically depleted, I withdraw to the bed Tina had made up for me on the second floor. Though it is still early, I am unable to resist the fatigue, and even so throughout the night my sleep is

FIGURE 9.5. coca, seedling bed

choppy. I am beginning to feel the weight of encroaching horizons as my time here slips away. Toward the end of the night, I dream a long dream that upon waking leaves me without a trace.

Upon waking . . . it is morning, and I descend the ladder to discover Chara set up in the kitchen with tools poring over a weed-cutter machine. Black horn-rimmed glasses accentuate his demeanor of serious concentration: tinkering, adjusting, seeing what might be cared for, and, if need be, fixed. I find Tina out by the little stream that courses along the southern edge of the farm en route to the Magdalena River. On a little raft near water's edge, she is finishing up some washing. I go down to talk with her, and there we strike up a conversation, which continues as we head back up the bank. When she stops to hang five or six garments on a line strung along the back side of the cabin, near the stove, I ask her about a name I have heard she and Wilson, but also Chara, mention several times over the last few days: Cara Cortada (Scarface).

Tina says, oh that was Pablo, the local Sendero leader who opposed letting her return to Magdalena and recover the farm. And it was also that same Pablo who would later insist she could have no more than five hectares. But now Tina says it was Artemio himself who later took away the two parcels. Yet I had thought Rayo had done that. And here Tina deflects, or else simply following the wander of thoughts sparked upon hearing Rayo's name, she reminds me again that Rayo, oh how different he was from his brother, who not only belonged to Sendero but was among Artemio's most trusted. Rayo's brother, he always treated me well, telling me, don't you worry, Doña, I'll stand up for you. As long as I am around, to you I won't let them do anything. But of course, not long after, the police tracked him down, and in the firefight that ensued, Rayo's brother chose to surrender rather than lose his life. And Cara Cortada? I ask again. Oh, the police arrested him too. No, no, not here, but in the Carabayllo district of Lima, a good two years after that.

Seeing us approach and enter the cabin, Chimbo comes over to sit at the table, followed by Wilson. Tina invites me to take a seat, and soon she is bringing over plates of spaghetti noodles sparsely mixed with chunks of canned tuna: one for each of us, plus a fourth for herself, before joining us as well. Chara has now retired to the hammock but is still tinkering on the machine. Tina says he has already had breakfast, and I can feel him listening in on our talk as we sip at mugs of hot watery coffee. Once we have finished eating and dishes are washed, Tina and Chimbo will carry the weed cutters out to clear the fields. She is in the midst of telling us this, when the neighbor Shanty appears once again out on the trail, yet rather than passing right through, he stops and calls over. And once again Tina gets up and walks out to him to see what he might want.

From where I am seated, I have my back toward them. To catch what is going on, I have to twist my body around. Wilson has a better, more comfortable, vantage from his place at the table, able to take in everything. And so I watch him as he looks on. And as he looks, and as he listens, I see a glower of annoyance and displeasure begin to creep across his face. Soon he too is rising from his seat, walking over to join the conversation. I stay put but continue to watch and listen from a distance. Enough to make out that only under direct questioning from Wilson does the neighbor admit he did throw Chimbo off his plot. Admits he told Chimbo to leave. Alleges Chimbo threatened him. Claims he has always tried to give Chimbo helpful advice. But what can you do with a child?

This is how he speaks of Chimbo, even though he can see Chimbo sitting over here in the cabin, and well within earshot.

The neighbor says: Chimbo wastes his money on beer and liquor. First he gets drunk. Then he gets aggressive.

And Tina, now pulling the conversation elsewhere, can't resist the cut: When you walk by, don't go twisting your neck the other way no more!

And Shanty too can't resist the cut: Tina for living here *first* really should be the one to set an example of neighborly behavior.

And Tina, ignoring the slight but not missing the opportunity, opened by his unwitting reference to those times before he and his brother had settled in Magdalena, turns instead to recounting what has now become the refrain of how she had to fight, put her life on the line, to recover her land, and how, soon after, Sendero had seized the very parcels Shanty and his brother Rober now own and work. Tina intones once again, framing what for her are ongoing ties to fields she insists were unjustly taken. And again, it is clear these two brothers do not wish to know anything about what happened before they acquired what Tina says pertained to her. No less sure they deny that upon their properties there could be any outstanding claim.

That people from Sendero forcibly seized fields and then sold them to others is, Shanty insists, of little relevance. *Eso son tiempo de ellos*, I hear him say all the way back to where I am sitting and straining to follow. What *ellos*, the Party, Sendero, might had done before, all that belongs to another era, affirms Shanty, pushing away precisely what is not in his interest to entertain.

Eso son tiempo de ellos.

As if . . . Sendero's demise and departure had ushered in a different political time.

As if . . . recalling what had been suffered before and at their hands were now somehow prescribed.

As if . . . a strict severance and the complete discontinuity of historically contiguous moments blocked in no uncertain terms any and all continued assertions of prior rights to land.

As if . . . for the contemporary, ongoing relations between these neighbors and these neighboring farms, made possible, thanks in part to shady bills of sale, Tina's plaints of injuries previously received could have no bearing,

And here and now she makes no headway with her claim. How to respond to what is all too evident: Sendero is no longer around to impose its will and law. How to respond to the contention that all disputes arising during that other time when they were in charge, disappeared with them. Even though precisely what Tina asserts is a harm they exacted on her in the name of their authority, which in no moment did the Peruvian state ever cease to disallow. To Shanty's words she has no effective reply, not to what succeeds here in heading off Tina's refrain, leaving her silent, if only for a moment.

All the while, I am thinking how it must be for Tina to live pressed between these two brothers, who each day cross back and forth over what remains of her land, each time scraping at the scars of a wound, keeping its memory fresh, keeping traces of what happened viscerally present. I think too of the ways these encounters on her farm come to be filtered by the distinct perspectives of each one who takes part, encounters that directly transpire from the crisscross of neighbors, who themselves would not be walking back and forth if not for the histories of how the conflict had shaped the ways plots of land would ultimately change hands.

This morning Tina complains to Shanty about how Rober had been overbearing yesterday. Tina is emphatic about how arrogant and worked up he got. Yet from what I saw, Rober had not seemed condescending or especially angry. Not to me. Instead I saw him firm, trying to seek some kind of understanding, if expressed solely on terms that would best align with his own interests. Now that I have watched both brothers talk and interact with Tina, it is clear to me that their opinion of who Tina is is not only unflattering but well-defined and essentially set in stone. But even so, all must find some way to live side by side, such that tensions do not overflow into open hostilities, here where enmity feels deep and explosive. And that is why each of these conversations concludes with some sort of verbal reaffirmation, even when indirect and subtle, of how neighbors must strive to stay on good terms. And so in this conversation, before parting ways, Tina abruptly shifts toward matters less contentious, haggling now to my surprise with Shanty over the exact price she would be willing to sell him a seedling bed of coca.

And with that Shanty heads off toward Rober's farm, and Tina and Wilson walk back to the table, where Wilson expresses exasperation at the behavior of the two brothers, adding that he does not think for a moment that their intentions are friendly.

FIGURE 9.6. *mesa de chacra*

After breakfast, everyone except me goes out to work in the fields. Tina goes to collect *bijao* leaves and to help Chara whack weeds with the machine he has apparently now fixed to his satisfaction. I stay behind in the hammock to pore over what I have seen and heard this morning and to draft from that detailed notes. A couple of hours later Tina returns, carrying a bundle of bijao leaves on her back. Bushed, she says, laying her bulto beside the stove, but also wanting to prepare *limonada* to take out to everyone else, who are working in the heat, which is surprisingly strong for a day when the sky is completely overcast. I am still in the hammock, and Tina, from the table where she cuts and squeezes limes, shares lingering thoughts about this morning's encounter. She remarks that Chimbo had previously told her he had lost his national ID card or DNI. But she now learns that, according to Shanty, Chimbo pawned it for drink money! Shanty says he gave Chimbo fifty soles to recover his DNI but that Chimbo spent that money on getting drunk again and then in that altered state began chasing people around Shanty's farm with a knife. Chimbo denies Shanty gave him fifty soles, insisting it was only ten. Tina does not know whose version of events to believe.

Chimbo. Man of multiple facets, divergent faces: always talking, always spinning out stories. Which one will be a lie? When can anyone know he is telling the truth?

And now, as if announced, Chimbo appears with a weed-whacking machine in tow, which he sets down outside the cabin before pulling a stool up to the table. Tina pours him a glass of limeade from a plastic pitcher and then mentions that recently a narco, whom she does not name, approached her about setting up a maceration pit on the farm but that she had refused. She says narcos always ask for permission. They will pick an area on the farm hidden from view to place their makeshift lab, where they will work for about week and then be gone. For this they pay handsomely. As she tells us this, I see her moving pots and tending to the fire. Tina is always in motion, and soon she is putting lunch on the table for Chimbo and for me: canned tuna mixed with rice and beans. And now Chimbo begins talking of his own experiences working maceration pits, near Pampa Hermosa, Aguaytía. He say that *soplos*, leaks, to the police are rare. But whenever they happen, it's always because the patrón, the boss, tried to cheat his workers.

Wilson arrives, sits down at the table. Tina serves him a plate of food and then shifts her attention to the bundle of bijao leaves, which she now begins to separate and arrange in neat stacks, before tying them with twine into individual packets of ten. Chimbo keeps talking, spinning out stories.

Wilson finishes eating just as Chara appears, ready for lunch. Chara sits down, and Chimbo goes back to work, and Tina, as soon as he has walked off a ways, says she listens to Chimbo when he speaks but does not believe anything he has to say. She never contradicts him; she just listens. Later, she will recall out loud a part of the conversation this morning with her neighbor. Tina will express amazement that Chimbo stayed so quiet when Shanty spoke about him, explicitly criticizing him, calling him a child. Through it all, Chimbo said not a word.

Chara, Tina, and Wilson then begin talking about the clan of brothers, expressing begrudging admiration at how they put the Party's dwindling control over the area to their advantage. And only then do I realize I had misunderstood. The brothers are hardly recent migrants to the

286

FIGURE 9.7. Tina, packets of bijao

Alto Huallaga. They have lived in the region for many years. Only to Magdalena are they new. Which provides, to me at least, some plausible explanation about how they ended up buying the two parcels sold behind Tina's back.

And Tina, now turning to me, asks if I want to go see how Chimbo is clearing the fields. And so I put on my boots and I follow her out to where he is working. She leaves me there and walks on. Yet it does not take long for me, watching Chimbo with the weed whacker, with the noise and the repetitive motions, to get bored. So I go find Tina, where she is cutting and collecting bijao. I ask her about the nearby black metal cross that marks, atop a cement base, her brother's grave. When did she place it there? I wonder. Oh, she says, we did that one month after his death. And when she recovered the farm, she found the cross there still. No one had touched the grave, not in the roughly ten years she had been away, residing almost entirely in the town.

Drops of rain begin to fall in the late afternoon, a little past five. And I am now alone in the hammock of the cabin once again, listening to a recording I made of Tina recounting how she recovered the farm and telling us about the thickset man. Soon, and with darkness approaching, everyone starts to return: Chimbo, then Chara and Tina. Only Wilson is out there working still.

And again the neighbor Shanty appears, strolling along the trail. But this time one of Tina's dogs growls softly before racing out to meet him and nip furiously at his legs. Tina calls out *Muñeca*!!! but the dog pays her no mind and heads back to the cabin only once Shanty has passed over into Rober's farm.

All the while, the drops of rain fall ever thicker, with increasing force. Soon Wilson will arrive, and then he and Tina will go out to the stream to bathe, next to the little raft. Surely there, they must have conferred about what they could and should not speak. Because when they return, Tina and Wilson tell me that they do not want to talk in front of *gente bocona*, nodding in the direction of Chimbo, and Chara too, who for the moment are not paying attention.

Then later, after nightfall, when we were all sitting at the table eating, Tina and Wilson begin to open up. First, I hear Tina say to Chimbo that these are things that should remain with us, never talked about with others. She then launches into a story about that time the police entered the farm in the wee hours of the morning. Theirs was a secret raid, and with them they had a man who was wearing a ski mask and who must have been their snitch. Again, Tina tells the story of how she recovered the farm, assuring us that only people who are tough are willing to confront things the way she did.

After dinner, Tina will keep working her bijao leaves late into the night: sorting, stacking, tying into little bundles. Once again, I will go upstairs to bed before everyone else. This time though I withdraw thinking how abundantly clear it is that I do not even begin to know the history of Tina's farm or even basic outlines of what really transpired, even if what I have heard, seen, and sensed here intimate a visceral something of how events from the war and its aftermaths still persist.

Cloud to clod gestures toward what happens after a massive fall, in afterlives where an extended bout of fury just keeps petering out. Cloud to clod pulls toward what cannot be undone. And also why, in the intractability of empirical limits, bultos appear to gather sense, to craft a semblance, in the facing of all faces, in the return of all that drops and of all that turbulence spinning up from the currents, whirling round upon round. Cloud to clod . . . to cloud and again, in what is unsettled: the river, the graves, the dreams, and those claims persisting in the land, then as now, at an ever-greater distance still.

What can the histories of this place disclose of themselves in a present that never ceases to open forth? How to fathom the crucial difference between *standing at the cusp of events* of a war as they unfolded and *looking back* from its aftermaths, while caught in the press of expedience of new political times and the retroactive transformations that expedience casts upon on all that's come before?

Ethnography begins in lived encounters. In this way circumstances of fieldwork are experientially positioned and pushed along a billowing present. When contending with a previous era, twenty years ago, let's say, ethnography has no ready means of actually returning to former events themselves, to take part in them as they transpired, as they actualized in singular places and times.

Toward deep pasts ethnography seemingly has no choice but to act from a distance and from within distinct political moments. From there one might trace lines. From there one might skirt along the surfaces of terrains, listening for their sense,

A radio. A wasps' nest, and stones.

scanning for minor breaks, subtle cracks, for the soft rumblings of depths,

Sandy banks and a waiting stack of crates.

but attentive no less—anywhere and everywhere that image, sensation, and matter weave together—to how time tangles,

A misty, Lima-like rain.

comes unglued or shakes off hard creases between the actual and what is said to be gone—

Those leafless branches of coca uprooted and strewn across a field.

Perhaps in this way historiography and ethnography might somehow merge around specific ways things and words could be gathered up again and with care rearranged.

A rodent's burrow.

Aching wire in a pig's snout.

Vultures circling high in a nearby sky.

Clods of dry earth that hang on dead roots.

Those holes punched with a digging stick.

That air dropping seeds and sweat.

Wobbly footbridge crossing.

One thickset man.

Another dense heavy sack.

A fall that threatens.

A welcome threadbare . . . then hopelessly torn.

Her diabetic bruising fears.

Shot through with his spirited laugh.

How to approach events from the deep past ethnographically?

If not in senses reversible

If not in traces of what remains irretrievable

If not in the semblance of all that insists

Eso es de otro tiempo . . . y no lo es.

"*Amor*, leave it all behind, the chainsaw, everything, because they are coming. They have seen me, and they are coming now to kill. Let's go." So Sabine grabbed just her clothes and a blanket. And with that she and everyone else began the retreat—Abel, Ítalo, and Machín. Together they began the trek back, but it was late, and they spent the whole night climbing in the dark. They did not have matches. They did not have anything. And without supplies of any kind, like that, they walked and could not stop, not until the break of dawn when they reached Tina's house on Malecón Huallaga.

"Mamá," Sabine called out, "something terrible has happened. We are not safe here. What are we to do? We have already lost everything."

Ítalo did not say a word but went straight for their room and immediately to sleep. That entire day he did not get out of bed. For two days he refused to eat or even take a sip of water. "My son in-law was sick," Tina told me. "He did not want anything at all."

Two days passed like that, and then on the third Tina was organizing a chest of drawers when she heard a knocking out front. When she went and opened the door to the street, two men stood before her. One of the men had long hair and was dark in complexion. The other, she said, was short and had on a black jacket. Both are wearing black rubber boots covered now in mud, the kind that come up to just below the knee and that everyone wears in the chacra. It was a partial scene, she shared, perhaps all that she recalled: little fragments moving against a blank field for me to try to fill in from the doorway of her house I know, shifting their feet on the tawny dust and small pebbled earth of days prior to the cementing of the street, the view of the Huallaga and the hills beyond as one can still glimpse from the malecón.

"It surprised me when I heard a knocking, I went to the door: ¿Sí?"

"Señora, buenos días, buenos días. Señora. Where is Ítalo?"

"Ítalo is in the *monte*," Tina told them.

"Right, *en el monte,* if you say so, Señora, but you know what? We have come to tell you that he has done something that will *not* be forgiven."

"What did he do?" asked Tina, feigning ignorance but then quickly adding, "He is not in town."

"Well, you would know, Señora, but to us *ese concha de su madre,* is already dead.

"So, you tell him that, Señora. And you tell him this too,

"if it's actually true he has not yet returned from la chacra,

"that we are going to look for him,

"and that when we find him, we are going to cut him to bits.

"Now listen, Señora, to what we are telling you. We know you are his mother-in-law."

And with that they turned around and walked down the malecón.

They had been standing, right there, before her, yet only as her glance lingered on in their slow drift away did she notice that one of the men was carrying a bag—a black gunny sack, that now seemed to dangle between them in their retreat toward the port. And as she watched them withdraw, she had this terrible thought: perhaps inside that bag, they were hiding a weapon of some kind. A gun they would have surely used to shoot and kill Ítalo, right there, in the entrance of her house, if only, instead of her, her son-in-law had happened to answer the door.

In a glance, one sack dangled between two men she had never met before, and between those three bodies, dense forms moving away, no way of knowing for sure what they might contain, much less intend.

acknowledgments

And what if there is no end? Only a drifting away in the direction of somewhere else, that might allow, perhaps, for some lingering on, and for some noticing a bit more, in all that has transpired. Such are the traces, resonating across the foregoing pages, of so many people vital to this work.

Some appear under pseudonym to protect or to allow them some public distance from the histories they have shared. Tina, Wilson, and their children. Reynaldo (if only for Melissa who introduced us). Also, Shego and Mauro and Don Florentín and Chimbo. Chara too: always with a glower that's his alone, ever on the verge of breaking into a hearty laugh. Without their kindness, and so much that they conveyed, in words and in silence, this book would not have been or would surely have become something altogether else.

Others, whose circumstances permit me to mention them by given names, were no less generous in welcoming me into their homes during return trips to the Huallaga. I wish to thank Elías Soto, Cenith Vargas, Miller, Rowell, and Sally. Rosalía Stork and her family: Johnny, Adita, Freyla, and, in remembrance, Sonali (whose departure was far too soon, with giggles inimitable and a smile that will not dim). I thank Estela Isuiza and her dear mother, Doña Agripina, for their hospitality and for the many fortuitous things they put into play. To Dina Carrillo de Camacho and her now-late husband, Eulogio, sons Toño and Julio too: I am ever so grateful for their wealth of advice and more meals than I can now count. La familia Taboada, throughout, extended much warmth and cheer, especially Hugo and his daughter Pilar and her immediate family, Beto, Ana, Nicolás, who, in Lima, more than once put me up. Pilar from her home also transcribed many interviews from my fieldwork, and then we often sifted through together the insights they contained. Claudia Vega,

Eloy Neyra, Danitza Zevallos, Miguel Carpio, Laly Pinedo, Segundo Jara, Roberto Lay, Marie Manrique, and Tito Bracamonte all offered camaraderie, timely help, or simply exuded uncommon strength in ways I have secretly admired.

The National Endowment for the Humanities, the American Council of Learned Societies, and the University of Florida all provided generous assistance. Field research for the "Semblance in Terrain" project was made possible thanks to a Summer Stipend from NEH, a Humanities Scholarship Enhancement Fund Award from the UF College of Liberal Arts and Sciences, a Rothman Award from the UF Center for the Humanities and the Public Sphere, as well as travel assistance from the UF Center for Latin American Studies and the Department of Anthropology. An ACLS Fellowship allowed me to take a year off from teaching to dedicate myself full-time to writing the manuscript.

Manchester University Press kindly granted permission to reprint excerpts from my essay "Time as Weather," originally published in *Governing the Dead*, edited by Finn Stepputat (2014). I consider that earlier work to be a sibling to Chapter 5 of this book, and in two respects: they each trace their origins to overlapping moments from fieldwork, and ever since they have been conjoined along a shared track en route to Chara's farm: up a refurbished highway, across the Huallaga, before passing by the village of Venenillo. I likewise thank *Anthropological Quarterly* for permission to reprint my article "Oblivious Title," which reappears here as Chapter 8 in slightly modified form and without photographs.

Many other dear friends have accompanied this project through its various turns of fieldwork and writing, offering encouragement as well as keen commentary on chapter drafts at different stages of completion. Christophe Robert, Isaías Rojas-Perez, Sandra Rozental, Gabriela Zamorano, but also Olga González, Carmen Ilizarbe, Nancy Hunt, Enrique Mayer, Deborah Poole, Finn Stepputat, and Simón Uribe, all made critical contributions to my thinking and probably more than they realize. Along the way I benefited greatly from conversations and fine suggestions from many others, whom I wish to acknowledge: Daniel Barroca, Ulla Berg, Cristóbal Bonelli, Jon Horne Carter, Ponciano del

Pino, Tessa Farmer, Joseph Feldman, Elizabeth Ferry, Serra Hakyemez, Penny Harvey, Martin Holbraad, Alix Johnson, Catarina Laranjeiro, Alejandra Leal, Mariana Mora, Juan Obarrio, Neni Panourgia, Morten Axel Pederson, Annabel Pinker, Helene Risør, Jim Scott, Nitzan Shoshan, Sydney Silverstein, Rihan Yeh, and Caroline Yezer. And they are hardly alone.

On several occasions Makena Ulfe hosted me at La Católica in Lima for the public presentation of various works in progress, opportunities that always felt generative and affirming. Sandra Rozental also welcomed me into the rich, critically engaging *taller de etnografía* she has developed in Mexico City with Carlos Mondragón: not once but twice to discuss sections of the manuscript. Louisa Lombard surprised me as well with an invitation to share a draft of Chapter 7 for the "Political Violence and Its Legacies" seminar at Yale University. Tanmoy Sharma's prepared commentary on my work there was exceptional and resonates with me still.

Many students in my graduate seminars at the University of Florida have helped me think through ideas that became pivotal for this book. Several read chapter drafts as well, sharing their impressions and insights. Macarena Moraga, Patrick James, Heidi Jensen, Jason Mullen, Jeremy Frusco, Nolan Ruark, Aja Cacan, Netty Carey, Cady Gonzalez, Christine LeJeune, Neha Kohli, Alex Lowie, Shreemoyee Sil, Hannah Toombs, and Nicole Kinbarovsky all deserve special mention.

At Stanford University Press, my debt and gratitude to Senior Editor Kate Wahl for having seen me through two book projects now is infinite. Former anthropology editor Michelle Lipinsky encouraged me to imagine the future manuscript while I was still immersed in the early phases of research and then never lost patience with my measured pace. I thank the two anonymous reviewers for their finely detailed, thoughtful recommendations, which I drew on to refine and improve as much as I was able the final text. Incoming anthropology editor Dylan Kyung-lim White deftly guided the book to press, with the support of Sunna Juhn, Tim Roberts, Lizzie Haroldsen, Cynthia Lindlof, Nick Koenig, and the rest of the SUP team. In between and throughout, Kate Wahl has been the steady hand that made it all possible.

Over the years, I have been blessed at the University of Florida with many wonderful colleagues. For having directly engaged and facilitated my work, I wish especially to thank Sophia Acord, Brenda Chalfin, Pete Collings, Joel Correia, Carlos de la Torre, Susan DeFrance, (the deeply missed) Richard Freeman, Susan Gillespie, Rebecca Hanson, Mike Heckenberger, Ieva Jusionyte, Jack Kugelmass, Abdoulaye Kane, John Krigbaum, Carmen Martínez Novo, Augusto Oyuela-Caycedo, Susan Paulson, Gabriel Prieto, Rosana Resende, Ken Sassaman, Peter Schmidt, Maria Stoilkova, Phoebe Stubblefield, Marit Tolo Østebø, Catherine Tucker, Heather Vrana, and Phillip Williams.

My mother, Jane Kernaghan, read through the entire manuscript before it went out for review, noting passages that unnecessarily strained sense but also assuring me throughout how much the project really mattered. I am all the more appreciative for her efforts, as she did this but a few months after my father's sudden, unexpected passing. Now in an absence that startles still, I miss him deeply and recall so many years of his unwavering support.

Finally, I thank Angela Mesía Ruiz, who listened to each and every paragraph, multiple times, in various stages of composition. She also taught me to become a patient, more discerning photographer, while making pictures increasingly central to my own ethnographic practice. Then, she helped me select the images that have appeared in these pages. Even more important, through her influence I have learned to be a better father for our children, Orlando and Hazel, who have brought so much joy to our lives and who have animated the writing of this book in ways I could never have predicted.

notes

chapter 1

1. Concerning the linguistic emergence of *terruco*, Aguirre suggests some possible paths: most likely from the southern Andes region of Ayacucho, resulting from a crossover of the Spanish *terrorista* into Quechua, though he concedes there might have been a more profound entanglement as well with words of Quechua descent (2011:118–119). Aguirre's main concern, however, is with the racializing, stigmatizing, classificatory power that *terruco* acquired during the war: often as synonymous with the pejorative *indio* (Indian), designating people of Andean ancestry, presumed to be of darker complexion. For a genealogy of the term *terrorism* in Peru, tracked back to the country's beginnings as the republic in the early nineteenth century, see Méndez (2021), who lends clues as well for understanding more recent, less racially marked "postwar" political uses of *terruco* and variants (*terruquear, teruqueo*).

2. Though perhaps it's better to exercise caution with etymological inquiries and consider the advice of Anidjar, who specifically with regard to these two terms underscores the uncertain, "unsettled," and ultimately undecidable character of what might have linked them together at some, much earlier, time: where words for earth, land, territory, burn, dry, warding away by frightening, and others still, all appear somehow *but never definitively* connected (2004:54–55, 67).

3. "Oye, concha tu madre, ven acá."
"Tu eres terruco."
"No soy terruco."
"Tú eres maderero."
"Sí, soy maderero."
"Ya pues, los madereos son terrucos."

4. La Comisión de la Verdad y Reconciliación (CVR; Peruvian Truth and Reconciliation Commission). See notes 20–21.

5. On the popular mobilizations that led to Fujimori's demise at the start of his third term in office, see Ilizarbe 2017; and Poole and Rénique 2000.

6. If I had to name some of the expressions or places where I see the potential of that tradition, either realized or simply lingering, I might mention the ever-so-brief "Carnaval de Tambobamba" by José María Arguedas; Natalie Sarraute's early work on tropisms; fieldwork reports by Zora Neale Hurston; stories by Heinrich von Kleist; a handful of Robert Walser's microscripts; Kathleen Stewart's writing on Barton Springs, Appalachia, or New England; Lauren Berlant's reflections on intuition; various passages from Hugh Raffles's *Insectopedia* and others still from works by Michael Taussig; the cinematic projects of Rebecca Baron; numerous scenes from the films of Hou Hsiao Hsien or of Gianfranco An-

nichini Somalvico or from the first feature of Bi Gan; the dreamwork of Michel Leiris; and the most ethnographic of chapters in César Calvo Soriano's *Las tres mitades de Ino Moxo*.

7. The Communist Party of Peru–Shining Path / El Partido Comunista del Perú–Sendero Luminoso (PCP-SL) is a Marxist political-military organization, originally inspired by Mao and in particular by his Cultural Revolution. In the 1970s the group began to organize clandestinely in Ayacucho, one of the most economically and socially marginalized areas of the southern Peruvian highlands, in preparation for "armed struggle" against the Peruvian state. The launching of Shining Path's insurrection, or what it called "people's war," in 1980 was symbolically timed to begin as the country carried out elections for a civilian president. Widely cited as the pivotal event that would plunge Peru into an extended period of civil war, Shining Path's embrace of acts of violence also expressed its absolute rejection of the decision taken by other leftist parties to participate in electoral politics following twelve years of military rule. In retrospect, it is easy to overlook the degree to which Shining Path was once a hermetic, highly disciplined organization that spoke primarily and most stridently through sabotage and selective assassination, which the organization justified with pronouncements that could make sense only to those deeply versed in a Maoist reading and philosophy of history. Seemingly out of nowhere, from beginnings quite humble, and always on a shoestring budget, the Party's violent, often highly theatrical, actions would by the end of the 1980s achieve a territorial breadth that left few regions unscathed. Militarily, Shining Path would prove less able: tending to fare poorly in any direct engagements with the Peruvian Armed Forces. And yet it was the unexpected, and in many ways unplanned, police arrest of a majority of the Party's senior leadership, including Shining Path luminary Abimael Guzmán, aka Presidente Gonzalo, in September 1992 that would dramatically undermine its trajectory. From there everything would go downhill for the Maoist Party. Guzmán's subsequent attempts from captivity to enter into peace talks with the Fujimori government effectively split the movement between those favoring negotiations and those refusing to end the armed struggle. By the mid-1990s the insurgency, amid continual losses from military and police operations and increasingly divided, ceased to have the organizational and political capacity to threaten the stability of the Peruvian state. Vastly diminished pro-Guzmán and anti-Guzmán factions of the insurgency would survive, however, and for years to come: each in their own territorial areas, largely within separate geographic regions of the eastern tropical slopes of the Andes closely tied to the coca/cocaine trade.

The scholarly literature on Shining Path's rise is vast. The following are essential reading: Degregori 1989, 1990; Manrique 1989; del Pino 1996, 1998, 2017; La Serna 2012; Poole and Rénique 1992; CVR 2003, II:23–169; Stern 1998; and Heilman 2010. There has also been important work by Peruvian historians based on prison interviews with militants, including the principal leaders of the Party (i.e., Rénique 2003; Zapata Velasco 2017). The literature on Shining Path in the Upper Huallaga is much less robust, but see CVR 2003, V:186–208, 259–281. Sendero Luminoso was not the only leftist organization to carry out significant armed actions against the Peruvian state during the 1980s and 1990s. The Movimiento Revolucionario Túpac Amaru (MRTA)—ideologically less radical and cut from a more familiar Cuba-inspired mold—offered an alternative to Sendero for those who also felt electoral politics could not achieve significant social reforms. See La Serna 2020; and CVR 2003, II:254–288.

8. How imperatives of blending in with one's surroundings become a crucial feature of shifts in political time (from war into their aftermaths) will be an abiding concern going

forward, especially in Chapter 7. Here and there, I borrow the felicitous phrase "reciprocal topographies" from Roger Caillois's early work on animal mimicry (1984).

9. *Prehistory*, as I am using the word, would be akin to a "founding forgetting" of political time, such as Nicole Loraux (2002:10) described in *The Divided City* (on the aftermaths of civil war in the ancient Greek polis). A more direct inspiration comes from Nietzsche's elaboration of the notion in his *Genealogy of Morality* (1994) as the force of a violent past that runs unacknowledged alongside the ever-passing present: pressing, harassing, threatening to return. Prehistory for Nietzsche escapes historical accounting but secretly orients thinking and may even constitute thought itself.

10. I prefer the word *oblivion* to *forgetting* or even *amnesia*, because its semantic range seems to extend further and to accommodate a greater plurality of conditions: among them, the impossibility of anyone among "us" grasping much less holding on to what transpires when a political community confronts war; or that there might be whole groups of people within the same community who did not directly experience armed conflict, either because they lived at a safe distance or arrived later, generationally speaking. *Oblivion*, as a word, seems vast enough to admit those who never did know exactly what happened to them; also those who did then, but whose memories have since decayed; as well as those who still remember only a few things vividly; and many upon many others who had rather not share what they do recall or simply know better than to try. These distinct circumstances all seem worthy of acknowledgment. Yet, regardless of the actual words one prefers to refer to them, Anderson's keen reflections (2006) on the role of historical "forgetting" or "amnesia" in the creation of national political communities remain pertinent.

11. From the mid-1970s, lasting until 1995.

12. On the life of Vaticano, Hugo Coya (2011) has written an insightful chronicle.

13. Until his capture in 2012 Camarada Artemio directed the Party's Huallaga branch (Comité Regional Huallaga) from at least the mid-1990s and perhaps before. Little was publicly known about the Comité's leadership and organizational structure in the early years of the war, and it is still by no means clear at what point Artemio became the lone authority. When speaking with people who once lived in rural areas of Shining Path control, including those who participated in guerrilla actions, I have heard the names of many other important Comité leaders, such as Mancini, Jordán, and Ormeño. It was only later—once army counterinsurgency operations in the early to mid-1990s had winnowed insurgent ranks, through capture, killing, and disappearance, leaving the movement in tatters—that Artemio would emerge as the Comité's undisputed authority and voice. The regional Party that persisted and managed to reorganize in the late 1990s in the Upper Huallaga did so around Artemio as its figurehead and by most accounts under his guidance. Police first learned of Artemio much earlier through the analysis of a captured VHS tape, depicting a late 1980s clandestine meeting with Abimael Guzmán and the rest of the national Party's Central Committee. Artemio's presence at that meeting led to speculation he belonged to the highest echelons of Shining Path, perhaps an indication too of the growing influence, by the late 1980s, of the Huallaga branch within the Party, thanks to the ease with which the Comité could tax all levels of the cocaine trade. Following the capture of nearly all of Shining Path's Central Committee in September 1992, and then, seven years later, of Óscar Ramírez Durand (Camarada Feliciano), Artemio would be described in the national press as the lone member of the "original" national leadership still at large. Journalists would marvel at the many times Artemio dodged army patrols or slipped through the fingers of the police, underscoring the resourcefulness and craft

with which he seemed to elude his adversaries. Artemio in time would take advantage of the media's fascination, making ever-more-revealing public pronouncements. During the presidential administration of Alejandro Toledo (2001–2006), he began to issue communiqués and gave interviews in which he acknowledged that Shining Path had committed "errors" yet affirmed his loyalty to Guzmán. All overtures Artemio made to the national government to negotiate terms for disarmament were rebuffed. After his arrest in 2012, Artemio would be tried on charges of terrorism and drug trafficking, subsequently convicted, and sentenced to life imprisonment.

14. This area to the south, commonly identified with the acronym VRAEM, is a series of steep valleys along the Apurímac, Ene, and Mantaro Rivers—a remote tropical borderlands overlapping the political regions of Apurímac, Cusco, Huancavelica, and Junín. There the Proseguir faction of the insurgency is led by Victor Quispe Palomino "Camarada José" (Ferreira 2016).

15. For a synthetic discussion of how and why, see Paredes and Manrique 2018. For a longer historical perspective on cocaine's legal transformation from licit to illicit commodity, see Gootenberg 2008. Rojas-Perez (2005), meanwhile, offers detailed analyses of US drug control policies in Peru during the national governments of Alberto Fujimori and Alejandro Toledo. In my own work (Kernaghan 2009) I have found it helpful to distinguish between the coca/cocaine economy—which in Peru has retained broad territorial connections to the tropical eastern slopes of the Andes, where it varies in intensity but without ever going away—and those extraordinary periods of boom when a region's economy may turn entirely on the illegal trade, as it did in the Upper Huallaga, even to the point of being practiced for a time in surprisingly open fashion. Of course, cocaine has many histories in Peru. A recent article by Heilman (2018) examining cocaine-related arrests and police torture in Ayacucho from the late 1970s into the early 1980s provides one fascinating glimpse, suggestive too for parallels to contemporaneous experiences in the Upper Huallaga and for understanding the later emergence of the VRAEM (as a territorial margin of the state, critical to the illicit trade of cocaine in Peru and refuge for the Proseguir offshoot of Shining Path).

16. Despite acute differences in the respective regimes' political orientations and priorities, the Upper Huallaga would become a central target for rural settlement and colonization in the agrarian reform policies of both the presidential administration of Fernando Belaúnde Terry (1963–1968) and the Armed Forces Revolutionary Government of General Juan Velasco Alvarado (1968–1975). A vivid depiction of the era and its predicaments can be found in Armando Robles Godoy's *La muralla verde* (1970), a feature-length film about the fictional life of a settler and the afflictions faced in forests north of Tingo María when trying to make good on government promises. For a scholarly assessment from that era's immediate aftermath, see Aramburú 1981.

17. A loss that was never simple, of course, because historically encouraged by outside forces, whether the predatory predicaments of Spanish colonial rule (Santos Granero 1985) or, later, through Peruvian state policies that treated the eastern tropical forests as an internal frontier (Varese 1972). The early ethnological record of the Huallaga, from Franciscan missionary accounts in the seventeenth and eighteenth centuries, would attest to a region populated by numerous and diverse indigenous groups (Izaguirre 2001). Scholars now surmise—from scrutiny of these and other colonial-era documents—that such groups operated as cultural "hinges" or relational links (Santos Granero 1985; A. Taylor 1999; Barclay 2001) that facilitated trade and diplomatic communications between

peoples of the lowlands of Amazonia and of the central Andean highlands well before the arrival of the Spanish. As for what happened next, after the Franciscans definitively abandoned their missions in the late eighteenth century, and over the ensuing years, little documentary evidence exists. The eventual "disappearance" of the Upper Huallaga's prior inhabitants would be made productive, nonetheless, for others and for a long time to come. Indeed, by the mid-twentieth century, a perception that wide swaths of land across the region were *licit for reappropriation* rested in large part on claims that no "culturally distinct" Amazonian communities continued to reside in the area, as anthropologist Aníbal Buitrón (1948) would assert in his UNESCO-sponsored ethnological survey of the region (see also Sala 2019).

18. According to Jülich (1974), by the early 1970s approximately half of the population then living in the Upper Huallaga had migrated from sierra communities of Ancash, Huánuco, La Libertad, and San Martín, while up to a third had relocated from the central and lower portions of the valley.

19. Differences from one micro-area to another become apparent as well in ethnographic studies: see especially van Dun 2009, 2014, drawing upon extended research in hamlets north of Tocache; for my own fieldwork farther south, see Kernaghan 2009, 2013, 2014.

20. The CVR studied the circumstances that had given rise to and shaped an extended period of political violence between May 1980 and November 2000. After its legal creation (initially as La Comisión de la Verdad) in June 2001, during the final days of the transitional government of Valentín Paniagua Corazao, the commission assumed the enormous task of issuing a comprehensive report within approximately two years. On the political contexts that permitted the commission's formation, along with reflections on the challenges subsequently faced, see the 2004 brief essay by anthropologist (and former CVR "commissioner") Carlos Iván Degregori.

21. The CVR received widespread collaboration from local communities, grassroots victims-rights associations, educational institutions, teams of forensic archeologists, and human rights organizations. It is crucial to bear in mind, nonetheless, that the commission could never have completed its charge, even partially, if not for the generous assistance and resolve of individuals and families most affected by the conflict, who responded to the call for an accurate, exhaustive accounting of the war. And yet there would be real limits, both political and material, to what the commission could in fact achieve. Given the depths of destruction in both lives and social worlds and given the vehemence of hostilities (still unresolved) that would continue in the wake of war, the idea that "reconciliation" could be promoted by ascertaining "the truth" and even more so by an entity of the Peruvian state was naïve and, worse, left itself open to cynical retort. On some of the flounders, when not outright failures, of that promise, see Coxshall 2005; Yezer 2008; Poole and Rojas-Perez 2010; and Agüero 2015. Specifically with regard to forensic archeology and postwar exhumations, see Rojas-Perez 2017. On the eventual CVR archive—its history, institutional locale, post-commission salience, and limits—see Aguirre 2009.

22. The preface was signed by Commission President Salomón Lerner Febres and was the actual text that Lerner read during the official presentation of the commission's results and recommendations. That public ceremony took place on August 28, 2003, in the Palace of Government in Lima, with Lerner personally handing over the multivolume report to then-president of Peru Alejandro Toledo.

23. The credibility of the commission's calculations is a lingering question. Doubts about numerical accuracy and attribution of responsibility have been raised on method-

ological grounds (Rendón 2019). It is also important to note that the CVR's figures refer solely to deaths and do not include persons disappeared during the conflict. That number continues to grow. As of December 2020, the national registry—RENADE (Registro Nacional de Búsqueda de Personas Desaparecidas)—had documented 21,334 cases of disappearance related to the conflict (https://www.gob.pe/11872-ministerio-de-justicia-y-derechos-humanos-registro-nacional-de-busqueda-de-personas-desaparecidas-renade). More attention could perhaps be given to the performative force of CVR numbers and the extent to which they reflected the commission's own political constraints as it attempted to navigate a very particular historical moment. The Armed Forces considered themselves "the victors" and for the foreseeable future would remain one of the most powerful institutions in the country. The concerns of Shining Path and MRTA, meanwhile, could in practice be ignored. They were "the defeated" and so drastically sidelined as to have no say in postwar conditions nationally. Only in a few territorial margins—where coca-cocaine economies still flourished—would remnant successors of the Maoist insurgency continue to influence the rhythms of daily life. Against this specific background of relations of force, the CVR's final report determined that Shining Path was not only the principal instigator (*causante*) but responsible for the largest share of deaths (54 percent). The commission also deemed the actions of the security apparatus of the state (Armed Forces and police), if slightly less mortal (43 percent), to have been excessive: finding evidence not only of a systematic pattern of violating human rights but of having done so with legal impunity. It framed state violence, however, in terms of "national defense," mobilized as a necessary response to unwarranted attacks and thus deserving to be judged on different conceptual and legal grounds than the actions of Shining Path. In the view, and underlying moral sense, of the commission, crimes committed by the state should be considered repugnant and cause for collective shame, but they were not without some redemptive value. They could motivate reflections on the part of all sectors of Peruvian society to acknowledge and learn from what had happened. The Armed Forces and police belonged to the nation, and through the implementation of key social, institutional, and legal recommendations outlined in the commission's final report, a better union could ostensibly be crafted for "all."

24. Volume V of the final report contains several case studies on the history of the armed conflict in the Upper Huallaga and territorially adjacent coca-growing areas across the political departments (now "regions") of Huánuco, San Martín, and Ucayali. See CVR 2003, V:186–208, 231–259, 259–281, as well as a chapter dedicated exclusively to examining ties between the cocaine trade, the armed conflict, and government corruption (485–506). Among these is a compressed version of the study I completed, which appears without author attribution in a section of "representative histories" titled "El PCP-SL durante el auge de la hoja de coca en el Alto Huallaga" (186–208).

25. During my own work for the commission, I remember being acutely aware of how preliminary these collective efforts felt, if the charge were not only to gauge but seriously contend with the war history of the Upper Huallaga. Between the enormity of the task and a rushed time frame, the CVR could at best make but an opening gesture toward what was sorely needed: a far more sustained inquiry. Some residents of the Huallaga who worked for the commission and made important contributions there have continued to craft and share important written reflections on the region's wartime past, notably Felipe Paucar Mariluz (2006) and Segundo Jara Montejo (2013).

26. This early state of emergency, imposed in March 1980 by the military government of Morales Bermudez through Legal Decree 22927, authorized the police, with support

from the Armed Forces, to intervene against the production of coca in the departments of Huánuco and San Martín, as well as in the Coronel Portillo province of the department of Ucayali. That first emergency decree proffered, as it were, a belated justification, since during the prior year the police had already begun to target coca farmers and their properties directly through aggressive military-style raids. Decree 22927 did not acknowledge the police actions that were already under way but instead cited two separate juridical bases for what purportedly was still to come: the 1961 UN Single Convention on Narcotic Drugs, which required signatory nations to destroy illicit coca cultivations; and Legal Decree 22095 of 1978, through which the Peruvian government had set forth specific criteria for registering, eliminating, and substituting coca crops in compliance with that prior international convention.

Subsequent legal states of emergency in the Upper Huallaga would, however, be imposed in response to insurgent activity. From 1984 to 2000, the army would hold absolute authority over actions taken against Shining Path, a leading role that in later years, from 2005 to 2015, would fall to the police. By then, the territorial threat of the insurgency had been contained, and what remained to be achieved, from the perspective of the Peruvian state, was little more than disrupting and taking down a criminal racket.

27. On the history of cocalero movements in the Upper Huallaga, including critical insight into their relations with cocalero movements elsewhere in Peru, see van Dun 2009. For a broader comparison between Peru and Bolivia, see Durand Ochoa 2014.

28. Notably Degregori et al. 1996; also Starn 1999.

29. These debates have reanimated ideological currents of the war, if within a reduced spectrum of speech legally permitted by Peru's postconflict system of electoral democracy (i.e., no voicing of agreement with the insurgencies or with political positions held by their supporters; to do so is to risk social transformation into a public enemy and to face criminal prosecution). Within this constrained realm of the legally sanctioned, battle lines have been drawn between recognizable, if asymmetric, counter-publics: on one side, those who defend without question the actions of the Armed Forces (called by their critics *negacionismo*/denialism or *la pugna por la impunidad*/fight for impunity); and on another, those who underscore the profound costs of state terror and who appeal for full acknowledgment of harms, while advocating for just reparations (*la pugna por la justicia*/fight for justice). See Ilizarbe 2015; and Ulfe and Ilizarbe 2019. Battle lines reappear in myriad ways, circulating above all through social media and related platforms as well as print and broadcast news. They often reappear in response to controversies sparked by efforts at war commemoration: whether the defilement of memorial sites (Drinot 2009; Milton 2011), political obstacles delaying the creation and completion of museums dedicated to the conflict and its broader social ramifications (Feldman 2021; O. González 2022), or protests that seek to direct and sustain national attention on the demands of victims and increasingly those of veterans groups, especially those who as young men were pressed into military service (Granados Moya 2021). Taken as a whole, these debates, by contesting the terms of what happened, or who lost the most, or who was most to blame, have presupposed a basic if entailed questioning of the sort of political community that should emerge in aftermaths of war.

The different armed factions of the conflict at different moments have weighed in as well with their own interpretations of what transpired. The Peruvian Armed Forces would publish a report in direct counter to that of the CVR (see Ejército del Perú 2010). Shining Path took a less consistent posture: hostile toward the CVR at first, calling for the creation of an "authentic truth commission." The surviving original leaders of the Party, because imprisoned, would articulate their perspectives on war history through the sole channels open to them: legal motions and challenges filed during their criminal prosecution and occasional access to researchers and journalists. Outside either the confines of prison or the purview of the courts, few sought to defend Shining Path and its ideological legacy publicly, until a new pro-Sendero political organization, el Movimiento por Amnistía y Derechos Fundamentales (MOVADEF), appeared in 2012 to take up that task, all the while seeking to participate in electoral politics (Valle Riestra 2019). For a close reading and meticulous critique of the CVR's final report from the perspective of a former member of the MRTA, see Gálvez Olaechea 2017.

30. Schmitt 2003:88.

31. The word *reference* is a fundamental concept in the philosophy of language and attendant theories of sense: see, for example, Nietzsche (1873) 1982; Russell 1905; Frege 1948; and Deleuze 1990. If in the view of linguistics *reference* belongs to a broader field of indexicals, within the philosophy of language it specifies a class of names that affirm a faithful relation between themselves and the reality of the things they would point to (Frege 1948). Affirmations of faith, however, invite skepticism, even scenes of judgment where such claims can be deemed worthy or not. Where reference is found to *actually* fulfill the claims it asserts, it might be called "denotation" (Deleuze 1990:12–13). Yet the problem of who decides, or what determines, "fulfillment" will always return to haunt.

32. Leach 1965:175.

33. Writing about legacies of conflict, María Victoria Uribe (2009) has drawn attention to the intense controversies that attempts to ascribe an origin date to the outbreak of political violence in Colombia have inspired. Others have made similar remarks with respect to distinct historical contexts of uncivil war and state terror elsewhere in the Americas. See, for example, Stern 2006; Nelson 2009; and Rojas-Perez 2017.

34. I recognize the significance of such reflections and the arduous work they demand. Such is not my purpose here. There are others better placed, and far more qualified, who have undertaken it and continue to do so with acuity and verve. See, among others, Agüero 2015; Cisneros 2016; Salazar 2016; and Gavilán Sánchez 2019.

35. If that were the aim of this book, then I might ask about the specific ways the CVR attempted to reimagine the political community of the nation and the extent to which such imagining wrestled with, and arguably ignored, "the forgetting that founds the political" (Loraux 2002:10, 43). I might ask too whether memory presupposes oblivion as its necessary if ever-changing counterpart, a companion even, that cannot simply be dismissed or dispelled by bringing things "into the light." Perhaps when it comes to political community, historical reckoning unfolds less as an exercise in remembering than in learning "how to agree to oblivion" (Loraux 2002:43) or, if phrased in terms of public secrecy, in knowing what not to know (Taussig 1999; O. González 2011).

36. See, for example, Sanford 2008; McAllister and Nelson 2013; and Weld 2014.

37. Carter 2022.

38. Rojas-Perez 2013:152. For keen ethnographic reflections on the predicaments that aftermaths of political violence have had in Colombia, see Orrantia 2009, 2012; also Taussig 2003b.

39. Rojas-Perez (2013) specifically cites legal instruments and emergency measures introduced in the context of counterinsurgency that, following the war, successive national governments in Peru would reprise and refine in order to counter local grassroots

opposition to neoliberal policies that have favored extractive industries (mining and oil) without concern for the social disruptions and environmental devastation they create and exacerbate. For analyses of those instruments and measures, see, for instance, Siles 2017; Lajtman and Mendoza 2019; and Tafur Sialer and Quesada Nicoli 2020.

40. Bergson's theory of perception is a critique of perception. Not a phenomenology, as Lawlor (2003) explains, because Bergson gives far more important roles to memory and to the past: indeed, memory and the past receive the brunt of analytical stress. Lawlor, furthermore, points out that Bergson's theory of perception is a critique of all forms of imaging, containing therein a theory of the image as well.

41. On how the work of recollection for Bergson establishes communications between present and past, a relation based in analogy or resemblance at the biding of present utility, see Hyppolite 1971.

42. Virilio 1994.

43. Blanchot 1989:254.

44. Cache (1995:33–34) pushes Bergson's suggestions toward the reliefs of terrain, questioning the tendencies of human perception to seek out extremes: it notices and grasps peaks and valleys, with far less regard to what falls in between them. By focusing instead on the curvature of reliefs, Cache attempts to extract an "ideal genetic element" (Deleuze 1993:14), prior to orientation or to vector (Cache 1995:17), that he calls "inflection." This is to say that while Cache begins with topography, the broader emphases and ultimate aims of his book *Earth Moves* are more properly topological.

45. Dupréel 1933, 1961.

46. See Cache 1995:142. And to which there are always exceptions, as Lurgio Gavilán Sánchez (2019:108–109) has eloquently shown.

47. See Cache 1995:142–143. Cache here shares some unacknowledged affinities with Michel Serres, who insisted that "the inference from the local to the global is always problematic" (2000:187).

48. Bergson 1988:201, 210.

49. Gordillo 2014.

50. Stoler 2013.

51. Bennett 2010.

52. Stengers 2018; de la Cadena 2010, 2015.

53. Serres and Latour 1995:60–61.

54. A legal concept that takes ambiguity to extremes, *Apología del delito de terrorismo* first appeared in the antiterrorism legislation of 1992 (Decree 25475, Article 7) and was later introduced into the Peruvian Penal Code as Article 316. Subsequent modifications to the code, Articles 316.2 and 316a, have attempted to clarify its application and possible penalties, which have ranged from four to fifteen years of incarceration.

55. Freud 1961; Nietzsche 1994; Deleuze 1983:112–114.

56. Augé 2004:20–21.

chapter 2

1. See Cache 1995:23; also Chapter 1.

2. State-sponsored colonization programs have been the subject of an extensive scholarly literature in Peru, so much so that writer and journalist Roger Rumrill García once remarked that the Upper Huallaga Valley became, during the 1970s at least, one of the

most studied areas of the Peruvian Amazon. For a helpful recent overview and analysis of the history of colonization programs in the Upper Huallaga, see Paredes and Manrique 2018. Less scholarly attention has been given to land appropriations prior to the era of agrarian reform—i.e., colonizations in the nineteenth and early twentieth centuries, which resulted in Amazonian indigenous communities in effect ceding the forest; land grants to former military officers, plantation concessions (coca, rubber, etc.)—and subsequently how agrarian reform programs from the late 1950s to early 1970s reappropriated, redistributed, and resignified prior land seizures while expanding their territorial reach.

3. In 2014, another suspension bridge was built just north of the village of Madre Mía, cutting that distance roughly in half. Only in 2021 would completion of Puente Megote give Nuevo Progreso road-access to the opposite shore. Meanwhile, along the 175-kilometer route north of Tocache to Juanjuí, the highway crosses the Huallaga only twice—at the towns of Pizana and Punta Arenas, just before the village of Campanilla. Both of those bridges predate the war.

4. Palmas del Espino was established in the late 1970s by one of Peru's wealthiest families, that of Dionisio Romero. Throughout the war and even immediately after, company trucks loaded with buckets of palm oil would become frequent targets of Shining Path sabotage, leaving their burning remains strewn along the Marginal Highway.

5. The escalation Pedro described was happening nationally, above all in the southern Andes, by then a well-known bastion of Shining Path. See Degregori et al. 1996; del Pino 2017; O. González 2011; Heilman 2010; Theidon 2004; La Serna 2012; and CVR 2003.

6. Bergson 1920:28–29.

7. Virilio 1994:19.

chapter 3

1. The hamlet of La Morada was situated several dozen kilometers north, but on the left bank not far from Magdalena.

2. For a critical interpretation of the occupation and siege that ended it, see Hidalgo Vega 2007. For the perspective of the military involved in organizing the raid, see Hermoza Ríos 1997. For a personal account of one of the hostages, a conservative Catholic religious leader who would subsequently become archbishop of Lima, see Cipriani Thorne 2012.

3. Press reports focused in the main on possible abuses committed by the former captain or soldiers under his command and then on suspicions that the 2006 presidential candidate's campaign was actively attempting to intimidate or buy off residents of Madre Mía, who could offer witness testimony about Humala during the years he was stationed in the Huallaga. Sometimes, however, the tone of investigative seriousness teetered toward gossip and the apparently frivolous, as when journalists began looking into Humala's one-time local loves. In one instance, a woman's response to reporters revealed the complicated local field their questions, which she tried simultaneously to explain and to elude, opened up and forced her to navigate in the present. These were very different times: the then of the early 1990s and the now of the 2006 national elections each brought its own operative common sense. Back then other loves mattered. Bringing them up now could be uncomfortable, perhaps costly ("Amiga confirma que Ollanta Humala estuvo en Madre Mía el año 1992," *La República*, February 6, 2006).

4. The Truth and Reconciliation Commission's final report has no mention of Humala in its discussion of army counterinsurgency operations in the Upper Huallaga Valley. Other military officers were notorious: see, for example, Kernaghan 2009, chap. 5.

5. *La pacificación*, as the Peruvian Army occasionally referred to its counterinsurgency campaigns, was very much "political language" in Orwell's sense, notable for its combination of "euphemism, question-begging and sheer cloudy vagueness," and on call for that specific pragmatic purpose of "nam[ing] things without calling up mental pictures of them." And indeed, Orwell mentioned "pacification" among other typical phrases, the likes of "transfer of population . . . rectification of frontiers . . . elimination of unreliable elements" (1968:136).

6. Ollanta Humala first gained national attention when he and his brother Antauro Humala, a retired army major, led a small, short-lived, and ultimately bloodless military revolt on October 29, 2000, in Locumba (southern department of Tacna) to demand the resignation of Alberto Fujimori. Both brothers voluntarily surrendered to authorities five weeks later, following the inauguration of the transitional government of Valentín Paniagua, and shortly thereafter received a congressional amnesty. Ollanta would go on to convert celebrity from Locumba into a political career, nearly winning his first bid for the presidency in 2006. It was during the 2006 electoral campaign that current and former residents of Madre Mía, La Morada, and the nearby hamlet of Pucayacu would identify Humala in testimonies, given to human rights lawyers and journalists, as an army captain known as "Carlos" (CNDDHH 2006). Legal investigations that followed would turn on eleven accusations of human rights violations, including five cases of disappearances, but also torture and humiliations, dating to his alleged tenure as the commander of the Madre Mía army base in 1992 and early 1993 (CNDDHH 2009). Humala largely managed to hold those charges at bay—amid allegations of bribes paid to key witnesses who abruptly changed their testimony to clear him of responsibility. Though prosecutors eventually terminated legal proceedings on dubious grounds, the accusations did not simply go away. They returned when Humala ran again for president in 2011, and after completing his six-year term in 2016, there have been renewed calls and efforts to reopen the case. In 2017 the forensics team of the Public Prosecutions Office (Equipo Forense Especializado del Ministerio Público) conducted exhumations in the general vicinity of the Madre Mía base and recovered remains of eighteen persons, which they have attempted to connect with testimonies implicating the former commander. Humala has faced far more legal jeopardy, however, from charges of corruption. Between 2017 and 2018 both he and his wife, former first lady Nadine Heredia, served thirteen months of preventive detention for illicit campaign contributions from the Venezuelan government and the Brazilian construction company Odebrecht. Though they were temporarily released from prison, the legal case on those charges continues. Humala is one of four Peruvian ex-presidents and twelve across Latin America, as well as numerous other politicians in Peru and regionally, who have been implicated in the Brazilian money-laundering investigation known as *Operação Lava Jato* for bribes paid by Odebrecht in exchange for large construction contracts.

7. Shining Path attempts to dictate when and where cocaine could be purchased were said to have pushed cocaine traders to turn against the Party and cast their lot with the army. This was reported contemporaneously by investigative journalists of *la Revista Sí* and the *diario La República*. I heard similar versions locally in the late 1990s and then in 2002, when I returned as a researcher for the CVR.

8. "Thus die the buyers of drugs."

9. Townspeople spoke of the brothers as if they were an undifferentiated muddle of rowdy young men, all belonging to Sendero. Tina would individuate them and then explain: not all had those ties, and none by choice.

10. Or simply too devastating and disturbing, as Rojas-Perez (2017) describes in his discussions of "necro-governmentality" and the controlled recovery of pasts of state atrocity.

chapter 4

1. Harvey and Knox 2012.
2. Harvey and Knox 2012, 523.
3. Belaúnde Terry 1959, 1965.
4. Peru 1967:50.
5. Peru 1965, XXVIII.
6. Scott 1998.
7. Uribe 2017.
8. Uribe 2017; also Campbell 2012.
9. Schmitt 2003, 70.
10. For an extended engagement, see Serres 2015; on army counterinsurgency and foundational events of state law in the Upper Huallaga Valley, see Kernaghan 2009:188–212.
11. For an insightful, ethnographically informed discussion of new roads in Peru as "state space," see Harvey and Knox 2015.
12. Lefebvre 2009:224.
13. Lefebvre 2009:234.
14. Lefebvre's Marxist orientation and Schmitt's conservative jural philosophy (with intellectual ties and commitments to early 1930s German fascism) could not be starker.
15. See Deleuze 1994:36–37, 309; and Deleuze and Guattari 1998:380–381, 557n51. The distinctions Deleuze makes between two different readings of *nomos* are analytically suggestive. First roads viewed as a means of enacting land appropriations and instituting legal-spatial regimes—a new "order and orientation"—fall squarely within Schmitt's rendering of *nomos* or what Deleuze calls "sedentary *nomos*." And yet, the legal effects are hardly constrained to the tasks of founding law, since after the phase of initial construction (the moment that for Schmitt could correspond with taking a "first measure" of earth), first roads go on to have immensely eventful lives.
16. Deleuze and Guattari 1986, 1998.
17. In an earlier article on the history of the Marginal Highway (Kernaghan 2012), I have discussed frontier roads as legal topographies. There I draw upon the notion of sedentary *nomos*. However, I also point out that sedentary *nomos* is but one register among many others through which frontier roads have territorial effects.
18. Kernaghan 2012.
19. On agrarian reform histories and repercussions, see Mayer 2009; and Seligmann 1995. On the power of landed elites (*gamonalismo*) and the figure of the *gamonal*, see Burga and Flores Galindo 1984; and Poole 1994, 2004.
20. On infrastructure sabotage in the context of Shining Path's *hambrear la ciudad* (starve the cities) strategy, see del Pino 1996; CVR 2003, IV:64, 78; and L. Taylor 2006.
21. Koselleck 2002:36.
22. Numerous registers emerge from roads, which might lend themselves in turn to readings other than the strictly historical. Stewart (2014), with concision and verve, sketches a sense of the stakes, showing how roads not only "form links between disparate phenomena, scales, and compositional modes from literature to ordinary prac-

tices to state thinking" but have an "energetic life" of their own that unfolds across multiple planes.

23. The closest hospital was in Tingo María, as was the closest university and court of law. Most official business involving the departmental or national government had to be done there, making it the nearest "hub" of the state.

24. R. González 1989:14–15.

25. For critical reflections on similar dynamics in rural areas of Peru affected by the counterinsurgency war, see O. González 2011; and Theidon 2004, 2010, 2012.

26. The relative importance accorded to roads vis-à-vis other public works, among provincial and specifically rural populations in Peru, demonstrates they are a crucial ethnographic site for understanding how relations between state authorities and political subjects are articulated and refashioned. For a nuanced analysis of the fundamental political role rural roads play in contemporary Peru, see Harvey 2005. Also see Wilson 2004, especially with regard to the often uncritical acceptance of the imperatives of road building in development studies.

27. See CVR 2003, VIII:34n39.

28. It was precisely the broad range of potential human targets, and the facility with which one could become an enemy of the Party, that differentiated Shining Path from other insurgent movements in Peru and Latin America.

29. Key dates in the Shining Path calendar were May 17 (the commencement of the armed struggle); June 19 (Heroes Day [el Día de la Heroicidad]); October 4 (Prisoners of War Day); and December 3 (anniversary of the formation of the People's Guerrilla Army [EGP] and the birthday of the movement's supreme leader, Abimael Guzmán).

30. Though paro armado is generally translated in English as "armed strike," a more literal rending of paro as "stoppage" emphasizes the tactic's crucial function of impeding and upsetting the regular, expected, and habitual movements of everyday life. "Stoppage" does not allude, however, to the many ways a paro could be generative of its own modes of habit.

31. Party documents of Shining Path described the paros armados as a new and advanced form of struggle combining the four principal means of conducting people's war: agitation and propaganda, sabotage, selective assassination, and guerrilla combat. See Comité Central Partido Comunista del Perú 1990; and CVR 2003, II:107.

32. See CVR 2003, IV:66.

33. Participatory justice at its makeshift extreme, the juicio popular compressed legal hearing and execution into a single, rapid proceeding (see also Chapter 8, "contracts and contemplations"). Though the means of actual killing could vary—gunshot, machete blows, strangulation, etc.—the format was often detailed as follows: armed insurgents would call upon a group of local residents to form a circle around the accused, charges would be declared, and then a knife would be passed around for each spectator to take a stab at the victim. Participation in the juicios was consistently described as coerced. Nonetheless, it would not be wrong to say that on an affective plane they were exceedingly ambiguous affairs—with degrees of legitimacy varying too, one would suspect, across distinct historical moments of the conflict.

34. On the comparison between Sendero Luminoso and Pol Pot's regime, see Hinojosa 1992.

35. Caminar como el cangrejo is a common Spanish idiomatic expression for a regressive movement, an antiprogress.

36. The act of being pressed into "road work" resonates with modern historical precedents in Peru, where the state obliged remote rural, and often indigenous, populations to build highways—notoriously under the terms of the 1920 *ley de conscripción vial* (road conscription law) during the administration of Augusto B. Leguía. However, Shining Path's enlistment of rural peoples in the deliberate destruction of road infrastructure arguably derives more directly from the presuppositions of revolutionary people's war, which blurs distinctions separating civilian from combatant and, by extension, conventional from total war.

37. Through such sabotage, Shining Path enforced its total ban on vicinal road construction—undermining therein a major policy goal of US-funded anti-coca rural development—from early the 1980s until the late 1990s.

chapter 5

1. See Kernaghan 2009, 2013.

chapter 6

1. Though travels along the Marginal Highway often took me through Nuevo Progreso in the mid- to late 1990s, largely on account of spatial interdictions I did not cross the river there until 2002. My photographs of this ferryman, however, were taken much later during a series of fieldwork visits to the town between 2011 and 2017.

2. Indeed, those concrete particulars may well render readings of time uncanny, as Rojas-Perez reveals in his compelling ethnographic study of postconflict forensic exhumations of human remains in the southern Andes of Peru. Aftermaths of war, he suggests, may sometimes unfold as a "strange temporality . . . simultaneously over and not over yet" (2017:32).

3. Taussig 2003b:21.

4. Taussig 1993; Poole 2005; Edwards 2005.

5. Sontag 2003:117.

6. Such possibilities have become a renewed area of concern among ethnographers. Seale-Feldman's (2018) introductory essay to the Fieldsights series "Images" in the journal *Cultural Anthropology* sets out some of the stakes; see too, and especially, the contribution there by Meyers (2018). Photographs from my fieldwork seem to point to other kinds of images, but obliquely: in terms of a "not present" that appeals to acts of memory or of writing. As the general characteristic linking different manifestations of images, that "not present" offers a shared trait with which to make comparisons, that is, through the specific types of absences they each express.

7. See Poole 2005.

8. As Serres 2015 suggests.

9. Blanchot 1989.

10. See Hertz's 1960 foundational treatise for an early synthesis; see Lomnitz-Adler 2005 and Stepputat 2014 for recent appraisals.

11. Kwon 2008; Rojas-Perez 2017.

12. Kernaghan 2014:187; also Kernaghan 2009 passim.

13. Poole 1997:8–13.

14. Stewart 2003:439.

15. Corpse mutilation in the Huallaga had profound sensorial, political, and legal effects. However, in terms of sinister artistry, the practice did not rival what had already historically obtained in Colombia's paramilitary violence, as described and explored by Taussig 2003a.

16. A stark symptom of that scarcity: prior to the year 2000 few photographs circulated in the public domain of members of the Huallaga faction of Sendero Luminoso. The rare exception was a handful of images taken by *Caretas* photojournalist Victor Vargas in 1987. Consequently, throughout the 1990s when the national press print media published a new journalistic report about Sendero in the Upper Huallaga, the photographs that would accompany it were frequently the very same ones Vargas had taken in 1987 and that over time had become iconic.

17. Kernaghan 2009.

18. Brighenti 2006:69.

19. Deleuze and Guattari 1998:310–350.

20. Munn 1996:451 (my emphasis).

21. And not just any bodies or bodies in general, since for Deleuze and Guattari (1998:319) the manners in which critical distances are crafted are always specific (i.e., they happen between "two beings of the same species"), even while territorializing practices are broad phenomena found across different and quite numerous classes of beings. The specificity of territorial practices that Munn describes belongs to a particular cultural milieu.

22. Deleuze and Guattari 1994:319–320.

23. Munn 1996:452.

24. On imagination as a crucial facet of territory, see Brighenti 2006, 2010.

25. See Cache 1995:70; also discussed in Chapter 1.

26. Video clip may be viewed here: https://www.crossingthecurrent.net/6-video.

27. And indeed here, in only a few years' time (2021), a bridge would be built to the north of this town. "Puente Megote" now bypasses the port, siphoning off some of its social life and many of the livelihoods it once made possible.

28. Deleuze 1988:18. I thank Chris Fraga for raising this possible objection but also for phrasing it in terms that aligned with my own thinking.

29. Spyer and Steedly 2013.

30. Mitchell 1984.

31. For Blanchot (1989) the "formlessness" of matter did not entail absence of form but rather a state of neutrality, freed from human-imposed interests and designs.

32. Blanchot 1989:256.

33. Blanchot 1989:254.

34. Rephrased within the register of sense: what returns for Blanchot is reversible. In other words, "image" returns to affirm a sense of what cannot.

35. Blanchot 1989:254.

36. Blanchot 1989:254.

37. Blanchot 1989:255.

38. Blanchot 1989:255–256 (my emphasis).

39. Barthes 1981:45.

40. Barthes 1981:88. Which of course, is not to say that photography has not always offered numerous possibilities for manipulation and deception, something that Barthes

(1977:21–22) readily acknowledged and that Sontag (2003:46) also stressed. For a recent ethnographic reflection on this theme, see Zamorano 2022.

41. Poole 2005.

42. Orrantia 2009, 2012.

43. Siegel 1983, 2006.

44. On some of those other sorts of images, see Taussig's (2011) compelling discussion of fieldwork drawings and watercolors.

45. Barthes 1981:76.

46. Blanchot 1989:263; see also Blanchot 2003:184.

47. For sharp, eloquent reflections on this point, see O. González 2011, especially chap. 8, "Behind the Visible."

48. Spyer and Steedly 2013:8.

49. Paraíso began as a government-subsidized settler community for families displaced by the 1970 Yungay earthquake. A decade and a half later it had transformed into a rural center of the cocaine trade and a social base of Shining Path. See CVR 2003, IV:263–264, V:109–195, 494, 498–499.

50. In that regard, Goldenberg and Watanabe's *Memorías del Paraíso* (2003), a video documentary filmed at the end of the Truth Commission's two-year tenure, offers a valuable chronicle of Paraíso's place in the Huallaga Valley. Prefaced by an extended segment on the community's origins as an agricultural colony for earthquake refugees, *Memorías* draws on taped interviews with contemporary residents to craft what can, and perhaps should, be read as a village-level "official story" of the war and its aftermaths.

51. See Fortes 1975:243.

52. See Ansión et al. 1992; and Reátegui 2009.

53. Pitt-Rivers 2012:504.

54. Simmel 1971:146.

55. Fortes 1975:246.

56. Pitt-Rivers 2012:514.

57. Such "local" differences would always crop up to belie easy claims about the war or its separation from what followed in its wake. Circumstances could change fast in the Huallaga and were rarely the same from place to place. At any rate, two years *back then* was a long stretch of time.

chapter 7

1. The figure of *despliegue/repliegue*, as well as some of the conceptual reflections I offer here on the relation between counterinsurgency bases and political states of emergency in Peru, owes a profound debt to conversations with Isaías Rojas-Perez. Those conversations initially sparked a series of conference panels, which we co-organized, but more recently have led to participation in a vibrant interdisciplinary group of scholars and lawyers convened by Carmen Ilizarbe, who are studying the history of emergency measures in Peru as well as the broad implications of ongoing government reliance on states of legal exception.

2. As mentioned in Chapter 1, the Upper Huallaga initially became a zone of Shining Path expansion for reasons directly related to widespread police operations against coca farms and farmers in the late 1970s and early 1980s. Those operations were given legal authorization in part through recourse to an emergency zone decree (see Chapter 1, note 26), ostensibly focused on disrupting the cocaine trade. States of emergency imposed in

response to the armed conflict specifically came later, beginning in October 1984. That decree from October 1984 would become the first in a series of declarations and extensions that, notwithstanding a four-year lapse following the Fujimori regime in late 2000, did not definitely cease until 2015. According to Peruvian constitutional law, states of emergency can be imposed for no more than sixty days. Then they can be prolonged and frequently are. In the Upper Huallaga from 1984 to 2000, emergency zone decrees stipulated the army's leading role in counterinsurgency operations, granting it ultimate authority over local civilian affairs and state institutions, including the police. Subsequent decrees, from late 2005 to mid-2015, would expressly place the Peruvian National Police (PNP) in charge of counterinsurgency, with the military authorized to provide support as needed. Even though the national government did not declare any states of emergency in the Upper Huallaga from November 2000 to December 2005, during that stretch the Peruvian Army and the police continued to carry out surveillance, detentions, and occasional operations against Shining Path, as remnants of the insurgency attempted to reorganize and step up attacks.

3. On some temporal implications of the material remains of modern warfare, albeit from the ostensible perspective of universal history, see Paul Virilio's *Bunker Archeology* (1994). While Virilio makes only passing references to counterinsurgency—his concerns dwell with the late twentieth-century arms race of "superpowers" ever haunted by specters of total annihilation—his discussion of *switches* in the war's movement (23) run in many ways parallel to the remarks above on the material unfolding / furling up of political emergency. I find particularly compelling Virilio's analysis of how time in war relates to space and that there are moments when fortifications serve only to slow down the enemy's advance while "forts and blockhouses" become so many "alarms" to wake the armed forces out of their peacetime slumber (23). And yet the difference between enemies foreign and internal, and therefore the place from where imminent attacks on the nation might arise, is hardly minor.

4. Historically, studies of animal mimicry have influenced experiments in military camouflage, as seen most notably in the life and works of British zoologist Hugh B. Cott. French surrealist sociologist Roger Caillois would comment at length on Cott's coloration theories in his 1964 book *Mask of Medusa* (first English translation; originally published in 1960). And yet Caillois's most compelling engagement on the topic appears much earlier in a 1938 essay, where he introduces the notion of "reciprocal topography" to describe how certain insects blend into a surrounding milieu with such precision that it is possible to speak of a "mutual organization" between the two. In some cases, insects tend so close toward terrains that they take on their morphological features. Camouflage becomes at that point, he suggested, an "actual photography . . . of the form and the relief, a photography at the level of the object and not of that of the image, a reproduction in three-dimensional space with solids and voids" (Caillois 1984:23).

5. During the approximately same era, 1989 and over next few years, army bases also unfurled from Tingo María along the Central Highway up to kilometer 86, where jurisdiction subsequently shifted and was handed over to *la Marina* (navy), all the way to the city of Pucallpa. However, the histories that Yéssica recounted largely belonged to a time before the army attempted to occupy the Upper Huallaga.

6. Kernaghan 2009.

7. Ollanta Moisés Humala Tasso, president of Peru (2011–2016).

8. On the notion "frames of probability," as drawn from Bernard Cache's theory of architecture, see Chapter 1.

9. Across the Huallaga region the archipelago of counterinsurgency forts reached maximum extension in the mid-1990s. However, my discussion here is limited to the stretch of country north of Tingo María, beginning immediately after the Marginal Highway peels off from the Central Highway to follow the Huallaga River only as far as Tocache. Falling within the stretch were the bases situated directly on the road before Aucayacu at Tulumayo, Pendencia, Pueblo Nuevo, and Anda and then passing Aucayacu, above the Honoris Bridge, Pucayacu, Madre Mía, Nuevo Progreso, and Río Uchiza. With the exception of a permanent base in the town of Uchiza, from the late 1980s, and a temporary occupation of the caserío Paraíso (1990–1991) to the south of Tocache, only later would the army extend its base system to the Huallaga's left bank, historically Shining Path's rural rear guard and domain of greatest support—with forts in Merced de Locro (1995 approx.); Venenillo (1995 approx.), Primavera (2000), and then in Yanajanca (2013) much later still—that is to say, *after* the Peruvian state had the military situation well in hand.

10. The army took the heights too by controlling airspace—demonstrated by their helicopters but also when base commanders facilitated the landing and takeoff of drug planes transiting cocaine and money between Peru and Colombia (an army-narco—anti-Sendero alliance that endured for several years in the early to mid-1990s until the Peruvian Air Force imposed a no-fly zone over the entire area, with an assist from CIA contractors).

11. Taussig, in his *Magic of the State* (1997), describes the uncertainties, potentially unnerving, of passing before police/customs checkpoints. The intense forebodings that such moments may provoke might be tracked to an even more fundamental permeability, which Serres has ascribed to all social encounters. This, thanks in part to how hospitality always moves in close proximity to war: "The uncertainty principle *hostes hospites*, or better *hospites imbelles hostes*, causes the wall to be porous, blurs the boundaries, causes the definition to be fuzzy" (2015:125). And perhaps the most unnerving thing about times when political community is at war with itself is how lines of hostility end up crisscrossing those of hospitality, again and again, denying any surety that friend could be definitively distinguished from foe.

12. Sometimes checkpoints would crop up suddenly around a bend in the road, creating a kind of routinized surprise. Sometimes the base would not even come into view but be tucked high overhead (Tulumayo) behind the backs of travelers whose sight was oriented toward oncoming traffic. Sometimes the checkpoint would arise down a long straightaway (Anda, Pueblo Nuevo), slowly moving closer and closer until the driver brought the vehicle to a stop.

13. Indeed, Wilson called Ramal de Aspuzana *el ombligo* (umbilicus or crossroad) of Shining Path territory for the way the village communicated insurgent areas of influence and strength on the left bank with those on the right.

14. In October 1984; see note 2 in this chapter.

15. Canetti 1984:289.

16. CVR 2003, V:259–281.

chapter 8

1. The original, article version, of this chapter appeared in *Anthropological Quarterly* and is reproduced here with the journal's permission; see Kernaghan 2017.

2. Verdery 2003.

3. Koselleck 2004:97.

4. Anderson 2006:204.

5. Augé 2004.

6. On the importance of conceiving oblivion as operating at the level of connections and associations, "between memories or between traces," see Pontalis 1997:98–103, cited in Augé 2004:23.

7. In this specific use of the linguistic term *denotation*, I again follow Deleuze 1990:12–13, as discussed in Chapter 1, especially note 31.

8. See Caillois 1984; Povinelli 2011:30; and Lombard 2016.

9. Jusionyte 2015.

10. See Chapter 1, note 13.

11. Virilio 1994; Gordillo 2009, 2014.

12. Rojas-Perez 2008.

13. To demonstrate how postwar narrations of wartime events often demand strategic silences and creative forms of "forgetting," O. González (2011) builds on the notion of "public secrecy" theorized by Michael Taussig (1999) as the dramatic performance of concealment and revelation, which reanimates a secret and even reconceals it, if on a different register.

14. Indeed, duping and duplicity may appear in multiple and often surprising ways, as Diane Nelson (2009) shows in her work on postconflict Guatemala.

15. Cf. Rojas-Perez 2013; and Chapter 1.

16. For an insightful reassessment of how Sendero Luminoso responded to the devastating military and political setbacks of the early and mid-1990s, see L. Taylor 2015.

17. See L. Taylor 2015.

18. The Programa Especial de Titulación de Tierras (PETT) began on the coast in the late 1990s and subsequently extended to the highlands. The titling initiative did not reach the Upper Huallaga until 2007, when the Comisión de Formalización de la Propiedad Informal (COFOPRI) assumed PETT's work for a period of four years. Henceforth, rural titling became the administrative responsibility of the country's regional governments. For a detailed analysis of rural titling initiatives in Peru—their politics, claims, and limitations—during the 1990s Fujimori-era, see Lastarria-Cornhiel and Barnes 1999.

19. Humphrey and Verdery 2004.

20. Verdery 2003:357.

21. Alexander 2004:269.

22. See, for example, Povinelli 2011.

23. See Mayer 2002.

24. Humphrey and Verdery, 2004:5.

25. Rozental 2014.

26. Navaro-Yashin 2012:179.

27. From the early to mid-1990s the Peruvian Army treated the Huallaga's left bank as an indiscriminate kill zone without regard for age, gender, or affiliation of the rural populace. For a detailed description and analysis, see CVR 2003, V:259–281.

28. Hetherington 2014:200.

29. Das 2004:227.

30. Hull 2012:258–260. See also Holston's discussion of land-legalization subterfuges in Brazil, in particular, practices of "fraudulent subdivision [*loteamento grilado*]" and the figure of the *grileiro* (swindler) who draws on every possible trick to doctor documents,

"giv[ing] their operations a cloak of legality, sometimes so expertly woven that lawyers and judges are fooled" (Holston 1991:701). There is also a rich literature on faking documents in colonial Latin America, for instance, Wood 1998.

31. Deleuze and Guattari 1998; see also Brighenti 2010.

32. Deleuze and Guattari 1998:315–316.

33. Deleuze and Guattari 1998:315.

34. My analysis in this section is inspired by Deleuze's exegesis of the method of division in Plato's philosophy: "the essence of [which] . . . is to screen the claims (pretensions) and to distinguish the true pretender from the false one" (1990:254).

35. Siegel 1998.

36. "It is a feature of this sort of counterfeit that there are 'insiders' involved who furnish the genuine-but-false verification or mark; it might be, as in certain cases, government certificates" (Siegel 1998:54). See also Petrucci (1995) on "chancery forgeries" in European diplomatic history (cited in Hull 2008:513).

37. Mayer provides a concise account of agrarian reforms in Peru (2009:1–40).

38. Through a 1981 agreement (*convenio*) with the US Agency for International Development (USAID), the Peruvian government created the (expressly anti-coca) farm assistance agency known as the Proyecto Especial Alto Huallaga. Among its functions, it oversaw land surveys.

39. In 1983 Executive Degree D.S. 040-83-AG modified land law within the Peruvian Amazon (D.L. 22175): growing coca in agrarian reform areas is cited as legal grounds for denying title.

40. For discussions of Sendero's *batir el campo* strategy, see del Pino 1998 and L. Taylor 2006.

41. On that prerogative and its temporal, lawgiving implications, see Koselleck's vivid exegesis of the modern concept of revolution (2004:43–57). Revealingly he tracks the emergence of partisan assertions of "legitimate revolution" to nineteenth-century Europe. I find the following passage instructive: "For the modern professional revolutionary, the determined struggle by legal as well as illegal means belongs to *the anticipated course* of a revolution; the revolutionary feels free to use any means available because the revolution is, for him, legitimate" (2004:56; my emphasis). Even more to the point of my exposition here, Koselleck describes this self-justifying legitimacy as a *"legal title"* that stems from the temporal unfolding of revolution itself (my emphasis).

42. Base Huallaga 1999. Here the Spanish impersonal verbal form *se justifica* underscores the reflexive, auto-causative character of the action. In so doing, grammar provides felicitous support to the idea of self-legitimation.

43. See Arce Borja 1989 for relevant party documents. On the particular interpretation Guzman gave to "history as armed-struggle," see Guzmán 1988. On how his reading mixed "cosmic inevitability and armed agency," see Poole and Rénique 2003:156.

44. Koselleck 2004.

45. L. Taylor 2006.

46. In Peru this has been one widespread view of Sendero violence. For an early critical assessment, see Flores Galindo 1987, 1993. For a reappraisal, see Portocarrero Maisch 2012.

47. Lukács 1971.

48. See Kernaghan 2009. On the Huallaga cocalero movement and postwar coca/cocaine violence, see van Dun 2009.

49. See earlier discussion in Chapter 4, especially note 33.

50. Regarding Sendero land politics in the Huallaga, see CVR 2003, V:202. For Peru's northern highlands compared to the southern sierra, see L. Taylor 2006.

51. L. Taylor 2006:172–173.

52. Rojas-Perez 2005:191–194.

53. Hendrix 1991:22.

54. Hetherington 2011, 2014.

55. Krupa 2015.

56. Hetherington 2014:199.

57. Krupa 2015:103.

58. Hetherington 2014:97.

works cited

Agüero, José Carlos. 2015. *Los rendidos: Sobre el don de perdonar*. Lima: Instituto de estudios peruanos.

Aguirre, Carlos. 2009. "¿De quién son estas memorias? El Archivo de la Comisión de la Verdad y Reconciliación del Perú." *Jahrbuch für Geschichte Lateinamerikas–Anuario de Historia de America Latina* 46 (1): 135–166.

———. 2011. "Terruco de M . . . : Insulto y estigma en la guerra sucia peruana." *Histórica* 35 (1): 103–139.

Alexander, Catherine. 2004. "Value, Relations, and Changing Bodies: Privatization and Property Right in Kazakhstan." In *Property in Question: Value Transformation in the Global Economy*, edited by Katherine Verdery and Caroline Humphrey, 251–273. Oxford, UK: Berg.

Anderson, Benedict. 2006. *Imagined Communities: Reflections on the Origin and Spread of Nationalism*. London: Verso Books.

Anidjar, Gil. 2004. "Terror Right." *CR: The New Centennial Review* 4 (3): 35–69.

Ansión, Juan, Daniel del Castillo, Manuel Piqueras, and Isaura Zegarra. 1992. *La escuela en tiempos de guerra*. Lima: CEAPAZ/Tarea/IPEDEHP.

Aramburú, Carlos. 1981. "Problemas del desarrollo rural y la colonización en la Amazonía peruana." *Debates en Sociología* 6:41–70.

Arce Borja, Luis, ed. 1991. *Guerra popular en el Perú: El pensamiento Gonzalo*. Barcelona: Ediciones Bandera Roja.

Augé, Marc. 2004. *Oblivion*. Minneapolis: University of Minnesota Press.

Barclay Rey de Castro, Frederica. 2001. "Olvido de una historia: Reflexiones acerca de la historiografía andino-amazónica." *Revista de Indias* 61 (223): 493–511.

Barthes, Roland. 1977. "The Photographic Message." In *Image-Music-Text*, translated by Stephen Heath, 15–31. New York: Hill and Wang.

———. 1981. *Camera lucida*. Translated by Richard Howard. New York: Hill and Wang.

Base Huallaga Partido Comunista del Perú. 1999. "¡Luchar implacablemente contra la capitulación! ¡Desenmascarar y liquidar a los traidores! ¡Desenmascarar y aplastar la campaña de guerra psicológico de los fascistas reaccionarios!" http://www.solrojo.org/pcp_doc/pcp_luchar.htm.

Belaúnde Terry, Fernando. 1959. *La conquista del Perú por los peruanos*. Lima: Ediciones "Tawantinsuyu."

———. 1965. *Peru's Own Conquest*. Lima: American Studies Press.

Bennett, Jane. 2010. *Vibrant Matter: A Political Ecology of Things*. Durham, NC: Duke University Press.

Bergson, Henri. 1920. *Mind-Energy*. Translated by H. Wildon Carr. Westport, CT: Greenwood Press.

———. 1988. *Matter and Memory*. Edited by William Scott Palmer. Translated by Nancy Margaret Paul. New York: Zone Books.

Blanchot, Maurice. 1987. "Dreaming, Writing." In *Michel Leiris, Nights as Day, Days as Night*, translated by Richard Sieburth, xvii–xxviii. Hygiene, CO: Eridanos Press.

———. 1989. "Two Versions of the Imaginary." In *The Space of Literature*, 254–263. Lincoln: University of Nebraska Press.

———. 2003. "Diary and Story." In *The Book to Come*, 183–188. Stanford, CA: Stanford University Press.

Brighenti, Andrea. 2006. "On Territory as Relationship and Law as Territory." *Canadian Journal of Law and Society* 21 (2): 65–86.

———. 2010. "On Territorology towards a General Science of Territory." *Theory, Culture & Society* 27 (1): 52–72.

Buitrón, Aníbal. 1948. *Ethnological Survey of the Valley of the Rio Huallaga, Peru*. Paris: UNESCO.

Burga, Manuel, and Alberto Flores Galindo. 1984. *Apogeo y crisis de la república aristocrática*. Ediciones Rikchay Perú (Series) No. 8. Lima: Ediciones Rikchay Perú.

Cache, Bernard. 1995. *Earth Moves*. Cambridge, MA: MIT Press.

Caillois, Roger. 1960. *Méduse et Cie*. Paris: Gallimard, 1960.

———. 1964. *The Mask of Medusa*. Translated by George Ordish. New York: Clarkson N. Potter.

———. 1984. "Mimicry and Legendary Psychasthenia." Translated by John Shepley. *October* 31:16–32.

Campbell, Jeremy M. 2012. "Between the Material and the Figural Road: The Incompleteness of Colonial Geographies in Amazonia." *Mobilities* 7 (4): 481–500.

Canetti, Elias. 1984. *Crowds and Power*. New York: Farrar, Straus and Giroux.

Carter, Jon Horne. 2022. *Gothic Sovereignty: Street Gangs and Statecraft in Honduras*. Austin: University of Texas Press.

Cipriani Thorne, Juan Luis. 2012. *Doy fe: Testimonio del cardenal Cipriani sobre la crisis de los rehenes en la embajada de Japón*. Lima: Editorial Planeta Perú.

Cisneros, Renato. 2016. *La distancia que nos separa*. Mexico City: Editorial Planeta Mexicana.

CNDDHH (Coordinadora Nacional de Derechos Humanos). 2006. "Contexto de violencia en la región nororiental y sucesos de base militar de 'Madre Mía' (1992) (El caso del ex capitán EP Ollanta Humala Tasso)." Informe. Perú, 7 de Marzo 2006. CNDDHH: Lima, Perú.

———. 2009. "Violaciones a los derechos humanos en el Alto Huallaga El caso Madre Mía y la responsabilidad de Ollanta Humala." Documento de trabajo. November. Lima: CNDDHH.

Comisión de la Verdad y Reconciliación (CVR). 2003. *Informe final de la Comisión de la Verdad y Reconciliación*. 9 vols. Lima: Comisión de la Verdad y Reconciliación.

Comité Central Partido Comunista del Perú. 1990. "¡Elecciones, no! ¡Guerra popular, si!" May. http://www.solrojo.org/pcp_doc/pcp_0590.htm.

Coxshall, Wendy. 2005. "From the Peruvian Reconciliation Commission to Ethnography." *PoLAR: Political and Legal Anthropology Review* 28 (2): 203–222.

Coya, Hugo. 2011. *Polvo en el viento: Vaticano: Esplendor y miserias de un narcotrafi-cante*. Lima: Santillana.

Das, Veena. 2004. "The Signature of the State: The Paradox of Illegibility." In *Anthropol-ogy in the Margins of the State*, edited by Veena Das and Deborah Poole, 225–252. Santa Fe, NM: School of American Research.

de la Cadena, Marisol. 2010. "Indigenous Cosmopolitics in the Andes: Conceptual Reflec-tions beyond 'Politics.'" *Cultural Anthropology* 25 (2): 334–370.

———. 2015. *Earth Beings: Ecologies of Practice across Andean Worlds*. Durham, NC: Duke University Press.

Degregori, Carlos Iván. 1989. *Qué difícil es ser Dios: Ideología y violencia política en Sendero Luminoso*. Lima: El Zorro de Abajo Ediciones.

———. 1990. *El surgimiento de Sendero Luminoso Ayacucho 1969–1979: Del mov-imiento por la gratuidad de la enseñanza al inicio de la lucha armada*. Lima: Instituto de Estudios Peruanos.

———. 2004. "Heridas abiertas, derechos esquivos: Reflexiones sobre la Comisión de la Verdad y Reconciliación." In *Memorias en conflicto: Aspectos de la violencia política contemporánea*, edited by Raynald Belay, Jorge Bracamonte, Carlos Iván Degregori, and Jean Joinville Vacher, 75–85. Lima: Institut Français d'Études Andines.

Degregori, Carlos Iván, José Coronel, Ponciano del Pino, and Orin Starn, eds. 1996. *Las rondas campesinas y la derrota de Sendero Luminoso*. Estudios de la Sociedad Rural 15. Lima: Instituto de Estudios Peruanos.

del Pino, Ponciano. 1996. "Tiempos de guerra y de dioses: Ronderos, evangélicos y send-eristas en el valle del Río Apurímac." In *Las rondas campesinas y la derrota de Send-ero Luminoso*, edited by Carlos Iván Degregori, José Coronel, Ponciano del Pino, and Orin Starn, 117–188. Estudios de la Sociedad Rural. Lima: IEP Ediciones.

———. 1998. "Family, Culture and 'Revolution': Everyday Life with Sendero Lumi-noso." In *Shining and Other Paths: War and Society in Peru, 1980–1995*, edited by Steven Stern, 158–192. Durham, NC: Duke University Press.

———. 2017. *En nombre del gobierno: El Perú y Uchuraccay: Un siglo de política campesina*. Juliaca, Peru: Universidad Nacional de Juliaca.

Deleuze, Gilles. 1983. *Nietzsche and Philosophy*. Translated by Hugh Tomlinson. New York: Columbia University Press.

———. 1988. *Bergsonism*. Cambridge, MA: Zone Books.

———. 1990. *The Logic of Sense*. New York: Columbia University Press.

———. 1993. *The Fold: Leibniz and the Baroque*. Minneapolis: University of Minnesota Press.

———. 1994. *Difference and Repetition*. New York: Columbia University Press.

Deleuze, Gilles, and Félix Guattari. 1986. *Kafka: Toward a Minor Literature*. Minneapo-lis: University of Minnesota Press.

———. 1998. *A Thousand Plateaus: Capitalism and Schizophrenia*. Minneapolis: Univer-sity of Minnesota Press.

Drinot, Paulo. 2009. "For Whom the Eye Cries: Memory, Monumentality and the Ontol-ogies of Violence in Peru." *Journal of Latin American Cultural Studies* 18 (1): 15–32.

Dupréel, Eugène. 1933. "La cause et l'intervalle, ou ordre et probabilité." Archives de la Société Belge de Philosophie Cinquième Année (1932–33). Fascilicule No 2. Brussels: Maurice Lamertin.

———. 1961. "La consistance et la probabilité constructive." *Revue Internationale de Philosophie* 58 (4): 11–12.

Durand Ochoa, Ursula. 2014. *Political Empowerment of the Cocaleros of Bolivia and Peru*. New York: Palgrave Macmillan.

Edwards, Elizabeth. 2005. "Photographs and the Sound of History." *Visual Anthropology Review* 21 (1–2): 27–46.

Feldman, Joseph P. 2021. *Memories before the State: Postwar Peru and the Place of Memory, Tolerance, and Social Inclusion*. New Brunswick, NJ: Rutgers University Press.

Ferreira, Francisco. 2016. "De-demonizing the VRAEM: A Peruvian-Cocalero Area." *Substance Use & Misuse* 51 (1): 41–53.

Flores Galindo, Alberto. 1987. *Buscando un inca: Identidad y utopia en los Andes*. Lima: Instituto de Apoyo Agrario.

———. 1993. *Obras completas: Tomo VI*. Lima: Sur, Casa de Estudios del Socialismo.

Fortes, Meyer. 1975. "Strangers." In *Studies in African Social Anthropology*, edited by Meyer Fortes and Sheila Patterson, 229–253. New York: Academic Press.

Frege, Gottlob. 1948. "Sense and Reference." *Philosophical Review* 57 (3): 209–230.

Freud, Sigmund. 1961. "A Note upon the 'Mystic Writing-Pad' (1925)." In *Standard Edition of the Complete Psychological Works of Sigmund Freud*, edited and translated by James Strachey, 19:225–232. London: Hogarth Press.

Gálvez Olaechea, Alberto. 2017. "Sísifo en Perú. Reconciliación: Elusiones, ilusiones, elucubraciones." *Pacarina del Sur* 8 (30). www.pacarinadelsur.com/index.php?option=com_content&view=article&id=1434&catid=5.

Gavilán Sánchez, Lurgio. 2019. *Carta al Teniente Shogún*. Lima: Editorial Debate.

Goldenberg, Sonía, and José Watanabe. 2003. Documentary: *"Memorias del Paraíso."* Lima: Tramas.

González, Olga M. 2011. *Unveiling Secrets of War in the Peruvian Andes*. Chicago: University of Chicago Press.

———. 2022. "Imágenes 'sin sentido aparente' en el lugar de la memoria, la tolerancia y la inclusión social." *Encartes Revista Digital Multimedia* 4 (9).

González, Raúl. 1989. "Recuperar el Huallaga: Una estrategia posible." *Quehacer* 58 (April–May): 14–19.

Gootenberg, Paul. 2008. *Andean Cocaine: The Making of a Global Drug*. Chapel Hill: University of North Carolina Press.

Gordillo, Gastón. 2009. "Places That Frighten: Residues of Wealth and Violence on the Argentine Chaco Frontier." *Anthropológica* 51:343–351.

———. 2014. *Rubble: The Afterlife of Destruction*. Durham, NC: Duke University Press.

Granados Moya, Carla. 2021. "De la 'guerra contraterrorista' al Congreso: El activismo político de los militares excombatientes en el Perú posconflicto." In *La violencia no cesa: Huellas y persistencias del conflicto armado en el Perú contemporáneo*, edited by Ricardo Bedoya Forno, Dorothée Delacroix, Valérie Robin Azevedo, and Tania Romero Barrios, 231–256. Lima, Peru: Punto Cardinal Editores S.A.C.

Guzmán, Abimael. 1988. *Entrevista con el presidente Gonzalo*. http://www.solrojo.org/pcp_doc/pcp_0688.htm.

Harvey, Penelope. 2005. "The Materiality of State Effects: An Ethnography of a Road in the Peruvian Andes." In *State Formation: Anthropological Perspectives*, edited by Christian Krohn-Hansen and Knut G. Nustad, 123–141. London: Pluto Press.

Harvey, Penelope, and Hannah Knox. 2012. "The Enchantments of Infrastructure." *Mobilities* 7 (4): 521–536.

———. 2015. *Roads: An Anthropology of Infrastructure and Expertise*. Ithaca, NY: Cornell University Press.

Heilman, Jaymie Patricia. 2010. *Before the Shining Path: Politics in Rural Ayacucho, 1895–1980*. Stanford, CA: Stanford University Press.

———. 2018. "Peruvian Cocaine Tangles: Arrests and Assertions of Innocence in Ayacucho's Drug Trade, 1976–1981." *Hispanic American Historical Review* 98 (2): 257–292.

Hendrix, Steven E. 1991. *Interplay among Land Law and Policy, the Environment, the War on Drugs, Narco-Terrorism and Democratization: Perspectives on Peru's Upper Huallaga Valley*. Madison: Land Tenure Center, University of Wisconsin–Madison.

Hermoza Ríos, Nicolás de Bari. 1997. *Operación Chavín de Huántar: Rescate en la residencia de la Embajada del Japón*. Lima: Talleres Gráficos de Fimart S.A.

Hertz, Robert. 1960. "A Contribution to the Study of the Collective Representation of Death." In *Death and the Right Hand*, translated by Rodney Needham and Claudia Needham, 27–86. London: Cohen and West.

Hetherington, Kregg. 2011. *Guerrilla Auditors: The Politics of Transparency in Neoliberal Paraguay*. Durham, NC: Duke University Press.

———. 2014. "Waiting for the Surveyor: Development Promises and the Temporality of Infrastructure." *Journal of Latin American and Caribbean Anthropology* 19 (2): 195–211.

Hidalgo Vega, David. 2007. *Sombras de un rescate: Tras las huellas ocultas en la residencia del embajador japonés*. Lima: Planeta Perú.

Hinojosa, Iván. 1992. "Entre el poder y la ilusión: Pol Pot, Sendero y las utopías campesinas." *Debate Agrario* 15:69–93.

Holston, James. 1991. "The Misrule of Law: Land and Usurpation in Brazil." *Comparative Studies in Society and History* 33 (4): 695–725.

Hull, Matthew S. 2008. "Ruled by Records: The Expropriation of Land and the Misappropriation of Lists in Islamabad." *American Ethnologist* 35 (4): 501–518.

———. 2012. "Documents and Bureaucracy." *Annual Review of Anthropology* 41:251–267.

Humphrey, Caroline, and Katherine Verdery. 2004. "Introduction: Raising Questions about Property." In *Property in Question: Value Transformation in the Global Economy*, edited by Katherine Verdery and Caroline Humphrey, 1–25. Oxford, UK: Berg.

Hyppolite, Jean. 1971. "Aspects divers de la memoire chez Bergsons." In *Figures de la pensée philosophique*, 1:468–488. Paris: Presses Universitaires de France.

Ilizarbe Pizarro, Carmen. 2015. "Memoria, olvido y negacionismo en el proceso de recomposición política en el Perú de la posguerra del siglo XXI." In *Políticas en justicia transicional: Miradas comparativas sobre el legado de la CVR*, edited by Ludwig Huber and Ponciano del Pino, 231–259. Lima: Instituto de Estudios Peruanos.

———. 2017. "Hegemonic Struggles of the Democratic Imaginary Street Protests and the Public Sphere in Peru (1997–2006)." PhD diss., The New School, New York.

Izaguirre, Bernardino. 2001. *Historia de las misiones franciscanas y narración de los progresos de la geografía en el oriente del Perú: Relatos originales y producciones en lenguas indígenas de varios misioneros.* Vol. 1. Lima: Provincia Misionera de San Francisco Solano del Perú, Convento de los PP. Descalzos.

Jara Montejo, Segundo. 2013. *Le avisas al general.* Aucayacu, Perú: Segundo Jara Montejo.

Jülich, Volker. 1974. *Colonización como complemento de la reforma agraria en la selva peruana: El valle del Huallaga Central.* Santiago de Chile: Instituto Latinoamericano de Investigaciones Sociales.

Jusionyte, Ieva. 2015. "States of Camouflage." *Cultural Anthropology* 30 (1): 113–138.

Kafka, Franz. 1971. *The Complete Short Stories.* New York: Schocken.

———. 1998. *The Castle: A New Translation, Based on the Restored Text.* Translated by Mark Harman. New York: Schocken.

Kernaghan, Richard. 2009. *Coca's Gone: Of Might and Right in the Huallaga Post-boom.* Stanford, CA: Stanford University Press.

———. 2012. "Furrows and Walls, or the Legal Topography of a Frontier Road in Peru." *Mobilities* 7 (4): 501–520.

———. 2013. "Readings of Time." In *Times of Security: Ethnographies of Fear, Protest and the Future,* edited by Martin Holbraad and Morten Axel Pederson, 80–102. London: Routledge.

———. 2014. "Time as Weather: Corpse-Work in the Prehistory of Political Boundaries." In *Governing the Dead: Sovereignty and the Politics of Dead Bodies,* edited by Finn Stepputat, 179–202. Human Remains and Violence Series. Manchester, UK: Manchester University Press.

———. 2017. "Oblivious Title: On the Political Time of Land Tenure in Postwar Peru." *Anthropological Quarterly* 90 (3): 637–673.

Koselleck, Reinhart. 2002. "Social History and Conceptual History." In *The Practice of Conceptual History: Timing History, Spacing Concepts,* 20–37. Cultural Memory in the Present. Translated by Todd Samuel Presner, Kerstin Behnke, and Jobst Welge. Stanford, CA: Stanford University Press.

———. 2004. *Futures Past: On the Semantics of Historical Time.* New York: Columbia University Press.

Krupa, Christopher. 2015. "Cadastral Politics: Property Wars and State Realism in Highland Ecuador." In *State Theory and Andean Politics: New Approaches to the Study of Rule,* edited by Christopher Krupa and David Nugent, 99–125. Philadelphia: University of Pennsylvania Press.

Kwon, Heonik. 2008. *Ghosts of War in Vietnam.* Cambridge: Cambridge University Press.

La Serna, Miguel. 2012. *The Corner of the Living: Ayacucho on the Eve of the Shining Path Insurgency.* Chapel Hill: University of North Carolina Press.

———. 2020. *With Masses and Arms: Peru's Tupac Amaru Revolutionary Movement.* H. Eugene and Lillian Youngs Lehman Series. Chapel Hill: University of North Carolina Press.

Lajtman, Tamara, and Marina Mendoza. 2019. "La utilización del estado de emergencia como herramienta represiva en el Perú contemporáneo: Los casos del VRAEM y el Proyecto Minero Conga." *El@ Tina. Revista Electrónica de Estudios Latinoamericanos* 17 (67) 1–19.

Lastarria-Cornhiel, Susana, and Grenville Barnes. 1999. *Formalizing Informality: The*

Praedial Registration System in Peru. Vol. 131. Madison: Land Tenure Center, University of Wisconsin–Madison.

Lawlor, Leonard. 2003. *The Challenge of Bergsonism*. London: Continuum.

Leach, Edmund. 1965. "The Nature of War." *Disarmament and Arms Control* 3 (2): 165–183.

Lefebvre, Henri. 2009. "Space and the State." In *State, Space, World: Selected Essays*, edited by Neil Brenner and Stuart Elden, 223–253. Minneapolis: University of Minnesota Press.

Leiris, Michel. 1987. *Nights as Day, Days as Night*. Hygiene, CO: Eridanos Press.

Lombard, Louisa. 2016. "Camouflage: The Hunting Origins of Worlding in Africa." *Journal of Contemporary African Studies* 34 (1): 147–164.

Lomnitz-Adler, Claudio. 2005. *Death and the Idea of Mexico*. Cambridge, MA: Zone Books.

Loraux, Nicole. 2002. *The Divided City: On Memory and Forgetting in Ancient Athens*. Translated by Corinne Pache and Jeff Fort. New York: Zone Books.

Lukács, Georg. 1971. *History and Class Consciousness*. Cambridge, MA: MIT Press.

Manrique, Nelson. 1989. "La década de la violencia." *Márgenes* 3 (5–6): 137–182.

Mayer, Enrique. 2002. "Land Tenure and Communal Control in Laraos." In *The Articulated Peasant: Household Economies in the Andes*, 279–311. Boulder, CO: Westview Press.

———. 2009. *Ugly Stories of the Peruvian Agrarian Reform*. Durham, NC: Duke University Press.

McAllister, Carlota, and Diane M. Nelson, eds. 2013. *War by Other Means: Aftermath in Post-genocide Guatemala*. Durham, NC: Duke University Press.

Méndez, Cecilia. 2021. "The Paths of Terrorism in Peru: Nineteenth to Twenty-First Centuries*." In *The Cambridge History of Terrorism*, edited by Richard English, 420–452. Cambridge: Cambridge University Press. https://doi.org/10.1017/9781108556248.017.

Meyers, Todd. 2018. "Trespass." Society for Cultural Anthropology, Fieldsights, March 27. https://culanth.org/fieldsights/trespass.

Milton, Cynthia E. 2011. "Defacing Memory: (Un)Tying Peru's Memory Knots." *Memory Studies* 4 (2): 190–205.

Mitchell, W. J. T. 1984. "What Is an Image?" *New Literary History* 15 (3): 503–537.

Munn, Nancy C. 1996. "Excluded Spaces: The Figure in the Australian Aboriginal Landscape." *Critical Inquiry* 22 (3): 46–65.

Navaro-Yashín, Yael. 2012. *The Make-Believe Space: Affective Geography in a Postwar Polity*. Durham, NC: Duke University Press.

Nelson, Diane M. 2009. *Reckoning: The Ends of War in Guatemala*. Durham, NC: Duke University Press.

Nietzsche, Friedrich. (1873) 1982. "On Truth and Lie in an Extra Moral Sense." In *The Portable Nietzsche*, translated by Walter Kaufmann, 42–47. Reprint, London: Penguin Books.

———. 1994. *On the Genealogy of Morality*. Cambridge: Cambridge University Press.

Orrantia, Juan. 2009. *Aqueous Recollections: Moments of Banality, Intimacy and Unexpectedness in the Aftermath of Terror in Colombia*. New Haven, CT: Yale University Press.

————. 2012. "Where the Air Feels Heavy: Boredom and the Textures of the Aftermath." *Visual Anthropology Review* 28 (1): 50–69.

Orwell, George. 1968. "Politics and the English Language." In *The Collected Essays, Journalism, and Letters of George Orwell*, edited by Sonia Orwell and Ian Angos, 4:127–140. New York: Harcourt, Brace, Jovanovich.

Paredes, Maritza, and Hernán Manrique. 2018. "Ideas of Modernization and Territorial Transformation: The Case of the Upper Huallaga Valley of Peru." In *The Origins of Cocaine*, edited by Paul Gootenberg and Liliana Dávalos, 65–95. London: Routledge.

Paucar Mariluz, Felipe A. 2006. *La guerra oculta en el Huallaga, Monzón y Aguaytía*. Tingo María, Peru: Centro de Estudios y Promoción para el Desarrollo Agroindustrial, CEDAI.

Peru. 1965. *El Perú Construye. Mensaje del Presidente de la República Fernando Belaúnde Terry al Congreso Nacional*. July 28. Lima: Editorial Minerva.

————. 1967. *Discursos pronunciados por el Presidente de la República Arq. Fernando Belaúnde Terry en Actos Oficiales*. December. Lima: Imprenta Diario Oficial "El Peruano."

Perú, Ejército del. 2010. *En honor a la verdad: Versión del ejército sobre su participación en la defensa del sistema democrático contra las organizaciones terroristas*. Lima: Ejército del Peru.

Petrucci, Armando. 1995. *Writers and Readers in Medieval Italy: Studies in the History of Written Culture*. New Haven, CT: Yale University Press.

Pitt-Rivers, Julian. 2012. "The Law of Hospitality." *HAU: Journal of Ethnographic Theory* 2 (1): 501–517.

Pontalis, J.-B. 1997. *Ce temps qui ne passe pas, suivi de Le compartiment de chemin de fer*. Paris: Éditions Gallimard.

Poole, Deborah, ed. 1994. *Unruly Order: Violence, Power, and Cultural Identity in the High Provinces of Southern Peru*. Boulder, CO: Westview Press.

————. 1997. *Vision, Race, and Modernity: A Visual Economy of the Andean Image World*. Princeton, NJ: Princeton University Press.

————. 2004. "Between Threat and Guarantee: Justice and Community in the Margins of the Peruvian State." In *Anthropology in the Margins of the State*, edited by Veena Das and Deborah Poole, 35–65. Santa Fe, NM: School of American Research.

————. 2005. "An Excess of Description: Ethnography, Race, and Visual Technologies." *Annual Review of Anthropology* 34:159–179.

Poole, Deborah, and Gerardo Rénique. 1992. *Peru: Time of Fear*. London: Latin American Bureau.

————. 2000. "Popular Movements, the Legacy of the Left, and the Fall of Fujimori." *Socialism and Democracy* 14 (2): 53–74.

————. 2003. "Terror and the Privatized State: A Peruvian Parable." *Radical History Review* 85 (1): 150–163.

Poole, Deborah, and Isaías Rojas Pérez. 2010. "Memories of Reconciliation: Photography and Memory in Postwar Peru." *E-Misférica* 7 (2): 1–23.

Portocarrero Maisch, Gonzalo. 2012. *Profetas del odio: Raíces culturales y líderes de Sendero Luminoso*. Lima: Fondo Editorial de la Pontificia Universidad Católica del Perú.

Povinelli, Elizabeth A. 2011. *Economies of Abandonment: Social Belonging and Endurance in Late Liberalism*. Durham, NC: Duke University Press.

Reátegui, Félix. 2009. *El sistema educativo durante el proceso de violencia*. Colección cuadernos para la memoria histórica 1. Lima: IDEHPUCP.

Rendón, Silvio. 2019. "Capturing Correctly: A Reanalysis of the Indirect Capture–Recapture Methods in the Peruvian Truth and Reconciliation Commission." *Research & Politics* 6 (1). https://doi.org/10.1177/2053168018820375.

Rénique C., José Luis. 2003. *La voluntad encarcelada*. Lima: IEP, Instituto de Estudios Peruanos.

Rojas-Perez, Isaías. 2005. "Peru: Drug Control Policy, Human Rights, and Democracy." In *Drugs and Democracy in Latin America: The Impact of U.S. Policy*, edited by Coletta Youngers and Eileen Rosin, 185–230. Boulder, CO: L. Rienner.

———. 2008. "Writing the Aftermath: Anthropology and 'Post⬚conflict.'" In *A Companion to Latin American Anthropology*, edited by Deborah Poole, 254–275. Malden, MA: Blackwell, 2008.

———. 2013. "Inhabiting Unfinished Pasts: Law, Transitional Justice, and Mourning in Postwar Peru." *Humanity: An International Journal of Human Rights, Humanitarianism, and Development* 4 (1): 149–170.

———. 2017. *Mourning Remains: State Atrocity, Exhumations, and Governing the Disappeared in Peru's Postwar Andes*. Stanford, CA: Stanford University Press.

Rozental, Sandra. 2014. "Stone Replicas: The Iteration and Itinerancy of Mexican Patrimonio." *Journal of Latin American and Caribbean Anthropology* 19 (2): 331–356.

Russell, Bertrand. 1905. "On Denoting." *Mind* 14 (56): 479–493.

Sala, Núria. 2019. "La expedición científica al río Huallaga (Perú, 1948) y la búsqueda de la cohesión social." *Estudios Sociales Revista Universitaria Semestral* 57 (2): 185–207.

Salazar, Claudia. 2016. *La sangre de la aurora*. Lima: Animal de Invierno.

Sanford, Victoria. 2008. *Guatemala: Del genocidio al feminicidio*. Guatemala City: F&G Editores.

Santos Granero, Fernando. 1985. "Crónica breve de un etnocidio o génesis del mito del 'Gran Vacío Amazónico.'" *Amazonía Peruana* 11:9–38.

Schmitt, Carl. 2003. *The Nomos of the Earth in the International Law of the Jus Publicum Europaeum*. New York: Telos.

Scott, James. 1998. *Seeing like a State: How Certain Schemes to Improve the Human Condition Have Failed*. New Haven, CT: Yale University Press.

Seale-Feldman, Aidan. 2018. "Images." Society for Cultural Anthropology, Fieldsights, March 2. https://culanth.org/fieldsights/series/images.

Seligmann, Linda. 1995. *Between Reform and Revolution: Political Struggles in the Peruvian Andes, 1969–1991*. Program in Agrarian Studies. Stanford, CA: Stanford University Press.

Serres, Michel. 2000. *The Birth of Physics*. Manchester, UK: Clinamen Press.

———. 2015. *Rome: The First Book of Foundations*. Translated by Randolph Burks. London: Bloomsbury Publishing.

Serres, Michel, and Bruno Latour. 1995. "A Different Theory of Time." In *Conversations on Science, Culture, and Time*, 57–62. Ann Arbor: University of Michigan Press.

Siegel, James T. 1983. "Images and Odors in Javanese Practices Surrounding Death." *Indonesia* 36:1–14.

———. 1998. *A New Criminal Type in Jakarta: Counter-revolution Today*. Durham, NC: Duke University Press.

———. 2006. *Naming the Witch*. Stanford, CA: Stanford University Press.

Siles, Abraham. 2017. "Problemática constitucional del estado de emergencia en Perú: Algunas cuestiones fundamentales." *Estudios Constitucionales* 15 (2): 123–166.

Simmel, Georg. 1971. "The Stranger." In *Georg Simmel on Individuality and Social Forms: Selected Writings*, edited by Donald N. Levine, 143–149. Chicago: University of Chicago Press.

Sontag, Susan. 2003. *Regarding the Pain of Others*. New York: Farrar, Straus and Giroux.

Spyer, Patricia, and Mary Margaret Steedly. 2013. *Images That Move*. Santa Fe, NM: School for Advanced Research Press.

Starn, Orin. 1999. *Nightwatch*. Durham, NC: Duke University Press.

Stengers, Isabelle. 2018. "The Challenge of Ontological Politics." In *A World of Many Worlds*, edited by Marisol de la Cadena and Mario Blaser, 83–111. Durham, NC: Duke University Press.

Stepputat, Finn. 2014. *Governing the Dead: Sovereignty and the Politics of Dead Bodies*. Human Remains and Violence Series. Manchester, UK: Manchester University Press.

Stern, Steve J. 1998. *Shining and Other Paths: War and Society in Peru, 1980–1995*. Durham, NC: Duke University Press.

———. 2006. *Battling for Hearts and Minds: Memory Struggles in Pinochet's Chile, 1973–1988*. Durham, NC: Duke University Press.

Stewart, Kathleen. 2003. "Arresting Images." In *Aesthetic Subjects*, edited by Pamela R. Matthews and David McWhirter, 431–448. Minneapolis: University of Minnesota Press.

———. 2014. "Road Registers." *Cultural Geographies* 21 (4): 549–563.

Stoler, Ann Laura. 2013. "Introduction 'the Rot Remains': From Ruins to Ruination." In *Imperial Debris: On Ruins and Ruination*, 1–35. Durham, NC: Duke University Press.

Tafur Sialer, Andrea, and Diego Quesada Nicoli. 2020. "El estado de emergencia en el Perú democrático post-conflicto: Un estudio empírico preliminar de las normas de emergencia." *Anuario de Derechos Humanos* 16 (2): 205–234.

Taussig, Michael. 1997. *The Magic of the State*. New York: Routledge.

———. 1993. *Mimesis and Alterity: A Particular History of the Senses*. New York: Routledge.

———. 1999. *Defacement: Public Secrecy and the Labor of the Negative*. Stanford, CA: Stanford University Press.

———. 2003a. "The Language of Flowers." *Critical Inquiry* 30 (1): 98–131.

———. 2003b. *Law in a Lawless Land: Diary of a "Limpieza" in Colombia*. New York: New Press.

———. 2011. *I Swear I Saw This: Drawings in Fieldwork Notebooks, Namely My Own*. Chicago: University of Chicago Press.

Taylor, Anne-Christine. 1999. "The Western Margins of Amazonia from the Early Sixteenth to the Early Nineteenth Century." In *The Cambridge History of the Native Peoples of the Americas*, part 2, edited by Frank Salomon and Stewart Schwartz III, 188–256. Cambridge: Cambridge University Press.

Taylor, Lewis. 2006. *Shining Path: Guerrilla War in Peru's Northern Highlands, 1980–1997*. Liverpool Latin American Studies. Liverpool: Liverpool University Press.

———. 2015. "Sendero Luminoso in the New Millennium: Comrades, Cocaine and

Counter-insurgency on the Peruvian Frontier." *Journal of Agrarian Change* 17 (1). doi:10.1111/joac.12137.

Theidon, Kimberly. 2004. *Entre prójimos: El conflicto armado interno y la política de la reconciliación en el Perú*. Vol. 24. Lima: Instituto de Estudios Peruanos.

———. 2010. "Histories of Innocence: Post-war Stories in Peru." In *Localizing Transitional Justice: Interventions and Priorities after Mass Violence*, edited by Rosalind Shaw, Lars Waldorf, and Pierre Hazan, 92–110. Stanford, CA: Stanford University Press.

———. 2012. *Intimate Enemies: Violence and Reconciliation in Peru*. Philadelphia: University of Pennsylvania Press.

Ulfe, María Eugenia, and Carmen Ilizarbe. 2019. "El indulto como acontecimiento y el asalto al lenguaje de la memoria en Perú." *Colombia Internacional* 97:117–143.

Uribe, María Victoria. 2009. "Memory in Times of War." *Public Culture* 21 (1): 3–7.

Uribe, Simón. 2017. *Frontier Road: Power, History, and the Everyday State in the Colombian Amazon*. Hoboken, NJ: Wiley Blackwell.

Valle Riestra, Esteban. 2019. "De la 'guerra popular' a la amnistía. Movadef y la reaparición de Sendero Luminoso: 1992–2012." *+MEMORIA(S) Revista Académica del Lugar de la Memoria, la Tolerancia y la Inclusión Social*. Lima 2:21–47.

van Dun, Mirella. 2009. *Cocaleros: Violence, Drugs and Social Mobilization in the Postconflict Upper Huallaga Valley, Peru*. Amsterdam: Rozenberg Publishers.

———. 2014. "Exploring Narco-Sovereignty/Violence: Analyzing Illegal Networks, Crime, Violence, and Legitimation in a Peruvian Cocaine Enclave (2003–2007)." *Journal of Contemporary Ethnography* 43 (4): 1–24.

———. 2019. "Narco-Territoriality and Shadow Powers in a Peruvian Cocaine Frontier." *Terrorism and Political Violence* 31 (5): 1026–1048.

Varese, Stefano. 1972. *The Forest Indians in the Present Political Situation of Peru*. IWGIA-8. Copenhagen: International Work Group for Indigenous Affairs.

Verdery, Katherine. 2003. *The Vanishing Hectare: Property and Value in Postsocialist Transylvania*. Ithaca, NY: Cornell University Press.

Virilio, Paul. 1994. *Bunker Archeology*. New York: Princeton Architectural Press.

Weld, Kirsten. 2014. *Paper Cadavers: The Archives of Dictatorship in Guatemala*. Durham, NC: Duke University Press.

Wilson, Fiona. 2004. "Towards a Political Economy of Roads: Experiences from Peru." *Development and Change* 35 (3): 525–546.

Wood, Stephanie. 1998. "The Social vs. Legal Context of Nahuatl Títulos." In *Native Traditions in the Postconquest World: A Symposium at Dumbarton Oaks, 2nd through 4th October 1992*, edited by Elizabeth Hill Boone and Tom Cummins, 16:201–231. Washington, DC: Dumbarton Oaks.

Yezer, Caroline. 2008. "Who Wants to Know? Rumors, Suspicions, and Opposition to Truth-Telling in Ayacucho." *Latin American and Caribbean Ethnic Studies* 3 (3): 271–289.

Zamorano, Gabriela. 2022. "Remendar la imagen: Subjetividades y anhelos en los archivos fotográficos de Michoacán, México." *Encartes Revista Digital Multimedia* 5 (9). https://encartes.mx/zamorano-subjetividad-fotografia-familia-michoacan.

Zapata Velasco, Antonio. 2017. *La guerra senderista. Hablan los enemigos*. Lima: Taurus.

index

185–87, 191, 194–97, 198, 201–2,
205–8, 228; on snitching, 8, 24,
124, 182, 183, 198, 200, 201–2,
203–5, 288; on speaking, 19–20,
46, 56, 124–25, 179–80, 199
public works, 118–19, 135–36, 309n26
Pucallpa, 8, 126
Pueblo Nuevo, 107, 160, 314n12
Punta Arenas, 72, 306n3
Pucayacu, 75; location, 17

Quechua speakers, 28–29, 30
Quispe Palomino, Victor, 300n14

rafts, 71–72
Ramal de Aspuzana, 102, 215, 230,
276; location, 17; during Shining
Path insurgency, 223–28, 314n13
Ramírez Durand, Óscar, 299n13
recollection, 13–14, 41, 45–46, 109,
110–11, 129–30, 174, 305n41
RENADE, 302n23
Rendón, Silvio, 302n23
road building, 117, 121, 125–26, 179, 213
Robles Godoy, Armando: La
muralla verde, 300n16
Rojas-Perez, Isaías, 304n39, 312n1; on
necro-governmentality, 308n10;
on postwar Peru, 35, 310n2
Romania: decollectivization in, 246
Rumrill García, Roger, 305n2

San José de Pucate, 102, 232
San Martín, 27, 302n23, 303n26
San Martín de Pucate, 102, 232, 234
Santa Lucía, Huánuco, 97, 99, 261
Santa Lucía, San Martín, 73
Santos Granero, Fernando, 300n17
Sarhua, 244
Schmitt, Carl: on nomos, 121–22; on
politics, 32; on spatial dimensions
of law, 121–22; and ties to fascism,
308n14; on visuality, 122
Seale-Feldman, Aidan, 310n6
semblance, 34, 40, 45, 46, 90–91,
183–88, 209, 273, 289, 290
Sendero Luminoso. See Shining Path

sequential ordering, 41–42, 46, 193
Serres, Michel, 305n47, 314n11;
on time as handkerchief, 42
Servicio de intelegencia, 5
Shining Path (Sendero Luminoso), 20, 21,
182, 188, 202, 303n29, 306nn4,5,
309n28, 311n16; armed strikes
(paros armados) against Marginal
Highway by, 131, 137–46, 149, 165,
245, 309nn30,31, 310n36; in Bijao,
3–5; bridges destroyed by, 66, 142,
144, 145, 146, 148, 149; Camarada
Artemio, 26, 66, 199, 239, 242,
245–46, 249, 250, 261, 262, 281,
299n13; and cocaine trade, 30–31,
52, 112, 138, 165, 171–72, 244,
257, 267, 298n7, 299n13, 300n15,
302n23, 307n7, 310n37, 312n2;
commemorative calendar of, 137,
309n29; defeat of, 35, 44, 105, 183,
198–99, 211–12, 240, 241, 242–43,
244, 245–46, 247–48, 254–55, 261,
266, 276, 298n7, 313n2, 340n23;
emergence of, 14, 18, 27, 28, 30–31,
42, 74–76, 96, 103, 112, 127, 138,
163–64, 165, 170, 198, 232, 233,
256–58, 298n7, 312n2; Abimael
Guzmán, 243, 256, 298n7, 299n13,
309n9; high-voltage wires disrupted
by, 128, 137, 259–60; juicio popular
(people's trial), 76, 141–42, 203–5,
258–59, 260, 309n33; and land
titles, 238–43, 245–46, 247, 248–49,
250–52, 254–55, 256–57, 258, 261,
266–67; la Urbana, 109, 111, 307n9;
and left bank of Huallaga River, 52,
74–75, 139, 161–62, 163–64, 170,
179, 184, 198–99, 201, 207, 220,
223, 224, 232, 257–58, 314nn9,13,
315n27; Madre Mía fort attacked
by, 165, 222–23; in Magdalena,
112–13, 162, 164, 169, 223, 270–71,
281, 283; Maoism of, 14, 26, 136,
298n7; national strategy of, 128–29,
146–48, 308n20; redistribution of
land by, 242, 245, 248–49, 250–52,
254–55, 259, 260, 262, 263, 266–67,

The authorized representative in the EU for product safety and compliance is:
Mare Nostrum Group
B.V Doelen 72
4831 GR Breda
The Netherlands

www.ingramcontent.com/pod-product-compliance
Lightning Source LLC
Chambersburg PA
CBHW020822270326
41928CB00006B/407